Trends in Embedded Design
Using Programmable Gate Arrays

Trends in Embedded Design Using Programmable Gate Arrays

Dennis Silage
Electrical and Computer Engineering
Temple University

Bookstand Publishing
www.BookstandPublishing.com

Published by
Bookstand Publishing
Morgan Hill, CA 95037
3917_2

ISBN 978-1-61863-541-9

Printed in the United States of America

Acknowledgements

This second text in embedded design using programmable gate arrays would not have been possible without the support of the Xilinx University Program (XUP, *www.xilinx.com/univ*) and Digilent, Inc. (*www.digilentinc.com*) and their commitment to assist Faculty to prepare the future workforce in the face of a sea change in electrotechnology. Parimal Patel of XUP has provided able assistance to our undergraduate and graduate curriculum and research efforts in the paradigm of the coarse grained programmable gate array. Alex Wong of Digilent, Inc. has provided encouragement for this second edition. Timothy Boger, Robert Esposito and John Ruddy are my recent graduate students who have contributed to this research at the System Chip Design Center in the Department of Electrical and Computer Engineering at Temple University (*www.temple.edu/scdc*).

This text, though, is dedicated to Ryan Erhardt and Alex Silage to whom the future belongs.

The only way to discover the limits of the possible is to go beyond them to the impossible.

–Arthur C. Clarke

Table of Contents

Chapter 3   Programmable Gate Array Hardware

Chapter 4   Digital Signal Processing, Communications and Control

Preface

Trends in Embedded Design Using Programmable Gate Arrays describes the analysis and design of modern embedded processing systems using the field programmable gate array (FPGA). The FPGA has traditionally provided support for embedded design by implementing customized peripherals, controller and datapath constructs and finite state machines (FSM). Although microprocessor-based computer systems have usually been used for the design of larger scale embedded systems, the paradigm of the FPGA now challenges that notion of such a fixed architecture especially with the constraints of *real-time*.

This new paradigm in embedded design utilizes the Verilog hardware description language (HDL) behavioral synthesis of controller and datapath constructs and the FSM for digital signal processing , communications and control with the FPGA, external interface *hard core* peripherals, custom internal *soft core* peripherals and the *soft core processor*. The transition to embedded design with the parallel processing capabilities and coarse grained architecture of the modern FPGA is described by in-part by the translation of C/C++ program segments for real-time processing to a controller and datapath construct or an FSM. However, the availability of the Xilinx 8-bit PicoBlaze™ and 32-bit MicroBlaze™ soft core processors and the emergence of the ARM® hard core processor and AMBA bus for the Xilinx Zynq™ Extensible Processing Platform (EPP) now also challenges the conventional microprocessor with its fixed architecture for embedded design.

The prior text entitled *Embedded Design Using Programmable Gate Arrays* featured the Xilinx Spartan®-3E FPGA on the Digilent Basys™ Board and the Spartan-3E Starter Board and presents some, but not all, of the material and Verilog HDL projects in this text. The Xilinx 8-bit PicoBlaze™ soft core processor and projects are presented in the prior text.

Trends in Embedded Design Using Programmable Gate Arrays features the Xilinx Spartan®-6 FPGA on the Digilent Nexys™ 3 Board and the Atlys™ Board evaluation hardware, the Xilinx Integrated Synthesis Environment (ISE®) electronic design automation software tool in the Verilog HDL, Xilinx CORE Generator for LogiCORE™ blocks and an introduction to the Xilinx Zynq EPP. The complete Xilinx ISE projects and Verilog HDL modules described in the Chapters are available (see the Appendix).

Trends in Embedded Design Using Programmable Gate Arrays, as was the prior text, is intended as a supplementary text and laboratory manual for undergraduate students in a contemporary course in digital logic and embedded systems. Professionals who have not had an exposure to the coarse grained FPGA, the Verilog HDL, an EDA software tool or the new paradigm of the controller and datapath and the FSM will find that this text facilitates an expansive experience with the tenets of digital signal processing, communications and control in embedded design. The References sections at the end of each Chapter contain a list of suitable undergraduate and graduate texts and reference books.

1

Verilog Hardware Description Language

The evolution of the programmable gate array (PGA) from the nascent programmable logic device is facilitated by the concurrent development of a hardware description language (HDL) and electronic design automation (EDA) software tools, such as the Xilinx Integrated Synthesis Environment (ISE®), as described in Chapter 2 Verilog Design Automation. Programmable gate arrays have progressed from logic arrays with a fine grained architecture of regular macrocells and simple non-volatile local interconnections to the now complex PGA with a coarse grained architecture of dissimilar but specialized subsidiary units and advanced but volatile routing interconnections.

An HDL can *model* and *simulate* both the functional behavior and critical timing of digital logic. The Advanced Boolean Expression Language (ABEL) HDL provided combination and sequential logic equations early on (1983) that implemented complex digital logic functions and finite state machines. A contemporary HDL (1995) is Verilog with syntax similar to the C programming language. Verilog HDL concepts and syntax are surveyed here to support the development of an embedded design using programmable gate arrays.

Structural models in the Verilog HDL are presented in this Chapter which portrays a digital logic design as a model similar to a schematic. Several of these simpler structural models can be encapsulated in a high-level architectural description, which provides a less obtrusive structure for implementation. However, a behavioral model is more intuitive and evocative of the process. The finite state machine and the controller and datapath constructs provide this behavioral description in the Verilog HDL design implementation.

The translation of an algorithm in the conversational C language to the Verilog HDL facilitates the implementation of an embedded design using programmable gate arrays. Behavioral synthesis Verilog is both conversational and ultimately executes rapidly at the programmable gate array hardware level. However, the Verilog HDL is not a computer language and common arithmetic functions are problematical.

Finally, the PGA and the microprocessor are functionally compared. Unlike a PGA, operations cannot be performed in parallel by a microprocessor and the throughput rate in real-time processing is then limited by the clock period and the complexity of the task. However, the microprocessor efficiently implements large stored instructions for sequential tasks and can be programmed in the conversational C language. With the availability of the configurable hard and soft core processors within the PGA, embedded designs can advantageously incorporate the sequential processor, essentially a microprocessor, and the inherently parallel and effective controller-datapath construct.

Programmable Logic Devices

The programmable gate array (PGA) contains basic logic components and programmable interconnections that can be configured to functionally replicate a network of combinational or sequential digital logic. The earliest programmable integrated circuits (IC) (1978) were the programmable array logic (PAL) devices which implemented combinational logic using a *sum-of-products* (AND-OR) configuration. Combination logic and registered output PAL devices were then configured as *macrocells* (1983) which facilitated the design of sequential logic.

The original PAL devices were programmed by electrically destroying the connections in a *fuse map*, which produced a non-volatile logic circuit. The generic array logic (GAL) provided the same logic elements as a PAL device but could be electrically erased and reprogrammed (1987). Complex programmable logic devices (CPLD) combined several macrocells and a programmable interconnection system (1988). The CPLD exhibited a *fine grained* architecture in which the logic

Trends in Embedded Design Using Programmable Gate Arrays

circuit elements were highly regular and implemented as an array of several PAL devices on a single IC.

Although this configuration produces predictable timing delays, the fine grained architecture of the CPLD results in a restrictive structure with the sum-of-products logic as an input to registered output. As an alternative architecture, the early PGA (1994) provided an array of configurable logic blocks (CLB) dominated by a complex routing scheme. The simplified CLB consists of a multiple input *look-up-table* (LUT), a type D (or data) *flip-flop* as a storage element and a *multiplexer* (MUX) which selects the logic output, as shown in Figure 1.1.

However, the early PGA remained substantially fine gained with a regular architecture, albeit with a complex interconnection of these CLB elements. The Xilinx Spartan® field programmable gate array (FPGA) (1998) utilized a matrix of routing channels surrounding the CLB, a perimeter of programmable input-output blocks (IOB) and a static memory cell for the interconnection (data sheet DS060, *www.xilinx.com*), as shown in the simplified depiction in Figure 1.2. The *boundary scan* hardware is compatible with the IEEE Standard 1149.1 and allows the programming of any number of devices. The oscillator (OSC) is the hardware responsible for the generation and distribution of the synchronizing clock signals. The *start-up* hardware sets the initial configuration of the flip-flops in the CLBs and the *read back* hardware allows the verification of the programming of the FPGA.

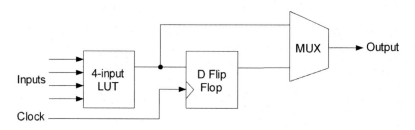

Figure 1.1 Simplified configurable logic block

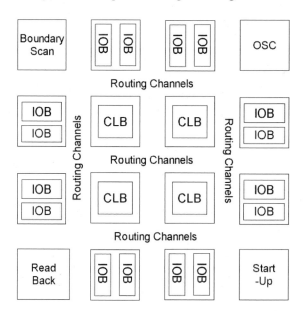

Figure 1.2 Simplified depiction of the Xilinx Spartan FPGA architecture

In the Spartan FPGA the CLB consists of three LUTs which are used as logic function generators, two flip-flops and two groups of multiplexers which select the logic signals. The Spartan CLB also included the capability to function as a 32 bit distributed random access memory (RAM). The largest Spartan FPGA provides a 28 by 28 CLB matrix with 224 input-output (IO) pins.

The Xilinx Spartan II FPGA (2000) introduced dedicated RAM in blocks of 4096 bits and delay-locked loops (DLL) for clock distribution delay compensation (data sheet DS001, *www.xilinx.com*). The DLL can also function as a clock frequency doubler. The largest Spartan II FPGA provided a 28 by 42 CLB matrix with 284 input-output (IO) pins and 56 Kb of block RAM.

The evolutionary *coarse grained* architecture of the FPGA was exemplified by the Xilinx Spartan-3E FPGA (2003). This FPGA included high level logic functions, such as input-output blocks (IOB), digital clock managers (DCM), multipliers, and block and distributed random access memory (RAM) (data sheet DS312, *www.xilinx.com*), as shown in the simplified depiction of a corner segment in Figure 1.3.

The DCM of the Spartan-3E FPGA supported clock *skew* elimination, phase shift and frequency synthesis. While the DCM incorporated the DLL of the Spartan II FPGA it also included a digital frequency synthesizer (DFS) and status logic. The DCM is capable of generating a wide range of clock output frequencies by multiplying or dividing the clock input frequency.

In the Spartan-3E FPGA the CLB consisted of four *slices* and each slice contained two LUTs and two flip-flops. The two LUTs in each slice can function as either a 16-bit distributed RAM or a 16-bit shift register. The four interconnected slices of the CLB are grouped into a conceptual left and right pair. The left pair of slices supports both logic and memory functions, while the right pair supports only logic functions. The Spartan-3 and the Spartan-3E PGA also have adjacent *dual-ported* 18 kb block RAM and 18-bit multipliers with a 36-bit two's complement product, as shown in Figure 1.3.

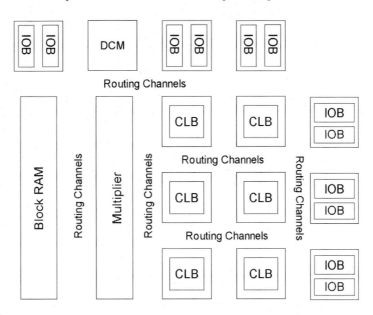

Figure 1.3 Simplified depiction of a corner segment of the Xilinx Spartan-3E FPGA architecture

The Spartan-6 device (2009) is the target FPGA architecture for the embedded design applications here in this text, as described in Chapter 3 Field Programmable Gate Array Hardware. The Spartan-6 continues the evolution of the coarse grained FPGA architecture by providing a more efficient dual register 6-input LUT, second generation hardware multipliers, improved clock management and external dynamic memory controller blocks (MCB) (data sheet DS160, *www.xilinx.com*). The enhanced coarse grained elements of the Spartan-6 FPGA architecture contribute to robust and efficient digital logic but may also increase the difficulty of the advanced design process.

Finally, the interconnection of the either the fine or coarse grained elements of the FPGA is provided by a *switch network*. The pattern of the switch is essentially binary data and is stored in either non-volatile fuses, electrically programmable read-only memory (EPROM), electrically erasable read-only memory (EEPROM), and block-oriented flash memory or volatile static RAM (SRAM). If the volatile SRAM is used internally for the switch configuration, the pattern is *downloaded* to the FPGA on *power-up* from an external device, such as an EEPROM or flash memory device. A standard Joint Test Action Group (JTAG) port for remote programming of the switch configuration by this *bit stream* data is provided on the FPGA, as described in Chapter 2 Verilog Design Automation.

Hardware Description Languages

The complexity of the CPLD required the early development of a hardware description language (HDL) and an associated set of software electronic design automation (EDA) tools. An HDL can *model* and *simulate* both the functional behavior and critical timing of complex digital logic [Ciletti99]. Although an HDL can portray a digital logic design as an inherent structural model similar to a schematic, it can also describe the intrinsic behavioral function of the logic using constructs and procedures [Botros06]. In either instance, the digital logic signal output of the design generated by the HDL can be simulated with *test vectors* providing the logic signal stimulus input for verification. The resulting HDL model can then be *bound* to the interconnections of the programmable logic device for execution as part of a hardware system, as described in Chapter 2 Verilog Design Automation for the Xilinx ISE EDA software tool.

An early HDL is ABEL (Advanced Boolean Expression Language) (1983), which provided combination and sequential logic equations that implemented complex logic functions and finite state machines (FSM). Other early HDLs for PAL and CPLD programmable logic devices include CUPL (1981) and PALASM (1982).

VHDL (Very high speed integrated circuit Hardware Description Language) originally provided documentation for application specific integrated circuits (ASIC). VHDL is a subset of the Ada programming language and, like the Ada language, is case insensitive and strongly typed. Strong typing implies that additional statements are required to convert from one data type to another. VHDL first appeared as IEEE standard 1076 (1987) but was extended (1993) to multi-valued logic and with more consistent syntax.

Verilog is an HDL with syntax similar to the C programming language, but Verilog, unlike the C language, does not have structures, pointers or recursive subroutines. Verilog, like the C language, is also weakly typed. Common to all HDLs but missing in programming languages that execute on sequential processors, Verilog has a different concept of the order of execution. The execution of its modules is not strictly linear, as Verilog has both sequential and concurrent statements [Botros06]. Modules can also execute in parallel and interact through semaphore logic signals and data. Verilog stems from a proprietary HDL (1985) but became IEEE Standard 1364 (1995) and was extended (2001) with an enhanced syntax [Ciletti04]. Verilog 2005 focused only on minor language corrections. A separate EDA development is SystemVerilog (IEEE Standard P1800-2005) which, although based on Verilog 2001, supports design verification.

ABEL

The structure of the ABEL source file supports a *compiler* that translates its HDL into the appropriate logic element interconnections and routing for the device input and output pins. The output of an HDL compiler is the bit stream of programming instructions for the device. An HDL provides an implicit concurrency of the logic operations that are unlike the instructions of a conversational programming language, such as the C or Java, that execute on sequential processors.

Although an early implementation of an HDL, a survey of the ABEL source file structure is instructive to describe as a precursor of the Verilog HDL that is utilized here for embedded design using the programmable gate array. Both a short description of the ABEL HDL (Xilinx application note XAPP075, *www.xilinx.com*) and a complete language reference [Pellerin94] is available.

An ABEL source file for a combination logic 1-bit adder with carry as a *structural* model, derived from the logic diagram in Figure 1.4, is given in Listing 1.1. The ABEL source file consists of a header, declarations, and logic descriptions. Reserved words or *keywords* indicate the various subsections. The keywords *module* and *end* indicate the extent of the ABEL declaration. Source files can consist of multiple modules with concurrency of the logic operations and communication between the modules. Source file lines are terminated with a semicolon (;) and a comment statement begins with a quotation mark (") and terminates with either another quotation mark or an end-of-line.

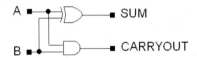

Figure 1.4 Logic diagram for a combination logic one bit adder with carry

The optional keyword *title* provides a documentation of the module. The optional keyword *device* provides the identification and type of the device to be used (the XC4003E is a Xilinx FPGA). Recent EDA tools specify the type of programmable logic in a project description, rather than an HDL source file, so that the design is more independent of the device, as described in Chapter 2 Verilog Design Automation for the Xilinx ISE EDA software tool.

The keyword *pin* instructs the compiler to associate logic signals with external device pins. The keyword *node*, although somewhat superfluous in Listing 1.1, has the same format but is used for an internal logic signal connection. The keywords *istype* and *com* indicate that these signals are combinatorial logic and an alternative description is *reg* for registered logic (a flip-flop output). Recent EDA tools assign the logic signals to pins in a *user constraint file* (UCF), rather than an HDL source file, for flexibility in interfacing the device, again as described in Chapter 2 Verilog Design Automation for the Xilinx ISE EDA software tool. Finally, the keyword *equations* indicate the logical operations for the module.

Listing 1.1 ABEL structural model of a 1-bit adder with carry

```
module onebitadder;
title '1 bit adder';
U1 device 'XC4003E';

" input and output pins
A, B pin 3, 5;
SUM, CARRYOUT pin 15, 18 istype 'com';

" internal node
AandB node istype 'com';

" equations
SUM = (A & !B) # (!A & B);
AandB = A & B;
CARRYOUT = AandB;

end onebitadder;
```

Trends in Embedded Design Using Programmable Gate Arrays

The logic operators (& (AND), ! (NOT), and # (OR)) in the *equations* section for the one bit adder with carry in Listing 1.1 mimic the logic diagram (or schematic) in Figure 1.4 and do not indicate the robustness of ABEL as an HDL. The construct *when-then-else* can be used in the *equations* section to describe a logic function, as given in Listing 1.2. The ABEL *else* clause is optional. The logical equality operator (= =) or inequality operator (! =) specifies the condition for the combinational logic signal assignment (=) here or registered logic signal assignment (: =).

Listing 1.2 ABEL *when-then-else* logic function

```
when (A == B) then D = !A & !B;
    else when (A != B) then D = A & B;
```

In addition to structural models as equations, ABEL can utilize *behavioral* truth tables and state descriptions for logic design. A partial ABEL module, truth table description for the 1-bit adder with carry combinational logic function is given in Listing 1.3. The keyword *truth_table* and the bracketed term ([...]) indicates a *set* of logic signals for the function. The assignment operator (- >) is for a combinational logic output.

Listing 1.3 ABEL 1-bit adder with carry combinational logic truth table

```
truth_table ([A, B] -> [SUM, CARRYOUT])
    [0, 0] -> [0, 0];
    [0, 1] -> [1, 0];
    [1, 0] -> [1, 0];
    [1, 1] -> [1, 1];
```

The ABEL truth table construct can also be used to describe sequential logic behavior. Listing 1.4 is a three bit counter which generates output logic 1 when the count reaches seven (binary 111).

Listing 1.4 ABEL three bit counter sequential logic truth table

```
module counter;
title '3 bit counter'
U1 device 'XC4003E';
CLOCK pin 12;
RESET pin 22;
OUTPUT pin 18 istype 'com';
QC, QB, QA pin 14, 15, 16 istype 'reg';
[QC,QB,QA].CLK = CLOCK;
[QC,QB,QA].AR = RESET;

truth_table ([QC, QB, QA] :> [QC, QB, QA] -> OUTPUT)
    [0, 0, 0] :> [0, 0, 1] -> 0;
    [0, 0, 1] :> [0, 1, 0] -> 0;
    [0, 1, 0] :> [0, 1, 1] -> 0;
    [0, 1, 1] :> [1, 0, 0] -> 0;
    [1, 0, 0] :> [1, 0, 1] -> 0;
    [1, 0, 1] :> [1, 1, 0] -> 0;
    [1, 1, 0] :> [1, 1, 1] -> 0;
    [1, 1, 1] :> [0, 0, 0] -> 1;

end counter;
```

6

The assignment operator (: >) is for a registered logic output. The ABEL *dot extensions* are used to mimic the logic diagram of the counter. The dot extension *.CLK* is the clock input to an edge-triggered flip-flop and *.AR* is the asynchronous reset for the flip-flop. There are also a variety of other dot extensions for specific hardware flip-flop registers [Pellerin94].

Finally, ABEL provides a behavioral finite state machine (FSM) construct for logic design. A partial ABEL module for an arbitrary FSM is given in Listing 1.5. The keywords *state_diagram* and *state* describe an FSM with two input logic signals (Y, and LASTX), one logic output signal (X) and four states (INIT, LOCK, OK and RESET). The construct *if-then-else* is used in the FSM description, rather than *when-then-else* which is used for logic functions. The ABEL *else* clause is optional.

Listing 1.5 ABEL finite state machine

state_diagram datalock

state INIT: if RESET then INIT else LOOK;

state LOCK: if RESET then INIT
     else if (X == LASTX) then OK
     else LOCK;

state OK: if RESET then INIT
     else if Y then OK
     else if (X == LASTX) then OK
     else LOCK;

state RESET: goto INIT

The ABEL combinational logic function in Listing 1.1 represents a design process that is allied to the underlying structural model as a hardware logic diagram or schematic. The ABEL HDL there merely translates the structural model to the programming bit stream for the interconnections of the logic elements of the programmable gate array. The ABEL truth table construct in Listing 1.4 approaches a behavioral description of the sequential logic function, but it also utilizes the dot extensions for the specific hardware flip-flop registers. However, the ABEL FSM in Listing 1.5 closely describes the essential behavior of the logic without a requisite structural model. Xilinx ABEL (XABEL) as an HDL is supported by the Xilinx ISE EDA software tool.

Verilog

The Verilog HDL provides all the structural and behavioral models available in the ABEL HDL with additional extensions for a higher level of behavioral abstraction [Ciletti99]. Similarly, the structure of the Verilog source file supports a *compiler* that translates its HDL into the appropriate logic element interconnections and routing for the device input and output pins. Verilog sustains a structured design methodology with a *top-down* or hierarchically representation of a digital logic design as simpler functional units. Alternatively, the verification of the digital logic design can proceed *bottom-up*, in which the lower level of functions are individually simulated and tested.

A Verilog HDL behavioral description consists of procedural statements without reference to available *primitives* which model combinational logic gates. A Verilog source file for the one bit adder with carry as a behavioral description is given in Listing 1.6.

The Verilog source file consists of a module declaration and description. The keywords *module* and *endmodule* indicate the extent of the Verilog HDL declaration. As in the ABEL HDL, source files can consist of multiple modules with concurrency of the logic operations and communication between the modules. Source file lines are terminated with a semicolon (;) and a comment statement begins with a double forward stroke (//) and terminate with an end-of-line. Verilog also accepts a comment statement that begins with the C language convention of a forward stroke and asterisk (/*) and ends with an asterisk and forward stroke (*/).

The revised Verilog HDL standard (Verilog 2001) introduced a less verbose, C language style declaration of the ports of the module which also provided the mode and size (in bits) of the ports [Ciletti04]. The keywords *input* and *output* indicate the direction of the port and the keyword *reg* indicates that the port is an abstraction of a hardware storage element or register. The port size by default is one bit. The logic operators (^ (exclusive or) and & (and)) are not the primitives which directly model combinational logic gates in the Verilog HDL.

The one bit adder with carry in Listing 1.6 is a Verilog behavioral description because its functionality is described by an *event* triggered by changes in the logic levels of the data input signal. The keyword *always@* indicates the concurrent event. The keyword *or* here is part of the event syntax and is not the Verilog primitive for the combinational logic OR gate. The event executes statements contained within the keywords *begin* and *end*.

Listing 1.6 Verilog behavioral description of a one bit adder with carry

```
module half_add(output reg sum, output reg carry, input a, b);

always@(a or b)          // event
     begin
          sum = a ^ b;      // exclusive OR
          carry = a & b;    // and
     end

endmodule
```

Verilog as an HDL is supported by the Xilinx ISE EDA software tool. Rather than a cursory description of structural and behavioral modeling and the implementation of finite state machines, a concise but more systematic discussion of the Verilog HDL is provided in this Chapter. Other more extensive references for Verilog can provide support of these concepts and additional topics [Botros06] [Ciletti99] [Navabi06] [Zeidman99].

Verilog Syntax and Concepts

Verilog concepts and syntax are surveyed here to support the development of an embedded design using programmable gate arrays. Verilog is a hardware description language (HDL) and, although the syntax is similar to the C language, its concepts are quite different. The description of the Verilog HDL concept and syntax here concentrates on the exacting hardware synthesis in a programmable gate array (PGA) and not the simulation task [Navabi06].

Number Formats

Verilog is a hardware description language and integer numbers are represented in binary without reference to any fixed organization, such as bytes or words. For convenience in the source depiction, integer numbers can be specified as *<sign><size><base format><number>*. The *<sign>* is optional and is a minus sign (–) for a two's complement representation of the number. The *<size>* provides the number of bits and is optional. If the *<size>* is not given, then the number of bits is a default minimum of 32. However, if the number of bits required is greater than that specified then only the least significant bits (LSB) of *<size>* is stored and the most significant bits (MSB) are truncated.

The *<base format>* consist of an apostrophe (') followed by *b* (binary, base-2), *d* (decimal, base-10), *o* (octal, base-8) or *h* (hexadecimal, base-16) for integer numbers. If the *<base format>* is not used, the base is assumed to be decimal. The *<number>* must contain only digits which are valid for the specified base format. Digits can include *x* (unknown) and *z* (high impedance). Examples of valid and invalid integer number formats are given in Listing 1.7.

Real numbers are only specified in the Verilog HDL for simulation. In hardware synthesis, floating point numbers are usually implemented as signed, single precision 32 bit numbers using the IEEE-754 standard. In this standard there are 23 bits for the mantissa, 8 bits for the exponent and one sign bit. Other real number representations include IEEE-754 double precision floating point with 52 bits for the mantissa, 11 bits for the exponent and one sign bit and a fixed point number (for example, -123.456) with a sign bit and a variable number of bits for the integer and fractional part. The conversion and manipulation of floating point numbers is facilitated by a Xilinx LogiCORE HDL construct, as described in Chapter 2 Verilog Design Automation (data sheet DS335, Floating Point Operator, *www.xilinx.com*).

Listing 1.7 Examples of valid and invalid integer number formats in Verilog

```
138        // decimal number, 32 bit as 00000000000000000000000010001010
10′d138    // decimal number, 10 bit as 0010001010
6′o74      // octal number, 6 bits as 111100
24′h25F    // hexadecimal number, 24 bit as 000000000000001001011111
8′hxB      // hexadecimal number, 8 bit as xxxx1011
3′b010     // binary number, 3 bits as 010
-6′b101    // 6 bit, two's complement of 000101 or 111011
-10′d15    // 10 bit, two's complement of 0000001111 or 1111110001
5′d124     // decimal number, 5 bits as 11100 since 7 bits are required
12′oF2     // invalid, F is not a octal digit
```

Signal Data Types

Binary encoded logic signals in the Verilog HDL represent information such as loop indices, input data or a computed value [Cilletti04]. The value of a signal can be either a constant or a variable. Constants in Verilog are declared with the keyword *parameter* and can include arithmetic expressions with other constants, as given in Listing 1.8. Such declared constants are useful to describe the global characteristics of a Verilog module and to facilitate change during development, as in the constructs of the C language.

The keyword *defparam* is used to redefine a parameter within a module [Citelli04]. The redefinition can be specifically applied to the parameters of a specific (M2) nested module (auxbus), as given in Listing 1.8 and described in Chapter 1. However, this parameter redefinition may be evoked unnoticed anywhere within the design hierarchy and thus could cause problems to occur. Other Verilog HDL keywords and constructs that constraint the definition of parameter include the keywords *specparam* and *localparam* and the parameter redefinition by name association (#.*name*(*value*)(*port*);).

Listing 1.8 Constant *parameter* declaration and *defparam* redefinition with in Verilog

```
parameter BUS_WIDTH = 32;               // integer
parameter XMAX=640, YMAX = 480;         // integers
parameter START_VALUE = 8′b00001111;    // register
parameter SIZE = XMAX*YMAX;             // arithmetic expression

defparam auxbus.M2.BUS_WIDTH = 16;      // redefinition of BUS-WIDTH in instance M2
                                        // of nested module auxbus
```

Trends in Embedded Design Using Programmable Gate Arrays

Signal variables in Verilog are either of the type *net* or *register*. Net variables provide connectivity between objects in a Verilog module or between modules. Several of the net variable types available are specific for connection of Verilog primitives, which model combinational logic gates, and are not generally used in a Verilog HDL behavioral description [Navabi06]. However, the net variable type *wire* establishes behavioral connectivity with logic values of 0, 1, *x* (unknown) or *z* (high impedance) determined by the module *port* that drives the signal variable. The keyword *wire* declaration is followed by an optional array range and variable name, as given by Listing 1.9.

Listing 1.9 Net variable *wire* declaration in Verilog

```
wire glbrst;             // scalar net signal
wire mclk, dav;          // scalar net signals
wire [31:0] average;     // 32-bit vector net signal
wire [0:7] adc_value;    // 8-bit vector net signal, reversed MSB
```

Register variables are used in behavioral modeling, are assigned values by procedural statements and store information [Ciletti04]. Register variables that are used in a Verilog HDL behavioral description are declared by the keywords *reg* and *integer*. The keyword *reg* is the abstraction of a hardware storage element and has a default size of one bit and an initial logic value of *x*. The register variables can be declared to utilize signed arithmetic with the keyword *signed*. The keyword *reg* declaration is followed by an optional array range and variable name, as given by Listing 1.10.

Listing 1.10 Register variable *reg* declaration in Verilog

```
reg clock;               // register signal
reg reset, read_data;    // register signals
reg signed [7:0] sum;    // 7-bit plus sign register signal
reg [15:0] accum;        // 16-bit register signal, reversed MSB
```

The integer type of register variable supports numerical computation in Verilog behavioral synthesis. Integer variables are declared by the keyword *integer*, have a default but fixed size of 32 bits in signed two's complement format and a default initial value of zero [Ciletti04]. Integers are *true abstractions* that must have a numerical value, but the procedures that they comprise are compiled by the Verilog HDL to synthesizable hardware. The keyword *integer* declaration is followed the variable name then by an optional array range, as given by Listing 1.11.

Listing 1.11 Register variable *integer* declaration in Verilog

```
integer data;            // integer
integer i, j, k;         // multiple integers
integer data[1:1000]     // integer array
```

Strings and Arrays

Verilog utilizes the register variable with the *reg* declaration to store ASCII character strings as 8-bit values. The string can be initially assigned to the register variable *reg* declaration by enclosing it within quotation marks ("), as given by Listing 1.12. If the string assignment uses less than the available number of bits, the unused register variable *reg* declaration bits are filled with zero. The assignment of a string to a register variable with the *reg* declaration is a single address *memory*. Multiple addressable register variables of the same size can be accommodated with the format <*word size*><*variable name*><*memory size*>, as given by Listing 1.12.

The revised Verilog HDL standard (Verilog 2001) supports the selection of a word or the contiguous part of a word for net or register variables with the part select operators (*<start bit>* +: *<width>* and *<start bit>* –: *<width>*). The parameter *width* specifies the size of the selection which is obtained by either incrementing (+:) or decrementing (–:) the index of the bits in the register. In Listing 1.12, the integer register variable i sets the parameter *start bit* as the starting position for the selection [Ciletti04]. A fixed selection of a part of the register utilizes fixed parameters with the separation operator (:). Finally, a register variable can be concatenated from either the entire or a portion of two or more smaller register variables. The concatenation is enclosed by the brace symbols ({ }) and separated by a comma, as given in Listing 1.12.

Listing 1.12 String and memory register variable *reg* declaration in Verilog

```
parameter STRING_LENGTH = 11;          // parameter declaration
reg [8 * STRING_LENGTH] string_data;   // arithmetic calculation of size
reg [7:0] byte_memory [0:511];         // MSB bit first, 512 byte memory
strdata = "hello world";               // string assignment to a register
lcddata[7:0] = strdata[i–:8];          // variable selection of a register
lcddata[7:0] = strdata[87:80];         // fixed selection of a register
reg [3:0] data = {adata[1:0], bdata[1:0]};  // concatenation
```

Although Verilog 2001 supports multidimensional array, the Xilinx ISE EDA software tool only supports arrays with no more than three dimensions. Listing 1.13 shows a two-dimensional array of register variables with the *reg* declaration and the selection of a fixed word and a fixed part of a word in the array.

Listing 1.13 Multidimensional arrays and word selection in Verilog 2001

```
reg [7:0] pix_data [0:639] [0:479];        // two dimensional array of bytes
wire [7:0] pixout [120] [330];             // fixed word of pixel (120,330)
wire msb_pix = pix_data [120] [330] [7];   // MSB of pixel (120,330)
```

Signal Operations

Verilog provides intrinsic signal operations which describe logic symbolically in behavioral synthesis, rather than by Verilog primitives in a structural model which utilize combinational logic gates [Botros06]. The *bitwise* operators combine two signal operands to form a signal result. The symbols utilized in the Verilog HDL standard and the operations are patterned after those in the C language, as given in Table 1.1. The *exclusive not or* bitwise operation is not available in the C language.

Table 1.1 Bitwise operations in Verilog

~	Negation (one's complement)
&	And
|	Inclusive Or
^	Exclusive Or
~^	Exclusive Not Or
^~	Exclusive Not Or

The *reduction* operators produce a scalar with logic values of 0, 1, or *x* (unknown) from a single signal operand, as given in Table 1.2. Each bit of the signal operand participates in the reduction operation to produce the result. For example, if x = 1001, then &x = 0 and |x = 1. The scalar value is x (unknown) if the operand contains at least a single bit which is unknown.

The *relational* operators compare two signal operands and produce a scalar with logic values of 0 (false), 1 (true), or x (unknown), as given in Table 1.3. The scalar value is x (unknown) if either operand contains at least a single bit which is unknown or z (high impedance).

The *logical equality* and *logical inequality* operators compare two signal operands *bit-by-bit* and produce a scalar with logic values of 0 (false), 1 (true), or x (unknown), as given in Table 1.4. The scalar value is x (unknown) if the operand contains at least a single bit which is unknown or z (high impedance). If the operands are not the same length, logic 0 is added as the most significant bits of the smaller operand. The *case equality* and *case inequality* operators compare two signal operands *bit-by-bit* utilizing the four logic values (0, 1, x, z) and produce a scalar with logic values of 0 (false) and 1 (true), as given in Table 1.4.

Table 1.2 Reduction operations in Verilog

&	And
~ &	Not And
|	Or
~ |	Not Or
^	Exclusive Or
~ ^	Exclusive Not Or
^ ~	Exclusive Not Or

Table 1.3 Relational operations in Verilog

<	Less Than
< =	Less Than or Equal To
>	Greater Than
> =	Greater Than or Equal To

Table 1.4 Equality operations in Verilog

= = =	Case Equality
! = =	Case Inequality
= =	Logical Equality
! =	Logical Inequality

The *logical* operators are similar to the reduction operators but produce a scalar with logic values of 0, 1, or x (unknown) from two signal operands, as given in Table 1.5. Each bit of the two signal operands participates in the logical operation to produce the result. For example, if x = 1001 and y = 0110 then x && y = 0 and x || y = 1. The scalar value is x (unknown) if either of the operands contains at least a single bit which is unknown. The operation is evaluated from left to right and ends as soon as result is unequivocally true or false [Ciletti04].

Table 1.5 Logical operations in Verilog

& &	Logical And
| |	Logical Or
!	Logical Negation

The logical shift operator shifts the bits in a signal operand to the right or left and fills the vacated bits with a logic value of 0, as given in Table 1.6. For example, if x = 10011100 then x << 2 =

01110000. The revised Verilog HDL standard (Verilog 2001) supports the arithmetic shift operator which shifts the bits in a signal to the right or left and fills the vacated bits with the most significant bit (MSB) if a right shift and a logic value of 0 if a left shift, as given in Table 1.7 [Ciletti04]. For example, if x = 10011100 then x >>> 2 = 11100111. The left shift arithmetic operator is functionally the same as the left shift logical operator.

Table 1.6 Logical shift operations in Verilog

> >	Logical Shift Right
< <	Logical Shift Left

Table 1.7 Arithmetic shift operations in Verilog

> > >	Arithmetic Shift Right
< < <	Arithmetic Shift Left

Arithmetic Operations

The common arithmetic operations in Verilog 2001 manipulate the register variable *reg* declaration as signed or unsigned integers of any bit size [Ciletti04]. The keyword *signed* is used to declare that the register variable *reg* declaration is signed, as given in Listing 1.14. The register variable *integer* declaration has a default but fixed size of 32 bits for signed two's complement arithmetic. The common arithmetic operations for the Verilog HDL are listed in Table 1.8.

The division operation (/) is somewhat problematical with register variable *reg* declarations because in hardware synthesis the Xilinx ISE EDA software tool only supports division by a signed power of two ($\pm 2^n$). Precedence for the arithmetic operations in Verilog, as in the C language, occurs from left to right on a source line with the multiplication, division and modulus operations at a higher precedence level than the addition and subtraction operations.

Table 1.8 Arithmetic operations in Verilog

*	Multiplication
/	Division
%	Modulus
+	Addition
–	Subtraction

The conditional operation in the Verilog HDL can utilize the logic true or false of a Boolean expression to select one of two possible arithmetic expressions, as given in Listing 1.14. The form of the conditional operation is *<Boolean expression>* ? *<result if true>* : *<result if false>*.

Listing 1.14 Conditional operation in Verilog

```
reg signed [15:0] c;
reg signed [7:0] a;
reg signed [7:0] b;

c = (a > b) ? 1 : 0;              // c will be either 1 or 0
c = (a == b) ? a – b : a + b;     // c will be either a – b or a + b
c = (a – b) > 4 ? a : b;          // c will be either a or b
```

Trends in Embedded Design Using Programmable Gate Arrays

The conditional operation also supports the logical implementation of a bidirectional signal or data bus in which one of the expressions that occur when the Boolean expression is true or false is a signal with a defined high impedance state (*z*). Verilog 2001 also provides for assignment width extension for the signed 16-bit register variable *reg* declaration c from the signed 8-bit register variable *reg* declarations a and b in Listing 1.14.

If the expression of the right hand side is signed, then the sign bit is used to fill the addition bits of the left hand side of the assignment. If the expression on the right hand side is unsigned, then the additional bits of the left hand side are filled with logic 0.

Structural Models in Verilog

Structural models in the Verilog HDL portray a digital logic design as a model similar to a schematic [Navabi06]. Several of these simpler structural (or even behavioral) models can be encapsulated in a high-level architectural description, which provides a less obtrusive structure for implementation in an embedded design using a programmable gate array. A simple structural model is a *netlist* or connection of logic gates and is often inferred from an existing design in combinational or sequential digital logic [Zeidman99].

The intrinsic Verilog HDL primitives consists of a logic gate construct that operates on one, two or more 1-bit input signals and provides a one 1-bit output signal, as given in Table 1.9. Verilog primitives can be combined to describe sequential digital logic *flip-flop* operation and other complex functions, such as an arithmetic logic unit (ALU).

Table 1.9 Intrinsic combinational logic Verilog primitives.

and (output, input1, input2)	And
nand (output, input1, input2)	Not And
or (output, input1, input2)	Or
nor (output, input1, input2)	Not Or
xor (output, input1, input2)	Exclusive Or
xnor (output, input1, input2)	Exclusive Not Or
buf (output, input)	Non-inverting Buffer
not (output, input)	Inverter

Additional Verilog HDL primitives are used to model logic operation at the *gate level* of abstraction in hardware synthesis for specific FPGA devices. These additional Verilog primitives are FPGA device and EDA implementation dependent and model *tri-state*, *bi-directional* and *open collector* logic gates [Ciletti99]. The remaining Verilog primitives model the critical path timing of the logic operation at the *switch level* of abstraction, based on the transistor fabrication technique in use.

The Verilog HDL switch level primitives are usually not utilized in an initial structural model of an embedded design using a programmable gate array. The EDA tools provide support for critical path timing determinations. If timing anomalies are detected by the Verilog synthesizer warning messages are produced. Finally, the Verilog gate level primitives can also be inferred in structural FPGA hardware synthesis with the output logic signal *z* (high impedance) that is available for each of the intrinsic combinational logic Verilog primitives, as given in Table 1.9.

Modules

The Verilog HDL structural (or a behavioral) model consists of declarations beginning with the keyword *module* and ending with the keyword *endmodule*. The declarations specify the signal inputs and outputs of the model at the *port* and the manipulation of the signals using the Verilog primitives. The order of the input and the output ports of the module are irrelevant. However, the order of the output and input signals for the Verilog primitives in Table 1.9 is relevant. The Verilog

HDL structural model of the 1-bit adder with carry, similar to that of the one in the ABEL HDL in Listing 1.1, is given in Listing 1.15.

The module name is case sensitive and the names *half_adder* and *Half_adder* are assumed by the Verilog compiler to be different modules. A comparison can be made of this structural model with the Verilog *event-driven* cyclical behavioral description of the one bit added with carry in Listing 1.6. The declarations define whether the module is a structural or a behavioral model or a combination of the two descriptions.

Listing 1.15 Verilog structural model of a 1-bit adder with carry

```
module half_add (output sum, carry, input a, b);

    xor (sum, a, b);      // exclusive OR
    and (carry, a ,b);    // and

endmodule
```

Ports

The ports of a Verilog HDL structural (or a behavioral) module describe the interface to other modules or the external environment. The mode of a port can be unidirectional, with the keywords *input* or *output*, or bidirectional, with the keyword *inout*. If the mode of a port is input, then it must appear only as the input of a Verilog primitive (or only on the right hand side of a behavioral assignment statement (=)). If the mode of a port is output, then it must appear only as the output of a Verilog primitive. The port functions as both and input and output if the mode of a port is bidirectional [Botros06]. Finally, the input and output ports of a Verilog HDL module can be modified by the keyword *signed* which declares that signed arithmetic is to be used for the net and register variables and integers of the port.

The ports of a module must be associated in a consistent manner with the declaration of the module. The position and size in bits of the net or register variables are directly mapped in the hierarchical structure of nested modules that form the interconnections. In this *connection by position* option for the ports of a module the formal name in the declaration need not be the same as the actual name evoked in the hierarchical structure, as given in Listing 1.16.

However, this connection by position method with its direct mapping is problematical when the number of the port variables is large and their bit size is diverse. An alternative is the *connection by name* convention in which ports are associated in the nested module port list by the syntax .*formal_name(actualname)*, as given in Listing 1.17. This option connects the *actual_name* to the *formal_name* regardless of the position of the entry in the list [Ciletti04].

Nested Modules

The *top-down* design of a complex logic architecture implemented in a programmable gate array implies that the system is partitioned into functionally smaller structural (or behavioral) modules. Although these inherently smaller modules are easier to design and test, their utility extends to their *design reuse* and the lessening on the interconnection constraints placed on the place and route operations of the HDL compiler and synthesizer. Nested modules in the Verilog HDL support such a top-down design.

The top-down design methodology using nested modules and Verilog primitives is illustrated by the binary full-adder with carry, as given in Listing 1.16. The Verilog HDL hierarchical model of the design contains two instances of the half_add module that structurally models the 1-bit adder with carry, as given in Listing 1.15, and an *or* gate Verilog primitive [Ciletti04]. Each instance of the half_add module is given a module name (M1 and M2) for identification by the Verilog compiler.

Trends in Embedded Design Using Programmable Gate Arrays

In Listing 1.16 the *wire* net variable type establish the 1-bit *connection by position* for signals between the half_add modules and the *or* gate Verilog primitive. In the first instance of the half_add module (M1), wire w1 represents the output signal sum, which is connected to the input signal b of the second instance (M2) of the half_add module. This nested module 1-bit full adder with carry can be in turn be nested to form a multiple bit adder.

The ports of the nested Verilog HDL modules in the *full_add.v* module in Listing 1.16 are identified as either input or output by their position in the declaration of the module. Although this is adequate for a small number of ports, a large number of ports can generate confusion. Wire w1 is both an output signal to one of the half_add modules and an input signal to the other.

Verilog ports can also use *connection by name* for the unambiguous association of the signals of the *half_add.v* modules, which does not require that the port connections be listed in the same relative position. The nested 1-bit full adder with carry module with *connection by name* port mapping is given in Listing 1.17.

Listing 1.16 Verilog nested structural model of a 1-bit full-adder with carry with port *connection by position*

```
module full_add (output sum_out, carry_out, input a_in, b_in, carry_in);

    wire w1, w2, w3;

    half_add M1 (w1, w2, a_in, b_in);
    half_add M2 (sum_out, w3, carry_in, w1);
    or (carry_out, w2, w3);

endmodule
```

Listing 1.17 Verilog nested structural model of a 1-bit full-adder with carry with port *connection by name*

```
module full_add (output sum_out, carry_out, input a_in, b_in, carry_in);

    wire w1, w2, w3;

    half_add M1 (.a(a_in), .sum(w1), .b(b_in), .carry(w2));
    half_add M2 (.sum(sum_out), .b(w1), .carry(w3), .a(carry_in));
    or (carry_out, w2, w3);

endmodule
```

User Defined Primitives

User defined primitives (UDP) in the Verilog HDL facilitate the implementation of complex structural models. The UDP is not a Verilog module and must be incorporated within a module to be instantiated. The UDP is encapsulated by the keywords *primitive* and *endprimitive*, all the input ports must be 1-bit signals and only one 1-bit output port, which must be the first entry, is allowed. Verilog provides the *behavioral* truth table, similar to that in ABEL in Listing 1.3, which is versatile and can describe complex combinational and sequential logic.

The scalar values 0 (false), 1 (true), x (unknown) and any transitions between these logic values are indicated in the table. The scalar logic value z (high impedance) is not supported by the UDP. The register variable *reg* declaration defines a sequential logic construct, but only the single 1-bit output port can be a *reg* declaration. The keyword *initial* indicates the *power-up* state for the UDP and only the scalar logic values 0 (false), 1 (true) and x (unknown) can be used. The default initial state is x (unknown).

The Verilog truth table declaration begins with the keyword *table* and ends with the keyword *endtable*. The entries for a combinational logic truth table are specified as *<input logic value>* : *<output logic value>*. A whitespace must separate each input entry in the table. The order of the table entries for the inputs is associated with the declaration of the ports of the Verilog primitive. The question mark (?) entry in the truth table indicates that a *don't care* condition occurs for the scalar logic input value, which can be 0, 1 or x. A combinational logic UDP using a truth table for a 2-bit multiplexer is given in Listing 1.18.

The entries for a sequential logic truth table are specified as *<input logic value>* : *<previous logic value>* : *<output logic value>*. The 1-bit output port must be declared a register variable *reg*. Only one input logic signal can have an edge transition for each entry in the truth table. If any input logic signal entry has an edge transition, then all other input logic signal must be have truth table entries to account for their transitions. A sequential logic UDP for a type D (data) flip-flop is given in Listing 1.1

Listing 1.18 Combinational logic UDP using truth table for a 2-bit multiplexer

primitive mux (output y, input a, b, sel);

```
    table
      // a  b  sel : y
        0 ?  0 : 0;      // select a
        1 ?  0 : 1;      // select a
        ? 0  1 : 0;      // select b
        ? 1  1 : 1;      // select b
    endtable

endprimitive
```

Listing 1.19 Sequential logic UDP for a type D flip-flop

primitive dff (output reg q, input d, clk, rst);

```
    table
      // d  clk rst:state:q
        ? ?  0 : ? : 0;      // active low reset
        0 R  1 : ? : 0;      // rising clock edge, data = 0
        1 R  1 : ? : 1;      // rising clock edge, data = 1
        ? N  1 : ? : -;      // ignore clock negative edge
        * ?  1 : ? : -;      // ignore all edges on d
        ? ?  P : ? : -;      // ignore reset positive edge
    endtable

endprimitive
```

In Listing 1.19 the rising edge of the *clock* signal is the desired transition and the negative edge of the clock, the positive and negative edges of the d input and the positive edge of the reset input is ignored. A level sensitive truth table entry, such as that for reset, has precedence over edge sensitive entries. The truth table input entry R indicates a rising transition (logic 0 to 1), N indicates a negative transition (logic 1 to 0, logic 1 to x or logic x to 0), P indicates a positive transition (logic 0 to 1, logic 0 to x or logic x to 1), and asterisk (*) indicates any possible transition (logic 0 to 1, logic 0 to x, logic x

to 1, logic x to 0, logic 1 to 0 or logic 1 to x). Here the truth table output entry dash ($-$) indicates no change in state for the register variable.

Other truth table input entries are available but not used in Listing 1.19. The truth table input entry x indicates an unknown logic value, B indicates a *don't care* condition if the logic value is 0 or 1 and F indicates a falling transition (logic 1 to 0).

Behavioral Models in Verilog

Although a digital logic design can be rendered entirely in a structural model in the Verilog HDL, a behavioral model is more intuitive and evocative of the process. Structural models do provide an architectural partition of the design and are often provided as *building blocks* for a more complex behavioral model. The Xilinx LogiCORE building blocks are efficient in the use of FPGA resources and can be integrated with Verilog modules, as described in Chapter 2 Verilog Design Automation. This partitioning facilitates the digital logic design process by allowing different levels of abstraction [Ciletti99] [Navabi06].

Continuous Assignment

Continuous assignment statements in the Verilog HDL are Boolean equations that describe combination logic using the bitwise signal operations, as given in Table 1.1. These bitwise operations are implicit descriptions of combinational logic and have structural or gate level equivalences and can be easily synthesized. The continuous assignment statement is declared with the keyword *assign* followed by a net variable name and the equal sign ($=$) as the operator. Net variables not only provide connectivity between objects in a Verilog module, using the *wire* construct, but between the output and input objects between Verilog modules.

The Verilog HDL nested structural model of a 1-bit full-adder with carry, as given in Listing 1.16, utilized the wire construct and is difficult to discern without recourse to the schematic. The 1-bit full-adder with carry can also be described with continuous assignment statements for the two output net variables and is more concise, as given in Listing 1.20.

Listing 1.20 Verilog continuous assignment model of a 1-bit full-adder with carry

```
module full_add (output sum_out, carry_out, input a_in, b_in, carry_in);

    assign sum_out = a_in ^ b_in ^ carry_in;
    assign carry_out = (a_in & b_in) | (b_in & carry_in) | (a_in & carry_in);

endmodule
```

The Verilog continuous assignment statement is not like a program statement in the C language because it is sensitive to the signal variables on the right hand side of the assignment operator and execute concurrently. Whenever a signal variable changes logic state the assignment is reevaluated and the result is updated. The continuous assignment statement cannot utilize a register variable *reg* declaration.

Continuous assignment statements are used with the conditional operator, as given in Listing 1.14, to model *tri-state* digital logic. The Verilog continuous assignment model of a 1-bit full-adder with carry can be augmented with a conditional operator on an *enable* input signal to provide a tri-state output using the high impedance (z) logic level, as given in Listing 1.21. The conditional assignment statement with the inclusion of the high impedance logic level is also used for the implementation of external bidirectional signal or data busses.

Continuous assignment statements with the conditional operator and feedback can model a logic level sensitive *transparent latch*, as given in Listing 1.22. The output signal of a transparent latch follows the input signal when the latch is enabled. The net variable output signal qout is fedback to itself and will be synthesized in the Verilog HDL as a hardware latch [Zeidman99].

Listing 1.21 Verilog continuous assignment model of a 1-bit full-adder with carry and enable

module full_add (output sum, carry_out, input a, b, carry_in, enable);

    assign sum = enable ? a ^ b ^ carry_in : 1'bz;
    assign carry_out = enable ? (a & b) | (b & carry_in) | (a & carry_in) : 1'bz;

endmodule

Listing 1.22 Verilog continuous assignment model of a transparent latch

module tlatch (output qout, input data, enable);

    assign qout = enable ? data : qout;

endmodule

Single Pass Behavior

Single pass behavior in the Verilog HDL for simulation utilizes the keyword *initial* which executes the associated statements then expires [Ciletti04]. The single pass behavior is useful for setting the initial value of register variables declared by the keywords *reg* and *integer*, as given in Listing 1.23. However, single pass behavior is not a hardware synthesizable construct and is only used in simulation. For hardware synthesis, register variables can be given a value in a declaration or reset by an external event, such as an input signal derived from a push button [Lee06].

Listing 1.23 Verilog single pass behavior in simulation using the keyword *initial*

reg [4:0] rstate;
reg dav, sclk, ackdata;

initial
    begin
        rstate = 0;
        dav = 0;
        sclk = 0;
        ackdata = 1;
    end

Cyclic Behavior

Cyclic behavior is an abstract model of logic functionality and is not related to gate level primitives in the Verilog HDL. Rather, cyclic behavior executes procedural statements which generate output signals from input signals, as does the C language for variables. However, the difference between the Verilog HDL and any programming language such as C is that the procedural statements can execute either unconditionally and concurrently or with an event control statement [Ciletti04]. The event control statement has a list of input signals that are sensitive to either logic level or edges. The cyclic behavior is declared by the keyword *always* followed by the *at sign* (@) as the event control operator and the comma (,) separated sensitivity list of signals in Verilog 2001. The 1-bit full-adder

Trends in Embedded Design Using Programmable Gate Arrays

with carry, as given in Listing 1.20, can also be described as a logic level sensitive cyclic behavior, as given in Listing 1.24.

The event control statement is sensitive to changes in the logic level of the net variable input signals a, b, and carry_in. The procedural statements are a block encapsulated by the keywords *begin* and *end* and execute within the block only sequentially here because of the *blocking* assignment operator (=). Here the output signal sum is updated only when the logic level changes for either or all of the input signals and before the output signal carry_out is updated. The output signals sum and carry_out are register variable *reg* declarations here which hold the event control statement assignment until they are changed.

Listing 1.24 Verilog level sensitive cyclic behavior of a 1-bit full-adder with carry

```
module full_add (output reg sum, output reg carry_out, input a, b, carry_in);

always@(a, b, carry_in)
      begin
            sum = a ^ b ^ carry_in;
            carry_out = (a & b) | (b & carry_in) | (a & carry_in);
      end

endmodule
```

Sequential digital logic, such as most implementations of the flip-flop, has edge sensitive cyclic behavior and operates synchronously with a *clock* signal. The Verilog HDL has the qualifiers *posedge* (positive edge) and *negedge* (negative edge) with the event control statement in the sensitivity list to model edge sensitive cyclic behavior. The sequential logic type D flip-flop, as given in listing 1.19 as a UDP, can be also be described as a cyclic behavior, as given in Listing 1.25. The keywords *if* and *else* are Verilog HDL control flow statements.

Listing 1.25 Verilog cyclic behavioral model for a type D flip-flop

```
module dff (output reg q, input d, clk, rst);

always@(posedge clk)
      begin
            if (rst == 0)
                  q = 0;
            else
                  q = data;
      end

endmodule
```

The event control statement uses the positive edge of the input signal clk. Here the logic level of the reset input signal rst clears the register variable *reg* declaration of the output signal q with a control flow (*if*) statement. The sequential logic UDP, as given in Listing 1.19, provides more possibilities for the logical functionality of the type D flip than the cyclic behavioral model, as given in Listing 1.25. Thus the UDP type D flip flop model may be more suited for robust embedded designs using programmable gate arrays.

Finally, sequential digital logic designs may require repetitive procedures distributed over multiple clock cycles [Botros06]. This operation can be modeled as *multicyclic* behavior using nested edge sensitive event control statements. A multicyle processor that receives four 4-bit net variable

20

input signals data[3:0]on the positive edge of a clock signal and places them into a 16-bit register variable output signal outdata[15:0] is given in Listing 1.26. The multicyclic behavior is aborted with the reset signal rst by naming the process rcvrloop and using the keyword *disable*. A data available signal dav is used to verify that the complete data transfer has occurred.

Listing 1.26 Verilog multicyclic behavioral model for a processor

```
module rcvrdata (output reg [15:0] outdata, input [3:0] data, input clk, rst, output reg dav);

always@(posedge clk)
    begin: rcvrloop
        dav = 0;
        if (rst == 0) disable rcvrloop;
            else outdata[3:0] = data[3:0];
        @(posedge clk)
            if (rst == 0) disable rcvrloop;
                else outdata[7:4] = data[3:0];
        @(posedge clk)
            if (rst == 0) disable rcvrloop;
                else outdata[11:8] = data[3:0];
        @(posedge clk)
            if (rst == 0) disable rcvrloop;
                else
                    begin
                        outdata[15:12] = data[3:0];
                        dav = 1;
                    end
    end

endmodule
```

Blocking and Non-Blocking Assignments

Verilog HDL statements that use the procedural assignment operator (=) execute in the order listed which is a *blocking assignment* [Botros06]. The net or register variable blocking assignment occurs immediately but before the next statement executes. Although this can be interpreted as a sequential execution as in the C language, Verilog also has a concurrent procedural assignment operator (<=) which is a *non-blocking assignment*.

Listing 1.27 Verilog structural model of a four bit shift register with blocking assignments

```
module shiftreg (output reg [3:0] Q, input data, clk);

always@(posedge clk)
    begin
        Q[0] = Q[1];
        Q[1] = Q[2];
        Q[2] = Q[3];
        Q[3] = data;
    end

endmodule
```

Trends in Embedded Design Using Programmable Gate Arrays

However, the Xilinx ISE EDA software tool provides an error on compilation if a net or register variable or different portions (*bit slices*) of a register variable are assigned through both blocking and non-blocking statements.

The group of net or register variable non-blocking assignments occur in parallel and the order listed implies no precedence of any kind. Positive or negative edge sensitive cyclic behavior, as in sequential logic, is usually described by non-blocking assignments, while combinational logic is described with blocking assignments. This practice prevents a logic *race condition* from occurring [Ciletti04]. However, there are specific exceptions to this practice. Listing 1.27 is a sequential logic four bit serial shift register using blocking assignments to assure the correct transfer of data for this structural model.

Control Flow

Verilog HDL statements for the control of execution flow are similar to those found in the C language [Ciletti99]. The keyword *case* has a counterpart in the C language *switch* statement and searches for the first occurrence of an exact match between the *case expression*, which is a net or register variable, and the *case item*, which can be expressed as logic values of 0 (false), 1 (true), *x* (unknown) or *z* (high impedance). The *case* construct is terminated with the keyword *endcase*.

Listing 1.28 is a four channel multiplexer using the *case* statement with an expression as the net variable select to output one of four signal inputs if an exact bit-wise match occurs. Since only four *case items* (00, 01, 10, and 11) of the sixteen possible (00, 01, 10, 11, 0x, 0z, 1x, 1z, x0, z0, x1, z1, xx, xz, zx, and zz) are provided in Listing 1.27, the keyword *default* determines what the output of the multiplexer should be is no match occurs.

Listing 1.28 Verilog behavioral model of a four channel multiplexer using the *case* statement

```
module mux4ch (output reg data, input [1:0] select, input a, b, c, d);

always@(a or b or c or d or select)
        case (select)
            0: data = a;
            1: data = b;
            2: data = c;
            3: data = d;
            default data = 1'bz;
        endcase

endmodule
```

The Xilinx ISE EDA software tool may provide unpredictable results with unsized integers in the *case expression*. In Listing 1.28 the net variable select is sized to two bits.

The exact match requirement of the *case* statement can be eased by the Verilog HDL keywords *casex* and *casez*. The *casex* statement ignores values in the case expression or the case item which are *x* (unknown) or *z* (high impedance) and effectively considers these values are *don't cares*. The *casez* statement ignores values in the case expression or the case item which are *z* (high impedance). The *casez* also utilizes the *question mark* (?) as an explicit don't care. Listing 1.29 is an address decoder which provides a RAM output enable register variable ram_oe for a 12-bit range of valid addresses for the 16-bit net variable input address signal addr, event triggered by the positive edge of the address latch enable net variable input signal ale.

The Verilog HDL keywords *if...else* and *if...else...if* for flow control have a direct counterpart in the C language. The use of these conditional statements, which alter the sequence of activity, is illustrated for cyclic and multicyclic behavior in Listing 1.245 and Listing 1.26.

The Verilog HDL keyword *for* supports repetitive flow control also has a direct counterpart in the C language. The initial statement of the *for loop* construct executes once to set a register variable declared by the keywords *reg* or *integer*. If the *end of loop* expression is true, the statement or block of statements is executed and afterwards the *loop update* expression is executed. The common C language construct k++ for post-incrementation of a variable is not a valid syntax in the Verilog HDL and the construct k = k +1 is used instead in the *for loop* in Listing 1.30.

Listing 1.29 Verilog behavioral model of an address decoder using the *casez* statement

```
module addrdec (output reg ram_oe, input [15:0] addr, input ale);

always@(posedge ale)
        casez (addr)
                16′b0100????????????: ram_oe = 1;
                default: ram_oe = 0;
        endcase

endmodule
```

The *for loop* construct executes repeatedly until the *end of loop* expression is no longer true [Botros06]. Listing 1.30 is an odd parity generator using the *for loop* construct with the integer variable k which counts the number of logic 1s in an 8-bit net variable input signal (data). The odd parity output register variable parity is logic 1 if data contains an even number of logic 1s and logic 0 if otherwise.

Listing 1.30 Verilog behavioral model of an odd parity generator using the *for loop* construct

```
module oddparity_for (output reg parity, input [7:0] data);

integer k;

always@(data)
    begin
        parity = 1;
        for (k = 0; k <= 7; k = k + 1)
        begin
            if (data[k] == 1)
                parity = ~parity;
        end
    end

endmodule
```

The Verilog HDL keyword *repeat* supports repetitive flow control for a specific number of times determined by the *repeat expression* and has no direct counterpart in the C language. Listing 1.31 is the odd parity generator of Listing 1.30 using the *repeat loop* construct. The *repeat expression* must be a constant in the Xilinx ISE EDA software tool. Note that the integer variable k is still declared and incremented as an index separately here.

Trends in Embedded Design Using Programmable Gate Arrays

Listing 1.31 Verilog behavioral model of an odd parity generator using the *repeat loop* construct

```
module oddparity_repeat (output reg parity, input [7:0] data);

integer k;

always@(data)
    begin
        parity = 1;
        k = 0;
        repeat (8)
            begin
                if (data[k] == 1)
                    parity = ~parity;
                k = k + 1;
            end
    end

endmodule
```

The Verilog HDL keyword *while* supports repetitive flow control as long as the *while expression* is true. Listing 1.32 is a generator that outputs a gated clock register variable gclk derived from the net variable signals clk and clkgate.

However, such valid Verilog HDL constructs as the *while loop* do not have an explicit termination, are not necessary synthesizable in the hardware of an FPGA and should be avoided. The repetitive *for loop* and *repeat loop* constructs with an explicit termination can also be terminated early by using the keyword *disable*. An external or internal signal, such as the net variable reset signal rst in Listing 1.26, can be used to abort a repetitive flow control loop by naming the process and using the keyword *disable* [Ciletti04].

Listing 1.32 Verilog behavioral model of a gated clock generator using the *while loop* construct

```
module gated_clock (output reg gclk, input clk, clkgate);

always@(clk or clkgate)
    begin
        while (clkgate)
            gclk = clk;
    end

endmodule
```

Functions and Tasks

The Verilog HDL can organize and improve the rendering of a structural or behavioral description with a function or a task [Botros06]. Verilog functions and tasks are intended to support blocks used in multiple instances. A Verilog function is declared within a module but exhibits only combinational behavioral. A function returns a value, must have at least one input argument and cannot declare an output or bidirectional input and output argument.

The keywords *function* and *endfunction* encapsulate the function, which contains a declaration of the implied output, followed by the inputs associated by the order in which they are declared and optional local variables. Verilog functions cannot invoke a Verilog task nor recursively call other functions in the Xilinx ISE EDA software tool. Listing 1.33 is a Verilog module with a function which returns the greater of two 8-bit signed net variables as an argument.

Listing 1.33 Verilog module with a function which returns the greater of two 8-bit signed variables

```
module greater (input signed [7:0] a, b, output reg signed [7:0] c);

always @(a, b)
    begin
        c = great(a, b);
    end

function [7:0] great (input signed [7:0] x, y);
    begin
        if (x >= y)
            great = x;
        else
            great = y;
    end
endfunction

endmodule
```

A Verilog task is declared within a module and can have parameters passed to it and one or more results returned. The arguments of the task are passed by value and associated by the order in which they are declared. The keywords *task* and *endtask* encapsulate the task, which contains a declaration of the implied output, input and optional local variables. Verilog tasks cannot recursively call other functions in the Xilinx ISE EDA software tool. Listing 1.34 is a Verilog module of a 1-bit adder, as in Listing 1.20, but here with a task which implements two 1-bit half adders.

Listing 1.34 Verilog module of a 1-bit full adder with a task implementing two 1-bit half adders

```
module full_add (output reg sum, output reg carry_out, input a, b, carry_in);

reg psum, p1carry, p2carry;

always@(a, b, carry_in)
    begin
        half_adder(psum, p1carry, b, carry_in);
        half_adder(sum, p2carry, psum, a);
        carry_out = p1carry | p2carry;
    end

task half_adder(output half_sum, half_carry, input x, y);
    begin
        half_sum = x ^ y;
        half_carry = x & y;
    end

endtask

endmodule
```

Trends in Embedded Design Using Programmable Gate Arrays

Finite State Machines

The finite state machine (FSM) is used in embedded design in Verilog using the field programmable gate array (FPGA) to represent sequential behavior. In the traditional FSM the logic output depends not only on a combination of the current logic input but on the *sequence* of past logic inputs. This past sequence or present *state* completely characterizes the FSM without regard to the past logic inputs [Mano07]. The number of states is assumed to be *finite* and can be described by the contents of a multiple bit state register [Navabi06].

The traditional FSMs are described by the Moore State Machine and the Mealy State Machine, as shown by the block diagrams in Figure 1.5 and Figure 1.6. The *next state* (NS) of either of the traditional FSMs are formed from the logic inputs and the state register stored value of the *present state* (PS). Every *state transition* must be logically explicit or the FSM will exhibit unpredictable behavior. [Zeidman99]. The logic outputs of the Moore Machine depend only upon the state register which is synchronized to the input clock. However, the outputs of the Mealy Machine depend on the state register and the logic inputs which may not be synchronized to the input clock.

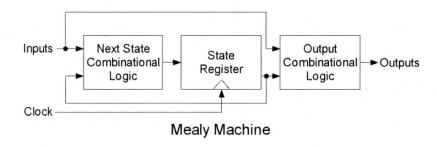

Figure 1.5 Block diagram of the traditional Mealy FSM

Listing 1.35 is Verilog module for a 4-state Mealy FSM with *binary state encoding* using a 2-bit state register. Binary state encoding utilizes the minimum number of bits require for the number of states. However, binary state encoding requires more combination logic decoding than the *one-hot state encoding*, as given in Listing 1.36, which uses a bit for each state [Mano07].

Listing 1.35 Verilog module for the Mealy FSM with binary state encoding

```
parameter <state1> = 2'b00;
parameter <state2> = 2'b01;
parameter <state3> = 2'b10;
parameter <state4> = 2'b11;

reg [1:0] state = <state1>;

always@(posedge <clock>)
     begin
          if (<reset>
               state <= <state1>;
          else
               case (state)
                    <state1> : begin
                              if (<condition>)
                                   state <= <next_state>;
```

```
                                else if (<condition>)
                                        state <= <next_state>;
                                else
                                        state <= <next_state>;
                        end
                <state2> : begin
                                if (<condition>)
                                        state <= <next_state>;
                                else if (<condition>)
                                        state <= <next_state>;
                                else
                                        state <= <next_state>;
                        end
                <state3> : begin
                                if (<condition>)
                                        state <= <next_state>;
                                else if (<condition>)
                                        state <= <next_state>;
                                else
                                        state <= <next_state>;
                        end
                <state4> : begin
                                if (<condition>)
                                        state <= <next_state>;
                                else if (<condition>)
                                        state <= <next_state>;
                                else
                                        state <= <next_state>;
                        end
        endcase

        assign <output1> = <logic_equation_based_on_states_and_inputs>;
        assign <output2> = <logic_equation_based_on_states_and_inputs>;
end
```

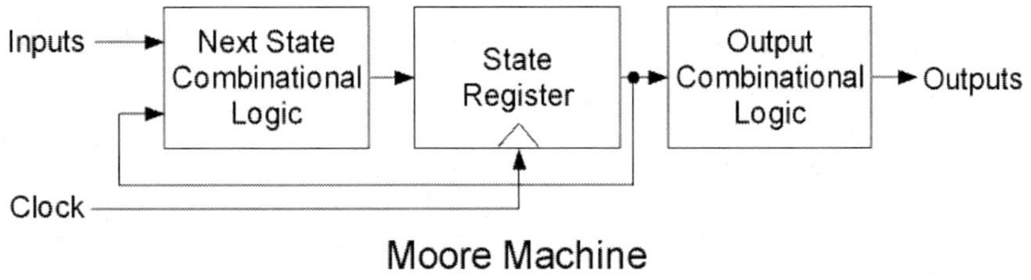

Figure 1.6 Block diagram of the traditional Moore FSM

Listing 1.36 is a Verilog module for a 4-state Moore FSM using a 4-bit state register with one-hot state encoding, which uses a bit for each state [Mano07].

Listing 1.36 Verilog module of the Moore FSM with one-hot state encoding

parameter <state1> = 4'b0001;

Trends in Embedded Design Using Programmable Gate Arrays

```verilog
parameter <state2> = 4'b0010;
parameter <state3> = 4'b0100;
parameter <state4> = 4'b1000;

reg [3:0] state = <state1>;

always@(posedge <clock>)
    begin
        if (<reset>)
            begin
                state <= <state1>;
                    <outputs> <= <initial_values>;
            end
        else
            case (state)
                <state1> : begin
                        if (<condition>)
                            state <= <next_state>;
                        else if (<condition>)
                            state <= <next_state>;
                        else
                            state <= <next_state>;
                        <outputs> <= <values>;
                    end
                <state2> : begin
                        if (<condition>)
                            state <= <next_state>;
                        else if (<condition>)
                            state <= <next_state>;

                        else
                            state <= <next_state>;
                        <outputs> <= <values>;
                    end
                <state3> : begin
                        if (<condition>)
                            state <= <next_state>;
                        else if (<condition>)
                            state <= <next_state>;
                        else
                            state <= <next_state>;
                        <outputs> <= <values>;
                    end
                <state4> : begin
                        if (<condition>)
                            state <= <next_state>;
                        else if (<condition>)
                            state <= <next_state>;

                        else
                            state <= <next_state>;
                        <outputs> <= <values>;
```

```
                           end
              endcase
    end
```

An arbitrary FSM as a Moore Machine with five states, where each state transition is logically explicit, is shown in Figure 1.7. The asynchronous RESET signal is used to set the present state to State 1. The synchronous CLOCK signal, which is not explicitly shown, initiates the determination of a state transition. The input logic signals are A, B, C and D and the output logic signals are X, Y and Z. State transitions occurs with a synchronous clock and the assertion of the combinational logic of the signals as AND (&), OR (|) and NOT (!) . The equivalent Verilog logic operations can process input logic signals even with multiple bits and use the symbols &&, || and !, as listed in Table 1.5.

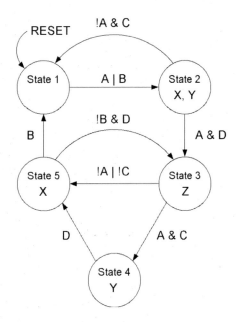

Figure 1.7 An arbitrary state diagram of a Moore FSM

The positive edge clock event driven Verilog HDL module for behavioral synthesis of the arbitrary Moore FSM of Figure 1.7 is given in Listing 1.39. The non-blocking assignment operator (<=) is used here to concurrently designate the output logic signals and the next state. The state register state requires three bits to provide binary state encoding for the five states. The Verilog statement default is required to insure that the unused state register values (0, 6, and 7) are determined. The Xilinx ISE EDA software tool configures an optimum decoding of the state register in Verilog HDL and one-hot state encoding is not explicitly required.

Listing 1.39 Verilog HDL of the arbitrary Moore FSM

```
reg [2:0] state;

  always@(posedge CLOCK)
    begin
        if (RESET)
            begin
                state <= 1;
```

```
                    X <= 0;
                    Y <= 0;
                    Z <= 0;
            end
    else
        case (state)
            1:   begin
                        if (A || B)
                            state <= 2;
                        X <= 0;
                        Y <= 0;
                        Z <= 0;
                 end
            2:   begin
                        if (!A && C)
                            state <= 1;
                        else if (A && D)
                            state <= 3;
                        X <= 1;
                        Y <= 1;
                        Z <= 0;
                 end
            3:   begin
                        if (!A || !C)
                            state <= 5;
                        else if (A && C)
                            state <= 4;

                        X <= 0;
                        Y <= 0;
                        Z <= 1;
                 end
            4:   begin
                        if (D)
                            state <= 5;
                        X <= 0;
                        Y <= 1;
                        Z <= 0;
                 end
            5:   begin
                        if (!B && D)
                            state <= 3;
                        else if (B)
                            state <= 1;
                        X <= 1;
                        Y <= 0;
                        Z <= 0;
                 end
            default: state <= 1;
        endcase
    end
```

Controller-Datapath Construct

Embedded design in Verilog using programmable gate arrays can utilize controller and datapath modules to facilitate the implementation of complex task. The controller module accepts external control signals and status signals from the datapath module and uses one or more finite state machine (FSM) to coordinate the process. The controller module sets the datapath module control input signals that route input data, perform any processing on the data and output the data to a functional unit [Navabi06]. The datapath module stores and manipulates data in registers using combinational logic and can use one or more FSM to output data but not autonomously. The controller can also accept external control signals from and return status signals to a sequential processor to augment the performance of the embedded system.

The controller and datapath construct partition the design into modules that can be separately verified in simulation, as described in Chapter 2 Verilog Design Automation. Rather than one module that encapsulates the entire process, the controller and datapath modules then each have a reduced number of interconnections which facilitates the Verilog behavioral synthesis into programmable gate array hardware. Datapath modules also support the concept of *design reuse*, as described in Chapter 3 Programmable Gate Array Hardware.

The controller module can be easily modified to accommodate a new task, which can then even include additional datapath modules. The configuration of a typical controller and datapath construct is shown in Figure 1.8. The synchronous clock inputs schedule the state transitions of the FSMs of the controller and datapath, if any. Registers can be initialized by a global reset signal, a local reset signal or by a declaration in the behavioral synthesis of the controller and datapath [Lee06]. The reset signal is not shown in Figure 1.8.

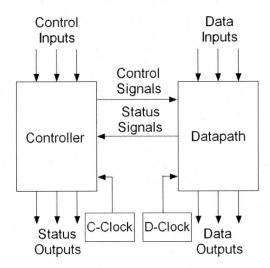

Figure 1.8 Configuration of a typical controller and datapath construct

The controller has *control input* logic signals that initiate the process and *status output* logic signals that signify the completion of the process. The datapath has only *data* as an input and output and no external process *control* logic signals other than those derived from the controller [Zeidman99]. The datapath outputs *status* logic signals to the controller to coordinate the process. A controller module can utilize many control signals but usually only one is evoked at a time which then waits for its status signal.

The controller and datapath can use either a single clock or clocks at different frequencies if warranted because coordination is only affected by the control and status logic signals. The clock

Trends in Embedded Design Using Programmable Gate Arrays

signals are used to provisionally evoke a state transition in the finite state machines (FSM) if utilized in the controller and datapath. The controller control signals and the datapath status signals usually are derived during a state transition of the FSM.

C to Verilog Translation

Embedded design has often relied upon the vast experience of utilizing the conversational language C to affect a process. If real-time processing is required, as in digital signal processing, digital communication or digital control, assembly language subroutines are used to augment the C language routines [Brown94]. However, although assembly language routines execute rapidly and are virtually at the microprocessor hardware level, they are not as discernible.

The translation of C language algorithms to the Verilog HDL can facilitate embedded design because behavioral synthesis Verilog is both conversational and ultimately executes rapidly at the programmable gate array hardware level [Smith00]. Selected algorithms available in the conversational C language can be readily translated to the and finite state machines (FSM) and then to the controller and datapath construct in the Verilog HDL, as shown in Figure 1.8. An example is the C algorithm for the greatest common denominator [Vahid02], as given in Listing 1.40.

Listing 1.40 Greatest common denominator C language algorithm

```
int gcd (int xin, int yin)
{
int x, y;

    x = xin;
    y = yin;
    while(x != y)
        {
        if (x < y)
            y = y - x;
        else
            x = x - y;
        }
    return x;
}
```

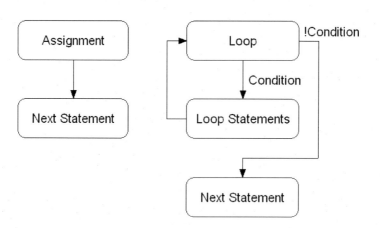

Figure 1.9 C language assignment and loop statement construct

The statements in the algorithm are first classified as assignment, loop or branch [Vahid02]. Assignment statements are mapped to an initial state which is immediate mapped to the next state in the FSM of the controller, as shown in Figure 1.9. Loop statements, derived from the C constructs *for* or *while*, are conditional statements which are mapped to either the loop statements and then a return to the conditional statement or to the next state if the condition is satisfied, as also shown in Figure 1.9 Finally, branch statements, derived from the C constructs *if-then-else* or *case*, are mapped separately to statements and then the next statement in FSM, as shown in Figure 1.10.

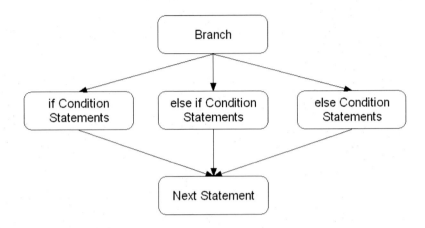

Figure 1.10 C language branch statement construct

The resulting five state FSM for the greatest common denominator algorithm is shown in Figure 1.11. Although this simple algorithm certainly does not require this level of complexity, for illustration the FSM can now be converted to Verilog HDL controller and datapath modules. The controller module incorporates the FSM and outputs commands to and inputs status signals from the datapath module, as shown in Figure 1.9. The datapath module is responsible for the input data (x and y) and output data (x), testing the loop statement (x ! = y) and the branch statement (x < y) and the data subtractions (y − x and x − y).

The Verilog HDL controller and datapath modules for the greater common denominator algorithm are given in Listing 1.41 and Listing 1.42. The controller module requires an external command signal that indicates that the process can start from another module. For the C language algorithm the subroutine merely is *called* from another routine but for the controller module an external signal gcddata is inputted for coordination. The controller module outputs the signal datagcd to the datapath module and the module that provided the external signal gcddata.

The command and status signals of the controller and datapath modules are shown in Figure 1.12. The controller signal lddata commands the datapath module to load the data xin and yin into the register variables x and y.

The datapath module sends the semaphore signal datald to the controller module to indicate that the data load has occurred. The other controller and datapath signals, subxy and xysub and subyx and yxsub, are for the arithmetic subtraction of the datapath register variables. The datapath modules also provides the xney and xlty signals to the controller module for the loop and branch statements.

Although this example of the greatest common denominator algorithm can be implemented as a controller and datapath construct in the Verilog HDL, an assembly or C language routine executing on a hard or soft core processor could be more discernable in practice because of the vast experience of utilizing these software paradigms.

However, the controller utilizes only a small number of event clock cycles, can execute a portion of the algorithm in parallel in each event state and does not require the multiple clock cycles of the instruction load, decode, and execute phase of a single processor instruction. Obviously, the design

Trends in Embedded Design Using Programmable Gate Arrays

tradeoff and selection of the controller and datapath construct verses a hard or soft core processor is a specific task in embedded design.

The ubiquitous nature of the conversational C programming language and the emerging paradigm of the programmable gate array in embedded design have provided the impetus to seek a hardware description language within the C syntax. SystemC is a system description language available as a set of library routines which makes it possible to simulate concurrent processes. SystemC has a hardware synthesis class subset and is now IEEE Standard 1066-2005.

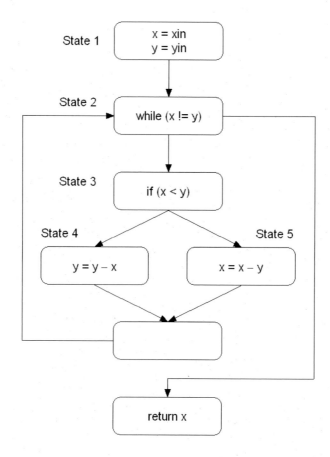

Figure 1.11 FSM for the greatest common denominator algorithm

Listing 1.41 Greatest common denominator C language algorithm Verilog controller module

```
module gcdcontroller (input clock, gcddata, lddata, xneqy, xlty, input xysub, yxsub, output reg gcdinit,
            output reg datagcd, output reg datald, output reg subxy, output reg subyx)

reg [2:0] gcdstate;

always@(posedge clock)
    begin
        if (gcddata == 0)
            begin
                gcdstate = 1;
                datagcd = 0;
```

```
                gcdinit = 1;
                datald = 0;
        end
    else
        case(gcdstate)
            1:    begin
                        gcdinit = 0;
                        datald = 1;
                        if (lddata)
                                begin
                                        datald = 0;
                                        gcdstate = 2;
                                end
                    end
            2:    begin
                        if (xneqy)
                                gcdstate = 3;
                        else
                                gcdstate = 6;
                    end
            3:    begin
                        if (xlty)
                                gcdstate = 4;
                        else
                                gcdstate = 5;
                    end
            4:    begin
                        subyx=1;
                            if (yxsub)
                                    begin
                                            subyx = 0;
                                            gcdstate = 2;
                                    end
                        end
            5:    begin
                        subxy = 1;
                        if (xysub)
                                begin
                                        subxy = 0;
                                        gcdstate = 2;
                                end
                    end
            6:    begin
                                datagcd = 1;
                                gstate = 6;
                            end
                default: gstate = 6;
        endcase
    end

endmodule
```

Trends in Embedded Design Using Programmable Gate Arrays

Listing 1.42 Greatest common denominator C language algorithm Verilog datapath module

```verilog
module gcddatapath (input clock, gcdinit, datagcd, datald, input subxy, subyx, output lddata,
                    output xneqy, xlty, xysub, yxsub,  inout [15:0] xdata, input signed ydata)
reg [15:0] x;
reg [15:0] y;

always@(posedge clock)
    begin
        if (gcdinit)
            begin
                lddata = 0;
                xney = 0;
                xlty = 0;
                xysub = 0;
                yxsub = 0;
            end
        if (datald)
            begin
                x = xdata;
                y = ydata;
                if (x != y)
                    xney = 1;
                if (x < y)
                    xlty = 1;
                lddata = 1;
            end
        if (subxy)
            begin
                x = x - y;
                if (x == y)
                    xney=0;
                if (x < y)
                    xlty = 1;
                xysub = 1;
            end
        if (subyx)
            begin
                y = y - x;
                if (x == y)
                    xney = 0;
                if (x < y)
                    xlty = 1;
                yxsub = 1;
            end
        if (datagcd)
            xdata = x;

    end

endmodule
```

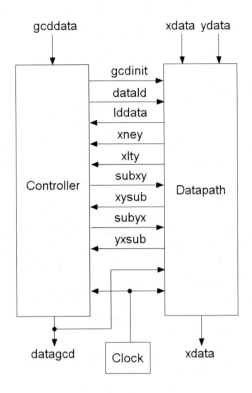

Figure 1.12 Controller and datapath modules for the greatest common
denominator algorithm

The Impulse C^{TM} design automation environment facilitates the execution of parallel algorithms that target programmable gate array and embedded, hard or soft core microprocessors for high performance computing (*www.impulseacclerated.com*). The Impulse C compiler generates an HDL for synthesizable hardware that implements streams, signals and memories. Impulse C extends standard ANSI C to support a communicating process parallel programming model (Pellerin05). Impulse C supports the Xilinx 32-bit embedded soft core MicroBlaze™ processor on the Spartan-6 FPGA.

Arithmetic Functions

The intrinsic arithmetic capabilities of the programmable gate array are similar to the conventional microprocessor because both are register based architectures [Smith00]. Signed and unsigned binary addition and subtraction are directly supported. Unlike the conventional microprocessor, the register size of the FPGA can be set to accommodate the task at hand. Microprocessors with an 8-bit register architecture, such as the Xilinx PicoBlaze soft core processor for the Xilinx Spartan-6 FPGA, require multiple byte arithmetic when processing analog-to-digital converter (ADC) and digital-to-analog converter (DAC) data with greater than 8 bits of resolution. However, the FPGA can provide registers for integer addition and subtraction suitable for the size in bits of the binary data and the arithmetic manipulation of the data.

Integer multiplication and division are often supported by conventional microprocessors. The 16-bit Intel 8086 microprocessor provides signed and unsigned integer multiplication, operational codes (*op codes*) IMUL and MUL, and division, op codes IDIV and DIV, through a *microcode* operation which requires multiple clock cycles [Brey05]. The Xilinx Spartan-6 FPGA supports rapid integer multiplication with the available of 18-bit hardware multipliers. Integer division, except by powers-of-two (2^n), is also supported by the use of the Xilinx CORE Generator and the LogiCORE blocks, as described in Chapter 2 Verilog Design Automation. The Multiplier LogiCORE block provides a parallel integer multiplier.

Floating-point arithmetic manipulations are usually not directly supported by conventional microprocessors. The Intel 8087 floating point coprocessor was an early adjunct to the 16-bit Intel 8086 microprocessor [Brey05]. The Xilinx Spartan-6 FPGA provides floating point operations with the Xilinx CORE generator LogiCORE block, as described in Chapter 2 Verilog Design Automation. These numbers are presented in both IEEE-754 Floating-Point Standard 32-bit and 64-bit format and non-standard size format. A floating-point number is represented using a sign bit, a w_e-bit exponent and a w_f-bit fraction, as shown in Figure 1.13. The value v of the floating-point number is determined by Equation 1.1.

$$v = (-1)^S \, 2^E \, b_0 b_1 b_2 ... b_{w_f-1} \qquad (1.1)$$

In Equation 1.1 S is the sign bit, E is the binary value of the w_e-bit exponent, and $b_i = 2^{-i}$. The sign bit causes the floating-point value to be negative if S = 1. The value of the biased unsigned exponent field e is determined by Equation 1.2.

$$e = \sum_{i=0}^{w_e-1} e_i \, 2^i \qquad (1.2)$$

In Equation 1.2 e_i represents the bits of the exponent, as shown in Figure 1.13. The exponent E in Equation 1.1 is obtained by removing the bias as determined by Equation 1.3.

$$E = e - (2^{w_e-1} - 1) \qquad (1.3)$$

The most significant bit b_0 is a *normalized* constant equal to 1 and is not represented in the floating-point number, as shown in Figure 1.13. The IEEE-754 Standard specifies a 32-bit format with a 24-bit fraction, an 8-bit exponent and a sign bit but only 23 bits are required for the fraction since b_0 is not represented. The IEEE-754 Standard also specifies a 64-bit format with a 53-bit fraction, an 11-bit exponent and a sign bit but again only 52 bits are required for the fraction.

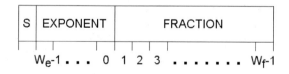

Figure 1.13 Floating-point number representation using a sign bit,
a w_e-bit exponent and a w_f-bit fraction

A fixed-point number is represented by a two's complement number weighted by a fixed power of two and an implied decimal point (■), as shown in Figure 1.14. The w-bit fixed-point number has a w_f-bit fraction, a $(w - w_f - 1)$-bit integer and a sign bit. The value u of the fixed-point number is determined by Equation 1.4 where $b_i = 2^{i - w_f}$. A signed integer number occurs when the fractional bit width is zero.

$$u = (-1)^S \, 2^{w-w_f-1} + b_{w-2} b_{w-3} ... b_{w_f+1} b_{w_f} \, b_{w_f-1} b_{w_f-2} ... b_1 b_0 \qquad (1.4)$$

The Xilinx CORE Generator LogiCORE Floating-Point block provides the floating-point operations of add, subtract, divide, square root and comparison and fixed-point to floating-point and floating-point to fixed-point conversion. The Coordinate Rotation Digital Computer (CORDIC) LogiCORE block provides vector rotation and translation, sine, cosine and tangent, arctangent, hyperbolic sine and cosine and square root calculations. The Multiplier and Pipelined Divider LogiCORE blocks support fixed-point arithmetic manipulations.

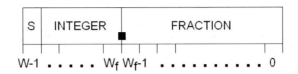

Figure 1.14 Fixed-point number representation using a sign bit,
A $(w - w_f - 1)$-bit integer and a w_f-bit fraction

These LogiCORE blocks for arithmetic functions and other LogiCORE blocks are described in Chapter 2 Verilog Design Automation. Chapter 4 Digital Signal Processing, Communications and Control present Xilinx ISE projects which survey the application of the Verilog HDL and programmable gate arrays in embedded design and use the FIR Compiler, Sine-Cosine Look-Up Table and the Direct Digital Synthesis Compiler LogiCORE blocks.

Programmable Gate Array and Microprocessor Comparison

The performance of a programmable gate array finite state machine (FSM) or controller and datapath construct for a task is quite noticeable when compared that of a conventional microprocessor. Microprocessors utilize operational codes (*op codes*) or instructions and data to sequentially perform the tasks required for an embedded design. The microprocessor is event driven by a master clock but requires several clock cycles to retrieve an op code instruction from random access or read-only memory and decode it, retrieve data if required, process the instruction and store the result. Usually operations cannot be performed in parallel by a conventional microprocessor and the throughput rate in real-time processing is then limited by the clock period and the complexity of the task.

Parallel operation of the Verilog HDL modules executing on a field programmable gate array (FPGA) facilitate real-time processing of diverse tasks. An example of an embedded design in Verilog for the Digilent Atlys™ board, which utilizes a Xilinx Spartan-6 FPGA, is an application which sets initiates a conversion of an analog input voltage to a 12-bit number and displays the results on the liquid crystal display (LCD). Four Verilog HDL modules are essentially operating simultaneously here, as given in Listing 1.43 The complete application is described in Chapter 3 Field Programmable Gate Array Hardware and given in Listing 3.31.

The analog-to-digital converter (ADC) Verilog datapath module *ad1adc.v* is operating in parallel with the LCD Verilog datapath modules *adclcd.v* and *lcd.v* while being supervised by the Verilog controller module *genadclcd.v*. In a microprocessor each of these tasks must be processed in sequence which often requires complex interrupt service routines [Vahid02].

The variable register size and bitwise logic operations of the FPGA also provide a performance increase compared to the fixed register size and register based logic operations of a conventional microprocessor. As an example of the performance comparison, the sequential transfer of 12 bits of data by a 16-bit microprocessor (Intel 8086) from the most significant bits (MSB) of a 16-bit general purpose register (bx) to a 12-bit digital-to-analog converter (DAC) input-output (I/O) peripheral in assembly language mnemonics (ASM) is given in Listing 1.44. This is a single task process that would be called as a subroutine.

Trends in Embedded Design Using Programmable Gate Arrays

Listing 1.43 Verilog HDL modules operating in parallel in an embedded design application

```
ad1adc M0 (CCLK, adcdav, davadc, adc0data, adc1data, adcsck, adcspod, conad);
adclcd M2 (CCLK, BTN0, resetlcd, clearlcd, homelcd, datalcd, addrlcd, initlcd, lcdreset, lcdclear,
           lcdhome, lcddata, lcdaddr, lcddatin, digitmux, data);
lcd M3 (CCLK, resetlcd, clearlcd, homelcd, datalcd, addrlcd, lcdreset, lcdclear, lcdhome, lcddata,
        lcdaddr, rslcd, rwlcd, elcd, lcdd, lcddatin, initlcd);
genadclcd M4 (CCLK, SW0, SW1, SW2, SW3, adcdav, davadc, adc0data, adc1data, digitmux, data);
```

The DAC here is assumed to be a 12-bit serial peripheral at I/O address 400h (hexadecimal) that inputs data (SDATA) at bit 0 of an 8-bit general purpose register (al) on the negative edge logic transition of the clock (SCLK) at bit 1 of the same register. The 8-bit I/O port is written to by the ASM command out dx,al and the ASM command mov is the register transfer instruction [Brey05]. The register bit manipulation ASM commands *and* and the ASM command *or* are similar to the intrinsic combinational logic Verilog HDL primitives, as listed in Table 1.9, but not as versatile as the bitwise logic operations, as listed in Table 1.1.

Listing 1.44 Sequential processor data transfer using Intel 8086 assembly language mnemonics

```
;SDATA from bx to DAC
;
sdato proc near
        mov ax,400H      ;IOW 400H
        mov dx,ax
        mov cl,12        ;count for 12 SDATA bits
sdatlp: rol bx,1
        mov al,bl
        and al,1         ;SDATA bit 0, SCLK=0 bit 1
        out dx,al
        or  al,2         ;SDATA bit 0, SCLK=1 bit 1
        out dx,al
        and al,0FDH
        out dx,al        ;SDATA bit 0, SCLK=0 bit 1
        dec cl           ;decrement count
        jnz sdatlp       ;jump if count is not zero
        ret
sdato endp
```

The finite state machine (FSM) in the Verilog HDL intrinsically provides a sequence of operations that is suited to convert sequential machine assembly language code that executes on a conventional microprocessor. If the DAC peripheral device sclk and sdata signals were interfaced to two I/O pins of an FPGA the resulting clock event driven Verilog HDL module for behavioral synthesis is rendered as given in Listing 1.45.

The I/O location of the logic signals for behavioral synthesis in an FPGA is set by a User Constraints File (UCF), as described in Chapter 2 Verilog Design Automation. The data transfer is affected by the positive edge of the signal clock and the semaphores dacdav and davdac are the controller command and datapath status signals. The data transfer is determined by sequence of the FSM which uses the dacstate state register. When the data transfer is completed the datapath sets the staus signal dacdac for the controller to logic 1.

Although there are 25 states in the FSM in Listing 1.45 for the datapath module, the Verilog hardware synthesis results produced with the FSM using blocking assigments are deterministic and the steps of the implementation have a constant latency. This is the same result as that for the ASM file for the sequential processor in Listing 1.44. However, for the Verilog HDL module several operations can occurring during a single state which require several ASM commands and a longer latency to accomplish.

Listing 1.45 Verilog HDL module for the data transfer

```
module sdat0 (input clock, dacdav, input [11:0] data, output reg sdata, output reg sclk,
          output reg davdac);

reg [4:0] dacstate;

always@(posedge clock)
    begin
        if (dacdav == 0)        ; controller command?
            begin
                dacstate = 0;
                sclk = 1;
            end
        else
            begin
            case (dacstate)
                0:    begin
                        davdac = 0;      // datapath status
                        sdata = data[11];
                        dacstate = 1;
                    end
                1:    begin
                        sclk = 0;
                        dacstate = 2;
                    end
                2:    begin
                        sdata = data[10];
                        sclk = 1;
                        dacstate = 3;
                    end
                3:    begin
                        sclk = 0;
                        dacstate=4;
                    end
{data bits 9 through 0 are sent similarly in states 4 through 23}
                24:   begin
                        davdac = 1;      // datapath status
                        sclk = 1;
                        dacstate = 24;
                    end
                default: dacstate = 24;
                endcase
            end
    end

endmodule
```

Trends in Embedded Design Using Programmable Gate Arrays

An alternative and seemingly more compact Verilog behavorial synthesis module for the data transfer is given in Listing 1.46. Here the repetitive states of the FSM for the loading of the data is replaced by an iteration of the integer variable i.

Listing 1.46 Alternative Verilog HDL module for the data transfer

```verilog
module sdat0 (input clock, dacdav, input [11:0] data, output reg sdata, output reg sclk,
              output reg davdac);

reg [1:0] dacstate;
integer i;

always@(posedge clock)
    begin
        if (dacdav == 0)
            begin
                i = 12;
                dacstate = 0;
                sclk = 1;
            end
        else
            begin
                davdac = 0;
                case (dacstate)
                    0:    begin
                              i = i – 1;
                              if (i == 0)
                                      dasstate = 3;
                              else
                                      sdata = data[i – 1];
                                      dacstate = 1;
                          end
                    1:    begin
                              sclk = 0;
                              dacstate = 2;
                          end
                    2:    begin
                              sclk = 1;
                              dacstate = 0;
                          end
                    3:    begin
                              davdac = 1;
                              dacstate = 3;
                          end
                endcase
            end
    end

endmodule
```

The Verilog hardware synthesis for the modules in Listing 1.45 and Listing 1.46 are observed to be nearly comparable in the number of resources required. However, the complexity and latency of the implementation of state 0 in Listing 1.46, in which all 12 bits of the data must be routed to, is problematic for FPGA hardware synthesis. Inclusion of additional signal or control processing tasks in that state then is limited and causes increased latency for high speed execution. For these reasons, the sequential FSM for serial data transfer, as given in Listing 1.45, is often utilized for such operations. However, the reduction in source code complexity for the alternative FSM in Listing 1.46 can be afforded in low speed execution if resources are available and signal or control routing is not problematic.

A comparison of the data transfer in Intel 8086 assembly language in Listing 1.44 and the Verilog HDL module in Listing 1.45 shows that the conversational nature of Verilog produces an easily discernable process. While a microprocessor could also employ a conversational language such a C to affect the same data transfer, the number of op codes and resulting execution time and may be even greater.

The command and status signals dacdav and davdac and the controller and datapath modules for the data transfer are shown in Figure 1.15. The logic signals dacdav and davdac provide parallelism and synchronization of the data transfer that is not available in a microprocessor executing a single task.

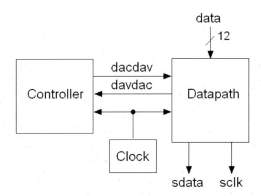

Figure 1.15 Controller and datapath modules for data transfer

A microprocessor would need to utilize a *multi-tasking operating system* to have this level of process coordination that is inherent in the Verilog HDL. Finally, the data to be transfer is inputted in parallel to the required number of bits and routing to the Verilog HDL module is provided by a *switch network* rather than a fixed path within a microprocessor. Such fixed paths readily led to bus contention and data transfer *stalls* [Smith00].

Soft Core Processors

The conventional microprocessor and a soft core processor implemented by an FPGA is a traditional architecture that is familiar to practitioners of embedded design. The limited internal program store for such a soft core processor, utilizing the Spartan-6 FPGA block random access memory (RAM), could be augmented by external non-volatile memory.

The soft core processor can utilize the datapath construct efficiently to *hand-off* such tasks as servicing both external hard core and internal soft core peripherals by effectively becoming the controller, as shown in Figure 1.15. Ultimately, several soft core processors could be instantiated in an embedded design on a single FPGA for either independent or cooperative operation.

The Xilinx ISE electronic design automation (EDA) software tool includes the Xilinx Embedded Development Kit (EDK) for the Xilinx 32-bit MicroBlaze soft core processor which can be programmed using the conversational C language. The architecture is described in the *MicroBlaze Processor Reference Guide* (UG081, *www.xilinx.com*).

Trends in Embedded Design Using Programmable Gate Arrays

Auxiliary EDA software for the Xilinx 8-bit PicoBlaze soft core processor is available. The 8-bit PicoBlaze is a *drop-in* module that can be easily instantiated in a Verilog behaviorial synthesis embedded design. However, programming of the PicoBlaze is accomplished in assembly language. The PicoBlaze architecture is described in Chapter 5 of the prior text [Silage08] and in the *PicoBlaze 8-Bit Embedded Microcontroller User Guide* (UG129, *www.xilinx.com*).

The Xilinx PicoBlaze is an 8-bit reduced instruction set computer (RISC) soft core processor optimized for efficiency and very low use of the available resources of the Xilinx field programmable gate arrays (FPGA). The PicoBlaze processor does not require any external resources, such as random access memory (RAM), and uses only 96 occupied slices and a single block RAM for program memory. The Xilinx PicoBlaze soft core processor architecture is shown in Figure 1.16.

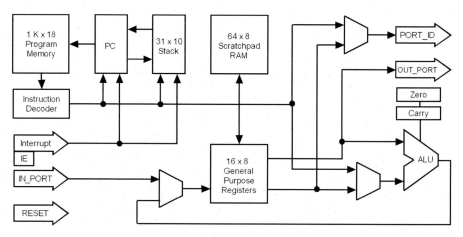

Figure 1.16 Xilinx PicoBlaze soft core processor architecture

The input-output (IO) interface signals to and from the PicoBlaze processor demonstrates the usefulness of this architecture as a controller, as shown in Figure 1.17. The 8-bit input data port IN_PORT provides data on the rising edge of the clock with the INPUT instruction.

Data appears on the 8-bit output port OUT_PORT for two clock cycles during the OUTPUT instruction. The input or output port address appears on the 8-bit PORT_ID during the INPUT or OUTPUT instruction. The INPUT and OUTPUT instructions can be either directly address as an 8-bit immediate constant or indirectly addressed as the contents of any of the general purpose registers.

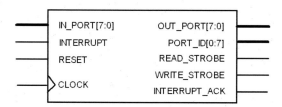

Figure 1.17 Xilinx PicoBlaze soft core processor interface signals

Chapter 5 Extensible Processing Platform introduces the Xilinx Zynq all programmable *system-on-chip* with a dual ARM Cortex™-A9 hard core processor, AMBA bus and integral FPGA. The Xilinx Zynq now provides the option to implement both a conventional hard core processor with programming in the C language and an FPGA with behaviorial synthesis in Verilog for embedded design.

Summary

In this Chapter the evolution of the Xilinx field programmable gate array (FPGA) and the concurrent development of a hardware description language (HDL) are described. Verilog HDL concepts and syntax are surveyed to support the development of an embedded design using programmable gate arrays. The finite state machine (FSM) and the controller and datapath constructs are presented as a behavioral description.

The translation of an algorithm in the conversational C language to the Verilog HDL facilitates the embedded design implementation. Behavioral synthesis Verilog is shown to be both conversational and ultimately executes rapidly at the FPGA hardware level. Finally, the conventional microprocessor and the FPGA are functionally compared. Unlike an FPGA, operations cannot be performed in parallel by a microprocessor and the throughput rate in real-time processing is then limited by the clock period and the complexity of the task.

Chapter 2 Verilog Design Automation presents the operation of the Xilinx Integrated Synthesis Environment (ISE) electronic design automation (EDA) tool for embedded design. Chapter 3 Programmable Gate Array Hardware describes two available Xilinx Spartan-6 FPGA hardware evaluation boards and peripherals in operation by complete Xilinx ISE projects. Chapter 4 Digital Signal Processing, Communications and Control presents complete Xilinx ISE projects in digital filtering, digital modulation in communication systems, data communication and digital process control.

These three Chapters survey the application of the Verilog HDL for programmable gate arrays in embedded design. Chapter 5 Extensible Processing Platform introduces the Xilinx Zynq all programmable *system-on-chip* with an ARM Cortex™-A9 hard core processor, AMBA bus and integral FPGA.

Trends in Embedded Design Using Programmable Gate Arrays

References

[Botros06]   Botros, Nazeih M., *HDL Programming Fundamentals*. Thomson Delmar, 2006.

[Brey05]   Brey, Barry M., *The Intel Microprocessors*. Prentice Hall, 2005.

[Brown94]   Brown, John F., *Embedded Systems Programming in C and Assembly*. Van Nostrand Reinhold, 1994.

[Ciletti99]   Cilletti, Michael D., *Modeling, Synthesis and Rapid Prototyping with the Verilog HDL*. Prentice Hall, 1999.

[Ciletti04]   Cilletti, Michael D., *Starter's Guide to Verilog 2001*. Prentice Hall, 2004.

[Lee06]   Lee, Sunggu., *Advanced Digital Logic Design*. Thomson, 2006.

[Mano07]   Mano, M. Morris and Michael D. Cilletti, *Digital Design*. Prentice Hall, 2007.

[Navabi06]   Navabi, Zainalabedin, *Verilog Digital System Design*. McGraw-Hill, 1999.

[Pellerin94]   Pellerin, David and Michael Holley, *Digital Design using ABEL*. Prentice Hall, 1994.

[Pellerin05]   Pellerin, David and Scott Thibault, *Practical FPGA Programming in C*. Prentice Hall, 2005.

[Silage08]   Silage, Dennis, *Embedded Design Using Programmable Gate Arrays*. Bookstand Publishing, 2008.

[Smith00]   Smith, David R. and Paul D. Franzon, *Verilog Styles for Synthesis of Digital Systems*. Prentice Hall, 2000.

[Vahid02]   Vahid, Frank and Tony Civargis, *Embedded System Design*, Wiley 2002.

[Zeidman99]   Bob Zeidman, *Verilog Designer's Library*. Prentice Hall, 1999.

2

Verilog Design Automation

Embedded design in the Verilog hardware description language (HDL) using a field programmable gate array (FPGA) is facilitated by software electronic design automation (EDA) tools which provide both simulation and hardware synthesis. The complexity of either the fine or coarse grained architecture of the FPGA, as described in Chapter 1 Hardware Description Language Verilog Hardware Description Language, requires EDA tools which can *route* the constructs of the Verilog HDL as an efficient, synthesizable interconnection of diverse logical elements.

The Xilinx (*www.xilinx.com*) Integrated Synthesis Environment (ISE®) is one such suite of EDA tools for the synthesis of embedded system applications in the FPGA from the Verilog HDL. This Chapter introduces the Xilinx ISE in a quick-start manner, with an emphasis on the project environment and the processes required to produce an embedded design for the Xilinx Spartan®-6 FPGA evaluation boards. The Verilog source and project file structure for the Xilinx ISE and FPGA hardware synthesis and configuration is described for an *elapsed time* example as a practical application. The FPGA evaluation boards and the *elapsed time* project are further described in Chapter 3 Field Programmable Gate Array Hardware.

This Chapter demonstrates the use of several additional components of the Xilinx ISE EDA. The Xilinx CORE Generator creates Verilog HDL modules as LogiCORE blocks that can be instantiated into a project to facilitate embedded design. A binary to binary coded decimal (BCD) converter Xilinx ISE project features the Divider Generator LogiCORE block. The Xilinx Floorplanner is an advanced software EDA tool that can in some instances improve the performance of an automatically placed and routed FPGA design. The Floorplanner is particularly useful for placing *critical path* logic to optimize timing performance in structural models and datapath modules. The Xilinx ISE Simulator provides behavioral and timing verification without hardware synthesis and implementation to the FPGA.

The Xilinx ISE Verilog Language Templates simply the process of implementing an embedded system design in an FPGA by providing a language implementation and syntax reference. The Xilinx Architecture Wizard is an advanced EDA tool that augments other Verilog HDL module creation tools such as the Xilinx CORE Generator. Finally, the Xilinx Timing Analyzer Xilinx Timing Analyzer provides a description of the timing constraint in error and design implementation suggestions to alleviate the error.

The Verilog source modules and project files are provided in the *Chapter 2* folder as subfolders identified by the name of the appropriate module. The complete contents and the file download procedure are described in the Appendix.

Xilinx Integrated Synthesis Environment

The registered and licensed electronic design automation (EDA) provided by Xilinx is the Integrated Synthesis Environment (ISE®) which supports the complete Xilinx complex programmable logic devices (CPLD) and field programmable gate arrays (FPGA). Xilinx also provides the registered but unlicensed ISE WebPACK™, which features the same functionality as ISE but with limited complex programmable logic device (CPLD) and FPGA support. However, the Xilinx Spartan®-6 FPGA devices are supported by ISE WebPACK. The evaluation boards, as further described in Chapter 3 Programmable Gate Array Hardware, both utilize the Xilinx Spartan-6 FPGA.

The Xilinx ISE is presented here in a *quick start* manner to begin the investigation of embedded system design in Verilog targeting the Xilinx Spartan-6 FPGA and the evaluation boards. The complete description of the Xilinx ISE is also available as an *In-Depth Tutorial* (UG695, *www.xilinx.com*). The Xilinx ISE WebPACK is freely available for download with software

Trends in Embedded Design Using Programmable Gate Arrays

registration (*www.xilinx.com*). The initial download for the Xilinx ISE or ISE WebPACK itself is relatively small but it administers the download of the entire application in the suggested directory *C:\Xilinx*.

The Xilinx ISE supports variety of design entry, simulation, synthesis, implementation, programming and verification tools including the HDL Editor, the Xilinx Synthesis Technology (XST), the CORE Generator, the iMPACT device programming environment, the FloorPlanner, the ISE Simulator and the Xilinx Embedded Development Kit (EDK). Also available are the Xilinx System Generator for DSP design entry tool, which is integrated with MATLAB/Simulink (*www.mathworks.com*), the architectural PlanAhead™ implementation tool and the ChipScope™ Pro verification tool.

The Xilinx EDK provides support for the advanced 32-bit MicroBlaze soft core processor, which pursues an alternative paradigm for embedded design using the conversational C language. Chapter 5 Extensible Processing Platform describes the Xilinx Zynq all programmable *system-on-chip* with dual ARM Cortex™-A9 hard core processors and FPGA.

The Xilinx PlanAhead EDA facilitates a hierarchical design methodology which minimizes routing congestion and interconnecting complexity for improved performance. The Xilinx ChipScope Pro EDA inserts logic analyzer, bus analyzer and virtual input-output (I/O) cores so that any internal signal or node can be captured or stimulated at system speed. The captured logic signals are then outputted through the programming interface without using normal I/O pins.

After the completion of the installation in the suggested directory *C:\Xilinx* for the Xilinx ISE and initial execution of the application, the *Project Navigator* design window is displayed, as shown in Figure 2.1. The bottom of the Project Navigator window shows a folder selection for console display of all process messages (Console), a display of only the fatal error messages (Error) or only warning messages (Warning) and the result of the *Find in Files* display which is evoked from the *Edit...Find in Files* menu command, as shown in Figure 2.2.

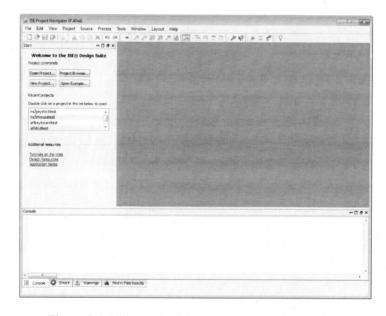

Figure 2.1 Xilinx ISE Project Navigator design window

The Xilinx ISE provides an on-line Help facility. Function key F1 provides Help for any highlighted tool or function and the *Help* menu command of the Project Navigator design window provides manuals and tutorials.

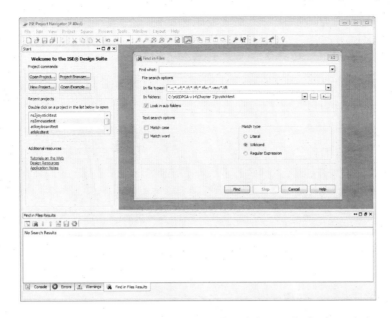

Figure 2.2 Find in Files menu command and the result display window

Project Creation

A new project can be created in the Xilinx ISE Project Navigator from the menu command *File…New Project* or from the *Project Command…New Project* button which opens the New Project Wizard – Create New Project window, as shown in Figure 2.3. The name of the Xilinx ISE project is *elapsedtimens3* (spaces are not allowed) and the location is the *C:\s6EDPGA-v14\Chapter 2\elapsedtimens3* folder.

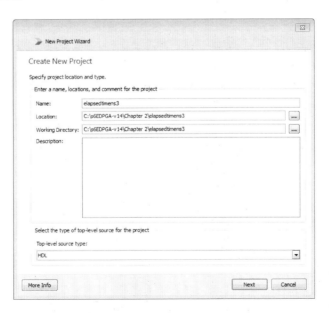

Figure 2.3 New Project Wizard – Create New Project window

Trends in Embedded Design Using Programmable Gate Arrays

The Nexys 3 Board (*www.digilentinc.com*) elapsed time or *stop watch* Verilog project is further described Chapter 3 Programmable Gate Array Hardware and given in Listing 3.15 as a test program for the seven segment LED display. However, it is used here to elucidate the requisite steps in the EDA process. The *Chapter 2\elapsedtimens3* folder is created automatically. The *Top-Level Source Type* should be HDL. Clicking *Next* opens the New Project Wizard – Project Settings window, as shown in Figure 2.4.

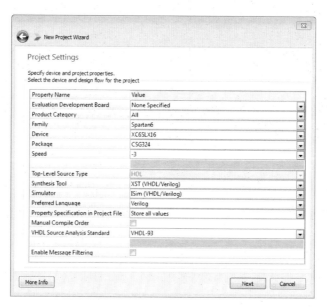

Figure 2.4 New Project Wizard – Project Settings window

Figure 2.5 New Project Wizard – Project Summary window

The FPGA device properties must match those of the device on the specific evaluator board, as described in Chapter 3 Programmable Gate Array Hardware. Here the Nexys 3 Board is used and the *Family* is Spartan6, the *Device* is XC6SLX16 (a Spartan-6 SLX16 FPGA), the *Package* is CSG324 (a fine pitch ball grid array package with 324 pins) and the *Speed* is -3 (standard speed grade).

The *Top Level Source Type* is HDL, the *Synthesis Tool* is XST and the *Simulator* is the ISim (ISE Simulator) and the Preferred Language is *Verilog*. Unchecking *Enable Message Filtering* provides an enhanced description of the design resources in use for the project.

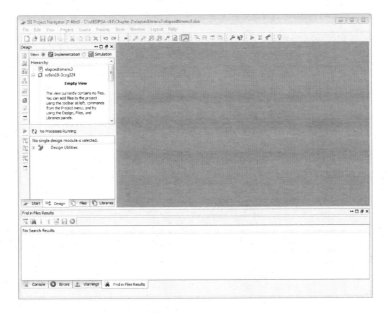

Figure 2.6 Project Navigator design window for the ISE project *elapsedtime.ise*

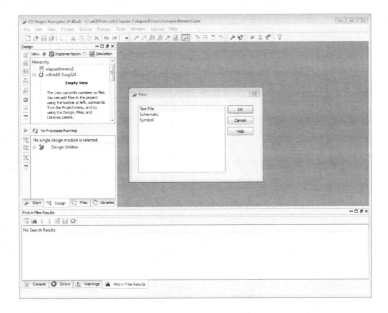

Figure 2.7 Project Navigator design window select Text File window

Clicking *Next* opens the New Project Wizard – Project Summary window, as shown in Figure 2.5. A summary of the specifications can be examined in this window before the project files are generated. Clicking *Finish* generates the project files and opens the Xilinx ISE Project Navigator

Trends in Embedded Design Using Programmable Gate Arrays

design window with the rudiments of the *elapsedtimens3.ise* project installed, as shown in Figure 2.6. Verilog source files can be created for the project by clicking on *File...New* which opens the select Text File window, as shown in Figure 2.7.

The editor of the Xilinx ISE Project Navigator design window then opens for the Verilog source file, as shown in Figure 2.8. The Verilog source text files must be added to the project after editing and saving them, as shown in Figure 2.9 and Figure 2.10. The Verilog source file association is for *All* which includes both *synthesis/implementation* and *simulation*.

Figure 2.8 Project Navigator design window source editor

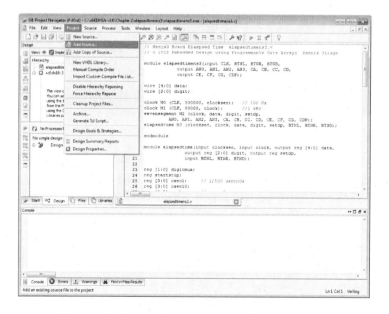

Figure 2.9 Project Navigator - Add Source… menu

The project has a designated top module and modules are implemented either by editing a new source or, through design reuse, adding an existing Verilog module. The top module can be set by highlighting then *right mouse button clicking* on the name of the module in the Sources window or from the Source menu of the taskbar of the Project Navigator.

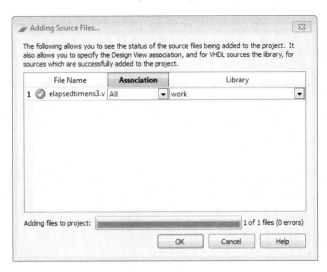

Figure 2.10 Project Navigator - Adding Source Files… window

Here the source modules for the elapsed time project are in folders and the *Project…Add Source* menu is used to add the top module *elapsedtimens3.v* and the template User Constraint File (UCF) is modified and saved as *elapsedtimens3.ucf* in the *Chapter 2\elapsedtime* folder. Also added to the project are the *clock.v* and the *sevensegment.v* datapath modules from the *Chapter 3\peripherals* folder. The controller module *elapsedtime.v* is in *elapsedtimens3.v*.

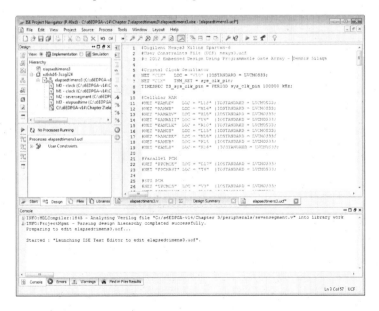

Figure 2.11 The template UCF in the Project Navigator design window source editor

The UCF is edited, saved and added to the project to assure that the input and output signals are routed to the proper pins, as described in Chapter 3 Programmable Gate Array Hardware.

Trends in Embedded Design Using Programmable Gate Arrays

Constraints can specify not only the naming, direction and pin placement of signals but can include electrical load, timing and implementation constraints [Ciletti04].

The template UCF for the FPGA evaluation boards, as described in Chapter 3 Programmable Gate Array Hardware in Listing 3.1 for the Nexys 3 Board and in Listing 3.2 for the Atlys Board, is opened as a file in the Project Navigator design window source editor, as shown in Figure 2.11.

The signals in the UCF used in the ISE project are uncommented (by removing the initial #) and the default signal names can be used in the Verilog module. The UCF is then saved with an appropriate new file name in the directory of the ISE project. The ISE project UCF must also be added to the project. The template UCF for the Nexys 3 Board is in the *Chapter 3\ucf* folder as the *nexys3.ucf* file. The template UCF for the Atlys Board, the other Spartan-6 FPGA evaluation board, is also in the same folder as the *atlys.ucf* file.

With the top module highlighted in the Hierarchy window of the Project Navigator, expanding Synthesis – XST in the Process window allows the syntax of the Verilog modules next to be checked by highlighting and *left mouse button clicking* the Check Syntax process, as shown in Figure 2.12.

Figure 2.12 Project Navigator - Synthesize - XST…Check Syntax design process

Project Implementation

Although any of the intermediate steps in the FPGA hardware synthesis process can be taken next, including design simulation, the project can readily be implemented as a configuration or *bit file* here targeting the specific Spartan-6 Nexys 3 Board. The process for the Spartan-6 Atlys Board is similar but not described here. The project UCF specifies the pin locations for the external signals that interface the Spartan-6 FPGA and its evaluation board peripherals, as described in Chapter 3 Programmable Gate Array Hardware.

The project can be synthesized and the FPGA can be programmed by highlighting and *left mouse button clicking* the Generate Programming File process, as shown in Figure 2.13. The Verilog structural or behavioral synthesis of a project can be a time-consuming process with numerous steps and intermediate file and console outputs. The progress and any warnings or errors of the hardware synthesis process can be followed in the Project Navigator console display, as shown in Figure 2.1. If the FPGA hardware synthesis process is successful, as shown in Figure 2.13, the configuration file *elapsedtimens3.bit* is generated in the project folder.

The Spartan-6 FPGA on the Nexys 3 Board is configured and programmed by the Adept application available from Digilent (*www.digilentinc.com*). Adept is a separate application and opens in its own window, as shown in Figure 2.14. The Spartan-6 Nexys 3 Board used here has three programmable devices, as described in Chapter 3 Programmable Gate Array Hardware. A USB cable from the host to the USB programming port of the Nexys 3 Board provides the configuration interface.

Figure 2.13 Project Navigator – Generate Programming File

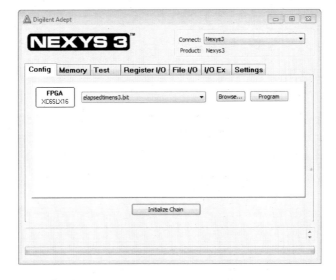

Figure 2.14 Digilent Adept Configuration menu tab

The Config (Configuration) menu tab in Adept identifies the Nexys 3 Board and the Xilinx XC6SLX16 Spartan-6 FPGA. After the assignment of the configuration file to the FPGA with the Browse… button, the Program button in Adept downloads the bit file via the USB cable to the USB programming port of the Nexys 3 Board.

Only the volatile FPGA is targeted for the configuration file here, although a bit file can be programmed into either the non-volatile parallel or serial phase change memories (PCM) and then

Trends in Embedded Design Using Programmable Gate Arrays

downloaded into the FPGA on *power up*. The Memory menu tab in Adept is used to program the parallel BPI Flash or serial SPI Flash memories, as shown in Figure 2.15.

The Spartan-6 Nexys 3 Board is now configured with the ISE project and begins executing. If the Xilinx ISE project source files or the UCF is modified it is only necessary to highlight and *left mouse button click* the Generate Programming File process to repeat the FPGA hardware synthesis process, as shown in Figure 2.13.

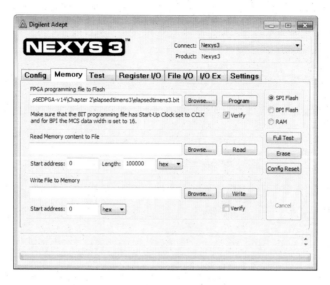

Figure 2.15 Digilent Adept Memory menu tab

Design Summary

The Xilinx ISE Project Navigator window provides a Design Summary tab for the synthesized ISE project, as shown in Figure 2.16. The Project Status window gives the name of the project, the Verilog hierarchical top module file name, the synthesis FPGA target device, the ISE version number, links to any errors or warnings and the date and time of the most recent project synthesis. The Device Utilization Summary window gives the logic utilization and distribution for the project synthesis.

The logic utilization is given as the number used and the percentage of the total available *slice registers* and *slice look up tables* (*LUT*) of the specific Spartan-6 FPGA, as described in Chapter 1 Hardware Description Language. The logic distribution is given as the number used and the percentage of the total available *slices* and their use in the design synthesis. The scrollable Design Summary window also provide the Performance Summary and the Detailed Reports both with links to more ISE project information, as shown in Figure 2.17.

All Implementation Messages of the Design Summary provides a listing of the warnings and errors encounters in the Xilinx ISE project synthesis and other salient information, as shown in Figure 2.18. The messages are grouped by the EDA tool that generated them. Warning and informational messages can be useful to the design process. Warning messages describe several signals as not changing or not used in the ISE project and were truncated. The Xilinx ISE informational messages describe the automatic steps taken in the ISE project synthesis.

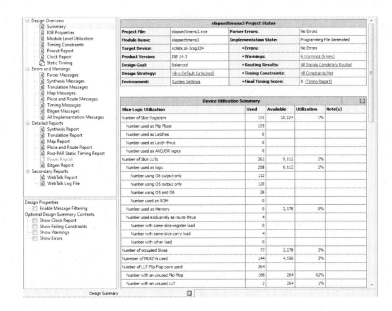

Figure 2.16 Project Navigator – Design Summary initial window

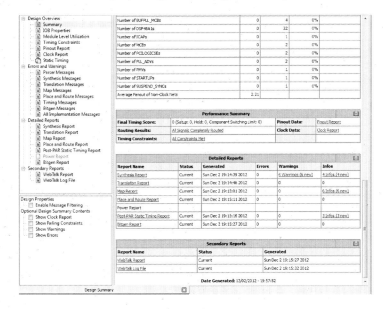

Figure 2.17 Project Navigator – Design Summary scrolled window

Figure 2.18 Project Navigator – Design Summary – All Implementation Messages window

Xilinx CORE Generator

The Xilinx CORE Generator™ System provides an optimized set of *building blocks* for common and specialized functions that facilitate embedded system design in Verilog using programmable gate arrays. The CORE Generator System provides access to the Xilinx LogiCORE™ intellectual property (IP) products. Several of the LogiCORE blocks for the Spartan-6 FPGA of the Nexys 3 Board and the Atlys Board are freely available. The implementation and inclusion of one such LogiCORE block into an ISE project is described here. Each LogiCORE product is provided with a descriptive data sheet, Verilog instantiation and a module description.

LogiCORE Creation

The name of the Xilinx ISE project is *binBCDdivider* and the location is the *Chapter 2\binBCDdivider* folder. This project reads the setting of the Nexys 3 Board eight slide switches as an 8-bit binary number. The 8-bit binary number is converted by a LogiCORE *pipelined divider* to a three digit (000 to 225) binary coded decimal (BCD) number, which is then outputted to the seven segment display. The 8-bit binary number read from the switches is also outputted to the light emitting diodes (LED). Further details of this project implementation as Verilog modules in support of the slide switches (SW), LED and the seven segment display of the Nexys 3 Board are described in Chapter 3 Programmable Gate Array Hardware.

The CORE Generator is installed as a part of the Xilinx ISE electronic design automation (EDA) tools and is accessible from the *Project…New Source* menu command, which opens New Source Wizard – Select Source Type window, as shown in Figure 2.19. Select *IP (Coregen & Architecture Wizard)* and enter the file name (*binbcddivider*) and project location for the LogiCORE Verilog instantiation and a module description. The file name cannot contain uppercase letters or start with a digit. The location for the LogiCORE module should be the same directory as that of the ISE project and the *Add to project* box should be checked.

Clicking *Next* opens the New Source Wizard – Select IP (Intellectual Property) window, as shown in Figure 2.20. Opening the *Math Functions…Dividers* directory folder shows the two LogiCORE products that are available. Select the Divider Generator 3.0 LogiCORE product for the project here. The Divider Generator 4.0 LogiCORE product is an AXI4-Stream compliant interconnection for the Advanced Microcontroller Bus Architecture (AMBA®), as described in Chapter 5 Extensible Processing Platform for the Xilinx Zynq all programmable *system-on-chip* device.

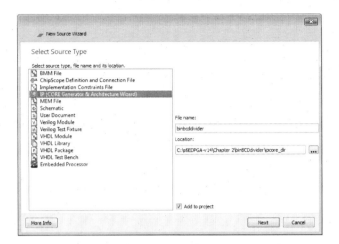

Figure 2.19 New Source Window – Select Source Type window

Figure 2.20 New Source Wizard – Select IP window

Clicking *Next* produces the New Source Wizard – Summary window, as shown in Figure 2.21. The summary describes the LogiCORE product selected, the file name and location and is customized for the Spartan-6 FPGA specified in the ISE project, as shown in the New Project Wizard – Project Settings window in Figure 2.4.

Clicking *Finish* opens the Divider Generator v3.0 LogiCORE design window, as shown in Figure 2.22. The Divider Generator LogiCORE block is a fixed-point divider based on radix-2 non-restoring division and is described in the data sheet DS530 (*www.xilinx.com*). The data sheet can be viewed (as a *pdf* file) by clicking the *Datasheet* button. The Divider is implemented as a fixed-point divider with a clock enable (CE) input signal, while the asynchronous clear (ACLR) and the synchronous clear (SCLR) input signals are not checked and are not used here.

The ready for data (RFD) output signal indicates the clock cycle in which input data is sampled. However, the RFD signal is only applicable if the number of cycles for the pipelined division is not 1. The dividend and divisor bus widths are both selected to be 8-bit, the number of clocks per division is 1, the operands are unsigned, and the remainder option is set.

Figure 2.21 New Source Wizard – Summary window

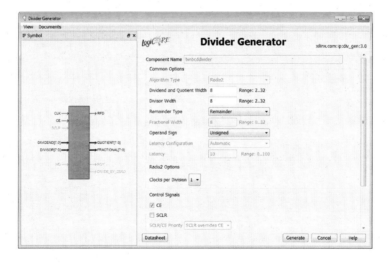

Figure 2.22 Design window of the LogiCORE Divider Generator v3.0

Clicking *Generate* produces the Divider LogiCORE block in the Xilinx CORE Generator which provides a *Readme File* with a description of the components. Here the file name is *binbcddivider_readme.txt* in the ISE project directory subfolder \ipcore_dir.

The Verilog components include the LogiCORE parameter file *binbcddivider.xco*, the instantiation template file *binbcddivider.veo* and the (so-called) wrapper file *binbcddivider.v* for functional implementation or simulation. The template file for each generated core must be instantiated into the parent design.

To instantiate a LogiCORE block into an Xilinx ISE project in Verilog, *copy and paste* the instantiation template file (*.veo*) into the appropriate area of the top module of the project. The module instantiation template file *binbcddivider.veo*, as shown in Listing 2.1, is in the project directory subfolder \ipcore_dir and opened in the Project Navigator design window by clicking on *File...Open*.

Listing 2.1 LogiCORE instantiation template file *binbcdcddivider.veo*

```
// The following must be inserted into your Verilog file for this
// core to be instantiated. Change the instance name and port connections
// (in parentheses) to your own signal names.

//----------- Begin Cut here for INSTANTIATION Template ---// INST_TAG
binbcddivider YourInstanceName (
    .clk(clk),   // input clk
    .ce(ce),     // input ce
    .rfd(rfd),   // output rfd
    .dividend(dividend),  // input [7 : 0] dividend
    .divisor(divisor),       // input [7 : 0] divisor
    .quotient(quotient),    // output [7 : 0] quotient
    .fractional(fractional)); // output [7 : 0] fractional

// INST_TAG_END ------ End INSTANTIATION Template ---------
```

YourInstanceName, a dummy name from the instantiation template *binbcdcddivider.veo* in Listing 2.1, must be changed and the port connections may need to change to reflect the actual connections in the ISE project. The *connection by name* is used in the instantiation template for the port connections, as described in Chapter 1 Verilog Hardware Description Language. Comment statements in *binbcdcddivider.veo* can be deleted. The Xilinx CORE generator parameter file *binbcddivider.xco* is automatically added to the ISE project, as shown in Figure 2.23.

Figure 2.23 Project Navigator window for the ISE project *binbcddivider.xise*

The LogiCORE binary to BCD pipelined divider module *binbcddivider.xco* is verified by the Verilog top module *binBCD.v* in Listing 2.2 which is in the *Chapter 2\binBCDdivider* folder. The instantiated LogiCORE module is copied from Listing 2.1 and inserted and modified, as shown in Listing 2.2. The module name for the pipelined divider is M2 in the top module and the default port connection names are used.

The complete Xilinx ISE project uses a User Constraints File (UCF) which uncomments the signals CLK, SW[0] to SW[7], LED[0] to LED[1], AN0, AN1, AN2, AN3, CA, CB, CC, CD, CE, CF, CG and CDP in the Nexys 3 Board UCF *nexys3.ucf* in Listing 3.2. The four Verilog modules operate

Trends in Embedded Design Using Programmable Gate Arrays

in parallel and some independently in the top module, as described in Chapter 3 Programmable Gate Array Hardware.

Listing 2.2 LogiCORE pipelined divider verification top module *binBCD.v*

```
// Nexys 3 Board
// LogiCORE Divider Binary to BCD binBCD.v
// c 2012 Embedded Design using Programmable Gate Arrays  Dennis Silage

module binBCD (input CLK, BTND, input [7:0] SW, output [7:0] LED,
               output AN0, AN1, AN2, AN3, CA, CB, CC, CD,
               output CE, CF, CG, CDP);

wire [7:0] bindata;
wire [7:0] divisor;
wire [7:0] dividend;
wire [7:0] quotient;
wire [7:0] fractional;
wire [4:0] data;
wire [2:0] digit;

assign LED = bindata;

gendata M0 (clock, BTND, SW, bindata, ce, rfd, dividend, divisor, quotient, fractional,
            data, digit, setdp);
sevensegment M1 (clock, data, digit, setdp, AN0, AN1, AN2, AN3, CA, CB, CC, CD, CE,
                 CF, CG, CDP);
binbcddiv M2 (.clk(CLK), .ce(ce), .rfd(rfd), .dividend(dividend), .divisor(divisor), .quotient(quotient),
              .fractional(fractional));
clock M3 (CLK, 50000, clock);       //1 kHz

endmodule
```

The structure and function of the controller module *gendata.v* and the seven segment LED display datapath module *sevensegment.v* are described for other specific embedded design applications in Chapter 3 Programmable Gate Array Hardware. The Xilinx ISE project here is intended to introduce the Xilinx CORE Generator System. The concept of a controller and datapath Verilog behavioral synthesis modules in embedded design is discussed in Chapter 1 Verilog Hardware Description Language.

The Design Utilization Summary for the top module *binBCD.v* for the LogiCORE pipelined divider shows the use of 233 slice registers (1%) and 250 slice LUTs (2%) in the XC6SLX16 Spartan-6 FPGA synthesis.

Implementation Comparison

The conversion of a binary number to a BCD representation is prevalent in embedded design applications [Botros06]. The Xilinx XST Verilog HDL compiler only supports division (/) by signed powers-of-two ($\pm 2^n$) so a direct conversion by dividing by powers-of-ten (10^n) is not possible [Ciletti04]. The LogiCORE pipeline divider, as given in Listing 2.1 and used in Listing 2.2, is a general solution that operates on any divisor and can produce its result in one clock cycle. Although the FPGA resource allocation of slice registers and slice LUTs is large, it can be reduced if 2, 4 or 8 clock cycles are specified for the pipelined divider.

However, embedded design in the Verilog HDL often requires a reasonable search for alternative structures that either may require less FPGA resources or present other desirable properties such as the data throughput rate [Ciletti99]. A top modular design for an ISE project also implies that other algorithms can be convenient inserted and synthesized.

The first alternative is the behavioral model in the Verilog HDL for binary to BCD conversion by iterative subtraction. The name of the Xilinx ISE project is *binBCDiterative.xise* and the location is the *Chapter 2\binBCDiterative* folder. The iterative subtraction algorithm is verified by the top module *binBCDiter.v*, which is similar to the top module for the LogiCORE pipelined divider *binBCD.v*, as given in Listing 2.2.

The behavioral model iterative subtraction Verilog module for binary to BCD conversion *iterative.v* is the datapath to the controller module *geniterdata.v* and is given in Listing 2.3. The controller-datapath signals are datadav and davdata, as described in Chapter 1 Hardware Description Language Verilog Hardware Description Language. The binary input data bindata is sequentially subtracted by powers-of-ten while incrementing the 4-bit BCD most significant and middle digit counters msdigit and middigit. The least significant digit lsdigit is the remainder. The 8-bit input signal bindata must be copied to an internal 8-bit register value for processing.

Listing 2.3 Iterative subtraction module for binary to BCD conversion *iterative.v*

```
// Binary to BCD Iterative Conversion iterative.v
// c 2012 Embedded Design using Programmable Gate Arrays  Dennis Silage

module iterative (input dav, input [7:0] bindata, output reg [3:0] msdigit, output reg [3:0] middigit,
                  output reg [3:0] lsdigit, output reg dataav);

reg [7:0] value;
integer i;

always@(posedge dav)
    begin
        dataav = 0;
        value = bindata;
        msdigit = 0;                // most significant digit
        for (i = 1; i <= 9; i = i + 1)
            begin
                if (value >= 100)
                    begin
                        msdigit = msdigit + 1;
                        value = value - 100;
                    end
            end

        middigit = 0;               // middle digit
        for (i = 1; i <= 9; i = i + 1)
            begin
                if (value >= 10)
                    begin
                        middigit = middigit + 1;
                        value = value - 10;
                    end
            end
```

Trends in Embedded Design Using Programmable Gate Arrays

```
            lsdigit[3:0] = value[3:0];    // least significant digit
            dataav = 1;
      end

endmodule
```

The Design Utilization Summary for the top module *binBCDiter.v* for the conversion by iterative subtraction for binary to BCD shows the use of 53 slice registers (<1%) and 135 slice LUTs (1%) in the XC6SLX16 Spartan-6 FPGA synthesis. This FPGA resource utilization is less than half that of the top module *binBCD.v* for the LogiCORE pipeline divider that accommodates any divisor.

The iterative subtraction algorithm produces its results for all three BCD digits in one clock cycle, although it uses a fixed scheme. The controller-datapath signals datadav and davdata can be assigned to one of the 4-bit output ports (6-bit header) of the Nexys 3 Board as *test points*, as described in Chapter 3 Programmable Gate Array Hardware. The latency of the controller-datapath signals can then be monitored by a logic analyzer or oscilloscope to assess its performance.

The second alternative for binary to BCD conversion in the Verilog HDL is the shift-and-add-3 behavioral model [Wakerly00]. The name of the Xilinx ISE project is *binBCDshiftadd3.xise* and the location is the *Chapter 2\binaryBCDshiftadd3* folder. The shift-and-add-3 binary to BCD conversion is verified by the top module *binBCDsadd3.v*, which is similar to the top module for the LogiCORE pipelined divider *binBCD.v*, as given in Listing 2.2.

The shift-and-add-3 Verilog module for binary to BCD conversion *shiftadd3.v*, as given in Listing 2.4, is itself a top module for the behavioral module *shiftadd.v*, which illustrates the concept of a hierarchical structure of nested modules, as described in Chapter 1 Verilog Hardware Description Language. The *shiftadd.v* datapath module is event driven on change in the input signal indata.

The binary input data bindata is processed by a *cascade* of seven shift-and-add-3 modules to produce the most significant msdigit. middle middigit and least significant lsdigit digits. Here the 8-bit input signal bindata does not need to be copied to an internal register in *shiftadd3.v* for processing, as it was in *interative.v* as given in Listing 2.3, and continuous assignment statements route the net variable signals.

Listing 2.4 Shift-and-add-3 module for binary to BCD conversion *shiftadd3.v*

```
// Binary to BCD Shift and Add 3 Conversion shiftadd3.v
// c 2012 Embedded Design using Programmable Gate Arrays  Dennis Silage

module shiftadd3 (input [7:0] bindata, output [3:0] msdigit, output [3:0] middigit, output [3:0] lsdigit);

wire [3:0] result1, result2, result3, result4, result5;
wire [3:0] result6, result7;
wire [3:0] value1, value2, value3, value4, value5;
wire [3:0] value6, value7;

assign value1 = {1'b0, bindata[7:5]};
assign value2 = {result1[2:0], bindata[4]};
assign value3 = {result2[2:0], bindata[3]};
assign value4 = {result3[2:0], bindata[2]};
assign value5 = {result4[2:0], bindata[1]};
assign value6 = {1'b0,result1[3], result2[3], result3[3]};
assign value7 = {result6[2:0], result4[3]};

shiftadd M1 (value1, result1);
shiftadd M2 (value2, result2);
```

```
shiftadd M3 (value3, result3);
shiftadd M4 (value4, result4);
shiftadd M5 (value5, result5);
shiftadd M6 (value6, result6);
shiftadd M7 (value7, result7);

assign msdigit[1:0] = {result6[3], result7[3]};
assign msdigit[3:2] = 0;
assign middigit = {result7[2:0], result5[3]};
assign lsdigit = {result5[2:0], bindata[0]};

endmodule

module shiftadd (input [3:0] indata, output reg [3:0] outdata);

always@(indata)
    case(indata)
        0:    outdata = 0;
        1:    outdata = 1;
        2:    outdata = 2;
        3:    outdata = 3;
        4:    outdata = 4;
        5:    outdata = 8;
        6:    outdata = 9;
        7:    outdata = 10;
        8:    outdata = 11;
        9:    outdata = 12;
        default: outdata = 0;
    endcase

endmodule
```

The Design Utilization Summary for the top module *binBCDsadd3.v* for the shift-and-add-3 algorithm for binary to BCD conversion shows the use of 43 slice registers (1%) and 127 slice LUTs (1%) in the XC6SLX16 Spartan-6 FPGA synthesis. This FPGA resource utilization is approximately the same as that of the top module *binBCDiter.v* for the iterative subtraction algorithm and less than half that of the top module *binBCD.v* for the LogiCORE pipeline divider for binary to BCD conversion. The shift-and-add-3 algorithm produces its results for all three BCD digits in one clock cycle, although it uses a fixed scheme.

The third alternative is the structural model for the serial conversion of binary to BCD in a complex programmable logic device (CPLD), as described in a Xilinx application note (XAPP029, *www.xilinx.com*) but not implemented here. The binary to BCD conversion is performed in a modified shift register that sequentially shifts the binary data serially into the register and successively doubles its contents. However, if during the conversion a BCD digit or 5 or greater is encountered, the shift register contents must be converted to the proper BCD value of its doubled contents and a logic 1 shifted into the next higher digit register [Navabi06].

Finally, the fourth alternative binary to BCD conversion is the *table look-up*. The obsolete 74185 medium scale integration (MSI) integrated circuit (IC) implemented a 6-bit binary to BCD conversion by using a 256-bit read-only memory (ROM). This does illustrate though another possible implementation for binary to BCD conversion using the block RAM (block random access memory, BRAM) feature of the Spartan-6 FPGA as a table look up in read-only memory (ROM).

Trends in Embedded Design Using Programmable Gate Arrays

ROM can be used for the conversion of 8-bit binary to three BCD digits. The three BCD digits are implemented as 12 bits, although only 10 bits are required since the most significant digit is 0, 1 or 2. The table look-up concept can also be used for other applications in embedded design such as the linearization of an analog transducer signal output after quantization.

The table look-up for binary to BCD conversion in the Verilog HDL is the Xilinx ISE project is *binBCDROM.xise* and the location is the *Chapter 2\binaryBCDROM* folder. The conversion is verified by the top module *binBCDROM.v*, which is similar to the top module for the LogiCORE pipelined divider *binBCD.v*, as given in Listing 2.2.

The conversion is a ROM implemented by the LogiCORE Distributed Memory Generator, whose initial design window is shown in Figure 2.24. The generated Verilog module is *ROMbinBCD.xco*. The BRAM is configured as ROM with 8 bits of address for 256 locations and 12 bits of data for the three BCD digits.

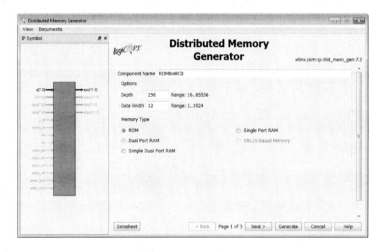

Figure 2.24 Initial design window of the Distributed Memory Generator v7.2

The second design window of the LogiCORE block specifies non-registered (latched) data for the input and output, as shown in Figure 2.25. The third design window specifies the coefficient file or data that determines the contents of the ROM, as shown in Figure 2.26. The coefficient file *binROMBCD.coe* is prepared by any text editor and specifies the memory_initialization_radix as 16 (hexadecimal) and then lists the 256 entries of the memory_initialization_vector for the conversion of binary to BCD by table look-up, as given in Listing 2.5. The data entries seem to be decimal but are actually BCD since the radix is hexadecimal. Comment statements in the coefficient file are preceded by a semi-colon (;), data entries are separated by a space and declarative statements also are terminated by a semi-colon.

Listing 2.5 LogiCORE Distributed Memory Generator coefficient file *ROMbinBCD.coe*

```
;initialization file for ROM
memory_initialization_radix = 16;
memory_initialization_vector =
0 1 2 3 4 5 6 7 8 9 10 11 12 13 14 15
16 17 18 19 20 21 22 23 24 25 26 27 28 29 30 31
32 33 34 35 36 37 28 29 40 41 42 43 44 45 46 47
48 49 50 51 52 53 54 55 56 57 58 59 60 61 62 63
64 65 66 67 68 69 70 71 72 73 74 75 76 77 78 79
80 81 82 83 84 85 86 87 88 89 90 91 92 93 94 95
96 97 98 99 100 101 102 103 104 105 106 107 108 109 110 111
```

112 113 114 115 116 117 118 119 120 121 122 123 124 125 126 127
128 129 130 131 132 133 134 135 136 137 138 139 140 141 142 143
144 145 146 147 148 149 150 151 152 153 154 155 156 157 158 159
160 161 162 163 164 165 166 167 168 169 170 171 172 173 174 175
176 177 178 179 180 181 182 183 184 185 186 187 188 189 190 191
192 193 194 195 196 197 198 199 200 201 202 203 204 205 206 207
208 209 210 211 212 213 214 215 216 217 218 219 220 221 222 223
224 225 226 227 228 229 230 231 232 233 234 235 236 237 238 239
240 241 242 243 244 245 246 247 248 249 250 251 252 253 254 255;

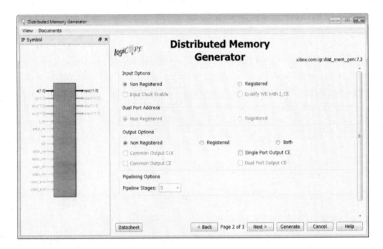

Figure 2.25 Second design window of the Distributed Memory Generator v7.2

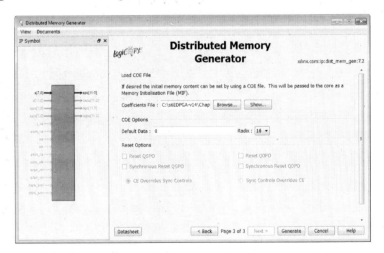

Figure 2.26 Third design window of the Distributed Memory Generator v7.2

The Design Utilization Summary for the top module *binBCDROM.v* for the table look-up binary to BCD conversion shows the use of 61 slice registers (<1%) and 130 slice LUTs (<1%) in the XC6SLX16 Spartan-6 FPGA synthesis. This FPGA resource utilization is approximately the same as that of the top module *binBCDiter.v* for the iterative subtraction algorithm and less than half that of the top module *binBCD.v* for the LogiCORE pipeline divider for binary to BCD conversion. The Summary also discloses that only look-up tables (LUT) are used in the LogiCORE block synthesis for the ROM.

Trends in Embedded Design Using Programmable Gate Arrays

Xilinx PlanAhead

The Xilinx ISE PlanAhead™ is an advanced software electronic design automation (EDA) tool for the entire FPGA design and implementation cycle. The PlanAhead tool is integrated with the Xilinx ISE, Core Generator and Simulator and can in some instances improve the performance of an automatically placed and routed FPGA design. This EDA tool is described in the *PlanAhead User Guide* (UG632, *www.xilinx.com*). PlanAhead is the starting point for the design with the Xilinx Zynq in Chapter 5 Extensible Processing Platform.

Floorplan Design

The Floorplan Design aspect of PlanAhead is particularly useful for placing *critical path* logic to optimize timing performance in structural models and datapath modules, as described in Chapter 1 Hardware Description Language Hardware Description Language. Floorplan Design is described in the *Floorplanning Methodology Guide* (UG633, *www.xilinx.com*).

Although the User Constraints File (UCF) determines the placement of logic to output pins, the Floorplan Design can add additional constraints on the routing, timing, grouping, initialization, synthesis and mapping. For example, the Floorplanner can be used to select the placement of logic in the control logic blocks (CLB), the location of CLBs on the FPGA, and the maximum delay between storage elements.

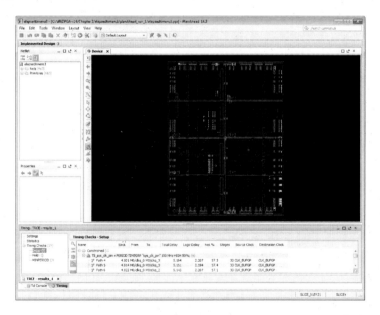

Figure 2.27 Floorplan Design window for the ISE project *elapsedtimens3.xise*

PlanAhead is installed as a part of the Xilinx ISE software EDA tools and Floorplan Design is accessible by expanding the *Processes...Implement Design...Place & Route* and left clicking on *Analyze Timing/Floorplan Design* tabular listing command, which here opens the Xilinx Floorplanner window for the ISE project *elapsedtimens3.xise* from the *Chapter 2\elapsedtimens3* folder, as shown in Figure 2.27. The utilization of the FPGA slice registers and slice LUTs for the specific register variable sec1 in the M3 module of the hierarchical nested modules in the ISE project is shown in Figure 2.28.

However, to utilize Floorplan Design to its best extent requires a detailed knowledge of the FPGA architecture and resources and the underlying structural model being implemented. Floorplan Design uses a manual and iterative approach to achieve realizable goals for routing, timing and synthesis. These factors become increasingly critical for real-time processes or an embedded design that utilizes a high degree of FPGA resources.

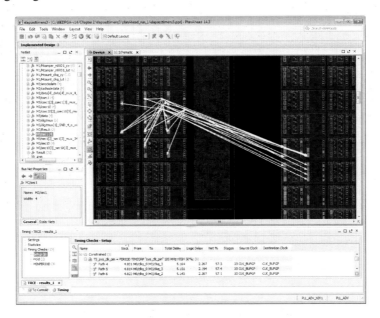

Figure 2.28 Floorplan Design window for the routing and slice register and slice LUT utilization for sec1 in module M3 of the ISE project *elapsedtimens3.xise*

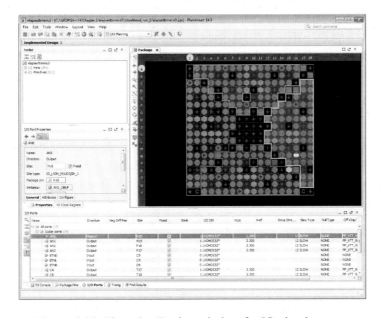

Figure 2.29 Floorplan Design window for IO pin placement

Figure 2.29 shows the package and pin placement for the ISE project *elapsedtimens3.xise* which is determined by the UCF. If the embedded system design has not fixed the input-output (IO) pins then Floorplan Design can be used to reroute the signals to meet the critical path specifications. However, the Spartan-6 Nexys 3 Board used here has fixed IO pins. This intricate process of

Trends in Embedded Design Using Programmable Gate Arrays

floorplanning can be obviated in many projects in embedded system design and is not used here. Additional details are available in the Xilinx *PlanAhead User Guide* (UG632, *www.xilinx.com*).

Xilinx Simulator

The Xilinx ISE Simulator (ISim) can provide behavioral and timing verification without hardware synthesis and implementation to the FPGA [Botros06] and is described in *the ISim User Guide* (UG660, *www.xilinx.com*). The elapsed time module for the Nexys 3 Board *elapsedtime.v*, one of the nested modules in the Xilinx project *elapsedtimens3.xise* in the *Chapter 2 \elapsedtimens3* folder, is used for the simulation, as given in Listing 3.19. Open the ISE Project Navigator and select the *elapsedtimes.v* Verilog HDL file in the *Sources* window in the *Implementation* mode, as shown in Figure 2.30.

Figure 2.30 Project Navigator selection of the *elapsedtime.v* module to simulate

Create a new source by selecting *Project...New Source* and the New Source Wizard – Select Source Type window opens, as shown in Figure 2.31. Select *Verilog Test Fixture* as the source type and input a file name (*ettest* is used here). Clicking *Next* and the New Source Wizard – Associate Source window opens which indicates which source file is associated with the test fixture, as shown in Figure 2.31.

Clicking *Next* New Source Wizard – Summary window opens, as shown in Figure 2.33. Clicking *Finish* and the ISE Project Navigator creates the initial stimulus Verilog source file *ettest.v*, as given in Listing 2.6. The Project Navigator in *Simulation* mode shows the generated Verilog module *ettest.v* and the designation of *uut* (unit under test) for the module *elapsedtime.v*, the associated module here, as shown in Figure 2.34.

The Verilog Fixture module *ettest.v* can be edited in the Project Navigator and saved to form an appropriate stimulus file, as shown in Figure 2.35 and as given in Listing 2.7. The input stimuli are the push button signals BTNL (start), BTNR (stop) and BTND (reset), the 100 Hz elapsed time clock (clocksec) and the 1 kHz seven-segment LED display multiplexer signal (clock). The output signal data for the simulation of the *elapsedtime.v* module is the 4-bit binary coded decimal (BCD) value (data), the 2-bit digit select signal (digit) and the decimal point logic signal (setdp) which is not used here.

In the edited Verilog Test Fixture in Listing 2.7 the time scale is arbitrary set to 10 μsec with a resolution of 10 ns. The time scale parameter can only be entered numerically as either 1, 10 or 100

70

with a scale of 1 to 10^{-15} in steps of 10^{-3} with the notation s, ms, us, ns, ps or fs (seconds, milliseconds, microseconds, nanoseconds, picoseconds or femtoseconds).

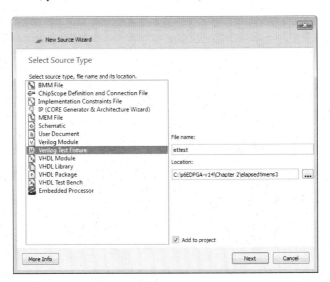

Figure 2.31 New Source Wizard – Select Source Type window

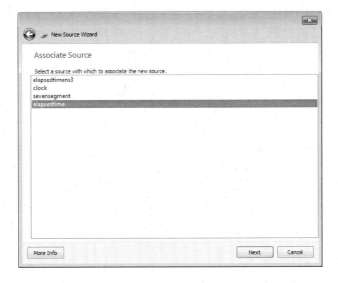

Figure 2.32 New Source Wizard – Associate Source window

The Verilog keyword *initial* defines three processes for the simulation in Listing 2.7. The first process uses the Verilog keyword *forever* to define clocksec as a 100 Hz elapsed time clock signal (500 × 2 × 10 µsec = 10 000 µsec). The next process defines the 1 kHz clock signal (50 × 2 × 10 µsec = 1000 µsec). The last process sets the stimulus signals BTND for reset and BTNL for start with an arbitrary delay of 2 msec (200 × 10 µsec = 2 msec).

After saving the ISE project, select *Simulate Behavioral Model* in the *Processes* window of the ISE Project Navigator, as shown in Figure 2.35. The simulation executes to the specified initial length of 100 msec, as shown in Figure 2.36. The resulting input stimulus and output response signals are displayed in the ISE Simulator. The waveform viewer can zoom-in or zoom-out and apply multiple markers for signal measurement using the ISE Simulator taskbar.

Trends in Embedded Design Using Programmable Gate Arrays

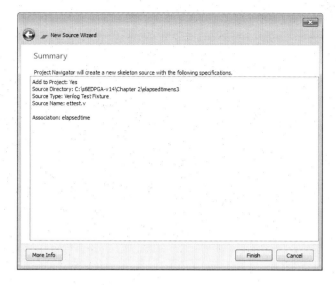

Figure 2.33 New Source Wizard – Summary window

Figure 2.34 Project Navigator for simulation

Listing 2.6 ISE Simulator Verilog Test Fixture initial stimulus file *ettest.v*

```
`timescale 1ns / 1ps
// Verilog Test Fixture created by ISE for module: elapsedtime

module ettest;

// Inputs
reg clocksec;
reg clock;
reg BTNL;
reg BTNR;
reg BTND;
```

```
// Outputs
wire [4:0] data;
wire [2:0] digit;
wire setdp;

// Instantiate the Unit Under Test (UUT)
elapsedtime uut (.clocksec(clocksec), .clock(clock), .data(data), .digit(digit), .setdp(setdp),
                .BTNL(BTNL), .BTNR(BTNR), .BTND(BTND));

initial
     begin
          // Initialize Inputs
          clocksec = 0;
          clock = 0;
          BTNL = 0;
          BTNR = 0;
          BTND = 0;
          // Wait 100 ns for global reset to finish
          #100;
          // Add stimulus here
     end

endmodule
```

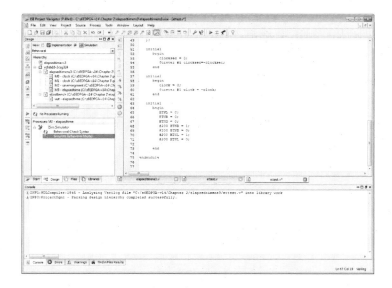

Figure 2.35 Project Navigator for editing the Verilog Test Fixture

Listing 2.7 ISE Simulator Verilog Test Fixture edited stimulus file *ettest.v*

```
`timescale 10 us / 10 ns
// Verilog Test Fixture created by ISE for module: elapsedtime

module ettest;
```

Trends in Embedded Design Using Programmable Gate Arrays

```
// Inputs
reg clocksec;
reg clock;
reg BTNL;
reg BTNR;
reg BTND;
// Outputs
wire [4:0] data;
wire [2:0] digit;
wire setdp;

// Instantiate the Unit Under Test (UUT)
elapsedtime uut (.clocksec(clocksec), .clock(clock), .data(data), .digit(digit), .setdp(setdp),
                 .BTNL(BTNL), .BTNR(BTNR), .BTND(BTND));

initial
     begin
          clocksec = 0;
          forever #500 clocksec = ~clocksec;
     end

initial
     begin
          clock = 0;
          forever #50 clock = ~clock;
     end

initial
     begin
          BTNL = 0;
          BTNR = 0;
          BTND = 0;
          #200 BTND = 1;
          #200 BTND = 0;
          #200 BTNL = 1;
          #200 BTNL = 0;
     end

endmodule
```

Behavioral simulation of a Verilog HDL embedded system design can be done on each module of an ISE project for verification of performance [Ciletti04]. Note that only the input and output signals are displayed and that internal net and register variables are not accessible, as described in Chapter 1 Verilog Hardware Description Language.

However, simulation requires stimulus test data and this step is somewhat time-consuming. Unless the test data is comprehensive, all possible conditions of operation may not be verified [Navabi06]. The simulation of the *elapsedtime.v* module here performs the same regardless of the clock frequency, although the ISE Simulator can utilize the input setup time and the output valid delay for the FPGA device being simulated. A characteristic of behavioral simulation (also known as *presynthesis simulation*) is that the clock, gate and routing propagation delays are not included [Navabi06].

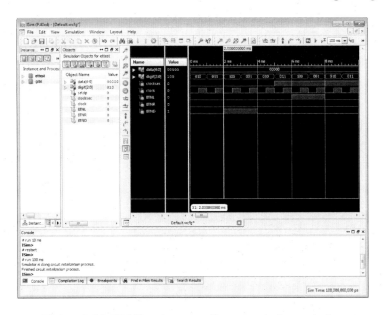

Figure 2.36 ISE Simulator test fixture waveform window

Behavioral simulation demonstrates that the Verilog HDL module functions as expected although the actual performance can only be verified after the embedded system design is synthesized to the FPGA. A timing simulation (also known as *postsynthesis simulation*) utilizes signal propagation information that is available after the *Implement Design...Place & Route* process of the ISE Project Navigator is executed. The Floorplan Design window displays the accurate setup and delay timing for the *elapsedtime.v* module, as shown in Figure 2.27.

Xilinx Verilog Language Templates

A Verilog language or *inference* template menu is evoked from the *Edit...Language Templates* taskbar of the Xilinx ISE Project Navigator, as shown in Figure 2.37. The Xilinx ISE provides such Language Templates in the Verilog HDL to possibly simply the process of implementing an embedded design in an FPGA.

The *Verilog...Common Constructs* language template menu provides terse reference material and Verilog HDL module segments for comment statements, compiler directives, arithmetic, logical and bitwise operators, and tasks and functions. The *Verilog...Device Primitive Instantiation...Spartan-6* provide arithmetic functions, clock components, configuration components, input-output (IO) components, RAM and ROM components, register, latches, look-up table (LUT) shift registers and slice and control logic block (CLB) primitives.

The *Verilog...Simulation Constructs* provide clock stimulus, configuration, delays, loops, mnemonics, procedural blocks, signal assignment, signal, constant and variable declarations and system task and functions. The *Verilog...Synthesis Constructs* provide *always* statement constructs and port, signal, constant and coding examples. The coding example synthesis constructs include accumulators, bidirectional IO, gates, counters, encoders and decoders, flip flops, logic shift, multiplexers, block and distributed RAM, ROM and LUT, shift registers, finite state machines (FSM) and tristate buffers.

An example of a 1-bit bidirectional IO module Verilog HDL language template with output enable is given in Listing 2.8. These language templates provide primitive but reasonable constructs and serve as a reference for incorporation into a Xilinx ISE project in embedded system design in Verilog using the FPGA. However, the incorporation of Verilog modules and the Xilinx LogiCORE blocks are generally more discernible and are used in the ISE projects here.

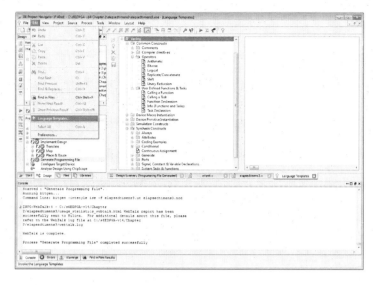

Figure 2.37 Language Template menu in the ISE Project Navigator

Listing 2.8 Xilinx Language Template for a 1-bit bidirectional IO with output enable

```
// IOBUFDS: Differential Bi-directional Buffer
//          Spartan-6                    Delete or comment out inputs/outs that are not necessary
// Xilinx HDL Language Template, version 14.3

IOBUFDS #(.IOSTANDARD("BLVDS_25"))    // Specify the I/O standard
IOBUFDS_inst (
                .O(O),        // Buffer output
                .IO(IO),      // Diff_p inout (connect directly to top-level port)
                .IOB(IOB),    // Diff_n inout (connect directly to top-level port)
                .I(I),        // Buffer input
                .T(T)         // 3-state enable input, high=input, low=output
                );
```

Xilinx Architecture Wizard

The Xilinx Architecture Wizard is an advanced software electronic design automation (EDA) tool that augments other Verilog HDL module creation tools such as the Xilinx CORE Generator. The only Architecture Wizards currently available for the Spartan-6 XC6SSLX16 FPGA on the Nexys 3 Board and the XC6SLX45 FPGA on the Atlys Board is the Clocking Wizard and the SelectIO Interface Wizard.

Clocking Wizard

The Xilinx Clocking Wizard provides flexibility in the selection and generation of synchronous clocks in an embedded system design in an FPGA and is described in *LogiCORE IP Clocking Wizard* (UG521, *www.xilinx.com*). The Clocking Wizard implements the digital clock manager (DCM), a coarse grain component of the Spartan-6 FPGA, as described in Chapter 1 Verilog Hardware Description Language. The DCM is used in the Nexys 3 Board and the Atlys Board applications described in Chapter 3 Programmable Gate Array Hardware and in Chapter 4 Digital Signal Processing, Communications and Control.

The Clocking Wizard is a convenient way to customize the relatively complex parameters and to precisely define the operation of the DCM. The Clocking Wizard has design rule checks to insure that the combination of parameters specified results in a valid configuration of the DCM.

The Architecture Wizard is installed as part of the Xilinx ISE software electronic design automation (EDA) tools and is accessible from the *Project…New Source* menu command, which opens New Source Wizard – Select Source Type window, as shown in Figure 2.38. Select *IP (Coregen & Architecture Wizard)* and enter the file name (*dacs6dcm*) and project location for the Architecture Wizard Verilog HDL instantiation.

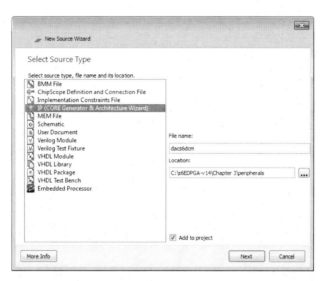

Figure 2.38 New Source Window – Select Source Type window

The file name cannot contain uppercase letters or start with a digit. Here the location for the Architecture Wizard block definition file (dac3sedcm.xaw) is the *Chapter 3\peripherals* folder. The resulting Verilog HDL module (*dacs6dcm.v*) is placed in the ISE project directory and the *Add to project* box should be checked. Clicking *Next* opens the New Source Wizard – Select IP (Intellectual Property) window, as shown in Figure 2.39.

Select the Clocking Wizard DCM IP for the project here. The DCM here is a *frequency synthesizer* which decreases the crystal clock frequency of the Nexys 3 Board or Atlys Board from 100 MHz to 83.33 MHz for an application utilizing the digital-to-analog converter (DAC), as described in Chapter 3 Programmable Gate Array Hardware.

Figure 2.40 is the Xilinx Clocking Wizard – Clocking Features/Input Clocks window in which reset (RESET), clock input (CLK_IN1), clock output (CLK_OUT1), delayed-locked loop (DLL) *lock-in* signal (LOCKED) and the external input clock frequency is specified. The Xilinx LogiCORE IP Clocking Wizard is also described in a Xilinx product guide (PG065, *www.xilinx.com*).

Clicking *Next* opens the Xilinx Clocking Wizard – Output Clock Settings window, as shown in Figure 2.41. The default clock buffer setting uses the global buffers for the clock output (BUFG) and the synthesized clock output is used. Clicking *Next* opens the Xilinx Clocking Wizard – – I/O and Feedback Clock window which confirms the settings for the optional input and output signals, as shown in Figure 2.42.

Clicking *Next* opens the Xilinx Clocking Wizard – DCM_SP Settings window, as shown in Figure 2.43. The DCM frequency synthesizer uses a clock input frequency of 100 MHz and a specified synthesized clock multiplier (CLKFX_MULTIPLY) of 5 and divider (CLKFX_DIVIDE) of 6 to produce a output frequency of 100 MHz × 5 / 6 = 83.333 MHz.

Trends in Embedded Design Using Programmable Gate Arrays

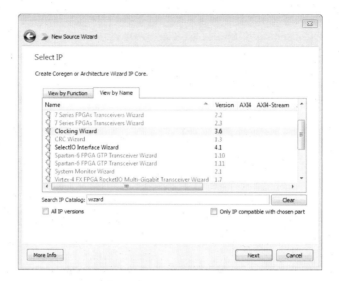

Figure 2.39 New Source Wizard – Select IP window

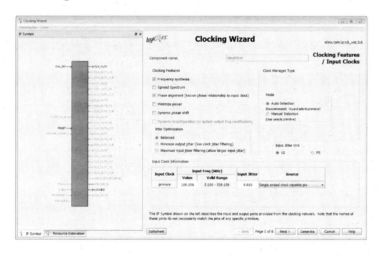

Figure 2.40 Xilinx Clocking Wizard – Clock Features/Input Clocks window

Clicking *Next* displays the Xilinx Clocking Wizard – Clock Summary, Port Naming, as shown in Figure 2.44. Finally, clicking *Next* displays the Xilinx Clocking Wizard – Core Summary which describes the files to be generated, as shown in Figure 2.45. Clicking *Generate* produces the specified files.

The Verilog components include the LogiCORE UCF *dacs6dcm.ucf*, the instantiation template file *dacs6dcm.veo* and the wrapper file *dacs6dcm.v* for functional implementation or simulation. To instantiate the LogiCORE block into an Xilinx ISE project in Verilog, *copy and paste* the instantiation template file (*dacs6dcm.veo*) into the appropriate area of the top module of the project.

The Verilog HDL module *dacs6dcm.v* generated is given in Listing 2.9. The module instantiations for the single-ended input global clock buffer IBUFG and the global clock buffer BUFG are generated automatically. The module ports in Listing 2.9 utilize the *connection by position* option where the formal name in the declaration need not be the same as the actual name evoked in the hierarchical structure, as described in Chapter 1 Hardware Description Language.

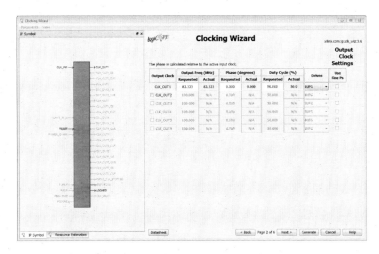

Figure 2.41 Xilinx Clocking Wizard – Output Clock Settings window

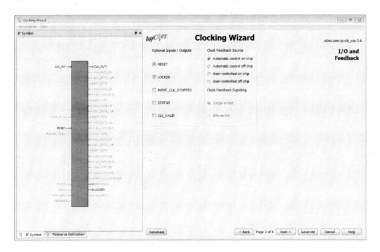

Figure 2.42 Xilinx Clocking Wizard – I/O and Feedback window

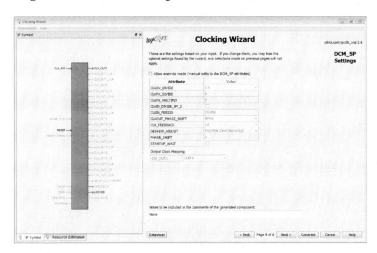

Figure 2.43 Xilinx Clocking Wizard – DCM_SP Settings window

Trends in Embedded Design Using Programmable Gate Arrays

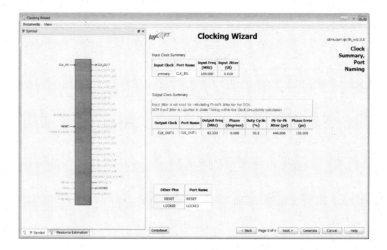

Figure 2.44 Xilinx Clocking Wizard – Clock Summary, Port Naming window

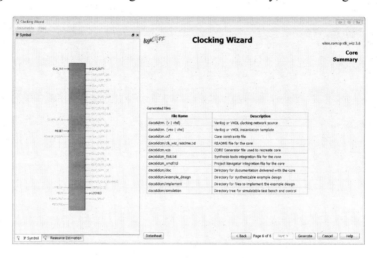

Figure 2.45 Xilinx Clocking Wizard – Core Summary window

Listing 2.9 Xilinx Clocking Wizard Verilog HDL module *dacs6dcm.v*

```
module dacs6dcm (// Clock in ports
            input      CLK_IN1,
            // Clock out ports
            output     CLK_OUT1,
            // Status and control signals
            input      RESET,
            output     LOCKED);

// Input buffering
IBUFG clkin1_buf (.O (clkin1), .I (CLK_IN1));

// Clocking primitive
// Instantiation of the DCM primitive
```

```verilog
wire    psdone_unused;
wire    locked_int;
wire [7:0] status_int;
wire clkfb;
wire clk0;
wire clkfx;

DCM_SP #(.CLKDV_DIVIDE       (2.000),
          .CLKFX_DIVIDE       (6),
          .CLKFX_MULTIPLY  (5),
          .CLKIN_DIVIDE_BY_2    ("FALSE"),
          .CLKIN_PERIOD       (10.0),
          .CLKOUT_PHASE_SHIFT  ("NONE"),
          .CLK_FEEDBACK      ("1X"),
          .DESKEW_ADJUST   ("SYSTEM_SYNCHRONOUS"),
          .PHASE_SHIFT       (0),
          .STARTUP_WAIT     ("FALSE"))

dcm_sp_inst
    // Input clock
    (.CLKIN          (clkin1),
    .CLKFB          (clkfb),
    // Output clocks
    .CLK0           (clk0),
    .CLK90          (),
    .CLK180         (),
    .CLK270         (),
    .CLK2X          (),
    .CLK2X180       (),
    .CLKFX          (clkfx),
    .CLKFX180       (),
    .CLKDV          (),
    // Ports for dynamic phase shift
    .PSCLK          (1'b0),
    .PSEN           (1'b0),
    .PSINCDEC       (1'b0),
    .PSDONE         (),
    // Other control and status signals
    .LOCKED         (locked_int),
    .STATUS         (status_int),
    .RST            (RESET),
    // Unused pin- tie low
    .DSSEN          (1'b0));

    assign LOCKED = locked_int;

    // Output buffering
    assign clkfb = CLK_OUT1;

    BUFG clkout1_buf (.O   (CLK_OUT1), .I   (clkfx));

endmodule
```

Trends in Embedded Design Using Programmable Gate Arrays

The module instantiation template file *dacs6dcm.veo* uses the *connection by name* convention, also described in Chapter 1, as given in Listing 2.10. Unspecified signals in the Clocking Wizard, as shown in Figure 2.45, are not implemented. The Clocking Wizard has the capability of providing clock signals at fixed phase shifts (CLK90, CLK180, CLK270). at double the input clock frequency with a phase shift (CLK2X, CLK2X180) in addition to the synthesis clock signals (CLKFX, CLKFX180).

Listing 2.10 Xilinx Clocking Wizard Verilog HDL instantiation template file *dacs6dcm.veo*

```
dacs6dcm instance_name
  (// Clock in ports
  .CLK_IN1(CLK_IN1),        // IN
  // Clock out ports
  .CLK_OUT1(CLK_OUT1),    // OUT
  // Status and control signals
  .RESET(RESET),            // IN
  .LOCKED(LOCKED));       // OUT
```

SelectIO Interface Wizard

The Xilinx SelectIO Interface Wizard implements an input, output and bidirectional busses with requisite buffering and delay elements, input and output serializer/deserializer (ISERDES and OSERDES) elements, registers, and the input/output (I/O) clock driver. The SelectIO Wizard is described in *LogiCORE IP SelectIO Interface Wizard* user's guide (UG700, *www.xilinx.com*).

The SelectIO Wizard generates datapath configurations and clock buffering and upon opening shows the first of three windows for data bus setup and delay, as shown in Figure 2.46. The data bus setup and delay windows set the size of the input and output data and the I/O signaling standard, evoke or bypass delay insertion, implement SERDES, register single or double data rate (DDR) data and enable control signals.

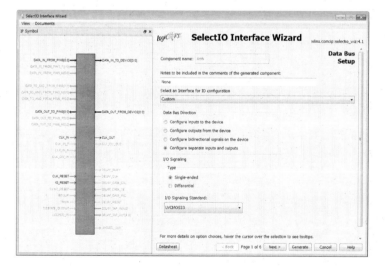

Figure 2.46 Xilinx SelectIO Interface Wizard – Data Bus Setup initial window

The next set of two windows of the SelectIO Wizard determines clock setup and delay, the first of which are shown in Figure 2.47. The clock setup window sets the I/O signaling standard, the type of clock buffer, the active clock edge and, if implemented, the alignment of the clock for DDR signaling. Further details for high speed, source synchronous ISERDES and OSERDES applications for the Spartan-6 FPGA are available (XAPP 1064, *www.xilinx.com*). The sixth and last window of the SelectIO Wizard is a summary and is not shown.

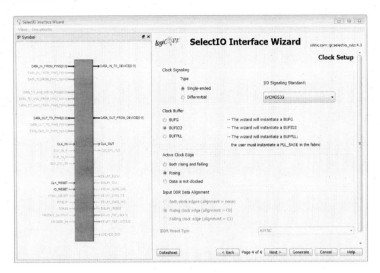

Figure 2.47 Xilinx SelectIO Interface Wizard – Clock Setup window

Xilinx LogiCORE Blocks

The Xilinx CORE Generator™ System and the LogiCORE blocks facilitate embedded design in the Verilog HDL using the programmable gate array. Several of the LogiCORE products for the Spartan-6 FPGA are freely available but subject to the LogiCORE site license agreement (*www.xilinx.com/ipcenter*). Other LogiCORE blocks are licensed intellectual property (IP) and not described here.

These structural LogiCORE blocks are optimized and are used in Xilinx ISE projects in Chapter 3 Field Programmable Gate Array Hardware and Chapter 4 Digital Signal Processing, Communications and Control. Each of the LogiCORE blocks is provided with design windows, as shown in Figure 2.22 for the LogiCORE Divider Generator v3.0. The LogiCORE block data sheets for the Spartan-6 XC6SSLX16 FPGA on the Nexys 3 Board and the XC6SLX45 FPGA on the Atlys Board are available (*www.xilinx.com*) and provide more detailed information. The LogiCORE base IP, basic element, memory and storage blocks provides accumulators, counter and memory and storage elements, as listed in Table 2.1 and shown in Figure 2.48.

Table 2.1 BaseIP, Basic Element, Memory and Storage LogiCORE blocks

Function	Data Sheet	Application
Accumulator	DS213	Adder/subtractor based accumulator
Multiply Accumulator	DS716	Multiply-accumulate (MAC) from DSP slices
Multiply Adder	DS717	Muliply-add from DSP slices
Binary Counter	DS215	Up, down and up/down counters
Block Memory Generator	DS512	Single/dual port RAM/ROM from BRAM
Distributed Memory Generator	DS322	Single and dual port RAM and ROM from LUTs
RAM-Based Shift Register	DS228	Parallel input and output N-bit shift register
FIFO Generator	DS317	First-in first-out memory queue
Memory Interface Generator	UG416	Memory controller block memory interface

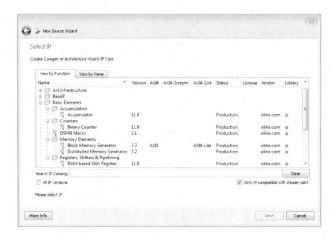

Figure 2.48 Xilinx LogiCORE BaseIP, Basic Element, Memory and Storage
blocks for the Spartan-6 FPGA

The Accumulator is an added/subtractor based accumulator using either look-up table (LUT) of DSP slice implementations while the Multiply Accumulator (MAC) and the Multiply Adder LogiCORE blocks use DSP slices exclusively. The Spartan-6 XC6SSLX16 FPGA on the Nexys 3 Board and the XC6SLX45 FPGA on the Atlys Board have respectively 32 and 58 DSP48A1 slices. These LogiCORE blocks form the basis for embedded DSP as described in Chapter 4 Digital Signal Processing, Communications and Control.

The Binary Counter implements an up, down and up/down counter where the upper limit of the count can be set, a count threshold signal can be outputted, asynchronous and synchronous set, clear and initialize input signals are available. The Block Memory Generator uses the available block random access memory (BRAM) of the coarse grained architecture of the Spartan-6 FPGA, as described in Chapter 1 Hardware Description Language. The Distributed Memory Generator LogiCORE block uses the look up tables (LUT) of the Spartan-6 FPGA.

The RAM-based Shift Register LogiCORE block uses BRAM to form optimized functions for variable length parallel digital data with synchronous set, clear and initialize input signals and clock enable logic signals [Wakerly00]. The FIFO Generator LogiCORE block provides first-in first-out (FIFO) N-bit parallel input and output shift registers, digital delay lines or time-skew buffers using block or distributed RAM.

The Memory Interface Generator (MIG) generates external memory interfaces using the memory control block (MCB) of the coarse grained architecture of the Spartan-6 FPGA, as described in Chapter 1 Verilog Hardware Description Language. The Spartan-6 XC6SSLX16 FPGA on the Nexys 3 Board and the XC6SLX45 FPGA on the Atlys Board each have two MCBs. MIG supports the DDR, DDR2 and DDR3 SDRAM (double data rate, synchronous dynamic random access memory) standards.

The LogiCORE communications and networking blocks provide error correction encoders and decoders, Ethernet media access controller (MAC), direct digital synthesizer (DDS) and an interweaver and de-interweaver, as listed in Table 2.2 and shown in Figure 2.49.

The Convolutional Encoder is a high speed implementation with parameterized *constrain lengths* and *puncturing* capability [Sklar01]. The Interweaver/De-interweaver randomizes data to mitigate the effect of burst errors in a data transmission using a convolutional or block structure.

The 10-Gigabit Ethernet MAC implements a 10 Gb/sec MAC compliant with the IEEE 802.3-2008 standard. The Tri Mode Ethernet MAC provides a 10 Mb/sec, 100 Mb/sec and 1 Gb/sec MAC that can be configured for half or full-duplex operation with flow control. However, the 10-Gigabit Ethernet Mac and the Tri Mode Ethernet MAC can only be simulated in the Xilinx ISE and are not available for hardware synthesis without a license.

Table 2.2 Communication and Networking LogiCORE blocks

Function	Data Sheet	Application
Convolutional Encoder	DS248	Encoder for Viterbi decoder
Interleaver/De-interleaver	DS250	Data randomizer for burst errors
10-Gigabit Ethernet MAC	DS201	10 Gb/sec Ethernet media access controller
Tri Mode Ethernet MAC	DS297	10/100/1000 Mb/sec media access controller
DDS Compiler	DS558	Direct digital synthesizer common interface
DUC/DDC Compiler	DS766	Digital up/down frequency converter

The Direct Digital Synthesizer (DDS) Compiler is a numerically controller oscillator (NCO) which provides a quadrature synthesizer for digital modulators and demodulators [Silage06]. The DDS consists of a phase generator and a sine/cosine look-up table (LUT) which can be used separately. The sine/cosine LUT can utilize distributed or block RAM in the Spartan-6 FPGA to produce the sine or cosine of an integer angle input and is utilized in Xilinx ISE projects in Chapter 4 Digital Signal Processing, Communication and Control. The Direct Digital Synthesizer Compiler is a common user interface for the DSS and NCO which simplifies the LogiCORE block implementation.

The DUC/DDC Compiler is a digital up and down frequency converter which compliments the DDS and provides support for wireless data communication. The DDS and DUC/DDC are utilized in Xilinx ISE projects in Chapter 4 Digital Signal Processing, Communication and Control.

Figure 2.49 Xilinx LogiCORE Communication and Networking
blocks for the Spartan-6 FPGA

The LogiCORE digital signal processing (DSP) blocks provide complex multiplication, the Coordinate Rotation Digital Computer (CORDIC), cascaded integrator-comb (CIC) and finite impulse response (FIR) digital filters and the Discrete and Fast Fourier Transform (DFT, FFT), as listed in Table 2.3 and shown in Figure 2.50.

The Complex Multiplier multiplies complex signal data in signed two's complement notation. The Coordinate Rotation Digital Computer (CORDIC) provides vector rotation and translation, sine, cosine and tangent, arctangent, hyperbolic sine and cosine and square root calculations. The Cascaded Integrator-Comb (CIC) Compiler implements the multiplierless, multirate Hogenauer filter for digital up converters (DUC) and digital down converters (DDC) [Mitra06].

Trends in Embedded Design Using Programmable Gate Arrays

The FIR Compiler is the common user interface for area efficient distributed arithmetic (DA) or multiply-and-accumulate (MA) FIR digital filters. The DA FIR digital filter implements the Hilbert transform and interpolated filters, including the polyphase and half-band decimator and interpolator [Mitra06]. The MA FIR digital filter is a parallel implementation with pipelining. The FIR Compiler is utilized in Xilinx ISE projects in Chapter 4 Digital Signal Processing, Communication and Control. The Discrete Fourier Transform (DFT) and the computationally efficient Cooley-Tukey algorithm for the Fast Fourier Transform (FFT) provides the discrete frequency transform of a sampled data signal.

Table 2.3 Digital Signal Processing LogiCORE blocks

Function	Data Sheet	Application
Complex Multiplier	DS291	Complex data multiplication
CORDIC	DS249	Vector rotation, sine and cosine, square root
CIC Compiler	DS613	Cascaded integrator-comb filter common interface
FIR Compiler	DS534	Finite impulse response (FIR) filter common interface
Discrete Fourier Transform	DS615	Discrete Fourier transform (DFT)
Fast Fourier Transform	DS808	Fast Fourier transform (FFT)

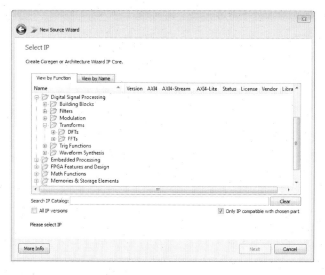

Figure 2.50 Xilinx Digital Signal Processing LogiCORE blocks

The LogiCORE math functions, first-in-first-out (FIFO) and memory interface generator blocks for the Spartan-3E FPGA provides an accumulator, adder/subtracter, dividers, floating-point operations, multipliers, memory generators and packet and FIFO buffers, as listed in Table 2.4 and shown in Figure 2.51.

Table 2.4 Math Functions LogiCORE blocks

Function	Data Sheet	Application
Adder Subtracter	DS214	Add, subtract or add and subtract
Divider Generator	DS530	Fixed-point or floating-point division
Floating-Point Operator	DS335	Floating-point operations
Multiplier	DS255	Parallel fixed-point multiplier

Figure 2.51 Xilinx Math Functions LogiCORE blocks

The Adder Subtractor can provide adders, subtractors and dynamically configurable adders/subtractors that operate on signed or unsigned data with *pipelining*. The Divider Generator is a fixed-point divider based on radix-2 non-restoring division or a high-radix divider with prescaling and is utilized previously in this Chapter.

The Floating Point Operator provides the floating-point operations of add, subtract, divide, square root and comparison and fixed-point to floating-point and floating-point to fixed-point conversion with close compliance to the IEEE-754 standard for floating-point arithmetic, as described in Chapter 1 Hardware Description Language.

The Multiplier LogiCORE accepts fixed-point data on two input busses and can utilize the hardware multiplier of the Spartan-6 FPGA, as described in Chapter 1. The Multiplier can also accept data on a single bus and multiply it by either a fixed integer constant or an integer constant that can be reloaded from the other input bus.

The Xilinx LogiCORE blocks provide *drop-in module* support for embedded design in the Verilog HDL using programmable gate arrays. The performance and applicability of the LogiCORE blocks are pre-verified and utilize optimal components of the coarse grained architecture of the Spartan-6 FPGA. The Divider Generator, FIR Compiler and the Direct Digital Synthesis Compiler LogiCORE blocks are used in the Xilinx ISE projects described in Chapter 3 Field Programmable Gate Array Hardware and Chapter 4 Digital Signal Processing, Communications and Control.

Warnings and Errors in Synthesis

The hardware synthesis of an embedded system application in a programmable gate array is subject to constraints which can generate implementation warnings and errors [Ciletti04]. The User Constraints File (UCF) not only assures that the input and output signals are routed to the proper pins of the FPGA but can include implementation and timing considerations. Warnings and errors appear in the Xilinx ISE Project Navigator – Design Summary window, as shown in Figure 2.18.

Warning are non-fatal descriptions of the design implementation process which consists of synthesizing, translating, mapping and placing and routing of the interconnections of the configurable logic and input-output blocks of the programmable gate array, as described in Chapter 1 Verilog Hardware Description Language.

Although non-fatal, warnings indicate design changes that are made autonomously by the Xilinx ISE during the implementation process. These warnings include signals that are inadvertently not used and other design implementation descriptions, as given in Listing 2.11.

Trends in Embedded Design Using Programmable Gate Arrays

The warning messages in Listing 2.11 are generated by the Xilinx ISE synthesizer (XST) for the project *ns3ad1test.xise*, as given in Listing 3.33. The warning messages here include that the control signal cmdlcd is used but never assigned (Xst:653) and that lcdhome is not used (Xst:647). This warning is generated because the controller module *genad1adc.v* does not utilize either the cmdlcd or lcdhome controller signals to datapath module for the LCD *clplcd.v* in this ISE project. Rather than modify the datapath module *clplcd.v* and complicate the design reuse of the Verilog HDL modules, the warning can be accepted and the signals set to logic 0.

Listing 2.11 Partial Xilinx XST synthesizer warning messages for the ISE project *ns3ad1test.xise*

WARNING:Xst:653 - Signal <cmdlcd> is used but never assigned. This sourceless signal will be automatically connected to value GND.

WARNING:Xst:647 - Input <lcdhome> is never used. This port will be preserved and left unconnected if it belongs to a top-level block or it belongs to a sub-block and the hierarchy of this sub-block is preserved.

WARNING:Xst:1710 - FF/Latch <lcddatin_7> (without init value) has a constant value of 0 in block <M1>. This FF/Latch will be trimmed during the optimization process.

WARNING:Xst:1710 - FF/Latch <homelcd> (without init value) has a constant value of 0 in block <M1>. This FF/Latch will be trimmed during the optimization process.

WARNING:Xst:1710 - FF/Latch <lcddatin_7> (without init value) has a constant value of 0 in block <adclcd>. This FF/Latch will be trimmed during the optimization process.

WARNING:Xst:1895 - Due to other FF/Latch trimming, FF/Latch <homelcd> (without init value) has a constant value of 0 in block <adclcd>. This FF/Latch will be trimmed during the optimization process.

WARNING:Xst:1710 - FF/Latch <lcdcmd> (without init value) has a constant value of 0 in block <clplcd>. This FF/Latch will be trimmed during the optimization process.

WARNING:Xst:1710 - FF/Latch <adc1_3> (without init value) has a constant value of 0 in block <genad1adc>. This FF/Latch will be trimmed during the optimization process.

WARNING:Xst:1293 - FF/Latch <adcstate_6> has a constant value of 0 in block <ad1adc>. This FF/Latch will be trimmed during the optimization process.

WARNING:Xst:2677 - Node <M2/lcdhome> of sequential type is unconnected in block <ns3ad1test>.

Warning messages can provide an alert to signals may be unintentionally not connected in the ISE project. The warnings concerning the unconnected controller and status signals homelcd (XST: 1710) and lcdhome (XST:674) should be reviewed to verify that this is correct. The Xilinx XST Verilog compiler trims unused signals during the optimization process.

Error messages generated by the Xilinx ISE project are fatal and interrupt the hardware synthesis of an embedded system design in a programmable gate array. Errors can occur for a variety of minor or severe causes. One minor cause of an error message is an active (uncommented) port in the User Constraints File (UCF).

Timing constraint errors are often prevalent in Verilog HDL implementation designs using multiple modules that are placed and routed at distances across the fine-grained architecture of the Spartan-6 FPGA. The Xilinx ISE Floorplanner can assist in identifying the placement of the modules of the design and the interconnection paths. The Xilinx ISE includes the Xilinx Timing Analyzer which provides a description of the timing constraint in error and design implementation suggestions to alleviate the error.

One severe error message occurs when timing constraints are not met in an implementation because of path delays in a design, as shown in Figure 2.52. Here the Synthesis and Translate processes of the Xilinx ISE are successful but the initial Map process at Place & Route process fails (Place:1108) for an error intentionally induced in the Xilinx ISE project *ns3keyboardtest.xise*, as given in Listing 3.22. The error message produced in part is in Listing 2.12.

Figure 2.52 Place & Route Properties window

Listing 2.11 Partial induced error message for the ISE project *ns3ad1test.xise*

ERROR:Place:1108 - A clock IOB / BUFGMUX clock component pair have been found that are not placed at an optimal clock IOB / BUFGMUX site pair. The clock IOB component <JA3> is placed at site <N10>. The corresponding BUFG component <JA3_BUFGP/BUFG> is placed at site <BUFGMUX_X3Y14>. There is only a select set of IOBs that can use the fast path to the Clocker buffer, and they are not being used…If this sub optimal condition is acceptable for this design, you may use the CLOCK_DEDICATED_ROUTE constraint in the .ucf file to demote this message to a WARNING and allow your design to continue...These examples can be used directly in the .ucf file to override this clock rule. < NET "JA3" CLOCK_DEDICATED_ROUTE = FALSE; >

The error occurs because the peripheral port JA3 is used for the PS/2 clock signal ps2clk for the Xilinx ISE project *ns3keyboardtest.xise*, as given in Listing 3.22. The message suggests that if this is an acceptable error then it can be mitigated with an override in the UCF file by using the CLOCK_DEDICATED_ROUTE constraint, as given in the partial UCF in Listing 2.12 used here.

Listing 2.11 Partial UCF for the ISE project *ns3ad1test.xise*

```
#Peripheral Port A
NET "JA1"        LOC = "T12" |IOSTANDARD = LVCMOS33;
#NET "JA2"       LOC = "V12" |IOSTANDARD = LVCMOS33;
NET "JA3"        LOC = "N10"  |IOSTANDARD = LVCMOS33;
NET "JA3" CLOCK_DEDICATED_ROUTE = FALSE;
```

Fortunately, a controller and datapath construct in the Verilog HDL is subjected less to actual timing constraint errors for an embedded design using a programmable gate array. The FSM of the controller and datapath, although event driven by a clock, essentially depends only upon the *data available* signals, as described in Chapter 1 Verilog Hardware Description Language. If the clock transition to the FSM is *late* then the state transition merely occurs on the next clock transition with a *design penalty* of only one clock cycle.

Trends in Embedded Design Using Programmable Gate Arrays

Summary

In this Chapter embedded system design in the Verilog HDL using a field programmable gate array (FPGA) is shown to be facilitated by software electronic design automation (EDA) tools which provide both simulation and hardware synthesis. The Xilinx ISE design process is presented using an embedded design stop watch project as a complete EDA tool in hardware synthesis for the Xilinx Spartan-6 FPGA and the Nexys 3 Board. Several additional components of the Xilinx ISE EDA are described, including PlanAhead and Floorplan Design, the Simulator, the Verilog Language Templates, the Architecture Wizard and the Core Generator.

Chapter 3 Programmable Gate Array Hardware describes two evaluation boards that utilize the Xilinx Spartan-6 FPGA. The integral components and available hardware modules of the evaluation boards are presented in operation by complete Xilinx ISE projects. Chapter 4 Digital Signal Processing, Communications and Control presents projects in digital filtering, digital modulation in communication systems, digital data transmission and digital control system design. These two Chapters survey the application of the Verilog HDL and programmable gate arrays in embedded design. Chapter 5 Extensible Processing Platform describes the Xilinx Zynq all programmable *system-on-chip* with an ARM Cortex™-A9 hard core processor, AMBA bus and integral FPGA.

References

[Botros06]   Botros, Nazeih M., *HDL Programming Fundamentals*. Thomson Delmar, 2006.

[Ciletti99]   Cilletti, Michael D., *Modeling, Synthesis and Rapid Prototyping with the Verilog HDL*. Prentice Hall, 1999.

[Ciletti04]   Cilletti, Michael D., *Starter's Guide to Verilog 2001*. Prentice Hall, 2004.

[Lee06]   Lee, Sunggu, *Advanced Digital Logic Design*. Thomson, 2006.

[Mitra06]   Mitra, Sanjit K., *Digital Signal Processing: A Computer Based Approach*. McGraw-Hill, 2006.

[Navabi06]   Zainalabedin Navabi, *Verilog Digital System Design*. McGraw-Hill, 1999.

[Silage06]   Silage, Dennis, *Digital Communication Systems using SystemVue*. Thomson Delmar, 2006

[Wakerly00]   Wakerly, John F. *Digital Design Principles and Practice*, Prentice Hall, 2000

3

Programmable Gate Array Hardware

Embedded design in the Verilog hardware description language (HDL) using a field programmable gate array (FPGA) is investigated with an electronic design automation (EDA) software tool, a hardware development and evaluation board and peripherals. The evaluation boards feature a Xilinx Spartan®-6 FPGA supported by a Joint Test Action Group (JTAG) port (IEEE 1149.1) for remote programming of the bit file provided by the EDA and a variety of external hardware components and ports. The ports allow the interconnection of analog and digital input-output hardware peripherals for interfacing to external signals and devices. These components, ports and peripherals facilitate real-time processing with the FPGA in digital signal processing, digital communications, data communications and process control, as described in Chapter 4.

The Verilog source modules and project files are located in the *Chapter 3* folder as subfolders identified by the name of the appropriate module or project. The complete contents and the file download procedure are described in the Appendix.

The Verilog HDL source and project file structure for the Xilinx Integrated Synthesis Environment (ISE) EDA software tool is described in Chapter 2 Verilog Design Automation. The projects in this Chapter illustrate not only the use of the components, ports and external hardware peripherals in applications, but the syntax, development and versatility of the Verilog HDL for embedded system design as an extension of the discussion in Chapter 1.

Evaluation Boards

The Xilinx Spartan-6 FPGA (data sheet DS160, *www.xilinx.com*) is a gate optimized device with up to 540 single-ended input/output (I/O) signals and 147 443 logic cells. The Xilinx Spartan-6 FPGAs are available as part of inexpensive development and evaluation boards and are used for the Verilog HDL hardware synthesis of an embedded design in this text.

Nexys 3 Board

The Digilent Nexys™3 Board (*www.digilentinc.com*) is an inexpensive Xilinx Spartan-6 FPGA development and evaluation board, as shown in Figure 3.1. The Xilinx Spartan-6 XC6SLX16-CSG324 FPGA on the evaluation board contains 14 579 logic cells. The coarse grained architecture of the Xilinx Spartan-6 XC6SLX16 FPGA includes thirty-two 18 kilobit (Kb) blocks of random access memory (RAM), thirty-two 18×18 bit hardware multipliers, two clock management tiles (CMT) digital clock managers and up to 232 I/O signals. The complete description of the Spartan-6 FPGA is available (user's guides UG380, UG381, UG382, UG383 and UG384, *www.xilinx.com*).

Available peripherals on the Nexys 3 Board are a Micron 128 megabit (Mb) M45W8MW16 Cellular RAM (pseudo-static dynamic RAM, PSDRAM), a Micron 128 Mb NP8P128A13T1760E parallel non-volatile PCM (phase-change memory), a Micron 128 Mb NP5Q128A13ESFC0E serial peripheral interface (SPI) non-volatile PCM and a 100 MHz crystal clock oscillator. External ports include a video graphics array (VGA) port, a USB HID (universal serial bus, human interface device) PS/2 mouse or keyboard port, a USB UART (universal asynchronous receiver transmitter), a USB programming port and a JTAG port.

The USB programming port is compatible with the Digilent Adept configuration system, as described in Chapter 2 Verilog Design Automation. The FPGA can be configured from the Adept USB or JTAG programming port, or either the parallel or serial non-volatile PCM, on power-up or by depressing the reset pushbutton. Jumper J8 selects either the Adept USB port or the PCMs for the configuration of the FPGA.

The Nexys 3 Board has hard-wired accessories, as shown in Figure 3.1. Five pushbuttons, eight slide switches, eight light emitting diodes (LED) and four LED seven-segment displays provide FPGA application support. The Nexys 3 Board provides power and configuration (Done) LED indicators. Four 12-pin hardware module connectors (JA, JB, JC and JD), a 68-pin very high density cable (VHDC) connector extend the capabilities of the Nexys 3 Board to additional external peripherals.

Figure 3.1 Digilent Spartan-6 Nexys 3 Board

The four 12-pin hardware module connectors each provide eight I/O signals from the FPGA, two power (+3.3 V) and two ground pins. The I/O signals are short-circuit protected with a series resistor and have electrostatic discharge protection (ESD) diodes. Two on-board regulators provide 3.3 V, 2.5 V, 1.8 V and 1.2 V digital logic power supplies. The Nexys 3 Board is described in detail in the publication *Nexys 3_rm.pdf* (*www.digilentinc.com*).

Atlys Board

The Digilent Atlys™ Board (*www.diligentinc.com*) is a more versatile but more expensive Xilinx Spartan-6 FPGA development and evaluation board, as shown in Figure 3.2. The Xilinx Spartan-6 XC6SLX45-CSG324 FPGA on the evaluation board contains 43 661 logic cells. The coarse grained architecture of the Xilinx Spartan-6 XC6SLX45 FPGA includes 116 18 kilobit (Kb) blocks of random access memory (RAM), fifty-eight 18 × 18 bit hardware multipliers, four CMT digital clock managers and up to 358 I/O signals.

Available peripherals on the Atlys Board are a Numonix 128 Mb N25Q12 SPI Flash non-volatile read-only memory (ROM) for the configuration of the FPGA and a Micron 1 gigabit (Gb) MT47H64M16-25E double data rate synchronous dynamic RAM (DDR2 DRAM) and a 100 MHz crystal clock oscillator. The DDR2 DRAM of the Atlys Board utilizes the integrated memory controller blocks available in the coarse grained architecture of the Spartan-6 FPGA. External ports include a high definition multimedia interface (HDMI) input and output ports, a USB HID PS/2 mouse or keyboard port, a USB UART, an audio coder-decoder (codec, AC-97), a USB programming port and a JTAG port.

The USB programming port is also compatible with the Digilent Adept configuration system, as described in Chapter 2 Verilog Design Automation. The FPGA can be configured from the Adept USB or JTAG programming port, or the serial non-volatile Flash ROM, on power-up or by depressing the reset pushbutton. Jumper JP11 selects either the Adept USB port or the Flash ROM for the configuration of the FPGA.

The Atlys Board also has hard-wired accessories, as shown in Figure 3.2. Five pushbuttons, eight slide switches and eight light emitting diodes (LED) provide FPGA application support. The Atlys Board provides power and configuration (Done) LED indicators. One 12-pin hardware module connector (JA) and a 68-pin very high density cable (VHDC) connector extend the capabilities of the Atlys Board to additional external peripherals.

Figure 3.2 Digilent Spartan-6 Atlys Board

The single 12-pin hardware module connectors provides eight I/O signals from the FPGA, two power (+3.3 V) and two ground pins. The I/O signals are short-circuit protected with a series resistor and have electrostatic discharge protection (ESD) diodes. Five on-board regulators provide 3.3 V, 2.5 V, 1.8 V, 1.2 V and 0.9 V digital logic power supplies. The Atlys Board is described in detail in the publication *Atlys_rm.pdf* (*www.digilentinc.com*).

Selection of an Evaluation Board

Since the Nexys 3 Board and Atlys Board are apparently complementary, both will be used extensively here. Many of the embedded design projects execute on either of these Xilinx Spartan-6 or even other Xilinx Spartan-3E FPGA evaluation boards. The Xilinx ISE project files targeting the Nexys 3 Board or Atlys Board are configured from project source files by substituting the appropriate User Constraints File (UCF) and modules that support their unique peripherals, such as the LED seven-segment display and the external ADC, DAC, rotary shaft encoder and other hardware modules that interface to the 12-pin connector. Project files for both the Nexys 3 Board and Atlys Board are available as described in the Appendix.

The salient differences between the Nexys 3 Board and the Atlys Board include the size of the Spartan-6 FPGA, four or one 12-pin hardware module connectors, VGA or HDMI port, PSDRAM or DDR2 DRAM and an integral LED seven-segment display or an AC-97 codec. The Nexys 3 Board

Trends in Embedded Design Using Programmable Gate Arrays

will be used for applications featuring the integral LED seven-segment display and VGA port or the availability of up to four 12-pin hardware module connectors. The Atlys Board will be used for applications utilizing the AC-97 codec, the USB HID port or only one 12-pin hardware module connector.

User Constraints File

   The User Constraints File (UCF) *nexys3.ucf* in Listing 3.1 provides the basic definitions for the hard-wired peripherals and accessories of the Digilent Nexys 3 Board and is located in the *Chapter 3\ucf* folder. The file download procedure is described in the Appendix.

   The net labels in the UCF, such as CLK for crystal clock oscillator, are arbitrary but are evocative of the peripheral or accessory function. Each net in this UCF is commented out with the asterisk (#) in Listing 3.1 and would be ignored. Active nets would be uncommented and the net label used in the UCF must also appear in the Verilog source modules of the project, as described in Chapter 2 Verilog Design Automation.

   Note that register variables are written as q<0> in the UCF, while they are written as q[0] in the Verilog source modules. The function of the specific pin locations for the peripherals and accessories of the Nexys 3 Board are described in this Chapter by the development of modules in Verilog and example application project files.

Listing 3.1 User Constraints File for the Digilent Nexys 3 Board *nexys3.ucf*

```
#Digilent Nexys 3 Xilinx Spartan-6
#User Constraints File (UCF) nexys3.ucf
#c 2012 Embedded Design Using Programmable Gate Array  Dennis Silage

#Crystal Clock Oscillator
#NET "CLK"   LOC = "V1"    |IOSTANDARD = LVCMOS33;
#NET "CLK"   TNM_NET = sys_clk_pin;
#TIMESPEC TS_sys_clk_pin = PERIOD sys_clk_pin 100000 kHz;

#Cellular RAM
#NET "RAMOE"        LOC = "L18"  |IOSTANDARD = LVCMOS33;
#NET "RAMWR"        LOC = "M16"  |IOSTANDARD = LVCMOS33;
#NET "RAMADV"       LOC = "H18"  |IOSTANDARD = LVCMOS33;
#NET "RAMWAIT"      LOC = "V4"   |IOSTANDARD = LVCMOS33;
#NET "RAMCLK"       LOC = "R10"  |IOSTANDARD = LVCMOS33;
#NET "RAMCS"        LOC = "L15"  |IOSTANDARD = LVCMOS33;
#NET "RAMCRE"       LOC = "M18"  |IOSTANDARD = LVCMOS33;
#NET "RAMUB"        LOC = "K15   |IOSTANDARD = LVCMOS33;
#NET "RAMLB"        LOC = "K16"  |IOSTANDARD = LVCMOS33;

#Parallel PCM
#NET "PPCMCE"       LOC = "L17"  |IOSTANDARD = LVCMOS33;
#NET "PPCMRST"      LOC = "T4"   |IOSTANDARD = LVCMOS33;

#SPI PCM
#NET "SPCMCS"       LOC = "V3"   |IOSTANDARD = LVCMOS33;
#NET "SPCMCLK"      LOC = "R15"  |IOSTANDARD = LVCMOS33;
#NET "SPCMSDI"      LOC = "T13"  |IOSTANDARD = LVCMOS33;

#Memory Address
```

```
#NET "ADDR<1>"      LOC = "K18"  |IOSTANDARD = LVCMOS33;
#NET "ADDR<2>"      LOC = "K17"  |IOSTANDARD = LVCMOS33;
#NET "ADDR<3>"      LOC = "J18"  |IOSTANDARD = LVCMOS33;
#NET "ADDR<4>"      LOC = "J16"  |IOSTANDARD = LVCMOS33;
#NET "ADDR<5>"      LOC = "G18"  |IOSTANDARD = LVCMOS33;
#NET "ADDR<6>"      LOC = "G16"  |IOSTANDARD = LVCMOS33;
#NET "ADDR<7>"      LOC = "H16"  |IOSTANDARD = LVCMOS33;
#NET "ADDR<8>"      LOC = "H15"  |IOSTANDARD = LVCMOS33;
#NET "ADDR<9>"      LOC = "H14"  |IOSTANDARD = LVCMOS33;
#NET "ADDR<10>"     LOC = "H13"  |IOSTANDARD = LVCMOS33;
#NET "ADDR<11>"     LOC = "F18"  |IOSTANDARD = LVCMOS33;
#NET "ADDR<12>"     LOC = "F17"  |IOSTANDARD = LVCMOS33;
#NET "ADDR<13>"     LOC = "K13"  |IOSTANDARD = LVCMOS33;
#NET "ADDR<14>"     LOC = "K12"  |IOSTANDARD = LVCMOS33;
#NET "ADDR<15>"     LOC = "E18"  |IOSTANDARD = LVCMOS33;
#NET "ADDR<16>"     LOC = "E16"  |IOSTANDARD = LVCMOS33;
#NET "ADDR<17>"     LOC = "G13"  |IOSTANDARD = LVCMOS33;
#NET "ADDR<18>"     LOC = "H12"  |IOSTANDARD = LVCMOS33;
#NET "ADDR<19>"     LOC = "D18"  |IOSTANDARD = LVCMOS33;
#NET "ADDR<20>"     LOC = "D17"  |IOSTANDARD = LVCMOS33;
#NET "ADDR<21>"     LOC = "G14"  |IOSTANDARD = LVCMOS33;
#NET "ADDR<22>"     LOC = "F14"  |IOSTANDARD = LVCMOS33;
#NET "ADDR<23>"     LOC = "C18"  |IOSTANDARD = LVCMOS33;
#NET "ADDR<24>"     LOC = "C17"  |IOSTANDARD = LVCMOS33;
#NET "ADDR<25>"     LOC = "F16"  |IOSTANDARD = LVCMOS33
#NET "ADDR<26>"     LOC = "F15"  |IOSTANDARD = LVCMOS33;


#Memory Data
#RAM or Parallel PCM DB<0>, or SPI PCM SDO
#NET "DATA<0>"      LOC = "R13"  |IOSTANDARD = LVCMOS33;
#RAM or Parallel PCM DB<1>, or SPI PCM WP
#NET "DATA<1>"      LOC = "T14"  |IOSTANDARD = LVCMOS33;
#RAM or Parallel PCM DB<2>, or SPI PCM HLD
#NET "DATA<2>"      LOC = "V14"  |IOSTANDARD = LVCMOS33;
#NET "DATA<3>"      LOC = "U5"   |IOSTANDARD = LVCMOS33;
#NET "DATA<4>"      LOC = "V5"   |IOSTANDARD = LVCMOS33;
#NET "DATA<5>"      LOC = "R3"   |IOSTANDARD = LVCMOS33;
#NET "DATA<6>"      LOC = "T3"   |IOSTANDARD = LVCMOS33;
#NET "DATA<7>"      LOC = "R5"   |IOSTANDARD = LVCMOS33;
#NET "DATA<8>"      LOC = "N5"   |IOSTANDARD = LVCMOS33;
#NET "DATA<9>"      LOC = "P6"   |IOSTANDARD = LVCMOS33;
#NET "DATA<10>"     LOC = "P12"  |IOSTANDARD = LVCMOS33;
#NET "DATA<11>"     LOC = "U13"  |IOSTANDARD = LVCMOS33;
#NET "DATA<12>"     LOC = "V13"  |IOSTANDARD = LVCMOS33;
#NET "DATA<13>"     LOC = "U10"  |IOSTANDARD = LVCMOS33;
#NET "DATA<14>"     LOC = "R8"   |IOSTANDARD = LVCMOS33;
#NET "DATA<15>"     LOC = "T8"   |IOSTANDARD = LVCMOS33;


#USB-HID Interface
#NET "USBHCLK"      LOC = "J13"  |IOSTANDARD = LVCMOS33;
#NET "USBSS"        LOC = "L12"  |IOSTANDARD = LVCMOS33;
#NET "USBSDI"       LOC = "K14"  |IOSTANDARD = LVCMOS33;
```

Trends in Embedded Design Using Programmable Gate Arrays

```
#NET "USBSDO"          LOC = "L13"    |IOSTANDARD = LVCMOS33;
#USB UART Interface
#NET "RXD"       LOC = "N17"   |IOSTANDARD = LVCMOS33;
#NET "TXD"       LOC = "N18"   |IOSTANDARD = LVCMOS33;


#Seven Segment Display
#NET "CA"        LOC = "T17"   |IOSTANDARD = LVCMOS33;
#NET "CB"        LOC = "T18"   |IOSTANDARD = LVCMOS33;
#NET "CC"        LOC = "U17"   |IOSTANDARD = LVCMOS33;
#NET "CD"        LOC = "U18"   |IOSTANDARD = LVCMOS33;
#NET "CE"        LOC = "M14"   |IOSTANDARD = LVCMOS33;
#NET "CF"        LOC = "N14"   |IOSTANDARD = LVCMOS33;
#NET "CG"        LOC = "L14"   |IOSTANDARD = LVCMOS33;
#NET "CDP"       LOC = "M13"   |IOSTANDARD = LVCMOS33;
#NET "AN0"       LOC = "N16"   |IOSTANDARD = LVCMOS33;
#NET "AN1"       LOC = "N15"   |IOSTANDARD = LVCMOS33;
#NET "AN2"       LOC = "P18"   |IOSTANDARD = LVCMOS33;
#NET "AN3"       LOC = "P17"   |IOSTANDARD = LVCMOS33;


#LEDs
#NET "LED<0>"    LOC = "U16"   |IOSTANDARD = LVCMOS33;
#NET "LED<1>"    LOC = "V16"   |IOSTANDARD = LVCMOS33;
#NET "LED<2>"    LOC = "U15"   |IOSTANDARD = LVCMOS33;
#NET "LED<3>"    LOC = "V15"   |IOSTANDARD = LVCMOS33;
#NET "LED<4>"    LOC = "M11"   |IOSTANDARD = LVCMOS33;
#NET "LED<5>"    LOC = "N11"   |IOSTANDARD = LVCMOS33;
#NET "LED<6>"    LOC = "R11"   |IOSTANDARD = LVCMOS33;
#NET "LED<7>"    LOC = "T11"   |IOSTANDARD = LVCMOS33;


#Slide Switches
#NET "SW<0>"     LOC = "T10"   |IOSTANDARD = LVCMOS33;
#NET "SW<1>"     LOC = "T9"    |IOSTANDARD = LVCMOS33;
#NET "SW<2>"     LOC = "V9"    |IOSTANDARD = LVCMOS33;
#NET "SW<3>"     LOC = "M8"    |IOSTANDARD = LVCMOS33;
#NET "SW<4>"     LOC = "N8"    |IOSTANDARD = LVCMOS33;
#NET "SW<5>"     LOC = "U8"    |IOSTANDARD = LVCMOS33;
#NET "SW<6>"     LOC = "V8"    |IOSTANDARD = LVCMOS33;
#NET "SW<7>"     LOC = "T5"    |IOSTANDARD = LVCMOS33;


#Push Buttons
#NET "BTNU"      LOC = "A8"    |IOSTANDARD = LVCMOS33;
#NET "BTNL"      LOC = "C4"    |IOSTANDARD = LVCMOS33;
#NET "BTND"      LOC = "C9"    |IOSTANDARD = LVCMOS33;
#NET "BTNR"      LOC = "D9"    |IOSTANDARD = LVCMOS33;
#NET "BTNC"      LOC = "B8"    |IOSTANDARD = LVCMOS33;


#VGA Display
#NET "RD<0>"     LOC = "U7"    |IOSTANDARD = LVCMOS33;
#NET "RD<1>"     LOC = "V7"    |IOSTANDARD = LVCMOS33;
#NET "RD<2>"     LOC = "N7"    |IOSTANDARD = LVCMOS33;
#NET "GR<0>"     LOC = "P8"    |IOSTANDARD = LVCMOS33;
#NET "GR<1>"     LOC = "T6"    |IOSTANDARD = LVCMOS33;
```

```
#NET "GR<2>"        LOC = "V6"    |IOSTANDARD = LVCMOS33;
#NET "BL<1>"        LOC = "R7"    |IOSTANDARD = LVCMOS33;
#NET "BL<2>"        LOC = "T7"    |IOSTANDARD = LVCMOS33;
#NET "HS"           LOC = "N6"    |IOSTANDARD = LVCMOS33;
#NET "VS"           LOC = "P7"    |IOSTANDARD = LVCMOS33;


#Peripheral Port A
#NET "JA1"          LOC = "T12"   |IOSTANDARD = LVCMOS33;
#NET "JA2"          LOC = "V12"   |IOSTANDARD = LVCMOS33;
#NET "JA3"          LOC = "N10    |IOSTANDARD = LVCMOS33;
#NET "JA4]"         LOC = "P11"   |IOSTANDARD = LVCMOS33;
#NET "JA7"          LOC = "M10"   |IOSTANDARD = LVCMOS33;
#NET "JA8"          LOC = "N9"    |IOSTANDARD = LVCMOS33;
#NET "JA9"          LOC = "U11"   |IOSTANDARD = LVCMOS33;
#NET "JA10"         LOC = "V11"   |IOSTANDARD = LVCMOS33;


#Peripheral Port B
#NET "JB1"          LOC = "K2"    |IOSTANDARD = LVCMOS33;
#NET "JB2"          LOC = "K1"    |IOSTANDARD = LVCMOS33;
#NET "JB3"          LOC = "L4"    |IOSTANDARD = LVCMOS33;
#NET "JB4"          LOC = "L3"    |IOSTANDARD = LVCMOS33;
#NET "JB7"          LOC = "J3"    |IOSTANDARD = LVCMOS33;
#NET "JB8"          LOC = "J1"    |IOSTANDARD = LVCMOS33;
#NET "JB9"          LOC = "K3"    |IOSTANDARD = LVCMOS33;
#NET "JB10"         LOC = "K5"    |IOSTANDARD = LVCMOS33;


#Peripheral Port C
#NET "JC1"          LOC = "H3"    |IOSTANDARD = LVCMOS33;
#NET "JC2"          LOC = "L7"    |IOSTANDARD = LVCMOS33;
#NET "JC3"          LOC = "K6"    |IOSTANDARD = LVCMOS33;
#NET "JC4"          LOC = "G3"    |IOSTANDARD = LVCMOS33;
#NET "JC7"          LOC = "G1"    |IOSTANDARD = LVCMOS33;
#NET "JC8"          LOC = "J7"    |IOSTANDARD = LVCMOS33;
#NET "JC9"          LOC = "J6"    |IOSTANDARD = LVCMOS33;
#NET "JC10"         LOC = "F2"    |IOSTANDARD = LVCMOS33;


#Peripheral Port D
#NET "JD1"          LOC = "G11"   |IOSTANDARD = LVCMOS33;
#NET "JD2"          LOC = "F10"   |IOSTANDARD = LVCMOS33;
#NET "JD3"          LOC = "F11"   |IOSTANDARD = LVCMOS33;
#NET "JD4"          LOC = "E11"   |IOSTANDARD = LVCMOS33;
#NET "JD7"          LOC = "D12"   |IOSTANDARD = LVCMOS33;
#NET "JD8"          LOC = "C12"   |IOSTANDARD = LVCMOS33;
#NET "JD9"          LOC = "F12"   |IOSTANDARD = LVCMOS33;
#NET "JD10"         LOC = "E12"   |IOSTANDARD = LVCMOS33;


#VHDC Connector
#NET "VHDCP<1>"     LOC = "B2"
#NET "VHDCN<1>"     LOC = "A2"
#NET "VHDCP<2>"     LOC = "D6"
#NET "VHDCN<2>"     LOC = "C6"
#NET "VHDCP<3>"     LOC = "B3"
```

```
#NET "VHDCN<3>"      LOC = "A3"
#NET "VHDCP<4>"      LOC = "B4"
#NET "VHDCN<4>"      LOC = "A4"
#NET "VHDCP<5>"      LOC = "C5"
#NET "VHDCN<5>"      LOC = "A5"
#NET "VHDCP<6>"      LOC = "B6"
#NET "VHDCN<6>"      LOC = "A6"
#NET "VHDCP<7>"      LOC = "C7"
#NET "VHDCN<7>"      LOC = "A7"
#NET "VHDCP<8>"      LOC = "D8"
#NET "VHDCN<8>"      LOC = "C8"
#NET "VHDCP<9>"      LOC = "B9"
#NET "VHDCN<9>"      LOC = "A9"
#NET "VHDCP<10>"     LOC = "D11"
#NET "VHDCN<10>"     LOC = "C11"
#NET "VHDCP<11>"     LOC = "C10"
#NET "VHDCN<11>"     LOC = "A10"
#NET "VHDCP<12>"     LOC = "G9"
#NET "VHDCN<12>"     LOC = "F9"
#NET "VHDCP<13>"     LOC = "B11"
#NET "VHDCN<13>"     LOC = "A11"
#NET "VHDCP<14>"     LOC = "B12"
#NET "VHDCN<14>"     LOC = "A12"
#NET "VHDCP<15>"     LOC = "C13"
#NET "VHDCN<15>"     LOC = "A13"
#NET "VHDCP<16>"     LOC = "B14"
#NET "VHDCN<16>"     LOC = "A14"
#NET "VHDCP<17>"     LOC = "F13"
#NET "VHDCN<17>"     LOC = "E13"
#NET "VHDCP<18>"     LOC = "C15"
#NET "VHDCN<18>"     LOC = "A15"
#NET "VHDCP<19>"     LOC = "D14"
#NET "VHDCN<19>"     LOC = "C14"
#NET "VHDCP<20>"     LOC = "B16"
#NET "VHDCN<20>"     LOC = "A16"
```

The UCF in Listing 3.2 provides the basic definitions for the hard-wired peripherals and accessories of the Digilent Atlys Board which are somewhat compatible with the Nexys 3 Board, as given in Listing 3.1. The Atlys Board UCF *atlys.ucf* is located in the *Chapter 3\ucf* folder. The file download procedure is described in the Appendix. The NET labels in this UCF for the Atlys Board, such as CLK, JA, LED, BTNS and VHDC, are the same as that for the Nexys 3 Board wherever possible. However, the some of the peripherals and accessories are functionally quite different including the inclusion of DDR2 RAM memory and USB HID on the Atlys Board.

Listing 3.2 User Constraints File for the Digilent Atlys Board *atlys.ucf*

```
#Digilent Atlys Xilinx Spartan-6
#User Constraints File (UCF) atlys.ucf
#c 2012 Embedded Design Using Programmable Gate Array  Dennis Silage

#Crystal Clock Oscillator
#NET "CLK"    LOC = "L15"   |IOSTANDARD = LVCMOS33;
```

```
#SPI Flash Memory
#NET "FMCLK"          LOC = "R15"    |IOSTANDARD = LVCMOS33;
#NET "FMCS"           LOC = "V3"     |IOSTANDARD = LVCMOS33;
#NET "FMDQ<0>"        LOC = "T13"    |IOSTANDARD = LVCMOS33;
#NET "FMDQ<1>"        LOC = "R13"    |IOSTANDARD = LVCMOS33;
#NET "FMDQ<2>"        LOC = "T14"    |IOSTANDARD = LVCMOS33;
#NET "FMDQ<3>"        LOC = "V14"    |IOSTANDARD = LVCMOS33;


#DDR2 DRAM
#NET "DDR2CLK0"       LOC = "G3"
#NET "DDR2CLK1"       LOC = "G1"
#NET "DDR2CKE"        LOC = "H7"
#NET "DDR2RASN"       LOC = "L5"
#NET "DDR2CASN"       LOC = "K5"
#NET "DDR2WEN"        LOC = "E3"
#NET "DDR2RZQ"        LOC = "L6"
#NET "DDR2ZIO"        LOC = "C2"
#NET "DDR2BA0"        LOC = "F2"
#NET "DDR2BA1"        LOC = "F1"
#NET "DDR2BA2"        LOC = "E1"

#NET "DDR2A0"         LOC = "J7"
#NET "DDR2A1"         LOC = "J6"
#NET "DDR2A2"         LOC = "H5"
#NET "DDR2A3"         LOC = "L7"
#NET "DDR2A4"         LOC = "F3"
#NET "DDR2A5"         LOC = "H4"
#NET "DDR2A6"         LOC = "H3"
#NET "DDR2A7"         LOC = "H6"
#NET "DDR2A8"         LOC = "D2"
#NET "DDR2A9"         LOC = "D1"
#NET "DDR2A10"        LOC = "F4"
#NET "DDR2A11"        LOC = "D3"
#NET "DDR2A12"        LOC = "G6"

#NET "DDR2DQ0"        LOC = "L2"
#NET "DDR2DQ1"        LOC = "L1\
#NET "DDR2DQ2"        LOC = "K2"
#NET "DDR2DQ3"        LOC = "K1"
#NET "DDR2DQ4"        LOC = "H2"
#NET "DDR2DQ5"        LOC = "H1"
#NET "DDR2DQ6"        LOC = "J3"
#NET "DDR2DQ7"        LOC = "J1"
#NET "DDR2DQ8"        LOC = "M3"
#NET "DDR2DQ9"        LOC = "M1"
#NET "DDR2DQ10"       LOC = "N2"
#NET "DDR2DQ11"       LOC = "N1"
#NET "DDR2DQ12"       LOC = "T2"
#NET "DDR2DQ13"       LOC = "T1
#NET "DDR2DQ14"       LOC = "U2"
#NET "DDR2DQ15"       LOC = "U1"
```

Trends in Embedded Design Using Programmable Gate Arrays

```
#NET "DDR2UDQS"       LOC="P2"
#NET "DDR2UDQSN"      LOC="P1
#NET "DDR2LDQS"       LOC="L4"
#NET "DDR2LDQSN"      LOC="L3"
#NET "DDR2LDM"        LOC="K3"
#NET "DDR2UDM"        LOC="K4"
#NET "DDR2ODT"        LOC="K6"
#NET "DDR2ZIO"        LOC="C2"
#NET "DDR2RZM"        LOC="L6"


#USB Controller
#NET "EppAstb"        LOC = "B9"    |IOSTANDARD = LVCMOS33;
#NET "EppDstb"        LOC = "A9"    |IOSTANDARD = LVCMOS33;
#NET "USBFLAG"        LOC = "C15"   |IOSTANDARD = LVCMOS33;
#NET "EppWait"        LOC = "F13"   |IOSTANDARD = LVCMOS33;
#NET "EppDB<0>"       LOC = "A2"    |IOSTANDARD = LVCMOS33;
#NET "EppDB<1>"       LOC = "D6"    |IOSTANDARD = LVCMOS33;
#NET "EppDB<2>"       LOC = "C6"    |IOSTANDARD = LVCMOS33;
#NET "EppDB<3>"       LOC = "B3"    |IOSTANDARD = LVCMOS33;
#NET "EppDB<4>"       LOC = "A3"    |IOSTANDARD = LVCMOS33;
#NET "EppDB<5>"       LOC = "B4"    |IOSTANDARD = LVCMOS33;
#NET "EppDB<6>"       LOC = "A4"    |IOSTANDARD = LVCMOS33;
#NET "EppDB<7>"       LOC = "C5"    |IOSTANDARD = LVCMOS33;
#NET "USBCLK"         LOC = "C10"   |IOSTANDARD = LVCMOS33;
#NET "USBOE"          LOC = "A15"   |IOSTANDARD = LVCMOS33;
#NET "USBWR"          LOC = "E13"   |IOSTANDARD = LVCMOS33;
#NET "USBPktEnd"      LOC = "C4"    |IOSTANDARD = LVCMOS33;
#NET "USBDIR"         LOC = "B2"    |IOSTANDARD = LVCMOS33;
#NET "USBMODE"        LOC = "A5"    |IOSTANDARD = LVCMOS33;
#NET "USBADR<0>"      LOC = "A14"   |IOSTANDARD = LVCMOS33;
#NET "USBADR<1>"      LOC = "B14"   |IOSTANDARD = LVCMOS33;


#USB HID Interface
#NET "USBHCLK"        LOC = "P17"   |IOSTANDARD = LVCMOS33;
#NET "USBSS"          LOC = "P18"   |IOSTANDARD = LVCMOS33;
#NET "USBSDI"         LOC = "N15"   |IOSTANDARD = LVCMOS33;
#NET "USBSDO"         LOC = "N18"   |IOSTANDARD = LVCMOS33;


# USB UART Interface
#NET "RXD"       LOC = "A16"   |IOSTANDARD = LVCMOS33;
#NET "TXD"       LOC = "B16"   |IOSTANDARD = LVCMOS33;


#LEDs
#NET "LED<0>"    LOC = "U18"   |IOSTANDARD = LVCMOS33;
#NET "LED<1>"    LOC = "M14"   |IOSTANDARD = LVCMOS33;
#NET "LED<2>"    LOC = "N14"   |IOSTANDARD = LVCMOS33;
#NET "LED<3>"    LOC = "L14"   |IOSTANDARD = LVCMOS33;
#NET "LED<4>"    LOC = "M13"   |IOSTANDARD = LVCMOS33;
#NET "LED<5>"    LOC = "D4"    |IOSTANDARD = LVCMOS33;
#NET "LED<6>"    LOC = "P16"   |IOSTANDARD = LVCMOS33;
#NET "LED<7>"    LOC = "N12"   |IOSTANDARD = LVCMOS33;
```

```
#Slide Switches
#NET "SW<0>"    LOC = "A10"   |IOSTANDARD = LVCMOS33;
#NET "SW<1>"    LOC = "D14"   |IOSTANDARD = LVCMOS33;
#NET "SW<2>"    LOC = "C14"   |IOSTANDARD = LVCMOS33;
#NET "SW<3>"    LOC = "P15"   |IOSTANDARD = LVCMOS33;
#NET "SW<4>"    LOC = "P12"   |IOSTANDARD = LVCMOS33;
#NET "SW<5>"    LOC = "R5"    |IOSTANDARD = LVCMOS33;
#NET "SW<6>"    LOC = "T5"    |IOSTANDARD = LVCMOS33;
#NET "SW<7>"    LOC = "E4"    |IOSTANDARD = LVCMOS33;


#Push Buttons
#NET "BTNU"    LOC = "N4"   |IOSTANDARD = LVCMOS33;
#NET "BTNL"    LOC = "P4"   |IOSTANDARD = LVCMOS33;
#NET "BTND"    LOC = "P3"   |IOSTANDARD = LVCMOS33;
#NET "BTNR"    LOC = "F6"   |IOSTANDARD = LVCMOS33;
#NET "BTNC"    LOC = "F5"   |IOSTANDARD = LVCMOS33;


#Peripheral Port A
#NET "JA1"    LOC = "T3"   |IOSTANDARD = LVCMOS33;
#NET "JA2"    LOC = "R3"   |IOSTANDARD = LVCMOS33;
#NET "JA3"    LOC = "P6"   |IOSTANDARD = LVCMOS33;
#NET "JA4"    LOC = "N5"   |IOSTANDARD = LVCMOS33;
#NET "JA5"    LOC = "V9"   |IOSTANDARD = LVCMOS33;
#NET "JA6"    LOC = "T9"   |IOSTANDARD = LVCMOS33;
#NET "JA7"    LOC = "V4"   |IOSTANDARD = LVCMOS33;
#NET "JA8"    LOC = "T4"   |IOSTANDARD = LVCMOS33;


#AC-97 Codec Interface
#NET "BITCLK"   LOC = "L13"   |IOSTANDARD = LVCMOS33;
#NET "AUDSDI"   LOC = "T18"   |IOSTANDARD = LVCMOS33;
#NET "AUDSDO"   LOC = "N16"   |IOSTANDARD = LVCMOS33;
#NET "AUDSYNC" LOC = "U17"   |IOSTANDARD = LVCMOS33;
#NET "AUDRST"   LOC = "T17"   |IOSTANDARD = LVCMOS33;


#VHDC Connector
#NET "VHDCP<1>"    LOC = "U16"
#NET "VHDCN<1>"    LOC = "V16"
#NET "VHDCP<2>"    LOC = "U15"
#NET "VHDCN<2>"    LOC = "V15"
#NET "VHDCP<3>"    LOC = "U13"
#NET "VHDCN<3>"    LOC = "V11"
#NET "VHDCP<4>"    LOC = "M11"
#NET "VHDCN<4>"    LOC = "N11"
#NET "VHDCP<5>"    LOC = "R11"
#NET "VHDCN<5>"    LOC = "T11"
#NET "VHDCP<6>"    LOC = "T12"
#NET "VHDCN<6>"    LOC = "V12"
#NET "VHDCP<7>"    LOC = "N10"
#NET "VHDCN<7>"    LOC = "P11"
#NET "VHDCP<8>"    LOC = "M10"
#NET "VHDCN<8>"    LOC = "N9"
#NET "VHDCP<9>"    LOC = "U11"
```

```
#NET "VHDCN<9>"     LOC = "V11"
#NET "VHDCP<10>"    LOC = "R10"
#NET "VHDCN<10>"    LOC = "T10"
#NET "VHDCP<11>"    LOC = "U10"
#NET "VHDCN<11>"    LOC = "V10"
#NET "VHDCP<12>"    LOC = "R8"
#NET "VHDCN<12>"    LOC = "T8"
#NET "VHDCP<13>"    LOC = "M8"
#NET "VHDCN<13>"    LOC = "N8"
#NET "VHDCP<14>"    LOC = "U8"
#NET "VHDCN<14>"    LOC = "V8"
#NET "VHDCP<15>"    LOC = "U7"
#NET "VHDCN<15>"    LOC = "V7"
#NET "VHDCP<16>"    LOC = "N7"
#NET "VHDCN<16>"    LOC = "P8"
#NET "VHDCP<17>"    LOC = "T6"
#NET "VHDCN<17>"    LOC = "V6"
#NET "VHDCP<18>"    LOC = "R7"
#NET "VHDCN<18>"    LOC = "T7"
#NET "VHDCP<19>"    LOC = "N6"
#NET "VHDCN<19>"    LOC = "P7"
#NET "VHDCP<20>"    LOC = "U5"
#NET "VHDCN<20>"    LOC = "V5"
```

Hardware Components and Peripherals

An embedded design using programmable gate arrays requires a variety of hardware components and peripherals which provide system support and facilitate the interface to the sensor and actuator environment and the operator. Some of the available integral and external peripherals for the Nexys 3 Board and the Atlys Board are described here.

Crystal Clock Oscillator

The 100 MHz crystal clock oscillator external peripheral on the Nexys 3 Board and the Atlys Board can function as the clock for synchronous logic operation of the FPGA. The clock oscillator has a 40% to 60% duty cycle and an accuracy of $\pm$ 2500 Hz or $\pm$ 50 parts per million (ppm). However, the minimum clock period of 10 nanoseconds (nsec) is exceedingly fast for projects that utilize the pushbuttons, slide switches, LEDs and the LED seven-segment display or an LCD peripheral. The module *clock.v* in Listing 3.3 is located in the *Chapter 3\peripherals* folder. The file download procedure is described in the Appendix.

Listing 3.3 Crystal clock oscillator module *clock.v*

```verilog
// Crystal Clock Oscillator  clock.v
// c 2012 Embedded Design using Programmable Gate Arrays  Dennis Silage

module clock (input CLK, input [31:0] clkscale, output reg sclclk);
                        // CLK master crystal clock oscillator 100 MHz

reg [31:0] clkq = 0;            // clock register, initial value of 0
```

```
always@(posedge CLK)
    begin
        clkq = clkq + 1;                 // increment clock register
            if (clkq >= clkscale)        // clock scaling
                begin
                    sclclk = ~sclclk;    // output clock
                    clkq = 0;            // reset clock register
                end
    end

endmodule
```

The module *clock.v* increases the period by comparing the 100 MHz master crystal clock input signal CLK accumulated in the register clkq to the input 32-bit variable clkscale to provide an external clk signal that is used in the application. The 32-bit register clkq is initialized to 0 here on global reset or power-up by a declaration, although the default value on power-up would also be 0 [Lee06].

The value of the clock scale factor net variable clkscale is determined by Equation 3.1, where *frequency* in Hertz (Hz) is the inverse of the period in seconds of the desired external clock signal. A square wave (50% duty cycle) clock signal with a frequency of 1 kHz requires that the input integer variable clkscale be 50 000.

$$clkscale = \frac{50\ 000\ 000}{frequency} \qquad (3.1)$$

The statement output reg sclclk defines and maps the scaled clock as a 1-bit register to the output net for use by other Verilog modules. The 32-bit clock register clkq can accommodate periods as long as 86 seconds with the 100 MHz master clock ($2^{32} - 1 = 4\ 294\ 967\ 296$) and matches the input 32-bit integer variable clkscale.

The clock oscillator module *clock.v* is verified by the Verilog top module *clocktest.v* in Listing 3.4. The Xilinx ISE project in the *Chapter 3\clocktest\ns3clocktest* folder uses the UCF *ns3clocktest.ucf* which uncomments the signals CLK, LED0, LED1 and LED2 in the Nexys 3 Board UCF of Listing 3.1. A Xilinx ISE project for the Atlys Board is located in the *Chapter 3\clocktest\atlclocktest* folder which illustrates the design reuse concept. The file download procedure is described in the Appendix.

Listing 3.4 Clock oscillator test top module for the Nexys 3 Board and Atlys Board *clocktest.v*

```
// Nexys 3 Board and Atlys Board
// Clock Oscillator Test  clocktest.v
// c 2012 Embedded Design using Programmable Gate Arrays  Dennis Silage

module clocktest (input CLK, output [2:0] LED);

clock M0 (CLK, 50000000, LED[0]);     // 1 Hz clock
clock M1 (CLK, 25000000, LED[1]);     // 2 Hz clock
clock M2 (CLK, 12500000, LED[2]);     // 4 Hz clock

endmodule
```

The LEDs are simply mapped in the *clocktest.v* module to the only output of each instance of the clock.v module and blink at rates of 1, 2, and 4 Hz. Unlike sequential processing, the three Verilog

Trends in Embedded Design Using Programmable Gate Arrays

modules operate in parallel and some independently, as described in Chapter 1 Verilog Hardware Description Language.

As described in Chapter 2 Verilog Design Automation, the Design Utilization Summary for the top module *clocktest.v* shows the use of use of 67 slice registers (<1%) and 237 slice LUTs ($\approx$2%) in the Nexys 3 Board XC6SLX16 Spartan-6 FPGA synthesis. Since the Nexys 3 Board and the Atlys Board have Spartan-6 FPGA devices of difference size, the maximum utilization is reported here for the smaller XC6SLX16 device.

Light Emitting Diodes

The LED hard-wired accessory on the Nexys 3 Board and the Atlys Board can function as an indicator in embedded applications of the FPGA. The module *bargraph.v* utilizes all eight available LEDs and provides a bar graph display useful for peak amplitude measurements in audio and communications signal processing.

The module demonstrates the simple mapping as a continuous assignment of an LED to a logic signal [Ciletti99]. The module is event driven on the positive edge of the input signal clk and uses the largest non-zero bit of the 8-bit input data to produce a bar graph display. The 8-bit LED data register leddata cannot be mapped directly to the eight LED output signals. In Listing 3.4 the 1-bit clock register could be mapped directly to a single LED. However, the eight continuous assignment Verilog statement assign performs the requisite 8-bit register mapping in Listing 3.5.

Listing 3.5 LED bar graph module *bargraph.v*

```
// LED Bar Graph  bargraph.v
// c 2012 Embedded Design using Programmable Gate Arrays  Dennis Silage

module bargraph (input clk, input [7:0] data, output reg [7:0] leddata);

always@(posedge clk)      // local clock event driven
    begin
        leddata = 8'b00000000;      // bar graph pattern based
        if (data[0] == 1)           // based on the least
            leddata = 8'b00000001;  // bit set to logic 1
        if (data[1] == 1)
            leddata = 8'b00000011;
        if (data[2] == 1)
            leddata = 8'b00000111;
        if (data[3] == 1)
            leddata = 8'b00001111;
        if (data[4] == 1)
            leddata = 8'b00011111;
        if (data[5] == 1)
            leddata = 8'b00111111;
        if (data[6] == 1)
            leddata = 8'b01111111;
        if (data[7] == 1)
            leddata = 8'b11111111;
    end

endmodule
```

The bar graph module has a resolution of 8-bits, but the most significant bit (MSB) is non-zero for 8-bit data greater than 128 or half the range (0 to 255). In an application the data might represent an analog signal that has been converted to a 12-bit digital signal by an analog-to-digital converter (ADC) peripheral. The most significant 8-bits would then be mapped to the 8-bits of the bar graph. To increase the resolution of the LED bar graph, a digital bias can be subtracted from the 12-bit data.

The bar graph module *bargraph.v* is verified by the Verilog top module *bargraphtest.v* in Listing 3.6. The Xilinx ISE project in the *Chapter 3\bargraphtest\ns3bargraphtest* folder uses a UCF *ns3bargraphtest.ucf* which uncomments the signals CLK, LED0 through LED7 in the Nexys 3 Board UCF of Listing 3.1. The three Verilog modules operate in parallel and some independently. A Xilinx ISE project for the Atlys Board is located in the *Chapter 3\bargraphtest\atlbargraphtest* folder. The file download procedure is described in the Appendix.

The data is generated as a simple ramp by the stimulus module *gendata.v* on the negative edge of the clock input signal. The wire net type establishes the 8-bit array connectivity for data between the *bargraph.v* and *gendata.v* module [Chu08]. The clock signal clk is outputted from the *clock.v* module and inputted to both the *bargraph.v* and *gendata.v* modules.

In Listing 3.6 the statement output reg [7:0] gdata defines and maps the generated data as an 8-bit register to the output array net for use by other Verilog modules. Note that the name of the generated signal data in the top module *bargraphtest.v* (data) does not have to agree with the name of the generated register data in the *gendata.v* module (gdata) since the connection by position option for the ports of a module is used here, as described in Chapter 1 Verilog Hardware Description Language.

As described in Chapter 2 Verilog Design Automation, the Design Utilization Summary for the top module *bargraphtest.v* shows the use of 49 slice registers (<1%) and 116 slice LUTs (≈1%) in the Nexys 3 Board XC6SLX16 Spartan-6 FPGA synthesis.

Listing 3.6 LED bar graph test top module for the Nexys 3 Board and Atlys Board *bargraphtest.v*

```
// Nexys 3 Board and Atlys Board
// LED Bar Graph Test  bargraphtest.v
// c 2012 Embedded Design using Programmable Gate Arrays  Dennis Silage

module bargraphtest (input CLK, output [7:0] LED);

wire [7:0] data;
wire [7:0] leddata;

assign LED = leddata;              // continuous assignment for LED data output

clock M0 (CLK, 1000000, clk);      // 50 Hz clock
bargraph M1 (clk, data, leddata);
gendata M2 (clk, data);

endmodule

module gendata (input clock, output reg [7:0] gdata);    // generate bar graph test data

always@(negedge clock)      // local clock event driven
    gdata = gdata + 1;      // increment generated data

endmodule
```

Trends in Embedded Design Using Programmable Gate Arrays

Push Buttons and Slide Switches

The hard-wired accessory push buttons and slide switches on the Nexys 3 Board and the Atlys Board function as asynchronous input signals in applications of the FPGA. Depressing the push buttons and setting the slide switches generate logic 1 on the associated FPGA pin, as given in the UCF of Listing 3.1 or Listing 3.2. They have no active debouncing circuitry.

The module *pbsswtest.v* in Listing 3.7 utilizes two of the five push buttons, the eight slide switches and the eight LEDs on the Nexys 3 Board or the Atlys Board. The Xilinx ISE project in the *Chapter 3\pbsswtest\ns3pbsswtest* folder uses a UCF *ns3pbsswtest.ucf* which uncomments the signals BTNL and BTNR, SW0 to SW7 and LED0 to LED3 in the Nexys 3 UCF of Listing 3.1. A Xilinx ISE project for the Atlys Board is located in the *Chapter 3\pbsswtest\atlpbsswtest* folder. The file download procedure is described in the Appendix.

The module is event driven on the asynchronous depression or release of either the left push button (BTNL) or right push button (BTNR) without the use of a synchronous clock. As in Listing 3.5, the continuous assignment Verilog statement assign performs the non-blocking mapping of leddata to the LED in Listing 3.7. Depressing BTNL reads the push button switches individually and maps their output to the LEDs. Depressing BTNR turns all the LEDs off.

As described in Chapter 2 Verilog Design Automation, the Design Utilization Summary for the module *pbsswtest.v* shows the use of no slice registers or slice LUTs but only a minimal number of logic gates and multiplexers in the Nexys 3 Board XC6SLX16 Spartan-6 FPGA synthesis.

Listing 3.7 Push button and slide switch test for the Nexys 3 Board and Atlys Board *pbsswtest.v*

```
// Nexys 3 Board and Atlys Board
// Push Button and Slide Switch Test  pbsswtest.v
// c 2012 Embedded Design using Programmable Gate Arrays  Dennis Silage

module pbsswtest (input BTNL, BTNR, input [7:0] SW, output [7:0] LED);

reg [7:0] leddata;          // LED data

assign LED = leddata;       // continuous assignment for LED data output

always@(BTNL or BTNR)       // pushbutton event driven
    begin
        if (BTNL == 1)
            begin
                leddata <= SW;      // non-blocking assignment
            end
        if (BTNR == 1)
            leddata <= 0;   // clear LEDs
    end

endmodule
```

The push buttons are often used for counting functions in FPGA applications where contact *bounce* can cause an aberrant result. The top module *pbdebouncetest.v* in Listing 3.8 illustrates the use of a serial shift register to insure that if a contact bounce occurs then only a single output pulse results. The module *pbdebounce.v* in Listing 3.9 is in the *Chapter 3\peripherals* folder and is utilized within the top module *pbdebouncetest.v*. The three Verilog modules operate in parallel and independently in the top module [Botros06].

A 4-bit register pbshift is logically (no wrap-around) left shifted on the positive edge of a 50 Hz clock provided by the *clock.v* module. The least significant bit of the shift register is set equal to the right push button (BTNR). If all four bits of pbshift contain logic 1 (1111 or 15 decimal), then the push button register output pbreg is set to logic 1. If all four bits contain logic 0, then the push button register output pbreg is set to logic 0. Any other 4-bit pattern indicates that a push button bounce has occurred and pbreg is unchanged.

Listing 3.8 Debounce test top module for the Nexys 3 Board and Atlys Board *pbdebouncetest.v*

```
// Nexys 3 Board and Atlys Board
// Push Button Debounce Test  pbdebouncetest.v
// c 2012 Embedded Design using Programmable Gate Arrays  Dennis Silage

module pbdebouncetest (input CLK, input BTNR, output [7:0] LED);

wire [3:0] leddata;
wire [3:0] dataled;

assign LED[7:4] = dataled[3:0];        // continuous assignment for LED data output
assign LED[3:0] = leddata[3:0];

clock M0 (CLK, 1000000, clk);        // 50 Hz clock
pbdebounce M1 (clk, BTNR, pbreg);
ledtest M2 (pbreg, BTNR, leddata, dataled);

endmodule

module ledtest (input pbreg, input button, output reg [3:0] leddata, output reg [3:0] dataled);

always@(posedge pbreg)  // debounced pushbutton event
    begin                              // driven
        leddata = leddata + 1;         // increment counter
    end

always@(posedge button) // chattering pushbutton event
    begin                              // driven
        dataled = dataled + 1;         // increment counter
    end

endmodule
```

Listing 3.9 Push button debounce *pbdebounce.v*

```
// Push Button Debounce  pbdebounce.v
// c 2012 Embedded Design using Programmable Gate Arrays  Dennis Silage

module pbdebounce (input clk, input button, output reg pbreg);

reg [3:0] pbshift;

always@(posedge clk)            // local clock event driven
    begin
```

```
        pbshift = pbshift << 1;     // shift register
        pbshift[0] = button;        // read button
        if (pbshift == 0)           // if a bounce occurs
            pbreg = 0;              // clear the register
        if (pbshift == 15)          // 15 local clock ticks without a bounce
            pbreg = 1;             //  sets the register
    end

endmodule
```

The module *ledtest.v* loads the rightmost four LEDs of the Nexys 3 Board or the Atlys Board with the 4-bit register leddata which increments on the positive edge of the register pbreg. The leftmost four LEDs are loaded with the 4-bit register dataled which increments on the positive edge of the same push button signal BTNL.

A comparison of the output of these two registers clearly indicates the deleterious nature of push button bounce on performance. The push button bounce mitigation is based on a time window that is the product of the number of bits in the shift register and the clock period.

The Xilinx ISE project in the *Chapter 3\pbdebouncetest\ns3pbdebouncetest* uses the UCF *ns3pbdebouncetest.ucf* which uncomments the signals CLK, BTNR and LED0 to LED7 in the Nexys 3 Board UCF of Listing 3.1. A Xilinx ISE project for the Atlys Board is located in the *Chapter 3\pbdebouncetest\atlpbdebouncetest* folder which illustrates design reuse. The file download procedure is described in the Appendix.

As described in Chapter 2 Verilog Design Automation, the Design Utilization Summary for the top module *pbdebouncetest.v* describes the use of 44 slice registers (<1%) and 110 slice LUTs (≈1%) in the Nexys 3 Board XC6SLX16 Spartan-6 FPGA synthesis.

PmodKYPD Keypad

The external accessory Digilent PmodKYPD™ keypad provides a standard 16 key input in applications of the FPGA, as shown in Figure 3.3. The operation of the PmodKYPD is referenced in the Digilent document 502-195 (*www.digilentinc.com*).

Figure 3.3 Digilent PmodKYPD keypad

The keypad is a matrix of interconnections that utilizes 4 column and 4 row signals or only 8 signals to determine which one of the 16 keys is depressed. The module *keypad.v* in Listing 3.10, which is also in the *Chapter 3\peripherals* folder, scans the 4 column pins with a logic 0 sequentially, reads the corresponding row pins and is event driven on the positive edge of the input signal clk provided by the *clock.v* module. The depressed key is identified by the column and row which are both logic 0. The module *keypad.v* returns the ASCII value of the most recent depressed key as the 8-bit data keydata with no key debouncing.

As described in Chapter 1 Verilog Hardware Description Language for the controller-datapath construct, the input net variable kpdreset resets keydata to 0 as the control input and the output net variable resetkpd is the status return. Control flow is effected by a finite state machine (FSM) and the *for loop* construct with the integer variable i. The ASCII code of the depressed key determined by an arithmetic expression of a fixed offset and the integer variable j.

Listing 3.10 Keypad module *keypad.v*

```
// Keypad   keypad.v
// c 2012 Embedded Design using Programmable Gate Arrays  Dennis Silage

module keypad (input clk, output reg [3:0] column, input [3:0] row, input kpdreset,
               output reg resetkpd, output reg [7:0] keydata);

reg [3:0] keystate;
integer i, j;

always@(posedge clk)
    begin
        case (keystate)
            0:   begin
                    if (kpdreset == 1)
                        begin
                            keydata =0;
                            resetkpd = 1;
                        end
                    keystate = 1;
                end
            1:   begin
                    if (kpdreset == 0)
                        begin
                            resetkpd = 0;
                            keystate = 2;
                        end
                    keystate = 2;
                end
            2:   begin
                    column = 14;
                    keystate = 3;
                end
            3:   begin
                    j = 0;
                    for (i = 0; i <= 2; i = i + 1)
                        begin
                            j = j + 3;
                            if (row[i] == 0)
                                keydata = 46 + j;
                        end
                    if (row[3] == 0)
                        keydata = 48;
```

```
                    keystate = 4;
            end
    4:  begin
                    column = 13;
                    keystate = 5;
            end
    5:  begin
                    j = 0;
                    for (i = 0; i <= 2; i = i + 1)
                            begin
                                    j = j + 3;
                                    if (row[i] == 0)
                                            keydata = 47 + j;
                            end
                    if (row[3] == 0)
                            keydata = 70;
                    keystate = 6;
            end
    6:  begin
                    column = 11;
                    keystate = 7;
            end
    7:  begin
                    j = 0;
                    for (i = 0; i <= 2; i = i + 1)
                            begin
                                    j = j + 3;
                                    if (row[i] == 0)
                                            keydata = 48 + j;
                            end
                    if (row[3] == 0)
                            keydata = 69;
                    keystate = 8;
            end
    8:  begin
                    column = 7;
                    keystate = 9;
            end
    9:  begin
                    for (i = 0; i <= 3; i = i + 1)
                            if (row[i] == 0)
                                    keydata = 65 + i;
                    keystate = 0;
            end
    default: keystate = 0;
    endcase
end

endmodule
```

The keypad module *keypad.v* is verified by the Verilog top module *keypadtest.v* in Listing 3.11 which is in the *Chapter 3\keypadtest\ns3keypadtest* folder. The 12-pin PmodKYPD is connected to one

(Peripheral Port A, JA) of the four 12-pin Pmod connectors on the Nexys 3 Board with a 12-pin connector cable (*www.digilentinc.com*).

Listing 3.11 Keypad top test module for the Nexys 3 Board and Atlys Board *keypadtest.v*

```
// Nexys 3 Board and Atlys Board
// Keypad Test keypadtest.v
// c 2012 Embedded Design using Programmable Gate Arrays  Dennis Silage

module keypadtest (input CLK, input JA7, JA8, JA9, JA10, output JA1, JA2, JA3, JA4,
                   output [7:0] LED);

wire [7:0] data;
wire [3:0] column;
wire [3:0] row;

assign LED = data;
assign JA1 = column[3];
assign JA2 = column[2];
assign JA3 = column[1];
assign JA4 = column[0];
assign row[3] = JA7;
assign row[2] = JA8;
assign row[1] = JA9;
assign row[0] = JA10;

clock M0 (CLK, 1000000, clk);        //50 Hz clock
keypad M1 (clk, column, row, 0, rstkpd, data);

endmodule
```

The wire net type establishes the 4-bit array connectivity for column and row net variables between the *keypad.v* and *keypadtest.v* modules. The 8-bit LED array external signals are assigned to the 8-bit register data since they are only referenced in the top module *keypadtest.v*. The *clock.v* module provides a 50 Hz clock signal. The keypad reset control input kpdreset is set to 0 and the status return is not used.

The PmodKYPD column signals are outputted on Peripheral Port A as JA1 to JA4 and the row signals are inputted as JA7 to JA10 in the top module *keypadtest.v*. This facilitates a conversational description of the process and is used here. The alternative is either to modify the UCF file with these names or use the less descriptive port nomenclature in the top module *keypadtest.v*.

The Xilinx ISE project in the *Chapter 3\keypadtest\ns3keypadtest* folder uses the UCF *ns3keypadtest.ucf* which uncomments the signals CLK, JA1 to JA10 and the 8-bit array LED in the Nexys 3 UCF of Listing 3.1. The two Verilog modules operate in parallel in the top module. A Xilinx ISE project for the Atlys Board is located in the *Chapter 3\keypadtest\atlkeypadtest* folder which illustrates design reuse. The file download procedure is described in the Appendix.

As described in Chapter 2 Verilog Design Automation, the Design Utilization Summary the top module *rotarytest.v* shows the use of 37 slice registers (<1%) and 112 slice LUTs ($\approx$1%) in the Nexys 3 Board XC6SLX16 Spartan-6 FPGA synthesis.

Trends in Embedded Design Using Programmable Gate Arrays

PmodENC Rotary Shaft Encoder

The external accessory Digilent PmodENC™ rotary shaft encoder provides asynchronous input signals in applications of the FPGA, as shown in Figure 3.4. The operation of the PmodENC is referenced in the Digilent document 502-117 (*www.digilentinc.com*).

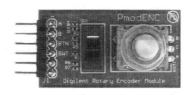

Figure 3.4 Digilent PmodENC rotary shaft encoder

Depressing the center shaft provides an additional push button switch which generates logic 1 on the rotCTR signal. An independent slide switch (SWT) is available but not utilized here. Rotating the shaft clockwise provides a logic 1 on the rotA signal before a logic 1 appears on the rotB signal. Rotating the shaft counter-clockwise provides a logic 1 on the rotB signal before a logic 1 appears on the rotA signal. When the shaft is stationary at the detent position both rotA and rotB are logic 0. The rotary shaft encoder signals rotA, rotB and rotCTR have no active debouncing circuitry.

The module *rotary.v* in Listing 3.12, which is also in the *Chapter 3\peripherals* folder, is event driven on the positive edge of the input signal clk provided by the *clock.v* module. Each of the rotary shaft encoder signals are debounced by the same process described in the module *pbdebounce.v* in Listing 3.9. The debounced shaft encoder signals here are the register variables rotAreg, rotBreg and rotCTRreg.

The rotary shaft encoder module *rotary.v* is verified by the Verilog top module *rotarytest.v* in Listing 3.13 which is in the *Chapter 3\rotarytest\s3erotarytest* folder. The 6-pin PmodENC is connected to one (Peripheral Port A, JA) of the four 12-pin Pmod connectors on the Nexys 3 Board using the upper 6 pins (JA1 to JA3). A slide switch on the PmodENC is connected to JA4 but is not used here.

The Xilinx ISE project in the *Chapter 3\rotarytest\ns3rotarytest* folder uses the UCF *ns3rotarytest.ucf* which uncomments the signals CLK, JA1, JA2, JA3, and LED7 to LED0 in the Nexys 3 UCF of Listing 3.1. The three Verilog modules operate in parallel and some independently in the top module. A Xilinx ISE project for the Atlys Board is located in the *Chapter 3\rotarytest\atlrotarytest* folder. The file download procedure is described in the Appendix.

Listing 3.12 Rotary shaft encoder module *rotary.v*

```
// Rotary Shaft Encoder rotary.v
// c 2012 Embedded Design using Programmable Gate Arrays  Dennis Silage

module rotary (input clk, rotA, rotB, rotCTR, output reg rotAreg, output reg rotBreg,
               output reg rotCTRreg);

reg [3:0] rotAshift;
reg [3:0] rotBshift;
reg [3:0] rotCTRshift;

always@(posedge clk)       // local clock event driven
    begin
          rotCTRshift = rotCTRshift << 1;       // debounce for rotCTR
          rotCTRshift[0] = rotCTR;
```

```
          if (rotCTRshift == 0)
              rotCTRreg = 0;
          if (rotCTRshift == 15)
              rotCTRreg = 1;

          rotAshift = rotAshift << 1;              // debounce for rotA
          rotAshift[0] = rotA;
          if (rotAshift == 15)
              rotAreg = 0;
          if (rotAshift == 0)
              rotAreg = 1;

          rotBshift = rotBshift << 1;              // debounce for rotB
          rotBshift[0] = rotB;
          if (rotBshift == 15)
              rotBreg = 0;
          if (rotBshift == 0)
              rotBreg = 1;
      end

endmodule
```

The wire net type establishes the 4-bit array connectivity for leddata and dataled between the *ledtest.v* and *rotarytest.v* modules. The LED external signals LED[7:4] and LED[3:0] are assigned to register dataled and leddata since they are only referenced in the top module *rotarytest.v*.

The PmodENC signals are inputted on Peripheral Port A as JA1, JA2 and JA3 and assigned to the signals rotA, rotB and rotCTR in the top module *rotarytest.v*. This facilitates a conversational description of the process and is used here. The alternative is either to modify the UCF file with these names or use the less descriptive port nomenclature in the top module *rotarytest.v*.

The module *ledtest.v* loads the rightmost four LEDs with the 4-bit register leddata which increments or decrements on the logic of the debounced register variable rotBreg on the positive edge of the debounced register variable rotAreg. The leftmost four LEDs are loaded with the 4-bit register dataled which increments or decrements on the logic of the chattering signal rotB on the positive edge of the chattering signal rotA.

The signal rotA is loaded into the register rotclk in the module *ledtest.v*. As described in Chapter 2 Verilog Design Automation event edge trigger signals often generate an irreconcilable error in Place and Route. The use of the register obviates this error here.

A clockwise rotation of the rotary shaft encoder increments the register, while a counterclockwise rotation decrements the register. These registers are cleared with the debounced register variable rotCTRreg or the chattering signal rotCTR which results from the depression of the shaft of the rotary encoder.

Listing 3.13 Rotary shaft encoder top module for the Nexys 3 Board and Atlys Board *rotarytest.v*

```
// Nexys 3 Board and Atlys Board
// Rotary Switch Test rotarytest.v
// c 2012 Embedded Design using Programmable Gate Arrays  Dennis Silage

module rotarytest (input CLK, JA1, JA2, JA3, output [7:0] LED);

wire [3:0] leddata;
wire [3:0] dataled;
```

```
assign LED[7:4] = dataled[3:0];
assign LED[3:0] = leddata[3:0];
assign rotA = JA1;
assign rotB = JA2;
assign rotCTR = JA3;

clock M0 (CLK, 50000, rotclk);        // 1 kHz clock
rotary M1 (rotclk, rotA, rotB, rotCTR, rotAreg, rotBreg, rotCTRreg);
ledtest M2 (CLK, rotA, rotB, rotAreg, rotBreg, rotCTR, rotCTRreg, leddata, dataled);

endmodule

module ledtest (input CLK, rotA, rotB, rotAreg, rotBreg, rotCTR, rotCTRreg,
                output reg [3:0] leddata, output reg [3:0] dataled);

reg rotclk;

always@(posedge CLK)
      begin
            rotclk = rotA;
      end

always@(posedge rotAreg)              // event driven on debounced
      begin                           // shaft encoder rotA
          if (rotBreg == 0 && rotCTRreg == 0)
                    leddata = leddata + 1;
                else
                    leddata = leddata – 1;
                if (rotCTRreg == 1)
                    leddata = 0;
      end

always@(posedge rotclk)               // event driven on chattering
      begin                           // shaft encoder rotA via rotclk
          if (rotB == 0 && rotctr == 0)
                dataled = dataled + 1;
          else
                dataled = dataled – 1;
          if (rotCTR == 1)
                dataled = 0;
          end

endmodule
```

A comparison of the output of these two registers clearly indicates the deleterious nature of rotary shaft encoder bounce on performance. The rotary shaft encoder bounce mitigation is based on a time window that is the product of the number of bits in the shift register and the clock period. As described in Chapter 2 Verilog Design Automation, the Design Utilization Summary the top module *rotarytest.v* shows the use of 35 slice registers (<1%) and 65 slice LUTs (<1%) in the Nexys 3 Board XC6SLX16 Spartan-6 FPGA synthesis.

Seven Segment Display

The hard-wired accessory seven segment LED display on the Nexys 3 Board functions as an annunciator in applications of the FPGA. The seven segment display is commonly used to indicate a numerical output with the digitals 0 through 9 and a decimal point, but can be extended to show several other patterns. For example, the additional characters that form the hexadecimal (base 16) number system can be displayed as A, b C, d, E and F. Other patterns can be formed which can be used in process control applications.

Any of the seven LED segments and the LED as a decimal point can be turned on separately by a logic 0 on the eight cathode signals CA, CB, CC, CD, CE, CF, CG and CDP. The Nexys 3 Board has four seven segment displays which are multiplexed by a logic 0 on the four anode signals AN0 (the rightmost seven segment display), AN1, AN2, and AN3 (the leftmost seven segment display). Multiplexing implies that the four seven segment displays must be scanned at a rate high enough to avoid flicker, but only 12 IO signals are used here rather than the 32 IO signals required if connected with the anodes grounded (logic 0).

The module *sevensegment.v* in Listing 3.14, which is in the *Chapter 3\peripherals* folder, is event driven on the negative edge of the input signal clk. A Verilog case statement assigns the 4-bit input signal data to the 8-bit cathode pattern signal cathodedata of the seven segment display for the normal 16 characters (the decimal numbers 0 through 9 and the extended hexadecimal digits A through F) and 15 special characters (including the minus sign and degree symbol). The decimal point as the least significant bit (LSB) is off (logic 1).

Another Verilog case statement assigns the 3-bit input signal digit to the 4-bit anode register anodedata to enable the seven segment display individually [Navabi06]. A 3-bit signal is used here because there are four digits and an all off condition (five states in all). The input signal setdp, if a logic 1, is used to logically AND (&) the 8-bit register cathodedata with FE hexadecimal (or 1111 1110 binary) to set the LSB of cathodedata to a logic 0 and turn the decimal point on. Finally, the continuous assignment Verilog statement assign performs requisite mapping of the cathode and anode signals to the output pins of the seven segment display, as given by the UCF of Listing 3.1.

Listing 3.14 Seven segment display module *sevensegment.v*

```
// Seven Segment Display  sevensegment.v
// c 2012 Embedded Design using Programmable Gate Arrays  Dennis Silage

module sevensegment (input clock, input [4:0] data, input [2:0] digit, input setdp, output AN0, AN1,
            output AN2, AN3, CA, CB, CC, CD, CE, CF, CG, CDP);

reg [7:0] cathodedata;          // cathode data
reg [3:0] anodedata;            // anode data
assign CA = cathodedata[7];
assign CB = cathodedata[6];
assign CC = cathodedata[5];
assign CD = cathodedata[4];
assign CE = cathodedata[3];
assign CF = cathodedata[2];
assign CG = cathodedata[1];
assign CDP = cathodedata[0];
assign AN3 = anodedata[3];
assign AN2 = anodedata[2];
assign AN1 = anodedata[1];
assign AN0 = anodedata[0];
```

Trends in Embedded Design Using Programmable Gate Arrays

```verilog
always@(negedge clock)   // local clock event driven
    begin
        case (data)
            0:    cathodedata = 8'b00000011;    // 0
            1:    cathodedata = 8'b10011111;    // 1
            2:    cathodedata = 8'b00100101;    // 2
            3:    cathodedata = 8'b00001101;    // 3
            4:    cathodedata = 8'b10011001;    // 4
            5:    cathodedata = 8'b01001001;    // 5
            6:    cathodedata = 8'b01000001;    // 6
            7:    cathodedata = 8'b00011111;    // 7
            8:    cathodedata = 8'b00000001;    // 8
            9:    cathodedata = 8'b00001001;    // 9
            10:   cathodedata = 8'b00010001;    // A
            11:   cathodedata = 8'b11000001;    // b
            12:   cathodedata = 8'b01100011;    // C
            13:   cathodedata = 8'b10000101;    // d
            14:   cathodedata = 8'b01100001;    // E
            15:   cathodedata = 8'b01110001;    // F
            16:   cathodedata = 8'b11111101;    // middle (minus sign)
            17:   cathodedata = 8'b01111111;    // top
            18:   cathodedata = 8'101111111;    // right top
            19:   cathodedata = 8'b11011111;    // right bottom
            20:   cathodedata = 8'b11101111;    // bottom
            21:   cathodedata = 8'b11110111;    // left bottom
            22:   cathodedata = 8'b11111011;    // left top
            23:   cathodedata = 8'b11011001;    // left top, middle, right bottom
            24:   cathodedata = 8'b10110101;    // left bottom, middle, right top
            25:   cathodedata = 8'b11000101;    // bottom small o
            26:   cathodedata = 8'b00111001;    // top small o (degree)
            27:   cathodedata = 8'b11010101;    // bottom, inverted small u
            28:   cathodedata = 8'b10111001;    // top, small u
            29:   cathodedata = 8'b11000111;    // bottom, small u
            30:   cathodedata = 8'b00111011;    // top, inverted small u
            31:   cathodedata = 8'b11111111;    // all OFF
        endcase

        if (setdp == 1)                          // decimal point
            cathodedata = cathodedata & 8'hFE;

        case (digit)
            0:    anodedata = 4'b1111;          // all OFF
            1:    anodedata = 4'b1110;          // AN0
            2:    anodedata = 4'b1101;          // AN1
            3:    anodedata = 4'b1011;          // AN2
            4:    anodedata = 4'b0111;          // AN3
            default:   anodedata = 4'b1111;     // all OFF
        endcase
    end

endmodule
```

The seven segment display module *sevensegment.v* is verified by the Verilog top module *sevensegtest.v* in Listing 3.15 which is in the *Chapter 3\sevensegtest\ns3sevensegtest* folder. The complete Xilinx ISE project uses a UCF *ns3sevensegtest.ucf* which uncomments the signals CLK, BTNL, BTNR, BTND and the cathode and anode signals in the Nexys 3 Board UCF of Listing 3.1. This project is the Verilog behavioral synthesis example that is used to illustrate the Xilinx ISE EDA software tool in Chapter 2 Verilog Design Automation.

The four Verilog modules operate in parallel and some independently in the top module. The file download procedure is described in the Appendix. There is no Xilinx ISE project for the Atlys Board because the PmodSSD external peripheral is only a two digit seven segment display and utilizes the only port available (Peripheral Port A, JA).

The wire net type establishes the 4-bit and 3-bit array connectivity for data and digit between the *elapsedtime.v* and *sevensegment.v* modules. The clock signals clka and clkb are outputted from the two instances of the *clock.v* module at a frequency of 100 Hz and 1 kHz and inputted to the *elapsedtime.v* module. The signal clka is also inputted to *sevensegment.v* module.

The module *elapsedtime.v* is a stop watch application with a resolution of 10 msec. The four seven segment displays are multiplexed on the negative edge of the signal clkb at a 1 kHz rate to avoid flicker using the 3-bit signal digit and the 4-bit signal data. The signal setdp is set to logic 1 for the third digit to signify the decimal point for the elapsed time in seconds. The blocking Verilog assignment statement (=) is used to set the seven segment display to insure that both the data and digit register variables are correct before the display is updated [Ciletti99].

The elapsed time is an event triggered process on the positive edge of the signal clock at a 100 Hz rate for a resolution of 10 milliseconds (msec). A digit is incremented and set to 0 if greater than 9 and the next digit is incremented. An overflow sets the elapsed time to 0. The push buttons BTN0, BTN1 and BTN3 starts, stops and resets the elapsed time clock process. Contact debounce, as shown in Listing 3.9, is not required here since the depression of the push button is a positive latch and not a counting function.

As described in Chapter 2 Verilog Design Automation, the Design Utilization Summary for the top module *sevensegtest.v* shows the use of 105 slice registers (<1%) and 262 slice LUTs (3%) in the Nexys 3 Board XC6SLX16 Spartan-6 FPGA synthesis.

Listing 3.15 Seven segment display test top module for the Nexys 3 Board *sevensegtest.v*

```
// Nexys 3 Board
// Seven Segment Display Test  sevensegtest.v
// c 2012 Embedded Design using Programmable Gate Arrays  Dennis Silage

module sevensegtest (input CLK, BTNL, BTNR, BTND, output AN0, AN1, AN2, AN3, CA, CB, CC,
                output CD, CE, CF, CG, CDP);

wire [4:0] data;
wire [2:0] digit;

clock M0 (CLK, 250000, clka);       // 100 Hz
clock M1 (CLK, 25000, clkb);        // 1 kHz
sevensegment M2 (clkb, data, digit, setdp, AN0, AN1, AN2, AN3, CA, CB,
            CC, CD, CE, CF, CG, CDP);
elapsedtime M3 (clka, clkb, data, digit, setdp, BTNL, BTNR, BTND);

endmodule

module elapsedtime(input clka, input clkb, output reg [3:0] data, output reg [2:0] digit,
                output reg setdp, input BTNL, BTNR, BTND);
```

Trends in Embedded Design Using Programmable Gate Arrays

```
reg [1:0] digitmux;
reg startstop;
reg [3:0] csec100;     // seconds 1/100s
reg [3:0] csec10;      // seconds 1/10s
reg [3:0] sec1;        // seconds 1s
reg [3:0] sec10;       // seconds 10s

always@(negedge clkb)    // local clock event driven
     begin
          digitmux = digitmux + 1;  // digit multiplexer
          setdp = 0;                 // clear decimal point
          data[4] = 0;
          case (digitmux)
               0:   begin
                         data[3:0] = csec100;
                         digit =1;
                    end
               1:   begin
                         data[3:0] = csec10;
                         digit = 2;
                    end
               2:   begin
                         data[3:0] = sec1;
                         digit = 3;
                         setdp = 1;       // set decimal point
                    end
               3:   begin
                         data[3:0] = sec10;
                         digit = 4;
                    end
          endcase
     end

always@(posedge clka)           // local clock event driven
     begin
          if (BTND == 1)        // clear and stop
               begin
                    startstop = 0;
                    csec100 = 0;
                    csec10 = 0;
                    sec1 = 0;
                    sec10 = 0;
               end
          if (BTNR==1)          // stop
               startstop = 0;
          if (BTNL == 1)        // start
               startstop = 1;

          if (startstop == 1)
               begin
                    csec100 = csec100+1;
                    if (csec100 > 9)
```

```
            begin
                  csec100 = 0;
                  csec10 = csec10+1;
            end
        if (csec10 > 9)
            begin
                  csec10 = 0;
                  sec1 = sec1 + 1;
            end
        if (sec1 > 9)
            begin
                  sec1 = 0;
                  sec10 = sec10+1;
            end
        if (sec10 > 9)
                  sec10 = 0;
      end
  end

endmodule
```

PmodCLP Parallel Liquid Crystal Display

The external accessory Digilent PmodCLP™ parallel liquid crystal display (LCD) function as an alphanumeric annunciator in applications of the FPGA. Although the interface is more complicated and inherently slower in response than the seven segment LED display, the LCD features a 2-line by 16-character display with fixed or user-defined fonts. Updating the LCD at even a 0.5 second interval produces diminished clarity.

The PmodCLP LCD uses an 8-bit data bus parallel interface and requires two ports which are only available on the Nexys 3 Board (peripheral ports C and D, JC and JD). The PmodCLP parallel LCD interface signals consist of the eight data bits lcdd[0] through lcdd[7], the read/write enable signal elcd, the register select signal rslcd and the read/write control signal rwlcd. Since the LCD requires a +5 V logic supply the PmodCLP includes a +3.3 V to +5 V boost regulator and a +5 V to +3.3 V logic buffer. The PmodCLP is referenced in the Digilent document 502-142 (*www.digilentinc.com*) and is shown in Figure 3.5.

The LCD has three internal memory regions. The display data (DD) RAM stores the reference to a specific character bitmap to be displayed on the screen. The DD RAM can hold 80 8-bit character codes as indices to the character bitmaps. The character bitmaps are stored in either the user-defined character generator (CG) RAM region or the CG ROM region. The CG RAM can hold 8 user defined 5×8 character patterns or bitmaps. The CG ROM has 192 preset 5×8 bitmaps and for these applications of the LCD in embedded system design is used to provide the fixed font bitmaps referenced by their ASCII character code.

The default hexadecimal DD RAM addresses for the 2-line by 16-character display are listed in Table 3.1. The actual DD RAM address range is 00h (hexadecimal) to 27h and 40h to 67h to accommodate other standard LCDs of up to 40 characters per line.

Table 3.1 Hexadecimal DD RAM addresses for the 2-line by 16-character parallel LCD

Position	1	2	3	4	5	6	7	8	9	10	11	12	13	14	15	16
Line 1	00	01	02	03	04	05	06	07	08	09	0A	0B	0C	0D	0E	0F
Line 2	40	41	42	43	44	45	46	47	48	49	4A	4B	4C	4D	4E	4F

Trends in Embedded Design Using Programmable Gate Arrays

Figure 3.5 Digilent PmodCLP parallel interface LCD module

The parallel LCD 8-bit commands in binary are listed in Table 3.2. The entry X indicates a don't care condition. The LCD read/write enable signal lcde must be logic 1 for the commands to be effective. The LCD register select signal lcdrs and the read/write control signal lcdrw are set, as listed in Table 3.2.

Table 3.2 Parallel LCD command set

Command	lcdrs	lcdrw	MSB							LSB
Clear Display	0	0	0	0	0	0	0	0	0	1
Cursor Home	0	0	0	0	0	0	0	0	1	X
Entry Mode	0	0	0	0	0	0	0	1	I/D	S
Display On/Off	0	0	0	0	0	0	1	D	C	B
Shift Mode	0	0	0	0	0	1	S/C	R/L	X	X
Function Set	0	0	0	0	1	L	N	F	X	X
Set DD RAM Address	0	0	1	A6	A5	A4	A3	A2	A1	A0
Set CG RAM Address	0	0	0	1	A5	A4	A3	A2	A1	A0
Read Busy Flag	0	1	BF	A6	A5	A4	A3	A2	A1	A0
Write Data to RAM	1	0	D7	D6	D5	D4	D3	D2	D1	D0
Read Data from RAM	1	1	D7	D6	D5	D4	D3	D2	D1	D0

The clear display command writes a space or ASCII character code 20 hexadecimal (h) into all DD RAM locations, clears all the option settings and sets the I/D bit to logic 1 and the DD RAM address counter to 00h or the top-left corner of the LCD. The cursor home command only sets the DD RAM address counter to 00h without clearing the LCD.

The entry mode command uses the increment/decrement (I/D) bit to auto-decrement with logic 0 or auto-increment with logic 1 the RAM address counter. This appears as though the invisible or blinking cursor is moving either left or right. The entry mode shift (S) bit shifts the display with logic 1 in the direction set by the I/D bit.

The display on/off command display (D) bit turns the LCD on with logic 1 or off with logic 0, the cursor (C) displays an underscore cursor with logic 1 or no cursor with logic 0 and the blink (B) bit blinks the cursor at an interval of 0.5 seconds or no cursor blink with logic 0.

The shift mode command uses the shift/cursor (S/C) bit and right/left (R/L) bit to provide four functions which shift the cursor or the entire display without affecting the RAM contents. If these di-bits are 00 the cursor shifts to the left and the RAM address counter is decremented by one. If these di-bits are 01 the cursor shifts to the left and the RAM address counter is incremented by one. If these di-bits are 10 the entire display and cursor shifts to the left and the DD RAM address counter is unchanged. Finally, if these di-bits are 11 the entire display and cursor shift to the right and the DD RAM address counter is unchanged.

The function set command sets the LCD interface data length (L), number of display lines (N) and character font (F). The default interface data length bit $L = 1$ for an 8-bit bus, the number of display lines bit $N = 1$ for 2 lines and the display font $F = 0$ for a 5×8 bitmap.

The set DD or CG RAM address command sets the initial value in the appropriate RAM address counter. Subsequent LCD RAM read or write commands are executed then with either the DD or CG RAM.

The read busy flag/address command reads the busy flag (BF) bit can be used to determine if an internal LCD interface operation is in progress and also returns the current DD RAM address if the set DD RAM address command was executed first. The BF can be used to test for completion of internal LCD operations which can require anywhere from 1 microsecond (μsec) to 1.6 millisecond (msec). However, this input requires the Verilog *inout* port mode directive and a fixed delay is used here.

The write data to RAM command writes the 8-bit data to the current DD or CG RAM address location and either increments or decrements the appropriate RAM address counter as set by the prior set RAM address and the entry mode commands. Finally, the read data from RAM command also requires the Verilog *inout* port mode directive and is not implemented here.

The parallel LCD power-on startup sequence begins with a delay of at least 20 msec, followed by the function set command, a delay of at least 37 μsec, the display set command, another delay of at least 37 μsec, the display clear command and a final delay of at least 1.52 msec.

The LCD interface requires a minimum setup time of 40 nsec for the signals lcdrs, lcdrw and the 8-bit data lcdd before the enable signal lcde becomes active logic 1. LCD commands and data must be held for a minimum of 220 nsec and for at least 20 nsec after the signal elcd becomes inactive logic 0. The 8-bit data lcdd and the LCD functions must be spaced, respectively, a minimum of 500 nsec and 37 μsec apart.

Finally, the clear display and cursor home commands require an additional delay of at least 1.64 msec. These LCD interface operations are event driven by the Nexys 3 Board crystal clock signal CLK with a frequency of 100 MHz or a period of 10 nsec.

The module *clplcd.v* in Listing 3.16, which is in the *Chapter 3\peripherals* folder, utilizes multiple finite state machines (FSM) as a datapath to perform the functions of the parallel LCD on the positive edge of the crystal clock oscillator (CLK) and provides status signals to the controller, as described in Chapter 1 Verilog Hardware Description Language. Since each parallel LCD function is somewhat unique with different commands and requisite delays, the multiple FSMs used here are efficient.

The state register lcdstate sets each of the operations within a given function of the LCD and the register variable lcdcount determines the fixed delays required by the operation. The delays are rounded up to the next power of two (2^n) for efficiency in the behavioral synthesis of the FSM. The default value of the state registers lcdstate and lcdcount on power-up would be 0 [Lee06].

Although the datapath module *clplcd.v* is lengthy and seemingly complicated, the multiple functions of the parallel LCD are essentially separate FSMs. The external controller should not evoke another LCD function until the corresponding status signal indicates that the function has completed.

The initialize LCD function occurs if the net variable initlcd is set to logic 1. The FSM state variable lcdstate and the delay count variable lcdcount are set to 0. The LCD datapath status signals lcdreset, lcdclear, lcdhome, lcdaddr and lcddata are cleared. The initialize LCD function synchronizes and coordinates the multiple FSMs that are used for the various functions.

The reset LCD function occurs if the net variable resetlcd is set to logic 1 which changes the configuration of the LCD to an 8-bit parallel interface, sets the LCD to automatically increment the DD RAM address pointer, and turns the LCD on and disables the display of the cursor.

The clear LCD function occurs if the net variable clearlcd is set to logic 1 which writes ASCII character code 20h or space to all DD RAM address locations, effectively clearing the LCD. The DD RAM address is set to 00h or a cursor location of the upper left corner as listed in Table 3.1. The I/D

Trends in Embedded Design Using Programmable Gate Arrays

bit is set to auto-increment the LCD. After 2 active states, the clear LCD function enters state 3 and waits there until the controller responds to the datapath status signal lcdclear as logic 1 by executing an initialization which resets the net variable clearlcd to logic 0.

Listing 3.16 Parallel interface liquid crystal display datapath module *clplcd.v*

```
// Parallel Interface Liquid Crystal Display clplcd.v
// c 2012 Embedded Design using Programmable Gate Arrays  Dennis Silage

module clplcd(input CLK, resetlcd, clearlcd, homelcd, datalcd, addrlcd, cmdlcd, initlcd,
            output reg lcdreset, output reg lcdclear, output reg lcdhome, output reg lcddata,
            output reg lcdaddr, output reg lcdcmd, output reg rslcd, output reg rwlcd,
            output reg elcd, output reg [7:0] lcdd, input [7:0] lcddatin);

reg [23:0] lcdcount;        // delay counter
reg [3:0] lcdstate;         // state register

always@(posedge CLK)
      begin

// initialize LCD
            if (initlcd == 1)
                  begin
                        lcdstate = 0;
                        lcdcount = 0;
                        lcdreset = 0;
                        lcdclear = 0;
                        lcdhome = 0;
                        lcdaddr = 0;
                        lcddata = 0;
                        lcdcmd = 0;
                  end

            else
                  lcdcount = lcdcount + 1;

// reset LCD
            if (resetlcd == 1 && lcdreset==0)      //LCD reset
                  begin
                        rslcd = 0;                 // register select for command
                        rwlcd = 0;                 // LCD read/write

                        case (lcdstate)
                              0:    begin           // wait 20 msec (2 000 000 clock cycles)
                                          elcd = 0;
                                          if (lcdcount == 2097152)
                                                begin
                                                      lcdcount = 0;
                                                      lcdstate = 1;
                                                end
                                    end
                              1:    begin           // function set '38h'
```

122

```
            lcdd = 56;
            lcdstate = 2;
        end
2:    begin
            elcd = 1;
            if (lcdcount == 32)          // >220 nsec
                begin
                    lcdcount = 0;
                    lcdstate = 3;
                end
        end
3:    begin
            elcd = 0;
            if (lcdcount == 4096)        // wait 37 usec (3700 clock cycles)
                begin
                    lcdcount = 0;
                    lcdstate = 4;
                end
        end
4:    begin              // display set '0Ch', no cursor or blink
            lcdd = 12;
            lcdstate = 5;
        end
5:    begin
            elcd = 1;
            if (lcdcount == 32)          // >220 nsec
                begin
                    lcdcount = 0;
                    lcdstate = 6;
                end
        end
6:    begin
            elcd = 0;
            if (lcdcount == 4096)        // wait 37 usec (3700 clock cycles)
                begin
                    lcdcount = 0;
                    lcdstate = 7;
                end
        end
7:    begin              // display clear '01h'
            lcdd = 1;
            lcdstate = 8;
        end
8:    begin
            elcd = 1;
            if (lcdcount == 32)          // >220 nsec
                begin
                    lcdcount = 0;
                    lcdstate = 9;
                end
        end
9:    begin
```

```
                                        elcd = 0;
                                        if (lcdcount == 262144)    // wait 1.52 msec
                                                begin              // (152 000 clock cycles)
                                                        lcdcount = 0;
                                                        lcdstate = 10;
                                                        lcdreset = 1;
                                                end
                                end
                        10:    lcdstate = 10;
                        default:    lcdstate = 10;
                    endcase
                end

// send 8-bit data to LCD
        if (datalcd == 1 && lcddata == 0)    //lcd data
            begin
                rslcd = 1;                        // register select for data
                rwlcd = 0;                        // LCD read/write

                case (lcdstate)
                    0:    begin
                                lcdd = lcddatin;
                                elcd = 0;
                                if (lcdcount == 8)            // >40 nsec
                                        begin
                                                lcdcount = 0;
                                                lcdstate = 1;
                                        end
                            end
                    1:    begin
                                elcd = 1;
                                if (lcdcount == 32)           // >220nsec
                                        begin
                                                lcdcount = 0;
                                                lcdstate = 2;
                                        end
                            end
                    2:    begin                // wait 37 usec (3700 clock cycles)
                                elcd = 0;
                                if (lcdcount == 4096)
                                        begin
                                                lcdcount = 0;
                                                lcdstate = 3;
                                                lcddata = 1;
                                        end
                            end
                    3:    lcdstate = 3;
                    default:    lcdstate = 3;
                endcase
            end

// return cursor home
```

```
if (homelcd == 1 && lcdhome == 0)          //lcd home
begin
        rslcd = 0;                      // register select for command
        rwlcd = 0;                      // LCD read/write

        case (lcdstate)
                0:    begin             // send '02h'
                              lcdd = 2;
                              elcd = 0;
                              if (lcdcount  == 8)           // >40 nsec
                                      begin
                                              lcdcount = 0;
                                              lcdstate = 1;
                                      end
                      end
                1:    begin
                              elcd = 1;
                              if (lcdcount == 32)           // >220 nsec
                                      begin
                                              lcdcount = 0;
                                              lcdstate = 2;
                                      end
                      end
                2:    begin             // wait 1.64 msec (164 000 clock cycles)
                              elcd = 0;
                              if (lcdcount == 262144)
                                      begin
                                              lcdcount = 0;
                                              lcdstate = 3;
                                              lcdhome = 1;
                                      end
                      end
                3:    lcdstate = 3;
                default:    lcdstate = 3;
        endcase
end

// clear display
        if (clearlcd  == 1 && lcdclear == 0)  //lcd clear
        begin
                rslcd = 0;                      // register select for command
                rwlcd = 0;                      // LCD read/write

                case (lcdstate)
                        0:    begin             // send '01h'
                                      lcdd = 1;
                                      elcd = 0;
                                      if (lcdcount == 8)            // >40 nsec
                                              begin
                                                      lcdcount = 0;
                                                      lcdstate = 1;
                                              end
                              end
```

```
                        end
            1:    begin
                        elcd = 1;
                        if (lcdcount == 32)          // >220 nsec
                              begin
                                    lcdcount = 0;
                                    lcdstate = 2;
                              end
                  end
            2:    begin                  // wait 1.64 msec (164 000 clock cycles)
                        elcd = 0;
                        if (lcdcount == 262144)
                              begin
                                    lcdcount = 0;
                                    lcdstate = 3;
                                    lcdclear = 1;
                              end
                  end
            3:    lcdstate = 3;
            default:    lcdstate = 3;
      endcase
end

// set 7-bit DDRAM display address
      if (addrlcd == 1 && lcdaddr == 0)      //lcd display address
            begin
                  rslcd = 0;                  // register select for command
                  rwlcd = 0;                  // LCD read/write

                  case (lcdstate)
                        0:    begin                  // send '10h' + 7 bit address
                                    lcdd[7] = 1;
                                    lcdd[6:0] = lcddatin[6:0];
                                    elcd = 0;
                                    if (lcdcount == 8)          // >40 nsec
                                          begin
                                                lcdcount = 0;
                                                lcdstate = 1;
                                          end
                              end
                        1:    begin
                                    elcd = 1;
                                    if (lcdcount == 32)          // >220 nsec
                                          begin
                                                lcdcount = 0;
                                                lcdstate = 2;
                                          end
                              end
                        2:    begin                  // wait 37 usec (3700 clock cycles)
                                    elcd = 0;
                                    if (lcdcount == 4096)
                                          begin
```

```
                                                lcdcount = 0;
                                                lcdstate = 3;
                                                lcdaddr = 1;
                                        end
                                end
                        3:    lcdstate = 3;
                        default:    lcdstate = 3;
                    endcase
                end

// enter LCD command
        if (cmdlcd == 1 && lcdcmd == 0)     //lcd command
            begin
                rslcd = 0;                      // register select for command
                rwlcd = 0;                      // LCD read/write

                case (lcdstate)
                    0:    begin                 // send 8-bit command
                                lcdd = lcddatin;
                                elcd = 0;
                                if (lcdcount == 8)            // >40 nsec
                                        begin
                                                lcdcount = 0;
                                                lcdstate = 1;
                                        end
                            end
                    1:    begin
                                elcd = 1;
                                if (lcdcount == 32)           // >220 nsec
                                        begin
                                                lcdcount=0;
                                                lcdstate=2;
                                        end
                            end
                    2:    begin              // wait 1.64 msec (164 000 clock cycles)
                                elcd=0;
                                if (lcdcount == 262144)
                                        begin
                                                lcdcount = 0;
                                                lcdstate = 3;
                                                lcdclear = 1;
                                        end
                            end
                    3:    lcdstate = 3;
                    default:    lcdstate = 3;
                endcase
            end
    end

endmodule
```

Trends in Embedded Design Using Programmable Gate Arrays

The home LCD function occurs if the net variable homelcd is set to logic 1 which sets the DD RAM address for the location of the cursor to 00h or the upper left corner. After 2 active states, the home LCD function enters state 3 and waits there until the controller responds to the datapath status signal lcdhome as logic 1 by executing an initialization which resets the net variable homelcd to logic 0.

The set DD RAM address LCD function occurs if the net variable addrlcd is set to logic 1. The 8-bit register variable lcddatin contains the address to be set as the cursor location. The most significant bit (MSB) of the register variable lcddatin is set to logic 1 and the remaining 7 bits contain the DD RAM address. After 2 active states, the set DD RAM LCD function enters state 3 and waits there until the controller responds to the datapath status signal lcdaddr as logic 1 by executing an initialization which resets the net variable addrlcd to logic 0.

The LCD data function occurs if the net variable datalcd is set to logic 1. The 8-bit register variable lcddatin contains the ASCII character to be displayed at the current DD RAM address of the LCD. After 2 active states, the LCD data function enters state 3 and waits there until the controller responds to the datapath status signal lcddata as logic 1 by executing an initialization which resets the net variable datalcd to logic 0. The 8-bit data as the register variable lcdd and the LCD control signals rslcd, rwlcd and elcd are outputted to a hierarchical Verilog top module.

Finally, the LCD command function is available to override any of the default settings of the configuration bits such as I/D and occurs if the net variable cmdlcd is set to logic 1. After 2 active states, the LCD command function enters state 3 and waits there until the controller responds to the datapath status signal lcdcmd as logic 1 by executing an initialization which resets the net variable cmdlcd to logic 0.

The parallel LCD datapath module *clplcd.v* is verified by the Verilog top module *plcdtest.v* and controller module *genlcd.v* in Listing 3.17 which is in the *Chapter 3\lcdtest\ns3plcdtest* folder. The 12-pin port of the PmodCLP LCD module is interfaced to Peripheral Port C (JC) of the Nexys 3 Board. The 6-pin port of the LCD is connected to the bottom 6 pins of Peripheral Port D (JD).

The complete Xilinx ISE project uses the UCF *ns3plcdtest.ucf* which uncomments the signals CLK, BTNR, JC1 to JC4, JC7 to JC10 and JD7 to JD9 in the Nexys 3 Board UCF of Listing 3.1. The four Verilog modules operate in parallel and some independently in the top module, as shown in Figure 3.6. There is no Xilinx ISE project for the Atlys Board because the PmodCLP external peripheral requires two ports and only one is available (Peripheral Port A, JA). The file download procedure is described in the Appendix.

The wire net type establishes the 8-bit array connectivity for lcddatin and lcdd between the *clplcd.v* and *genlcd.v* modules. The LCD external control signals JC1 to JC4, JC7 to JC10 and JD7 to JD9 are assigned to internal datapath register signals lcdd[0] through lcdd[3], lcdd[4] through lcdd[7], rslcd, rwlcd, and elcd in the top module *lcdtest.v*. Assignment of output signals to peripheral devices only in the top module provides a degree of flexibility in the FPGA hardware synthesis of an embedded system design [Navabi06].

The reset button BTNR signal asynchronously initializes the LCD controller signals. The button is debounced by the *pbdebounce.v* module, as given in Listing 3.8. The *genlcd.v* module utilizes an FSM as the LCD controller to the LCD datapath module *clplcd.v* to reset and clear the LCD, to set the DD RAM address to the second line at position 5 and to send the 11 character ASCII string *hello world*. The state register gstate sets each of the operations.

The LCD datapath is set to its initial state before each function by setting the register variable initlcd to logic 1 then resetting it to logic 0. Each LCD function in the datapath signals the controller when the function is completed. After 14 active states, the LCD test controller enters state 15 and waits there until a reset push button command is issued. The push button signal BTNR is processed by the contact debounce module *pbdebounce.v* of Listing 3.8. The 100 MHz crystal clock signal CLK is divided to a 1 kHz signal clk by the clock oscillator module clock of Listing 3.3.

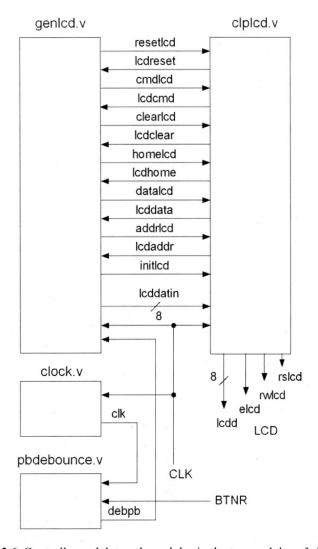

Figure 3.6 Controller and datapath modules in the top module *ns3plcdtest.v*

Listing 3.17 Parallel LCD test top module for the Nexys 3 Board *ns3plcdtest.v*

```
// Nexys 3 Board
// Parallel Liquid Crystal Display Test ns3plcdtest.v
// c 2012 Embedded Design using Programmable Gate Arrays  Dennis Silage

module ns3plcdtest(input CLK, BTNR, output JC1, JC2, JC3, JC4, JC7, JC8, JC9, JC10, JD7,
                   output JD8, JD9);

wire [7:0] lcddatin;
wire [7:0] lcdd;
wire rslcd, rwlcd, elcd;

assign JC10 = lcdd[7];
assign JC9 = lcdd[6];
assign JC8 = lcdd[5];
```

```
assign JC7 = lcdd[4];
assign JC4 = lcdd[3];
assign JC3 = lcdd[2];
assign JC2 = lcdd[1];
assign JC1 = lcdd[0];
assign JD7 = rslcd;
assign JD8 = rwlcd;
assign JD9 = elcd;


clplcd M0 (CLK, resetlcd, clearlcd, homelcd, datalcd, addrlcd, cmdlcd, initlcd, lcdreset, lcdclear,
            lcdhome, lcddata, lcdaddr, lcdcmd, rslcd, rwlcd, elcd, lcdd, lcddatin);
genlcd M1 (CLK, debpb, resetlcd, clearlcd, homelcd, datalcd, addrlcd, initlcd, cmdlcd, lcdreset,
            lcdclear, lcdhome,lcddata, lcdaddr, lcddatin);
pbdebounce M2 (clk, BTNR, debpb);
clock M3 (CLK, 50000, clk);          //50 Hz


endmodule

module genlcd(input CLK, debpb, output reg resetlcd, output reg clearlcd, output reg homelcd,
            output reg datalcd, output reg addrlcd, output reg initlcd, output reg cmdlcd,
            input lcdreset, lcdclear, lcdhome, lcddata, lcdaddr, output reg [7:0] lcddatin);

reg [3:0] gstate;          // state register
reg [87:0] strdata = "hello world";

integer i;

always@(posedge CLK)
    begin
        if (debpb == 1)
            begin
                resetlcd = 0;
                clearlcd = 0;
                homelcd = 0;
                datalcd = 0;
                initlcd = 0;
                cmdlcd = 0;
                gstate = 0;
            end
        else

        case (gstate)
            0:   begin
                    initlcd = 1;
                    gstate = 1;
                 end
            1:   begin
                    initlcd = 0;
                    gstate = 2;
                 end
            2:   begin
                    resetlcd = 1;
```

```
                if (lcdreset == 1)
                    begin
                        resetlcd = 0;
                        gstate = 3;
                    end
        end
3:      begin
            initlcd = 1;
            gstate = 4;
        end
4:      begin
            initlcd = 0;
            gstate = 5;
        end
5:      begin
            clearlcd = 1;
            if (lcdclear == 1)
                    begin
                        clearlcd = 0;
                        gstate = 6;
                    end
        end
6:      begin
            initlcd = 1;
            gstate = 7;
        end
7:      begin
            initlcd = 0;
            gstate = 8;
        end
8:      begin                    // DD RAM address 44h
            lcddatin[7:0] = 8'b01000100;
            addrlcd = 1;
            if (lcdaddr == 1)
                    begin
                        addrlcd = 0;
                        gstate = 9;
                    end
        end
9:      begin
            initlcd = 1;
            gstate = 10;
        end
10:     begin
            initlcd = 0;
            i = 87;
            gstate = 11;
        end
11:     begin
            lcddatin[7:0] = strdata[i−:8];
            datalcd = 1;
            if (lcddata == 1)
```

```
                              begin
                                  datalcd = 0;
                                  gstate = 12;
                              end
                    end
              12:  begin
                       initlcd = 1;
                       gstate = 13;
                   end
              13:  begin
                       initlcd = 0;
                       gstate = 14;
                   end
              14:  begin
                       i = i – 8;
                       if (i < 0)
                            gstate = 15;
                       else
                            gstate = 11;
                   end
              15:  gstate = 15;
              default:   gstate = 15;
         endcase
    end

endmodule
```

The 11 character ASCII string *hello world* is stored in the 88-bit register variable strdata with the first character stored in the MSBs. The 8-bit character to be sent to the LCD is obtained by the Verilog decrementing, variable part select operator (–:), as described in Chapter 1 Verilog Hardware Description Language. This simple method of character storage in a behavioral synthesis register is not the most efficient in the coarse grained architecture of the Xilinx Spartan-6 FPGA, as described in Chapter 2 Verilog Design Automation. Either the internal FPGA block RAM or an external ROM or RAM could be used to provide more efficient data storage for embedded design applications.

As described in Chapter 2 Verilog Design Automation, the Design Utilization Summary for the top module *lcdtest.v* shows the use of 116 slice registers (<1%) and 351 slice LUTs (3%) in the Nexys 3 Board XC6SLX16 Spartan-6 FPGA synthesis.

The elapsed time project designed for the seven segment display of the Nexys 3 Board in Listing 3.15 can be modified to execute on the PmodCLP LCD peripheral of the Nexys 3 Board. The top module *ns3elapsedtime.v* in Listing 3.18 is also in the *Chapter 3\elapsedtime \ns3elapsedtime* folder. There is no Xilinx ISE project for the Atlys Board because the PmodCLP external peripheral requires two ports and only one is available (Peripheral Port A, JA). The file download procedure is described in the Appendix.

The *elapsedtime.v* nested module in Listing 3.19 for the PmodCLP LCD is similar to the *elapsedtime.v* nested module in Listing 3.15 for the seven segment display on the Nexys 3 Board. The salient differences between the two modules are that only one 100 Hz clock signal eclk from the *clock.v* module for the elapsed time process is required and there is no required set decimal point signal setdp or signal digit. However, an input 2-bit register signal digitmux is used here to select which digit is returned to the controller module *etlcd.v*. This elapsed time project illustrates the relative ease of design reuse of modules in Verilog behavioral synthesis for embedded design [Ashenden08].

The complete Xilinx ISE project uses the UCF *ns3elapsedtime.ucf* which uncomments the signals CLK, BTNR, BTNL, BTNU, BTND, JC1 to JC4, JC7 to JC10 and JD7 to JD9 in the Nexys 3

Board UCF of Listing 3.1. The 8-bit LCD data signal lccd is connected to JC1 to JC4, JC7 to JC10. The LCD control signals rslcd, rwlcd and elcd are connected to JD7 to JD9. The four Verilog modules operate in parallel and some independently in the top module, as shown in Figure 3.7.

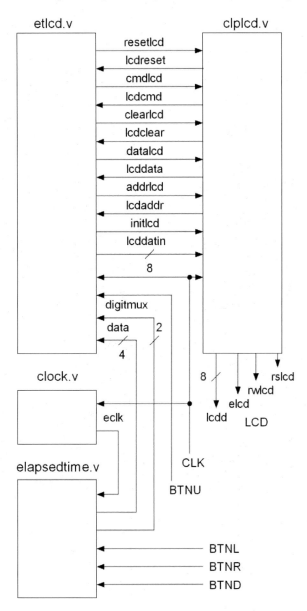

Figure 3.7 Controller and datapath modules in the top module *ns3elapsedtime.v*

Listing 3.18 Elapsed time top module for the Nexys 3 Board *ns3elapsedtime.v*

// Nexys 3 Board
// Elapsed Time Test ns3elapsedtime.v
// c 2012 Embedded Design using Programmable Gate Arrays Dennis Silage

Trends in Embedded Design Using Programmable Gate Arrays

```
module ns3elapsedtime(input CLK, BTNL, BTNR, BTND, BTNU, output JC1, JC2, JC3, JC4, JC7,
                output JC8, JC9, JC10, JD7, JD8, JD9);
wire [7:0] lcddatin;
wire [7:0] lcdd;
wire rslcd, rwlcd, elcd;
wire [3:0] data;
wire [1:0] digitmux;

assign JC10 = lcdd[7];
assign JC9 = lcdd[6];
assign JC8 = lcdd[5];
assign JC7 = lcdd[4];
assign JC4 = lcdd[3];
assign JC3 = lcdd[2];
assign JC2 = lcdd[1];
assign JC1 = lcdd[0];
assign JD7 = rslcd;
assign JD8 = rwlcd;
assign JD9 = elcd;

clock M0 (CLK, 250000, eclk);        // 100 Hz
clplcd M1 (CLK, resetlcd, clearlcd, homelcd, datalcd, addrlcd, cmdlcd, initlcd, lcdreset, lcdclear,
           lcdhome, lcddata, lcdaddr, lcdcmd, rslcd, rwlcd, elcd, lcdd, lcddatin);
elapsedtime M2 (eclk, BTNL, BTNR, BTND, digitmux, data);
etlcd M3 (CLK, BTNU, resetlcd, clearlcd, homelcd, datalcd, addrlcd, initlcd, lcdreset, lcdclear,
          lcdhome, lcddata, lcdaddr, lcddatin, digitmux, data);

endmodule

module etlcd(input CLK, BTNU, output reg resetlcd, output reg clearlcd,  output reg homelcd,
             output reg datalcd, output reg addrlcd, output reg initlcd, input lcdreset, lcdclear,
             input lcdhome, lcddata, lcdaddr, output reg [7:0] lcddatin, output reg [1:0] digitmux,
             input [3:0] data);

reg [4:0] gstate;        // state register

always@(posedge CLK)
    begin
        if (BTNU == 1)
            begin
                resetlcd = 0;
                clearlcd = 0;
                homelcd = 0;
                datalcd = 0;
                gstate = 0;
            end
        else

        case (gstate)
            0:    begin
                    initlcd = 1;
                    gstate = 1;
```

```
            end
1:      begin
                initlcd = 0;
                gstate = 2;
            end
2:      begin
                resetlcd = 1;
                if (lcdreset == 1)
                        begin
                                resetlcd = 0;
                                gstate = 3;
                            end
            end
3:      begin
                initlcd = 1;
                gstate = 4;
            end
4:      begin
                initlcd = 0;
                gstate = 5;
            end
5:      begin
                clearlcd = 1;
                if (lcdclear == 1)
                        begin
                                clearlcd = 0;
                                gstate = 6;
                            end
            end
6:      begin
                initlcd = 1;
                gstate = 7;
            end
7:      begin
                initlcd = 0;
                gstate = 8;
            end
8:      begin                // DD RAM start address 46h
                lcddatin[7:0] = 8'b01000110;
                addrlcd = 1;
                if (lcdaddr == 1)
                        begin
                                addrlcd = 0;
                                gstate = 9;
                            end
            end
9:      begin
                initlcd = 1;
                gstate = 10;
            end
10:     begin
                initlcd = 0;
```

```
                        gstate = 11;
            end
    11:  begin
                lcddatin[7:4] = 3;          // 30h
                digitmux = 3;               // sec10
                lcddatin[3:0] = data[3:0];
                datalcd = 1;
                if (lcddata == 1)
                        begin
                                datalcd = 0;
                                gstate = 12;
                        end
            end
    12:  begin
                initlcd = 1;
                gstate = 13;
            end
    13:  begin
                initlcd = 0;
                gstate = 14;
            end
    14:  begin
                digitmux = 2;               // sec1
                lcddatin[3:0] = data[3:0];
                datalcd = 1;
                if (lcddata == 1)
                        begin
                                datalcd = 0;
                                gstate = 15;
                        end
            end
    15:  begin
                initlcd = 1;
                gstate = 16;
            end
    16:  begin
                initlcd = 0;
                gstate = 17;
            end
    17:  begin
                lcddatin[7:0] = 58;         // ASCII :
                datalcd = 1;
                if (lcddata == 1)
                        begin
                                datalcd = 0;
                                gstate = 18;
                        end
            end
    18:  begin
                initlcd = 1;
                gstate = 19;
            end
```

```
            19:  begin
                        initlcd = 0;
                        gstate = 20;
                 end
            20:  begin
                        lcddatin[7:4] = 3;              // 30h
                        digitmux = 1;                   // csec10
                        lcddatin[3:0] = data[3:0];
                        datalcd = 1;
                        if (lcddata == 1)
                               begin
                                    datalcd = 0;
                                    gstate = 21;
                               end
                 end
            21:  begin
                        initlcd = 1;
                        gstate = 22;
                 end
            22:  begin
                        initlcd = 0;
                        gstate = 23;
                 end
            23:  begin
                        digitmux = 0;                   // csec100
                        lcddatin[3:0] = data[3:0];
                        datalcd = 1;
                        if (lcddata == 1)
                               begin
                                    datalcd = 0;
                                    gstate = 6;
                               end
                 end
            default:   gstate = 0;
         endcase
   end

endmodule
```

The wire net type establishes the 8-bit , 4-bit and 2-bit array connectivity for lcddatin, data, lcdd and digitmux between the *lcd.v*, *elapsedtime.v* and *etlcd.v* modules. The reset button BTNU signal asynchronously initializes the LCD controller signals [Ciletti04]. The *etlcd.v* module is similar to the *genlcd.v* of Listing 3.15.

The *etlcd.v* module utilizes an FSM as the LCD controller to the LCD datapath module *lcd.v* to reset and clear the LCD and set the DD RAM address to 46h or the second line at position 7 as listed in Table 3.1. The state register gstate sets each of the operations. Note that the parallel LCD command cmdlcd and the status lcdcmd are not used in the *etlcd.v* controller but are declared in the clplcd.v datapath. Unused port connections provide warning messages, as described in Chapter 2 Verilog Design Automation, and are removed during synthesis.

As described in Chapter 2 Verilog Design Automation Verilog Design Automation, the Design Utilization Summary for the top module *ns3elapsedtime.v* shows the use of 96 slice registers (1%) and 308 slice LUTs (3%) in the Nexys 3 Board XC6SLX16 Spartan-6 FPGA synthesis.

Trends in Embedded Design Using Programmable Gate Arrays

Listing 3.19 Elapsed time module *elapsedtime.v*

```verilog
// Elapsed Time Module elapsedtime.v
// c 2012 Embedded Design using Programmable Gate Arrays  Dennis Silage

module elapsedtime (input clk, BTNL, BTNR, BTND, input [1:0] digitmux, output reg [3:0] data);

reg startstop;          // start or stop
reg [3:0] csec100;      // seconds 1/100s
reg [3:0] csec10;       // seconds 1/10s
reg [3:0] sec1;         // seconds 1s
reg [3:0] sec10;        // seconds 10s

always@(digitmux)       // digit multiplex even driven
    begin
        case (digitmux)
            0:   data[3:0] = csec100;
            1:   data[3:0] = csec10;
            2:   data[3:0] = sec1;
            3:   data[3:0] = sec10;
        endcase
    end

always@(posedge clk)    // local clock event driven
    begin
        if (BTND == 1)// clear and stop
            begin
                startstop = 0;
                csec100 = 0;
                csec10 = 0;
                sec1 = 0;
                sec10 = 0;
            end

        if (BTNR == 1)// stop
            startstop=0;
        if (BTNL == 1) // start
            startstop=1;

        if (startstop == 1)
            begin
                csec100 = csec100 + 1;

                if (csec100 > 9)
                    begin
                        csec100 = 0;
                        csec10 = csec10 + 1;
                    end
                if (csec10 > 9)
                    begin
                        csec10 = 0;
                        sec1 = sec1 + 1;
```

```
                    end
             if (sec1 > 9)
                    begin
                          sec1 = 0;
                          sec10 = sec10 + 1;
                    end
             if (sec10 > 9)
                    sec10 = 0;
       end
end

endmodule
```

PmodCLS Serial Liquid Crystal Display

The external accessory Digilent PmodCLS™ serial LCD also functions as an alphanumeric annunciator in applications of the FPGA and features a 2-line by 16-character display with fixed or user-defined fonts. The PmodCLS LCD utilizes a 4-bit data bus serial peripheral interface (SPI) and requires a single port (Peripheral Port A, JA). The SPI protocol is described as one of the serial data link protocols in this Chapter. The PmodCLS LCD has an embedded microcontroller which also provides a universal asynchronous receiver transmitter (UART) or a two-wire interface (TWI) port which are not used here.

The PmodCLS SPI LCD interface consists of the serial clock sclk, master output/slave input mosi, master input/slave output miso and slave select ss signals. The SPI interface port is J1. The slave select signal ss is set by JP1 and the mode select port JP2 selects the SPI interface. Since the LCD requires a +5 V logic supply the PmodCLS includes a +3.3 V to +5 V boost regulator. The PmodCLS is referenced in the Digilent document 502-092 (*www.digilentinc.com*) and is shown configured with jumpers on JP1 and JP2 for the SPI interface in Figure 3.8.

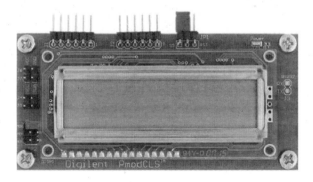

Figure 3.8 Digilent PmodCLS serial interface LCD module

The PmodCLS executes commands sent as ASCII character *escape sequences*, that is an escape (ESC decimal 27), followed by a left square backet ([decimal 91) and then ASCII parameters separated if required by semicolons (; decimal 59). The parameter <pr> is the row number (0 or 1), <pc> is the column number (0 to 39) and <ps> is the selection.

The parameters are sent as ASCII characters and not in binary. A two digit parameter is sent as two ASCII characters. If the command does not have a selection <ps> then 0 ASCII (decimal 48) must be sent before the ASCII character command. A portion of the serial LCD ASCII commands are listed in Table 3.3.

The module *clslcd.v* in Listing 3.20 which is in the *Chapter 3\peripherals* folder, utilizes multiple finite state machines (FSM) as a datapath to perform the functions of the serial LCD on the positive edge of the crystal clock oscillator (CLK) and provides signals to the controller, as described in Chapter 1 Verilog Hardware Description Language. The state register lcdstate sets each of the operations within a given function of the LCD and the default value on power-up would be 0 [Lee06].

Although the datapath module *clslcd.v* is lengthy and seemingly complicated, the multiple functions of the LCD are essentially separate FSMs. The external controller should not evoke another LCD function until the corresponding status signal indicates that the function has completed.

Table 3.3 Portion of the serial LCD command set

Command	Sequence	ASCII character (decimal)
Clear and Home Display	j	106
Set Cursor Position	<pr> ; <pc> H	72
Set Cursor Mode	<ps> c	99
	0 cursor off	
	1 curson on, blink off	
	2 cursor on, blink on	
Set Display Mode	<ps> h	104
	0 wrap line at 16 characters	
	1 wrap line at 40 characters	
Enable Display	<ps> e	101
	0 display off	
	1 display on	
Erase Line	<ps> K	75
	0 current cursor position to the end of the line	
	1 start of the line to the current cursor position	
	2 entire current line	

The initialize LCD function occurs if the net variable initlcd is set to logic 1. The FSM state variable lcdstate and the datapath status signals lcdreset, lcdclear, lcddata, lcdaddr and lcderase are cleared. The initialize LCD function synchronizes and coordinates the multiple FSMs that are used for the various functions and sets the SPI interface sclk, mosi and ss signals.

The reset LCD function occurs if the net variable resetlcd is set to logic 1 which turns the LCD on (enable display) and disables the display of the cursor (set cursor mode). The clear and home LCD function occurs if the net variable clearlcd is set to logic 1. The cursor address is set to 0 or a cursor location at the upper left corner. The LCD data function writes the ASCII character in the 8-bit parallel input net variable lcddatin to the current cursor location and increments the cursor position if the net variable datalcd is set to logic 1.

The LCD address function sets the row and column address of the cursor (set cursor position) if the net variable addrlcd is set to logic 1 from the contents of the 8-bit parallel input net variable lcddatin. The most significant bit (MSB) of lcddatin determines if the cursor is placed on the top (0) or bottom (1) row of the LCD. The remaining bits of lcddatin are the cursor column position in the range of 0 to 15 for the 16 character per line of the LCD here. The row and column parameters are converted to ASCII digits and sent by the SPI interface. Note that the cursor column position parameter is always two ASCII characters with a leading ASCII 0 if required.

The LCD erase function (erase line) writes an ASCII character 32 (space) from the current cursor position to the end of the line, from the start of the line to the to the current cursor position or the entire current line. The ASCII character parameter for 0, 1, or 2 (48, 49, 50) is in the contents of the 8-bit parallel input net variable lcddatin.

Delays inherent in the processing of the LCD command set for the PmodCLS are buffered by the embedded microcontroller. However, the clock frequency of the SPI interface, derived from an FSM and the datapath clock, should be comparable in magnitude to the maximum UART baud rate

(9600 b/sec). With the datapath clock lcdclk frequency of 100 kHz the derived SPI clock sclk frequency from the FSM here is 25 kHz.

Listing 3.20 Serial interface liquid crystal display datapath module *clslcd.v*

```
// Serial Interface Liquid Crystal display clslcd.v
// c 2012 Embedded Design using Programmable Gate Arrays  Dennis Silage

module clslcd (input lcdclk, initlcd, resetlcd, clearlcd, datalcd, addrlcd, eraselcd, output reg lcdreset,
            output reg lcdclear, output reg lcddata, output reg lcdaddr, output reg lcderase,
            output reg ss, output reg mosi, output reg sclk, input [7:0] lcddatin);

reg [4:0] lcdstate;            // state register
reg [2:0] prestate;            // prefix state register
reg [2:0] sndstate;            // send state register
reg [7:0] lcdd;                // LCD data
reg [3:0] ddat;                // data
reg snddat;                    // send data
reg datsnd;                    // data sent
reg predat;                    // send prefix data
reg datpre;                    // prefix data sent

integer i;

always@(posedge lcdclk)
        begin

//initialize
        if (initlcd == 1)
                    begin
                            lcdreset = 0;
                            lcdclear = 0;
                            lcddata = 0;
                            lcdaddr = 0;
                            lcderase = 0;
                            lcdstate = 0;
                            prestate = 0;
                            sndstate = 0;
                            snddat = 0;
                            datsnd = 0;
                            predat = 0;
                            datpre = 0;
                            ss = 1;
                            mosi = 0;
                            sclk = 1;
                    end

// reset LCD
            if (resetlcd == 1 && lcdreset == 0)
                    begin
                            case (lcdstate)
                                    0:    begin
```

```
                                    predat = 1;        //send prefix
                                    lcdstate = 1;
                            end
               1:    begin
                            if (datpre == 1)
                                    begin
                                            predat = 0;
                                            snddat = 0;
                                            lcdstate = 2;
                                    end
                     end
               2:    begin
                            datpre = 0;
                            datsnd = 0;
                            lcdd = 49;         //'1' LCD on
                            lcdstate = 3;
                     end
               3:    begin
                            snddat = 1;
                            lcdstate = 4;
                     end
               4:    begin
                            if (datsnd == 1)
                                    begin
                                            snddat = 0;
                                            lcdstate = 5;
                                    end
                     end
               5:    begin
                            datsnd = 0;
                            lcdd = 101;        //'e'
                            lcdstate = 6;
                     end
               6:    begin
                            snddat = 1;
                            lcdstate = 7;
                     end
               7:    begin
                            if (datsnd == 1)
                                    begin
                                            snddat = 0;
                                            lcdstate = 8;
                                    end
                     end
               8:    begin
                            datsnd = 0;
                            prestate = 0;
                            lcdstate = 9;
                     end
               9:    begin
                            predat = 1;        //send prefix
                            lcdstate = 10;
```

```
                        end
            10:  begin
                        if (datpre == 1)
                                begin
                                        predat = 0;
                                        snddat = 0;
                                        lcdstate = 11;
                                end
                        end
            11:  begin
                        datpre = 0;
                        datsnd = 0;
                        lcdd = 48;          //'0' cursor off, blink off
                        lcdstate = 12;
                        end
            12:  begin
                        snddat = 1;
                        lcdstate = 13;
                        end
            13:  begin
                        if (datsnd == 1)
                                begin
                                        snddat = 0;
                                        lcdstate = 14;
                                end
                        end
            14:  begin
                        datsnd = 0;
                        lcdd = 99;          //'c'
                        lcdstate = 15;
                        end
            15:  begin
                        snddat = 1;
                        lcdstate = 16;
                        end
            16:  begin
                        if (datsnd == 1)
                                begin
                                        snddat = 0;
                                        lcdstate = 17;
                                end
                        end
            17:  begin
                        datsnd = 0;
                        lcdreset = 1;
                        end
            default: lcdstate = 17;
        endcase
    end
// clear and home LCD
    if (clearlcd == 1 && lcdclear == 0)
        begin
```

```
case (lcdstate)
    0:  begin
            predat = 1;         //send prefix
            lcdstate = 1;
        end
    1:  begin
            if (datpre == 1)
                begin
                    predat = 0;
                    snddat = 0;
                    lcdstate = 2;
                end
        end
    2:  begin
            datpre = 0;
            datsnd = 0;
            lcdd = 48;          //'0'
            lcdstate = 3;
        end
    3:  begin
            snddat = 1;
            lcdstate = 4;
        end
    4:  begin
            if (datsnd == 1)
                begin
                    snddat = 0;
                    lcdstate = 5;
                end
        end
    5:  begin
            datsnd = 0;
            lcdd = 106;         //'j'
            lcdstate=6;
        end
    6:  begin
            snddat = 1;
            lcdstate = 7;
        end
    7:  begin
            if (datsnd == 1)
                begin
                    snddat = 0;
                    lcdstate = 8;
                end
        end
    8:  begin
            datsnd = 0;
            lcdclear = 1;
        end
    default: lcdstate = 8;
endcase
```

```
                end

// send 8-bit data to LCD
        if (datalcd == 1 && lcddata == 0)
            begin
                case (lcdstate)
                    0:    begin
                            datsnd = 0;
                            lcdd = lcddatin;        //8-bit character data
                            lcdstate = 1;
                        end
                    1:    begin
                            snddat = 1;
                            lcdstate = 2;
                        end
                    2:    begin
                            if (datsnd == 1)
                                begin
                                    snddat = 0;
                                    lcdstate = 3;
                                end
                        end
                    3:    begin
                            datsnd = 0;
                            lcddata = 1;
                            lcdstate = 3;
                        end
                    default: lcdstate = 3;
                endcase
            end

// set row and column LCD cursor address
        if (addrlcd == 1 && lcdaddr == 0)
            begin
                case (lcdstate)
                    0:    begin
                            ddat[3:0] = lcddatin[3:0];
                            predat = 1;                //send prefix
                            lcdstate = 1;
                        end
                    1:    begin
                            if (datpre == 1)
                                begin
                                    predat = 0;
                                    snddat = 0;
                                    lcdstate = 2;
                                end
                        end
                    2:    begin
                            datpre = 0;
                            datsnd = 0;
                            if (lcddatin[7] == 0)
```

```
                            lcdd = 48;        //row '0'
                    else
                            lcdd = 49;        //row '1'
                    lcdstate = 3;
            end
    3:      begin
                    snddat = 1;
                    lcdstate = 4;
            end
    4:      begin
                    if (datsnd == 1)
                            begin
                                    snddat = 0;
                                    lcdstate = 5;
                            end
            end
    5:      begin
                    datsnd = 0;
                    lcdd = 59;                // ';'
                    lcdstate = 6;
            end
    6:      begin
                    snddat = 1;
                    lcdstate = 7;
            end
    7:      begin
                    if (datsnd == 1)
                            begin
                                    snddat = 0;
                                    lcdstate = 8;
                            end
            end
    8:      begin
                    if (ddat >= 9)
                            begin
                                    lcdd = 49;        //column MS ASCII digit '1'
                                    ddat = ddat − 10;
                            end
                    else
                            lcdd = 48;        //column MS ASCII digit '0'
                    datsnd = 0;
                    lcdstate = 9;
            end
    9:      begin
                    snddat = 1;
                    lcdstate = 10;
            end
    10:     begin
                    if (datsnd == 1)
                            begin
                                    snddat = 0;
                                    lcdstate = 11;
```

```
                        end
                    end
            11:  begin
                    datsnd = 0;                  //column LS ASCII digit
                    lcdd[7:4] = 3;               //0011XXXX 30H ASCII bias
                    lcdd[3:0] = ddat[3:0];       //XXXXnnnn 0-9 ASCII
                    lcdstate = 12;
                 end
            12:  begin
                    snddat = 1;
                    lcdstate = 13;
                 end
            13:  begin
                    if (datsnd == 1)
                        begin
                            snddat = 0;
                            lcdstate = 14;
                        end
                 end
            14:  begin
                    datsnd = 0;
                    lcdd = 72;        //'H'
                    lcdstate = 15;
                 end
            15:  begin
                    snddat = 1;
                    lcdstate = 16;
                 end
            16:  begin
                    if (datsnd == 1)
                        begin
                            snddat = 0;
                            lcdstate = 17;
                        end
                 end
            17:  begin
                    datsnd = 0;
                    lcdaddr = 1;
                 end
            default: lcdstate = 17;
        endcase
    end

// erase LCD
    if (eraselcd == 1 && lcderase == 0)
        begin
            case (lcdstate)
            0:   begin
                    predat = 1;           //send prefix
                    lcdstate = 1;
                 end
            1:   begin
```

Trends in Embedded Design Using Programmable Gate Arrays

```
                    if (datpre == 1)
                        begin
                            predat = 0;
                            snddat = 0;
                            lcdstate = 2;
                        end
                end
        2:   begin
                datpre = 0;
                datsnd = 0;
                lcdd = lcddatin;        //'0', '1', or '2'
                lcdstate = 3;
             end
        3:   begin
                snddat = 1;
                lcdstate = 4;
             end
        4:   begin
                if (datsnd == 1)
                    begin
                        snddat = 0;
                        lcdstate = 5;
                    end
             end
        5:   begin
                datsnd = 0;
                lcdd = 75;             //'K'
                lcdstate = 6;
             end
        6:   begin
                snddat = 1;
                lcdstate = 7;
             end
        7:   begin
                if (datsnd == 1)
                    begin
                        snddat = 0;
                        lcdstate = 8;
                    end
             end
        8:   begin
                datsnd = 0;
                lcderase = 1;
             end
        default: lcdstate = 8;
    endcase
end

// send prefix ESC[
    if (predate == 1 && datpre == 0)
        begin
            case (prestate)
```

148

```
            0:   begin
                      datsnd = 0;
                      lcdd = 27;          //ESC
                      prestate = 1;
                 end
            1:   begin
                      snddat = 1;
                      prestate = 2;
                 end
            2:   begin
                      if (datsnd == 1)
                           begin
                                snddat = 0;
                                prestate = 3;
                           end
                 end
            3:   begin
                      datsnd = 0;
                      lcdd = 91;          // '['
                      prestate = 4;
                 end
            4:   begin
                      snddat = 1;
                      prestate = 5;
                 end
            5:   begin
                      if (datsnd == 1)
                           begin
                                snddat = 0;
                                prestate = 6;
                           end
                 end
            6:   begin
                      datsnd = 0;
                      datpre = 1;
                 end
            default: prestate = 6;
         endcase
      end

// reset send data state
      if (snddat == 0 && datsnd == 0)
         sndstate = 0;

// send SPI 8-bit data
      if (snddat == 1 && datsnd == 0)
         begin
            case (sndstate)
                 0:   begin
                           i = 0;
                           ss = 0;
                           sndstate = 1;
```

149

```
                              end
                    1:    begin
                                i = i + 1;
                                if (i <= 8)
                                        sndstate = 2;
                                else
                                        sndstate = 5;
                          end
                    2:    begin
                                mosi = lcdd[8−i];        //MSB first
                                sndstate = 3;
                          end
                    3:    begin
                                sclk = 0;
                                sndstate = 4;
                          end
                    4:    begin
                                sclk = 1;
                                sndstate = 1;
                          end
                    5:    begin
                                sclk = 0;
                                mosi = 0;
                                sndstate = 6;
                          end
                    6:    begin
                                ss = 1;
                                sclk = 1;
                                datsnd = 1;
                          end
                    default: sndstate = 6;
                endcase
            end
      end

endmodule
```

The serial LCD datapath module *clslcd.v* is verified by the Verilog top module *atlslcdtest.v* and controller module *genlcd.v* for the Atlys Board which is in the *Chapter 3\lcdtest\atlslcdtest* folder. The 6-pin port of the SPI interface of the PmodCLS LCD module is connected to the top 6 pins of Peripheral Port A (JA) of the Atlys Board.

The serial LCD test top module for the Atlys Board *atlslcdtest.v* uses two *clock.v* modules to generate the datapath clock lcdclk and the pushbutton debounce clock pbclk signals. However, it is otherwise similar to the parallel LCD test top module for the Nexys 3 Board *ns3plcdtest.v* in Listing 3.17 and is not listed here. The configuration of the controller and datapath, other modules and external peripherals in the top module *atlslcdtest.v* is shown in Figure 3.9.

The complete Xilinx ISE project uses the UCF *atlslcdtest.ucf* which uncomments the signals CLK, BTNR, JA1, JA2 and JA4 in the Atlys Board UCF of Listing 3.2. The file download procedure is described in the Appendix.

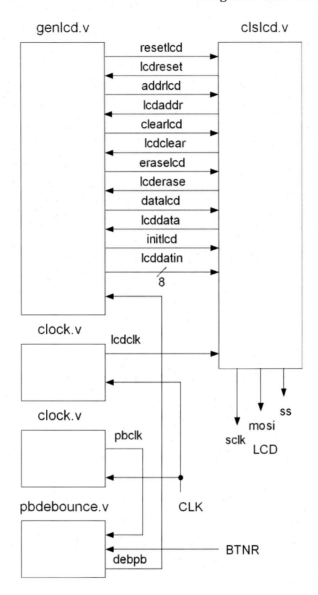

Figure 3.9 Controller and datapath modules in the top module *atlslcdtest.v*

As described in Chapter 2 Verilog Design Automation, the Design Utilization Summary for the top module *atlslcdtest.v* shows the use of use of 197 slice registers (1%) and 530 slice LUTs (1%) in the Atlys Board XC6SLX45 Spartan-6 FPGA synthesis.

As an example of design reuse, the serial LCD datapath module *clslcd.v* is also verified by the Verilog top module *ns3slcdtest.v* and controller module *genlcd.v* for the Nexys 3 Board which is in the *Chapter 3\lcdtest\ns3slcdtest* folder. Here the 6-pin port of the SPI interface of the PmodCLS LCD module is connected to the top 6 pins of Peripheral Port A (JA) of the Nexys 3 Board. Because only a single 6-pin peripheral port is required, Xilinx ISE projects for either the Nexys 3 Board or Atlys Board can be modified to utilize the PmodCLS LCD.

PS/2 Keyboard Port

Although the PS/2 serial peripheral protocol was first introduced in 1987, its use for data communication in an embedded system is less complicated that the more prevalent universal serial bus (USB) developed later. The self-synchronizing PS/2 protocol can be implemented easily with only two wires and does not require a significant amount of resources to process data. Both a PS/2 keyboard and mouse remain readily available.

The Digilent PmodPS2™ external connector for a PS/2 keyboard provides ASCII character input in applications of the FPGA as shown in Figure 3.10. A single PS/2 6-pin mini-DIN connector functions either as the input for a standard PC keyboard or mouse (but not at the same time). Neither the Nexys 3 Board or the Atlys Board has an integral PS/2 connector.

However, many PS/2 peripheral devices require a +5 VDC power supply and operate aberrantly or not at all on the +3.3 available on the Pmod connectors of the Nexys 3 Board or the Atlys Board. The JP2 connector of the Digilent PmodPS2 external connector can be set to use external power (VE) and JP1 can be connected to a +5 VDC power supply. The logic signal inputs and outputs on the Pmod connectors are tolerate of the voltage difference.

The PS/2 keyboard uses the two-wire (data and clock) PS/2 serial bus protocol to communicate with the host processor. The keyboard sends 11-bit data (ps2dat) on the synchronous negative edge of the PS/2 clock (ps2clk). The data is initially held as logic 1 and the first bit at the negative edge of ps2clk is the logic 0 start bit. Next, the 8-bit data keyboard scan code is sent with the LSB sent first followed by the odd parity bit and a stop bit that is logic 1. The number of logic 1s in the 8-bit data and the parity bit must be an odd number if the transmission is correct.

Figure 3.10 Digilent PmodPS2 PS/2 connector module

The module *keyboard.v* in Listing 3.21, which is also in the *Chapter 3\peripherals* folder, is event driven on the negative edge of the input signal ps2clk. A Verilog case statement uses the internal 4-bit register count as the state register of a finite state machine (FSM) to assess which of the 11 data bits are sent. The register count is initially set to 0 in a declaration [Lee06]. The output data available register dav is initially set to logic 0 by the start bit and a logic 1 by the stop bit. On the eleventh data bit the 4-bit state register count is reset to zero. The scan code of the depressed key is outputted in the 8-bit register kbddata with the separate register parity for the parity bit.

The PS/2 keyboard scan code of a key is not the ASCII character code and Table 3.4 lists their relationship in hexadecimal. If a key is depressed and held the PS/2 keyboard repeats the scan code approximately every 100 msec. Upon release of a key the keyboard first sends F0 hexadecimal (F0h) then a repeat of the scan code.

The left and right side shift keys actually have different scan codes and the application must keep track of the depression and release of the shift key for the upper case alphabetical characters and alternate symbols. The extended keys also send E0h before their scan code, even though the scan code for all of the keys are unique. If depressed and held the extended keys sends E0h and F0h then a repeat of the scan code.

The PS/2 keyboard module *keyboard.v* is verified by the Verilog top module *ns3keyboardtest.v* for the Nexys 3 Board in Listing 3.22, which is also in the *Chapter 3\keyboardtest \ns3keyboardtest* folder. The complete Xilinx ISE project uses the UCF *ns3keyboardtest.ucf* which uncomment the signals CLK, BTND, JA1, JA3, JC1 to JC4, JC7 to JC10 and JD7 to JD9 in the Nexys

3 Board UCF of Listing 3.1. The five Verilog modules operate in parallel and some independently in the top module, as shown in Figure 3.11. The file download procedure is described in the Appendix.

List 3.21 PS/2 keyboard module *keyboard.v*

```
// PS/2 Keyboard keyboard.v
// c 2012 Embedded Design using Programmable Gate Arrays  Dennis Silage

module keyboard (input ps2clk, input ps2dat, output reg dav, output reg [7:0] kbddata,
                 output reg parity);

reg [3:0] count = 0;

always@(negedge ps2clk)        // read keyboard data
     begin
          count = count + 1;
          case (count)
               1:    dav = 0;
               2:    kbddata[0] = ps2dat;
               3:    kbddata[1] = ps2dat;
               4:    kbddata[2] = ps2dat;
               5:    kbddata[3] = ps2dat;
               6:    kbddata[4] = ps2dat;
               7:    kbddata[5] = ps2dat;
               8:    kbddata[6] = ps2dat;
               9:    kbddata[7] = ps2dat;
               10:   parity = ps2dat;
               11:   begin
                          count = 0;
                          dav =1;          // data available
                      end
               default: count = 0;
          endcase
     end

endmodule
```

The wire net type in the *ns3keyboardtest.v* module for the Nexys 3 Board establishes the 8-bit connectivity for kbddata, lcddatin and lcdd between the *keyboard.v*, *genlcd.v* and *clplcd.v* modules, as given in Listing 3.22. The module *genlcd.v* is *event driven* on the positive edge of the data available signal dav from the *keyboard.v*. The data available event in the *genlcd.v* module checks the parity of the keyboard data with the Verilog exclusive or (xor) bit-wise operation (^) on the 8-bit keyboard data and the parity data.

The Verilog integer register variable i is used to sequentially index through the register variable kbddata to form the check parity register variable chkparity, which is a logic 1 for a correct data transmission. The clock event outputs the keyboard hexadecimal scan code, parity and check parity bits on the parallel LCD peripheral separted by colons (:).

As described in Chapter 2 Verilog Design Automation, the Design Utilization Summary for the top module *ns3keyboardtest.v* shows the use of 103 slice registers (1%) and 302 slice LUTs (3%) in the Nexys 3 Board XC6SLX16 Spartan-6 FPGA synthesis.

Assignment of output signals to peripheral devices only in the top module provides a degree of flexibility in the FPGA hardware synthesis of an embedded design. An Atlys Board project also in the *Chapter 3\keyboardtest\atlkeyboardtest* folder demonstrates this flexibility and the design reuse concept with the inclusion of the *clslcd.v* module, as given in Listing 3.20, with the *keyboard.v* module for a verification of the PS/2 keyboard performance.

Table 3.4 Hexadecimal scan code and ASCII code for the PS/2 keyboard characters

Character		Scan Code	ASCII Code		Character	Scan Code		ASCII Code	
a	A	1C	61	41	– _	4E		2D	5F
b	B	32	62	42	= +	55		3D	2B
c	C	21	63	43	BS	66		08	
d	D	23	64	44	TAB	0D		09	
e	E	24	65	45	[{	54		5B	7B
f	F	2B	66	46	] }	5B		5D	7D
g	G	34	67	47	\ |	5D		5C	7C
h	H	33	68	48	CAPS LOCK	58			
i	I	43	69	49	; :	4C		3B	3A
j	J	3B	6A	4A	' "	52		27	22
k	K	42	6B	4B	ENTER	5A			
l	L	4B	6C	4C	Left SHIFT	12			
m	M	3A	6D	4D	, <	41		2C	3C
n	*N*	*31*	*6E*	*4E*	. >	49		2E	3E
o	O	44	6F	4F	/ ?	4A		2F	3F
p	P	4D	70	50	Right SHIFT	59			
q	Q	15	71	51	Left CTRL	14			
r	R	2D	72	52	Left ALT	11			
s	S	1B	73	53	SPACE	29		20	
t	T	2C	74	54	Right ALT	E0	11		
u	U	3C	75	55	Right CTRL	E0	14		
v	V	2A	76	56	ESC	76		1B	
w	W	1D	77	57	F1	05			
x	X	22	78	58	F2	06			
y	Y	35	79	59	F3	04			
z	Z	1A	7A	5A	F4	0C			
`	~	0E	60	7E	F5	03			
1	!	16	31	21	F6	0B			
2	@	1E	32	22	F7	83			
3	#	26	33	23	F8	0A			
4	$	25	34	24	F9	01			
5	%	2E	35	25	F10	09			
6	^	36	36	5E	F11	78			
7	&	3D	37	26	F12	07			
8	*	3E	38	2A	↑	E0	75		
9	(	46	39	28	→	E0	74		
0	)	45	30	29	←	E0	6B		
					↓	E0	72		

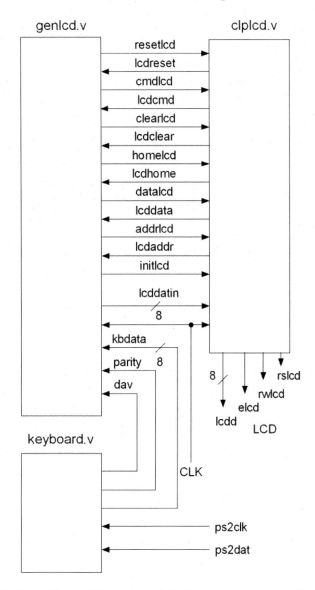

Figure 3.11 Controller and datapath modules in the top module *ns3keyboardtest.v*

Listing 3.22 Keyboard test top module for the Nexys 3 Board *ns3keyboardtest.v*

```
// Nexys 3 Board
// PS/2 Keyboard Test ns3keyboardtest.v
// c 2012 Embedded Design using Programmable Gate Arrays  Dennis Silage

module ns3keyboardtest(input CLK, JA1, JA3, BTND, output JC1, JC2, JC3,
                output JC4, JC7, JC8, JC9, JC10, JD7, JD8, JD9);


wire [7:0] kbddata;
wire [7:0] lcddatin;
wire [7:0] lcdd;
wire rslcd, rwlcd, elcd;
```

```
assign ps2dat = JA1;
assign ps2clk = JA3;
assign JC10 = lcdd[7];
assign JC9 = lcdd[6];
assign JC8 = lcdd[5];
assign JC7 = lcdd[4];
assign JC4 = lcdd[3];
assign JC3 = lcdd[2];
assign JC2 = lcdd[1];
assign JC1 = lcdd[0];
assign JD7 = rslcd;
assign JD8 = rwlcd;
assign JD9 = elcd;

keyboard M0 (ps2clk, ps2dat, dav, kbddata, parity);
clplcd M1 (CLK, resetlcd, clearlcd, homelcd, datalcd, addrlcd, cmdlcd, initlcd, lcdreset, lcdclear,
            lcdhome, lcddata, lcdaddr, lcdcmd, rslcd, rwlcd, elcd, lcdd, lcddatin);
genlcd M2 (CLK, debpb, resetlcd, clearlcd, homelcd, datalcd, addrlcd, initlcd, cmdlcd, lcdreset,
            lcdclear, lcdhome, lcddata, lcdaddr, lcddatin, dav, parity, kbddata);
pbdebounce M3 (clk, BTND, debpb);
clock M4 (CLK, 1000000, clk);        //50 Hz

endmodule

module genlcd(input CLK, depdb, output reg resetlcd, output reg clearlcd, output reg homelcd,
            output reg datalcd, output reg addrlcd, output reg initlcd, output reg cmdlcd,
            input lcdreset, input lcdclear, lcdhome, lcddata, lcdaddr, output reg [7:0] lcddatin,
            input dav, parity, input [7:0] kbddata);

reg [4:0] gstate;        // state register
reg chkparity;
integer i;

always@(posedge dav)            // calculate parity check
    begin
        chkparity = kbddata[0] ^ kbddata[1];
        for (i = 2; i <= 7; i = i + 1)
            chkparity = kbddata[i] ^ chkparity;
        chkparity = parity ^ chkparity;
    end

always@(posedge CLK)
    begin
        if (depdb == 1)
            begin
                resetlcd = 0;
                clearlcd = 0;
                homelcd = 0;
                datalcd = 0;
                gstate = 0;
            end
        else
```

```
case (gstate)
    0: begin
                initlcd = 1;
                gstate = 1;
        end
    1:    begin
                initlcd = 0;
                gstate = 2;
        end
    2:    begin
                resetlcd = 1;
                if (lcdreset == 1)
                        begin
                                resetlcd = 0;
                                gstate = 3;
                        end
        end
    3: begin
                initlcd = 1;
                gstate = 4;
        end
    4:    begin
                initlcd = 0;
                gstate = 5;
        end
    5:    begin
                clearlcd = 1;
                if (lcdclear == 1)
                        begin
                                clearlcd = 0;
                                gstate = 6;
                        end
        end
    6:    begin
                initlcd = 1;
                gstate = 7;
        end
    7:    begin
                initlcd = 0;
                gstate = 8;
        end
    8:    begin              // start address 44h
                lcddatin[7:0] = 8'b01000100;
                addrlcd = 1;
                if (lcdaddr == 1)
                        begin
                                addrlcd = 0;
                                gstate = 9;
                        end
        end
    9:    begin
                initlcd = 1;
```

```
                gstate = 10;
        end
10: begin
            initlcd = 0;
            gstate = 11;
        end
11: begin
            lcddatin[7:4] = 3;                  // ASCII digit 3Xh
            lcddatin[3:0] = kbddata[7:4];
            datalcd = 1;
            if (lcddata == 1)
                begin
                    datalcd = 0;
                    gstate = 12;
                end
        end
12: begin
            initlcd = 1;
            gstate = 13;
        end
13: begin
            initlcd = 0;
            gstate = 14;
        end
14: begin
            lcddatin[7:4] = 0;
            lcddatin[3:0] = kbddata[3:0];
            if (lcddatin <= 9)
                lcddatin[7:4] = 3;              // ASCII digit 3Xh
            else
                lcddatin = lcddatin + 55;       // ASCII A, B...
            datalcd = 1;
            if (lcddata == 1)
                begin
                    datalcd = 0;
                    gstate = 15;
                end
        end
15: begin
            initlcd = 1;
            gstate = 16;
        end
16: begin
            initlcd = 0;
            gstate = 17;
        end
17: begin
            lcddatin[7:0] = 58;           // ASCII :
            datalcd = 1;
            if (lcddata == 1)
                begin
                    datalcd = 0;
```

```
                        gstate = 18;
                end
        end
18:     begin
                initlcd = 1;
                gstate = 19;
        end
19:     begin
                initlcd = 0;
                gstate = 20;
        end
20:     begin
                lcddatin[7:4] = 3;        // 30h
                lcddatin[3:1] = 3'b000;
                lcddatin[0] = chkparity;
                datalcd = 1;
                if (lcddata == 1)
                        begin
                                datalcd = 0;
                                gstate = 21;
                        end
        end
21:     begin
                initlcd = 1;
                gstate = 22;
        end
22:     begin
                initlcd = 0;
                gstate = 23;
        end
23:     begin
                lcddatin[7:0] = 58;           // ASCII :
                datalcd = 1;
                if (lcddata == 1)
                        begin
                                datalcd = 0;
                                gstate = 24;
                        end
        end
24:     begin
                initlcd = 1;
                gstate = 25;
        end
25:     begin
                initlcd = 0;
                gstate = 26;
        end
26:     begin
                lcddatin[7:4] = 3;            // 30h
                lcddatin[3:1] = 3'b000;
                lcddatin[0] = parity;
                datalcd = 1;
```

```
                    if (lcddata == 1)
                        begin
                            datalcd = 0;
                            gstate = 6;
                        end
                end
            default: gstate = 0;
        endcase
    end

endmodule
```

PS/2 Mouse Port

The Digilent PmodPS2™ external connector, as shown in Figure 3.10, can also be used for a PS/2 mouse to provides positional information and button input in applications of the FPGA. A single PS/2 6-pin mini-DIN connector functions either as the input for a standard PC mouse or keyboard (but not at the same time).

Neither the Nexys 3 Board or the Atlys Board has an integral PS/2 connector. However, many PS/2 peripheral devices require a +5 VDC power supply and operate aberrantly or not at all on the +3.3 available on the Pmod connectors of the Nexys 3 Board or the Atlys Board. The JP2 connector of the Digilent PmodPS2 external connector can be set to use external power (VE) and JP1 can be connected to a +5 VDC power supply. The logic signal inputs and outputs on the Pmod connectors are tolerate of the voltage difference.

The mouse also uses the two-wire (data and clock) PS/2 serial bus protocol to communicate bidirectionally with the host processor and the clock (ps2clk) and data (ps2dat) signal is therefore defined with the Verilog type inout. The PS/2 mouse always generates the clock but, if the host is to send data, it must first inhibit communication by setting the clock to logic 0.

The PS/2 mouse enters the reset mode at initialization (power-up) and, unlike the PS/2 keyboard, data reporting is disabled. Although there are a variety of commands and resulting modes of operation for the PS/2 mouse, at the minimum the host should set the mouse to Enable Data Reporting with the 8-bit command code F4h.

The host first issues a Request to Send to the PS/2 mouse by setting the clock to logic 0 for at least 100 microseconds (μsec), setting the data to logic 0 and then setting the clock to logic 1. The host then sends an 11-bit data packet on the negative edge of the synchronous PS/2 clock consisting of a start bit (logic 0), 8-bit data command (F4h), an odd parity bit (logic 0) and a stop bit (logic 1). The PS/2 mouse responses with Acknowledge (FAh) as data, but this response can be ignored.

The PS/2 mouse then sends three 11-bit data packets (ps2dat) on the synchronous negative edge of the PS/2 clock (ps2clk) when either movement or button depression is sensed. The data is initially held as logic 1 and the first bit at the negative edge of ps2clk is the start bit (logic 0). Next, the PS/2 mouse 8-bit status data is sent followed by the odd parity bit and a stop bit (logic 1). The number of logic 1s in the 8-bit data and the parity bit must be an odd number if the transmission is correct. The X direction and Y direction 11-bit data packets are sent next.

Table 3.4 lists the contents of the 8-bit status and the X directional and Y directional data without the accompanying start, parity and stop bits. The L and R bits of the status are logic 1 when the left or right mouse button is depressed. The XS and YS bits indicate the sign of the mouse movement with respect to the last quiescent position and logic 0 indicates a positive sign. The XV and YV bits are logic 1 if an overflow in the movement in the x or y direction occurs. Finally, the X0 through X7 and Y0 through Y7 bits are the 8-bit mouse movement data.

The PS/2 mouse datapath module *mouse.v*, which is in the *Chapter 3\peripherals* folder, is given in Listing 3.23 and utilizes three finite state machines (FSM). The register reset is set to logic 1 and cleared to logic 0 on the positive edge of the crystal clock oscillator (CLK), but only initially by the first FSM using the 2-bit state register resstate.

Table 3.4 PS/2 mouse 8-bit data packets

Status	L	R	0	1	XS	YS	XV	YV
X Direction	X0	X1	X2	X3	X4	X5	X6	X7
Y Direction	Y0	Y1	Y2	Y3	Y4	Y5	Y6	Y7

After reset has occurred, the second FSM uses the 5-bit sent data state register sstate to send the command Enable Data Reporting (F4h) from the host to the PS/2 mouse. Finally, the third FSM uses the 6-bit received data state register rstate to report the movement of the mouse or button depression. The data is read on the negative edge of the PS/2 clock input signal ps2clk.

The 13-bit register count is used to set the PS/2 clock to logic 0 for at least 100 μsec. The 100 MHz crystal clock has a period of 0.01 μsec and a count of 11 000 (11 000 × 0.01 μsec = 110 μsec) assures that this occurs. The host then releases the PS/2 clock by setting it to a high impedance state (z).

A Verilog case statement uses the 5-bit state register sstate to send the Enable Data Reporting command from the host and to recognize the Acknowledge response from the PS/2 mouse. The 5-bit register sstate utilizes 22 states for the transmission and reception of these two 11-bit Enable Data Reporting and Acknowledge data packets.

A Verilog case statement uses the 6-bit state register rstate to assess which of the 33 data bits are sent. The output data available register dav is initially set to logic 0 by the start bit of the first data packet and to logic 1 by the stop bit of the third data packet. The PS/2 mouse X and Y directional data are outputted as a 9-bit signed (two's complement) binary number distributed in the 8-bit X direction data register mousexdata and the 8-bit Y direction data register mouseydata and the XS and YS sign bits, as listed in Table 3.4.

The sign bits are outputted in the 2-bit register sign. The 2-bit overflow register ovf and the two bit odd parity register parity are also provided for the PS/2 mouse X and Y directional data. Finally, the depression of the two PS/2 mouse buttons is outputted in the 2-bit register button.

Listing 3.23 PS/2 mouse datapath module *mouse.v*

```
// PS/2 Mouse mouse.v
// c 2012 Embedded Design using Programmable Gate Arrays  Dennis Silage

module mouse(input CLK, inout ps2dat, inout ps2clk, output reg dav, output reg [2:0] parity,
            output reg [1:0] button, output reg [1:0] ovf, output reg [1:0] sign,
            output reg [7:0] mousexdata, output reg [7:0] mouseydata);

reg [13:0] count = 0;       // delay counter
reg [1:0] restate = 0;      // reset state
reg [4:0] sstate = 0;       // sent data state
reg [5:0] rstate = 0;       // received data state
reg clkps2;
reg datps2;
reg reset = 0;
reg mclk = 0;

assign ps2clk = clkps2;
assign ps2dat = datps2;
```

```
always@(posedge CLK)
    begin
        resstate <= resstate + 1;
        if (resstate == 1)
            reset = 1;
        if (resstate == 3)
            begin
                resstate <= 2;
                reset = 0;
            end
    end

always@(count or reset)
    begin
        if (reset == 1)
            clkps2 = 1'bz;
        else if (count <= 11000 && reset == 0)
            clkps2 = 0;
        else
            clkps2 = 1'bz;
    end

always@(posedge CLK or posedge reset)
    begin
        if (reset == 1)
            count <= 0;
        else if (count == 12000)
            count <= count;
        else
            count <= count + 1;
    end

always@(count or reset)
    begin
        if (reset == 1)
            datps2 = 1'bz;
        else if (count > 10000 && sstate == 0)
            datps2 = 0;            // start bit
        else if (sstate == 1)      // F4h
            datps2 = 0;
        else if (sstate == 2)
            datps2 = 0;
        else if (sstate == 3)
            datps2 = 1;
        else if (sstate == 4)
            datps2 = 0;
        else if (sstate == 5)
            datps2 = 1;
        else if (sstate == 6)
            datps2 = 1;
        else if (sstate==7)
            datps2 = 1;
```

```
            else if (sstate == 8)
                    datps2 = 1;
            else if (sstate == 9)            // parity bit
                    datps2 = 0;
            else if (sstate == 10)           // stop bit
                    datps2 = 1;
            else
                    datps2 = 1'bz;
        end

always@(negedge ps2clk or posedge reset)
        begin
            if (reset == 1)
                    sstate <= 0;
            else if (sstate <= 21)
                    sstate <= sstate + 1;
            else if (sstate == 22)
                    sstate <= 22;
            else
                    sstate <= 0;
        end

always@(negedge ps2clk)                  // read mouse data
        begin
            if (reset == 1)
                    rstate = 0;
            else if (sstate == 22)
                    begin
                        rstate = rstate + 1;
                        case (rstate)
                            1:   dav = 0;
                            2:   button[1] = ps2dat;   // x button
                            3:   button[0] = ps2dat;   // y button
                            4:   dav = 0;
                            5:   dav = 0;
                            6:   sign[1] = ps2dat;     // x sign
                            7:   sign[0] = ps2dat;     // y sign
                            8:   ovf[1] = ps2dat;      // x overflow
                            9:   ovf[0] = ps2dat;      // y overflow
                            10:  parity[0] = ps2dat;
                            11:  dav = 0;
                            12:  dav = 0;
                            13:  mousexdata[0] = ps2dat;   // x data
                            14:  mousexdata[1] = ps2dat;
                            15:  mousexdata[2] = ps2dat;
                            16:  mousexdata[3] = ps2dat;
                            17:  mousexdata[4] = ps2dat;
                            18:  mousexdata[5] = ps2dat;
                            19:  mousexdata[6] = ps2dat;
                            20:  mousexdata[7] = ps2dat;
                            21:  parity[1] = ps2dat;   // x data parity
                            22:  dav = 0;
```

```
23:    dav = 0;
24:    mouseydata[0] = ps2dat;   // y data
25:    mouseydata[1] = ps2dat;
26:    mouseydata[2] = ps2dat;
27:    mouseydata[3] = ps2dat;
28:    mouseydata[4] = ps2dat;
29:    mouseydata[5] = ps2dat;
30:    mouseydata[6] = ps2dat;
31:    mouseydata[7] = ps2dat;
32:    parity[2] = ps2dat;   // y data parity
33:    begin
              rstate = 0;
              dav = 1;
          end
       default: rstate = 0;
    endcase
  end
 end

endmodule
```

The PS/2 mouse datapath module *mouse.v* is verified by the Verilog top module for the Nexys 3 Board *ns3mousetest.v*, which is in the *Chapter 3\mousetest\ns3mousetest* folder, is given in Listing 3.24. The complete Xilinx ISE project uses UCF *ns3mousetest.ucf* which uncomments the signals CLK, JA1, JA3, JC1 to JC4, JC7 to JC10 and JD7 to JD9 and four LEDs in the Nexys 3 Board UCF of Listing 3.1. The four Verilog modules operate in parallel in the top module. The file download procedure is described in the Appendix.

The wire net type establishes the 8-bit, 5-bit, 3-bit and 2-bit vector connectivity for mousexdata, mouseydata, data, digit, parity, button, sign and ovf between the *mouse.v*, *clplcd.v*, *checkmouse.v* and *genlcd.v* modules for the Nexys 3 Board as given in Listing 3.24 [Ciletti04]. The 2-bit PS/2 mouse button register button and the 2-bit data overflow register ovf are continuously assigned to the four LEDs for display.

The module *checkmouse.v* is event driven on the positive edge of the data available signal dav from the *mouse.v* module. The data available event extracts the PS/2 mouse X and Y directional data and calculates the absolute X and Y position for a standard Video Graphics Array (VGA) grid of 640 elements horizontally and 480 elements vertically. Depressing the two PS/2 mouse buttons simultaneously homes the absolute position to the center of the grid (X = 320, Y = 240).

The 9-bit X or Y directional data is converted to a magnitude in the 8-bit registers xvalue and yvalue with the original 2-bit register sign. If the X or Y directional data is negative, then the magnitude is calculated by the complement-and-increment Verilog statement mousedata = ~mousedata + 1; which converts the two's-complement binary number. The original 8-bit X and Y direction data registers mousexdata and mouseydata from the module mouse.v are inputted to the module checkmouse.v sequentially as the 8-bit register mousedata.

Unlike parameter passing in a conversational language such as C, mousexdata and mouseydata are signals and not registers and cannot be manipulated. The X and Y directional data is either added or subtracted from the 11-bit absolute position registers xpos and ypos, as determined by the sign bits.

An 11-bit absolute position register is required to check for underflow (X < 0 or Y < 0), which can occur after subtraction, by the value of the most significant bit (MSB). The MSB is a logic 1 for a negative two's complement binary number. The overflow value (X > 639 or Y > 479), which can occur after addition, is checked by the Verilog if statement. The Y absolute position register ypos need only be 10 bits but is 11 bits here for computational compatibility with the X absolute position register xpos.

Next, the absolute X and Y position registers xpos and ypos as binary numbers are converted to a three digit binary coded decimal (BCD) number. One structural model to do this is the serial binary to BCD conversion algorithm, as described in Chapter 2 Verilog Design Automation (Xilinx application note XAPP029, *www.xilinx.com*). However, this method is not intuitive and requires an understanding of the relationship of the binary and the BCD number systems.

Alternatively, Verilog can utilize a conversational language algorithm, as in the C language, to produce a behavioral model for the same result. This illustrates the salient concept that such algorithms can be used in Verilog for embedded design, as described in Chapter 1 Verilog Hardware Description Language.

The behavioral model iteratively subtracts 100 then 10 from the remaining binary number to form the most significant (msdigit), middle (middigit) and least significant (lsdigit) BCD digits. This behavioral model iterative subtraction algorithm is described in Chapter 2 Verilog Design Automation Verilog Design Automation.

Listing 3.24 Mouse test top module for the Nexys 3 Board *ns3mousetest.v*

```
// Nexys 3 Board
// PS/2 Mouse Test ns3mousetest.v
// c 2012 Embedded Design using Programmable Gate Arrays  Dennis Silage

module ns3mousetest (input CLK, inout JA1, inout JA3, output JC1, output JC2, JC3, JC4, JC7, JC8,
                output JC9, JC10, JD7, JD8, JD9, output [3:0]LED);

wire [7:0] lcddatin;
wire [7:0] lcdd;
wire rslcd, rwlcd, elcd;
wire [1:0] button;
wire [1:0] sign;
wire [1:0] ovf;
wire [2:0] parity;
wire [7:0] mousexdata;
wire [7:0] mouseydata;
wire [3:0] xmsdigit;
wire [3:0] xmiddigit;
wire [3:0] xlsdigit;
wire [3:0] ymsdigit;
wire [3:0] ymiddigit;
wire [3:0] ylsdigit;

assign JC10 = lcdd[7];
assign JC9 = lcdd[6];
assign JC8 = lcdd[5];
assign JC7 = lcdd[4];
assign JC4 = lcdd[3];
assign JC3 = lcdd[2];
assign JC2 = lcdd[1];
assign JC1 = lcdd[0];
assign JD7 = rslcd;
assign JD8 = rwlcd;
assign JD9 = elcd;
```

Trends in Embedded Design Using Programmable Gate Arrays

```
assign LED[1] = button[1];
assign LED[0] = button[0];
assign LED[3] = ovf[1];
assign LED[2] = ovf[0];

mouse M0 (CLK, JA1, JA3, dav, parity, button, ovf, sign, mousexdata, mouseydata);
clplcd M1 (CLK, resetlcd, clearlcd, homelcd, datalcd, addrlcd, cmdlcd, initlcd, lcdreset, lcdclear,
           lcdhome, lcddata, lcdaddr, lcdcmd, rslcd, rwlcd, elcd, lcdd, lcddatin);
checkmouse M2 (button, dav, sign, mousexdata, mouseydata, dataav, xmsdigit, xmiddigit, xlsdigit,
               ymsdigit, ymiddigit, ylsdigit);
genlcd M3 (CLK, dataav, resetlcd, clearlcd, datalcd, addrlcd, initlcd, lcdreset, lcdclear, lcddata,
           lcdaddr, lcddatin, xmsdigit, xmiddigit, xlsdigit, ymsdigit, ymiddigit, ylsdigit);

endmodule

module genlcd (input CLK, dataav, output reg resetlcd = 0, output reg clearlcd = 0,
               output reg datalcd = 0, output reg addrlcd = 0, output reg initlcd,
               input lcdreset, input lcdclear, lcddata, lcdaddr, output reg [7:0] lcddatin,
               input [3:0] xmsdigit, input [3:0] xmiddigit, input [3:0] xlsdigit,
               input [3:0] ymsdigit, input [3:0] ymiddigit, input [3:0] ylsdigit);

reg [4:0] gstate = 0;

always@(posedge CLK)
    begin
        case (gstate)
            0:   begin
                     initlcd = 1;
                     gstate = 1;
                 end
            1:   begin
                     initlcd = 0;
                     gstate = 2;
                 end
            2:   begin
                     resetlcd = 1;
                     if (lcdreset == 1)
                         begin
                             resetlcd = 0;
                             gstate = 3;
                         end
                 end
            3:   begin
                     initlcd = 1;
                     gstate = 4;
                 end
            4:   begin
                     initlcd = 0;
                     gstate = 5;
                 end
            5:   begin
                     clearlcd = 1;
```

```
                if (lcdclear == 1)
                        begin
                                clearlcd = 0;
                                gstate = 6;
                        end
        end
6:      begin
                if (dataav == 0)
                        gstate = 6;
                else
                        begin
                                initlcd = 1;
                                gstate = 7;
                        end
        end
7:      begin
                initlcd = 0;
                gstate = 8;
        end
8:      begin                   // start address 40h
                lcddatin[7:0] = 8'b01000000;
                addrlcd = 1;
                if (lcdaddr == 1)
                        begin
                                addrlcd = 0;
                                gstate = 9;
                        end
        end
9:      begin
                initlcd = 1;
                gstate = 10;
        end
10:     begin
                initlcd = 0;
                gstate = 11;
        end
11:     begin
                lcddatin[7:4] = 3;              // ASCII digit 3Xh
                lcddatin[3:0] = xmsdigit[3:0];
                datalcd = 1;
                if (lcddata == 1)
                        begin
                                datalcd = 0;
                                gstate = 12;
                        end
        end
12:     begin
                initlcd = 1;
                gstate = 13;
        end
13:     begin
                initlcd = 0;
```

```
                    gstate = 14;
          end
  14:   begin
                    lcddatin[3:0] = xmiddigit[3:0];
                    datalcd = 1;
                    if (lcddata == 1)
                          begin
                                  datalcd = 0;
                                  gstate = 15;
                          end
          end
  15:   begin
                    initlcd = 1;
                    gstate = 16;
          end
  16:   begin
                    initlcd = 0;
                    gstate = 17;
          end
  17:   begin
                    lcddatin[3:0] = xlsdigit[3:0];
                    datalcd = 1;
                    if (lcddata == 1)
                          begin
                                  datalcd = 0;
                                  gstate = 18;
                          end
          end
  18:   begin
                    initlcd = 1;
                    gstate = 19;
          end
  19:   begin
                    initlcd = 0;
                    gstate = 20;
          end
  20:   begin
                    lcddatin[7:0] = 8'h20;              // ASCII space
                    datalcd = 1;
                    if (lcddata == 1)
                          begin
                                  datalcd = 0;
                                  gstate = 21;
                          end
          end
  21:   begin
                    initlcd = 1;
                    gstate = 22;
          end
  22:   begin
                    initlcd = 0;
                    gstate = 23;
```

```
                end
        23:  begin
                    lcddatin[7:4] = 3;              // ASCII digit 3Xh
                    lcddatin[3:0] = ymsdigit[3:0];
                    datalcd = 1;
                    if (lcddata == 1)
                            begin
                                datalcd = 0;
                                gstate = 24;
                            end
                end
        24:  begin
                    initlcd = 1;
                    gstate = 25;
                end
        25:  begin
                    initlcd = 0;
                    gstate = 26;
                end
        26:  begin
                    lcddatin[3:0] = ymiddigit[3:0];
                    datalcd = 1;
                    if (lcddata == 1)
                            begin
                                datalcd = 0;
                                gstate = 27;
                            end
                end
        27:  begin
                    initlcd = 1;
                    gstate = 28;
                end
        28:  begin
                    initlcd = 0;
                    gstate = 29;
                end
        29:  begin
                    lcddatin[3:0] = ylsdigit[3:0];
                    datalcd = 1;
                    if (lcddata == 1)
                            begin
                                datalcd = 0;
                                gstate = 6;
                            end
                end
        default: gstate = 0;
    endcase
  end

endmodule
```

Trends in Embedded Design Using Programmable Gate Arrays

The data available event from the signal dataav in the *checkmouse.v* module displays the PS/2 mouse X or Y position on the PmodCLP parallel LCD peripheral in the *genlcd.v* module. Partial controller and datapath modules in the top module *ns3mousetest.v* are shown in Figure 3.12.

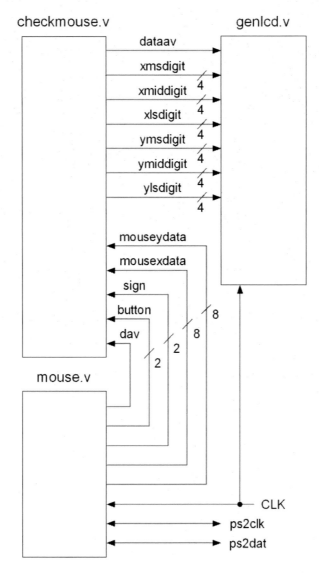

Figure 3.12 Partial controller and datapath modules in the top module *ns3mousetest.v*

Not shown to reduce the complexity of the Figure are the input and output connections to the *clplcd.v* module from the *genlcd.v* module, which are the same as those in Figure 3.11. Note that the controller signals resetlcd, clearlcd, datalcd and addrlcd from the *genlcd.v* module are initialized to logic zero at synthesis.

As described in Chapter 2 Verilog Design Automation Verilog Design Automation, the Design Utilization Summary for the top module *ns3mousetest.v* shows the use of 146 slice registers (1%) and 469 slice LUTs (5%) in the Nexys 3 Board XC6SLX16 Spartan-6 FPGA synthesis.

A Xilinx ISE project can be configured for the Atlys Board but, because of the availability of only one 12-pin Pmod connector, the PmodCLS serial LCD peripheral would be used instead. Such an ISE project would also utilize a controller for the serial LCD and the substitution of the Atlys Board

UCF, as was accomplished for the PS/2 keyboard test demonstrated by the project in the folder *Chapter 3\keyboardtest\atlkeyboardtest* but this is not implemented here.

PmodJSTK Joystick

The Digilent PmodJSTK™ peripheral provides a two axis joystick with a center pushbutton, two additional pushbuttons and two LEDs for applications of the FPGA as shown in Figure 3.13. The PmodJSTK module has an embedded microcontroller that provides an integral analog-to-digital converter to measure the center pin of the two potentiometers for the X-axis and Y-axis position of the joystick in the range from 0 to 1023 (10-bits).

Figure 3.13 Digilent PmodJSTK joystick module

The PmodJSTK module utilizes a 4-bit data bus serial peripheral interface (SPI) and requires a single port (Peripheral Port A, JA). The PmodJSTK SPI consists of the serial clock jstksclk, master output/slave input jstkmosi, master input/slave output jstkmiso and slave select jstkss signals. The SPI protocol is described as one of the serial data link protocols in this Chapter. The PmodJSTK is referenced in the Digilent document 502-116 (*www.digilentinc.com*).

The PmodJSTK SPI is initiated by setting the slave select signal jstkss to logic 0 for at least 16 μsec. The master then sends five data bytes to the joystick with a minimum delay of 10 μsec between the bytes. The master and the slave read data on the rising edge of the SPI clock signal jstksclk.

The first data byte transmitted by the master sets the condition of the two LEDs on the joystick, as listed in Table 3.5. The remaining four transmitted bytes from the master are required by the SPI protocol but are ignored by the slave. The first four received data bytes contain the X and Y axis data of the joystick position transmitted as low and high bytes and the fifth received data byte is the status of the three push buttons, as listed in Table 3.5. BTN1 and BTN2 are discrete push buttons and BTN0 is enable by a depression of the joystick itself.

Table 3.5 PmodJSTK joystick transmitted and received data packets

Transmitted data	1	0	0	0	0	0	JSTKLD2	JSTK LD1

Received data bytes	X (low)	X (high)	Y (low)	Y (high)	Button data			
Button data	0	0	0	0	0	BTN2	BTN1	BTN0

The datapath module *joystick.v*, which is in the *Chapter 3\peripherals* folder, is given in Listing 3.25 and utilizes two finite state machines (FSM). The joystick data command signal jstkdav resets parameters on logic 0 or initiates the transmission of five bytes of data from the master using an FSM on logic 1, including the value for the joystick LEDs, JSTKLD1 and JSTKLD2, contained in the 2-bit register jstkled. The slave responds with five received data bytes including the X-axis and Y-axis position data and the status of the push buttons. A joystick status signal davjstk indicates completion of the data transmission.

Trends in Embedded Design Using Programmable Gate Arrays

The send and receive SPI 8-bit data FSM is comparable to that in Listing 3.20 for the serial LCD module *clslcd.v*. Although the SPI data FSM is used routinely, placing it within a Verilog module promotes design reuse, simplifies data communication and FPGA hardware synthesis, as described in Chapter 2 Verilog Design Automation.

The datapath module *joystick.v* is verified by the Verilog top module for the Nexys 3 Board *ns3joysticktest.v*, which is in the *Chapter 3\joysticktest\ns3joysticktest* folder, is given in Listing 3.26. The complete Xilinx ISE project uses *ns3mousetest.ucf* which uncomments the signals CLK, BTNL, BTNR, JA1 to JA4, , JC1 to JC4, JC7 to JC10 and JD7 to JD9 and three LEDs in the Nexys 3 Board UCF of Listing 3.1. The five Verilog modules operate in parallel in the top module. The file download procedure is described in the Appendix.

Listing 3.25 Joystick datapath module *joystick.v*

```
// Joystick joystick.v
// c 2012 Embedded Design using Programmable Gate Arrays  Dennis Silage

module joystick (input jstkclk, output reg jstkss, output reg jstkmosi, input jstkmiso,
           output reg jstksck = 0, input jstkdav, output reg davjstk, input [1:0] jstkled,
           output reg [2:0] jstkbutton, output reg [9:0] jstkxdata, output reg [9:0] jstkydata);

reg [3:0] jstkstate = 0;     // joystick state register
reg [2:0] sndstate = 0;      // SPI state register
reg [7:0] jstktx;            // joystick transmit data register
reg [7:0] jstkrx;            // joystick receive data register
reg [7:0] jstktmp;           // temporary register
reg jstkspi = 0;             // SPI command
reg spijstk = 0;             // SPI command acknowledge

integer i;

always@ (posedge jstkclk)
     begin
          if (jstkdav == 0)           // joystick data?
               begin
                    davjstk = 0;
                    jstkstate = 0;
                    jstkss = 1;
                    jstkspi = 0;
                    spijstk = 0;
               end
          else
               begin
                    davjstk = 0;
                    case (jstkstate)
                    0:   begin
                              jstkss = 0;
                              jstktx[7:2] = 6'b100000;
                              jstktx[1:0] = jstkled[1:0];
                              jstkstate = 1;
                         end
                    1:   begin
                              jstkspi = 1;
```

172

```
                jstkstate = 2;
        end
2:      begin
            if (spijstk == 1)
                    begin
                        jstkspi = 0;
                        spijstk = 0;
                        jstktx = 0;
                        jstkxdata[7:0] = jstkrx[7:0];
                        jstkstate = 3;
                    end
        end
3:      begin
            jstkspi = 1;
            jstkstate = 4;
        end
4:      begin
            if (spijstk == 1)
                    begin
                        jstkspi = 0;
                        spijstk = 0;
                        jstkxdata[9:8] = jstkrx[1:0];
                        jstkstate = 5;
                    end
        end
5:      begin
            jstkspi = 1;
            jstkstate = 6;
        end
6:      begin
            if (spijstk == 1)
                    begin
                        jstkspi = 0;
                        spijstk = 0;
                        jstkydata[7:0] = jstkrx[7:0];
                        jstkstate = 7;
                    end
        end
7:      begin
            jstkspi = 1;
            jstkstate = 8;
        end
8:      begin
            if (spijstk == 1)
                    begin
                        jstkspi = 0;
                        spijstk = 0;
                        jstkydata[9:8] = jstkrx[1:0];
                        jstkstate = 9;
                    end
        end
9:      begin
```

```
                        jstkspi = 1;
                        jstkstate = 10;
                end
        10:   begin
                   if (spijstk == 1)
                        begin
                                jstkspi = 0;
                                spijstk = 0;
                                jstkbutton = jstkrx[2:0];
                                davjstk = 1;                // joystick DAV
                                jstkss = 1;
                                jstkstate = 11;
                        end
                end
        11: jstkstate = 11;
        default: jstkstate = 11;
        endcase
   end

// reset send and receive SPI data state
        if (jstkspi == 0 && spijstk == 0)
                sndstate = 0;

// send and receive SPI 8-bit data
        if (jstkspi == 1 && spijstk == 0)
                begin
                   case (sndstate)
                        0:   begin
                                i = 0;
                                sndstate = 1;
                             end
                        1:   begin
                                i = i + 1;
                                if (i < 8)
                                        sndstate = 2;
                                else
                                        sndstate = 6;
                             end
                        2:   begin
                                jstkmosi = jstktx[8-i];        //transmit, MSB first
                                sndstate = 3;
                             end
                        3:   begin
                                jstksck = 1;
                                sndstate = 4;
                             end
                        4:   begin
                                jstkrx[8-i] = jstkmiso;        //receive, MSB first
                                sndstate = 5;
                             end
                        5:   begin
                                jstksck = 0;
```

```
                            sndstate = 1;
                    end
        6:      begin
                    spijstk = 1;
                end
            default: sndstate = 6;
        endcase
    end
end

endmodule
```

The wire net type establishes the 10-bit, 8-bit, 4-bit, 3-bit and 2-bit vector connectivity for jstkxdata, jstkydata, the four BCD digits, jstkbutton, jstkled and the LCD data between the *joystick.v*, *clplcd.v*, *checkjstk.v* and *genlcd.v* modules for the Nexys 3 Board as given in Listing 3.26 [Ciletti04]. The module *checkjstk.v* is event driven on the positive edge of the data available signal jstkdav from the *joystick.v* module and response with the status signal davjstk [Ashenden08] .

Listing 3.26 Joystick test top module for the Nexys 3 Board *ns3joysticktest.v*

```
// Nexys 3 Board
// Joystick Test ns3joysticktest.v
// c 2012 Embedded Design using Programmable Gate Arrays  Dennis Silage

module ns3joysticktest (input CLK, BTNL, BTNR, output JA1, JA2, JA4, input JA3, output JC1, JC2,
                output JC3, JC4, JC7, JC8, JC9, JC10, JD7, JD8, JD9, output [2:0]LED);

wire [7:0] lcddatin;
wire [7:0] lcdd;
wire rslcd, rwlcd, elcd;
wire [1:0] jstkled;
wire [2:0] jstkbutton;
wire [9:0] jstkxdata;
wire [9:0] jstkydata;
wire [3:0] xthoudigit;
wire [3:0] xmsdigit;
wire [3:0] xmiddigit;
wire [3:0] xlsdigit;
wire [3:0] ythoudigit;
wire [3:0] ymsdigit;
wire [3:0] ymiddigit;
wire [3:0] ylsdigit;

assign JA1 = jstkss;
assign JA2 = jstkmosi;
assign jstkmiso = JA3;
assign JA4 = jstksck;
assign JC10 = lcdd[7];
assign JC9 = lcdd[6];
assign JC8 = lcdd[5];
assign JC7 = lcdd[4];
assign JC4 = lcdd[3];
```

Trends in Embedded Design Using Programmable Gate Arrays

```
assign JC3 = lcdd[2];
assign JC2 = lcdd[1];
assign JC1 = lcdd[0];
assign JD7 = rslcd;
assign JD8 = rwlcd;
assign JD9 = elcd;
assign jstkled[0] = BTNL;
assign jstkled[1] = BTNR;
assign LED[0] = jstkbutton[0];
assign LED[1] = jstkbutton[1];
assign LED[2] = jstkbutton[2];


joystick M0 (jstkclk, jstkss, jstkmosi, jstkmiso, jstksck, jstkdav, davjstk, jstkled, jstkbutton,
                jstkxdata, jstkydata);
clplcd M1 (CLK, resetlcd, clearlcd, homelcd, datalcd, addrlcd, cmdlcd, initlcd, lcdreset, lcdclear,
                lcdhome, lcddata, lcdaddr, lcdcmd, rslcd, rwlcd, elcd, lcdd, lcddatin);
checkjstk M2 (jstkxdata, jstkydata, jstkdav, xthoudigit, xmsdigit, xmiddigit, xlsdigit, ythoudigit,
                ymsdigit, ymiddigit, ylsdigit);
genlcd M3 (CLK, jstkdav, davjstk, resetlcd, clearlcd, datalcd, addrlcd, initlcd, lcdreset, lcdclear,
                lcddata, lcdaddr, lcddatin, xthoudigit, xmsdigit, xmiddigit, xlsdigit, ythoudigit, ymsdigit,
                ymiddigit, ylsdigit);
clock M4 (CLK, 1000, jstkclk);        // 50 kHz

endmodule

module genlcd (input CLK, output reg jstkdav = 0, input davjstk, output reg resetlcd = 0,
                output reg clearlcd = 0, output reg datalcd = 0, output reg addrlcd = 0,
                output reg initlcd, input lcdreset, lcdclear, lcddata, lcdaddr, output reg [7:0] lcddatin,
                input [3:0] xthoudigit, input [3:0] xmsdigit, input [3:0] xmiddigit, input [3:0] xlsdigit,
                input [3:0] ythoudigit, input [3:0] ymsdigit, input [3:0] ymiddigit, input [3:0] ylsdigit);

reg [5:0] gstate = 0;

always@(posedge CLK)
     begin
          case (gstate)
               0:   begin
                         initlcd = 1;
                         gstate = 1;
                    end
               1:   begin
                         initlcd = 0;
                         gstate = 2;
                    end
               2:   begin
                         resetlcd = 1;
                         if (lcdreset == 1)
                              begin
                                resetlcd = 0;
                                   gstate = 3;
                              end
                    end
```

```
3:      begin
            initlcd = 1;
            gstate = 4;
        end
4:      begin
            initlcd = 0;
            gstate = 5;
        end
5:      begin
            clearlcd = 1;
            if (lcdclear == 1)
                begin
                    clearlcd = 0;
                    gstate = 6;
                end
        end
6:      begin
            jstkdav = 1;
            if (davjstk == 0)
                gstate = 6;
            else
                begin
                    jstkdav = 0;
                    initlcd = 1;
                    gstate = 7;
                end
        end
7:      begin
            initlcd = 0;
            gstate = 8;
        end
8:      begin              // start address 40h
            lcddatin[7:0] = 8'b01000000;
            addrlcd = 1;
            if (lcdaddr == 1)
                begin
                    addrlcd = 0;
                    gstate = 9;
                end
        end
9:      begin
            initlcd = 1;
            gstate = 10;
        end
10:     begin
            initlcd = 0;
            gstate = 11;
        end
11:     begin
            if (xthoudigit == 0)
                lcddatin = 8'h20;      // ASCII space
            else
```

```
                            lcddatin = 8'h31;      // ASCII '1'
                    datalcd = 1;
                    if (lcddata == 1)
                            begin
                                    datalcd = 0;
                                    gstate = 12;
                            end
            end
12:     begin
                    initlcd = 1;
                    gstate = 13;
            end
13:     begin
                    initlcd = 0;
                    gstate = 14;
            end
14:     begin
                    lcddatin[7:4] = 3;             // ASCII digit 3Xh
                    lcddatin[3:0] = xmsdigit[3:0];
                    datalcd = 1;
                    if (lcddata == 1)
                            begin
                                    datalcd = 0;
                                    gstate = 15;
                            end
            end
15:     begin
                    initlcd = 1;
                    gstate = 16;
            end
16:     begin
                    initlcd = 0;
                    gstate = 17;
            end
17:     begin
                    lcddatin[3:0] = xmiddigit[3:0];
                    datalcd = 1;
                    if (lcddata == 1)
                            begin
                                    datalcd = 0;
                                    gstate = 18;
                            end
            end
18:     begin
                    initlcd = 1;
                    gstate = 19;
            end
19: begin
                    initlcd = 0;
                    gstate = 20;
            end
20:     begin
```

```
                lcddatin[3:0] = xlsdigit[3:0];
                datalcd = 1;
                if (lcddata == 1)
                        begin
                                datalcd = 0;
                                gstate = 21;
                        end
        end
21:     begin
                initlcd = 1;
                gstate = 22;
        end
22:     begin
                initlcd = 0;
                gstate = 23;
        end
23:     begin
                lcddatin[7:0] = 8'h20;              // ASCII space
                datalcd = 1;
                if (lcddata == 1)
                        begin
                                datalcd = 0;
                                gstate = 24;
                        end
        end
24:     begin
                initlcd = 1;
                gstate = 25;
        end
25:     begin
                initlcd = 0;
                gstate = 26;
        end

26:     begin
                if (ythoudigit == 0)
                        lcddatin = 8'h20;      // ASCII space
                else
                        lcddatin = 8'h31;      // ASCII '1'
                datalcd = 1;
                if (lcddata == 1)
                        begin
                                datalcd = 0;
                                gstate = 27;
                        end
        end
27:     begin
                initlcd = 1;
                gstate = 28;
        end
28:     begin
                initlcd = 0;
```

```
                        gstate = 29;
                end
        29:  begin
                lcddatin[7:4] = 3;              // ASCII digit 3Xh
                lcddatin[3:0] = ymsdigit[3:0];
                datalcd = 1;
                if (lcddata == 1)
                        begin
                                datalcd = 0;
                                gstate = 30;
                        end
                end
        30:  begin
                initlcd = 1;
                gstate = 31;
                end
        31:  begin
                initlcd = 0;
                gstate = 32;
                end
        32:  begin
                lcddatin[3:0] = ymiddigit[3:0];
                datalcd = 1;
                if (lcddata == 1)
                        begin
                                datalcd = 0;
                                gstate = 33;
                        end
                end
        33:  begin
                initlcd = 1;
                gstate = 34;
                end
        34:  begin
                initlcd = 0;
                gstate = 35;
                end
        35:  begin
                lcddatin[3:0] = ylsdigit[3:0];
                datalcd = 1;
                if (lcddata == 1)
                        begin
                                datalcd = 0;
                                gstate = 6;
                        end
                end
        default: gstate = 0;
    endcase
  end

endmodule
```

The data available event extracts the joystick 10-bit X-axis and Y-axis data and calculates the corresponding four BCD digits for display on the PmodCLP parallel LCD peripheral in the *genlcd.v* module. The 3-bit joystick button register jstkbutton are continuously assigned to the three LEDs for display.

The behavioral model checks for a number greater than 999 for the thousandths digit (thoudigit) then iteratively subtracts 100 then 10 from the remaining binary number to form the most significant (msdigit), middle (middigit) and least significant (lsdigit) BCD digits. This behavioral model iterative subtraction algorithm is described in Chapter 2 Verilog Design Automation Verilog Design Automation.

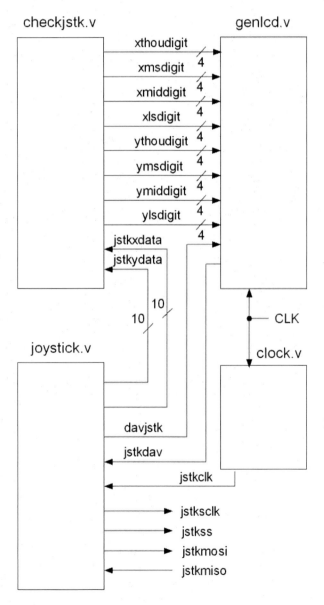

Figure 3.14 Partial controller and datapath modules in the top module *ns3joysticktest.v*

The *clock.v* module from the *Chapter 3\peripherals* folder divides the 100 MHz master clock CLK and outputs the 50 kHz (20 μsec period) joystick SPI clock jstkclk. This clock provides the

Trends in Embedded Design Using Programmable Gate Arrays

adequate delays specified for the slave select signal jstkss (16 μsec) and the transmission of SPI data (10 μsec).

Partial controller and datapath modules in the top module *ns3joysticktest.v* are shown in Figure 3.14. Not shown to reduce the complexity of the Figure are the input and output connections to the *clplcd.v* module from the *genlcd.v* module, which are the same as those in Figure 3.11, and the joystick buttons to the Nexys 3 Board LED and button connections. Note that the controller signals jstkdav, resetlcd, clearlcd, datalcd and addrlcd from the *genlcd.v* module are initialized to logic zero at synthesis.

As described in Chapter 2 Verilog Design Automation Verilog Design Automation, the Design Utilization Summary for the top module *ns3joysticktest.v* shows the use of 189 slice registers (2%) and 632 slice LUTs (6%) in the Nexys 3 Board XC6SLX16 Spartan-6 FPGA synthesis.

A Xilinx ISE project can be configured for the Atlys Board but, because of the availability of only one 12-pin Pmod connector, the PmodCLS serial LCD peripheral would be used instead. Such an ISE project would also utilize a controller for the serial LCD and the substitution of the Atlys Board UCF *atlys.ucf*, as was accomplished for the PS/2 keyboard test demonstrated by the project in the folder *Chapter 3\keyboardtest\atlkeyboardtest* but this is not implemented here.

Digital-to-Analog Converter

A digital-to-analog converter (DAC) provides a step-wise analog output signal from an n-bit binary data input signal for embedded system design in audio processing, analog and digital baseband and bandpass communication and digital process control. The analog output voltage resolution (or step size) ΔV for a DAC that inputs an unsigned n-bit binary values is determined by Equation 3.2.

$$\Delta V = \frac{V_{REF}}{2^n} \qquad (3.2)$$

V_{REF} is the precision DC voltage used as a reference. The maximum rate at which the DAC can accept binary data and update its analog voltage output is its throughput rate R_{DAC} in samples per second. The voltage output V_{OUT} of the DAC is determined by the n-bit binary data input D[n-1:0] and V_{REF}, as given by Equation 3.3.

$$V_{OUT} = \frac{D[n-1:0] \times V_{REF}}{2^n} \ V \qquad (3.3)$$

Pmod DAC

Neither the Nexys 3 Board or the Atlys Board have an integral digital-to-analog converter (DAC). However, the Digilent PmodDA1™, PmodDA2™, PmodDA3™ and Pmod DA4™ are available as an accessory DAC (*www.digilentinc.com*). Each of the Pmod DACs have different specifications, from the PmodDA1 with four channels, each with 8-bits of resolution, the PmodDA2 with two channels, each with 12-bits of resolution, the PmodDA3 with one channel with 16-bits of resolution and to the PmodDA4 with 8 channels, each with 12-bits of resolution.

PmodDA1

The Pmod DA1™ hardware module features two Analog Devices (*www.analog.com*) AD7303 two channel, 8-bit DACs, is referenced in the Digilent document 502-063 (*www.digilentinc.com*) and shown in Figure 3.15. The AD7303 DAC utilizes the serial peripheral interface (SPI) bus protocol with an active low SYNC signal, a SPI bus clock signal SCLK and two data signals DACD0 and DACD1. The SPI protocol is described as one of the serial data link protocols

182

in this Chapter. The DAC SPI data communication protocol begins with the sync signal SYNC set to logic 0.

The rising edge of the SPI bus clock signal SCLK is used to transmit a 16-bit data packet for each of the two AD7303 DAC, with the most significant bit (MSB) of the command, address and data sent first, as listed in Table 3.6. After all 16 bits have been sent, the sync signal SYNC is set to logic 1 whose rising edge starts the actual DAC process.

Figure 3.15 Digilent PmodDA1 module with two, two channel 8-bit DACs

The Pmod DA1DAC is connected to the top 6 pins of the 12-pin peripheral hardware module connector (JA). The SYNC signal is pin JA1, the two input data signals DACD0 and DACD1 are pins JA2 and JA3 and the SPI bus clock signal SCLK is pin JA4. Pins JA5 and JA6 are DC ground and power (VDD = +3.3 V DC). The analog output voltage for the 8-bit DAC is determined by Equation 3.3 with n = 8, D[7:0] ranging from 0 to 255 and V_{REF} = 3.3 V.

Table 3.6 PmodDA1 Analog Devices AD7303 DAC 16-bit data packet

Bits	Description	Contents (MSB…LSB)		
15	Internal (0) or external (1) reference voltage			
14	X (don't care)			
13	Load DAC	LDAC (see Control below)		
12-11	Power-down:	00	Both DAC A and DAC B active	
		01	DAC A powered-down, DAC B active	
		10	DAC A active, DAC B powered-down	
		11	Both DAC A and DAC B powered-down	
10	Address A/B:	0	Select DAC A (see Control below)	
		1	Select DAC B	
8-9	Control	(LDAC A/B)		
		00	0 X	DAC A and DAC B loaded from shift register
		01	0 0	Update DAC A input register from shift register
		01	0 1	Update DAC B input register from shift register
		10	0 0	Update DAC A from input register
		10	0 1	Update DAC B from input register
		11	0 0	Update DAC A from shift register
		11	0 1	Update DAC B from shift register
		XX	1 0	Load DAC A input register from shift register and update both DAC A and DAC B
		XX	1 1	Load DAC B input register from shift register and update both DAC A and DAC B
7-0	Data:	8-bit unsigned DAC data, MSB first		

If the PmodDA1 DAC internal reference voltage is selected with a logic 0 in bit 15 of the data packet, V_{REF} in Equation 3.3 is VDD/2 = 1.65 V DC. The four PmodDA1 DAC unipolar analog output voltages A1, B1, A2 and B2 appear on a 6-pin header at pins 1, 2, 3 and 4.

Trends in Embedded Design Using Programmable Gate Arrays

The module *da1dac.v* for the Pmod DA1 DAC, which is in the *Chapter 3\peripherals* folder, is given in abbreviated form in Listing 3.27. This module is a datapath utilizing a finite state machine (FSM) with the 6-bit state register dacstate and provides signals to the controller and the DAC device, as described in Chapter 1 Verilog Hardware Description Language.

The FSM has 34 states that sequentially inputs the 8-bit DAC command daccmd and the 8-bit DAC data dacdata. Because of this, the module *da1dac.v* is repetitive and the listing is truncated for brevity. The complete Verilog HDL source for this module is available and the file download procedure is described in the Appendix.

Listing 3.27 Datapath module for the PmodDA1 DAC *da1dac.v*

```
// Digital-to-Analog Converter da1dac.v
// c 2012 Embedded Design using Programmable Gate Arrays  Dennis Silage

module da1dac (input dacclk, input dacdav, output reg davdac, output reg dacout,
                output reg dacsck=0, output reg dacsync=0, input [7:0] daccmd, input [7:0] dacdata);

reg [5:0] dacstate = 0;

always@(posedge dacclk)
    begin
        if (dacdav == 0)            // DAC data?
                dacstate = 0;
        else
            begin
                davdac = 0;        // DAC data NAK
                case (dacstate)
                    0:    begin
                              dacsync = 1;
                              dacsck = 0;
                              dacstate = 1;
                          end
                    1:    begin        // DAC command
                              dacsync = 0;
                              dacout = daccmd[7];
                              dacstate = 2;
                          end
                    2:    begin
                              dacsck = 1;
                              dacstate = 3;
                          end
{DAC command bits 6 through 0 are sent similarly in states 3 through 16}
                    17:   begin        // DAC data
                              dacsck = 0;
                              dacout = dacdata[7];
                              dacstate = 18;
                          end
                    18:   begin
                              dacsck = 1;
                              dacstate = 19;
                          end
{DAC data bits 6 through 0 are sent similarly in states 19 through 32}
```

```
          33:  begin
                    dacsync = 1;
                    dacsck = 0;
                    davdac = 1;      // DAC data ACK
                    dacstate = 34;
               end
          34:  dacstate = 34;
          default: dacstate = 34;
        endcase
      end
  end

endmodule
```

The Analog Devices AD7303 DAC of the PmodDA1 hardware module has a maximum SPI clock frequency of 30 MHz, while the master clock oscillator CLK of the Nexys 3 Board or the Atlys Board is 100 MHz. Rather than using the Clock Management Technology (CMT) frequency module of the Xilinx Spartan-6 FPGA to output a 30 MHz clock signal, the 100 MHz master clock oscillator can be simply divided by two by the *clock.v* nested module in the top module. The clockscale parameter of the module *clock.v* is 1, which provides a 50 MHz clock signal, as determined by Equation 3.1.

The resulting 50 MHz clock signal is then divided by two again by the transitions of the FSM to produce a conservative 25 MHz SPI bus clock signal. The 8-bit AD7303 DAC requires a sync signal dacsync for a duration on one FSM transition and a 16-bit data packet to update a single analog output signal, so the approximate maximum throughput data rate R_{DAC} = 25 MHz/(1/2 +16 bits/packet) = 1.515 Msamples/sec

The data available signal dacdav from the controller sets the dacstate register to 0 if it is a logic 0 or activates the FSM on the positive edge of the clock signal dacclk if it is a logic 1. The datapath returns the status signal davdac as a logic 1 to the controller when the process of loading the DAC with a command and data is completed [Ciletti99]. The DAC SPI bus clock is set by the output register variable dacsck and on its positive edge clocks the 8-bit DAC command daccmd and the 8-bit DAC data dacdata as the DAC output signal dacout to either of the two data signals DACD0 and DACD1.

The PmodDA1 DAC datapath module *da1dac.v* is verified by the Verilog top module *ns3da1test.v* for the Nexys 3 Board, which is in the *Chapter 3\DACtest\ns3da1test* folder and is given in Listing 3.28. The file download procedure is described in the Appendix.

The top module file also includes the controller module *gendac.v*. The complete Xilinx ISE project uses *ns3da1test.ucf* that uncomments the signals CLK and JA1 to JA4 in the Nexys 3 Board UCF of Listing 3.1. The three Verilog modules operate in parallel and some independently in the top module. Only the first Analog Devices AD7303 DAC on the PmodDA1 hardware module is used.

The second DAC on the PmodDA1 hardware module can be processed by another *da1dac.v* module in the top module in Listing 3.28 but is not implemented here. The file download procedure is described in the Appendix. A PmodDA1 DAC Xilinx ISE project for the Atlys Board can be configured by replacing the UCF but also not implemented here.

Listing 3.28 Top module for the PmodDA1 DAC *ns3da1test.v*

```
// Nexys 3 Board
// Digital-to-Analog Converter Test ns3da1test.v
// c 2012 Embedded Design using Programmable Gate Arrays  Dennis Silage

module da1test (input CLK, output JA1, JA2, JA3, JA4);
```

```
wire dacdav, davdac, dacout, dacsck, dacsync, dacclk;
wire [7:0] dacdata;
wire [7:0] daccmd;
assign JA1 = dacsync;
assign JA2 = dacout;      // DACD0
assign JA3 = 0;           // DACD1, not used
assign JA4 = dacsck;

da1dac M0 (dacclk, dacdav, davdac, dacout, dacsck, dacsync, daccmd, dacdata);
gendac M1 (CLK, dacdav, davdac, daccmd, dacdata);
clock M2 (CLK, 1, dacclk);      // 25 MHz

endmodule

module gendac (input genclk, output reg dacdav, input davdac, output reg [7:0] daccmd = 19,
                 output reg [7:0] dacdata);

reg [1:0] gstate = 0;        // state register

always@(posedge genclk)
     begin
          case (gstate)
               0:   begin        // generate linear ramp
                         dacdata = dacdata + 1;
                         dacdav = 0;
                         gstate = 1;
                    end
               1:   begin
                         dacdav = 1;
                         gstate = 2;
                    end
               2:   begin
                         if (davdac == 0)
                         gstate = 2;
                    else
                         gstate = 0;
                    end
               default: gstate = 0;
          endcase
     end

endmodule
```

The DAC 8-bit command register daccmd is fixed at 0001 0011 binary or 19 decimal only for the first Analog Devices AD7303 DAC on the PmodDA1 hardware module. This command selects the internal reference, updates DAC A from the input shift register and activates DAC A, as listed in Table 3.6 . The DAC controller module *gendac.v* provides a signal and data to the DAC datapath using an FSM with the 2-bit state register gstate and generates an 8-bit (256 levels) linear ramp.

The direct measurement of the period of the 256 samples in the linear ramp voltage output at the PmodDA1 DAC header A1 is 189 μsec, which indicates that the actual data rate $R_{DAC} = 256/189 \times 10^{-6} \approx 1.354$ Msamples/sec (the maximum throughput data rate is 1.515 Msamples/sec).

As described in Chapter 2 Verilog Design Automation, the Design Utilization Summary for the top module *ns3da1test.v* shows the use of 54 slice registers (<1%) and 128 slice LUTs (≈1%) in the Nexys 3 Board XC6SLX16 Spartan-6 FPGA synthesis. A Xilinx ISE project can be easily configured for the Atlys Board with the substitution of the UCF *atlys.ucf* but is not implemented here.

PmodDA2

The PmodDA2™ hardware module features two National Semiconductor (now part of Texas Instruments, *www.ti.com*) DAC121S101 12-bit DACs, utilizes the SPI protocol described as one of the serial data link protocols in this Chapter, is referenced in the Digilent document 502-113 (*www.digilentinc.com*) and shown in Figure 3.16.

Figure 3.16 Digilent PmodDA2 module with two 12 bit DACs

For the PmodDA2 12-bit DAC the SPI data communication protocol begins with the sync signal SYNC set to logic 0. The falling edge of the SPI bus clock signal SCLK is used to transmit a 16-bit data packet, with the most significant bit (MSB) of the command and data sent first, as listed in Table 3.7. After all 16 bits have been sent, the sync signal SYNC is set to logic 1, whose rising edge starts the actual DAC process.

Table 3.7 PmodDA2 National Semiconductor DAC121S101 DAC 16-bit data packet

Bits	Description	Contents (MSB…LSB)	
15-14	X (don't care)		
13-12	Command:	00	Normal operation
		01	Power-down with 1 kΩ to ground
		10	Power-down with 100 kΩ to ground
		11	Power-down with high impedance to ground
11-0	Data:		12-bit unsigned DAC data, MSB first

The PmodDA2 DAC is connected to the top 6 pins of the 12-pin peripheral hardware module connector (JA). The SYNC signal is pin JA1, the two input data signals DACD0 and DACD1 are pins JA2 and JA3 and the SPI bus clock signal SCLK is pin JA4. Pins JA5 and JA6 are DC ground and power (VDD = +3.3 V DC). The analog output voltage for the 12-bit DAC is determined by Equation 3.3 with n = 12, D[11:0] ranging from 0 to 4095 and V_{REF} = 3.3 V. The two unipolar analog output voltages A and B appear on a 6-pin header at pins 1 and 3 and ground at pin 5.

The module *da2dac.v* for the PmodDA2 DAC, which is in the *Chapter 3\peripherals* folder, is given in abbreviated form in Listing 3.29. The file download procedure is described in the Appendix. This module is a datapath utilizing a finite state machines (FSM) with the 6-bit state register dacstate and provides signals to the controller and the DAC device, as described in Chapter 1 Verilog Hardware Description Language.

The National Semiconductor DAC121S101 of the PmodDA2 hardware module also has a maximum SPI bus clock frequency of 30 MHz, while the crystal clock oscillator of the Nexys 3 Board or the Atlys Board is 100 MHz. As for the PmodDA1 DAC hardware module, rather than using the

Trends in Embedded Design Using Programmable Gate Arrays

DCM frequency synthesizer module to output a 30 MHz clock signal, the 100 MHz crystal clock oscillator can be divided by two by the nested module *clock.v* and by two by the transitions of the FSM to produce a conservative 25 MHz SPI bus clock signal.

Listing 3.29 Datapath module for the PmodDA2 DAC *da2dac.v*

```verilog
// Digital-to-Analog Converter da2dac.v
// c 2012 Embedded Design using Programmable Gate Arrays  Dennis Silage

module da2dac (input dacclk, input dacdav, output reg davdac, output reg dacout, output reg dacsck,
              output reg dacsync, input [1:0] daccmd, input [11:0] dacdata);

reg [5:0] dacstate = 0;

always@(posedge dacclk)
    begin
        if (dacdav == 0)            // DAC data?
            dacstate = 0;
        else
            begin
                davdac = 0;             // DAC data NAK

                case (dacstate)
                    0:  begin
                            dacsync = 1;
                            dacsck = 1;
                            dacstate = 1;
                        end
                    1:  begin
                            dacsync = 0;
                            dacout = 0;      // X don't care
                            dacstate = 2;
                        end
                    2:  begin
                            dacsck = 0;
                            dacstate = 3;
                        end
                    3:  begin
                            dacsck = 1;
                            dacout = 0;      // X don't care
                            dacstate = 4;
                        end
                    4:  begin
                            dacsck = 0;
                            dacstate = 5;
                        end
                    5:  begin
                            dacsck = 1;
                            dacout = daccmd[1];
                            dacstate = 6;
                        end
                    6:  begin
```

```
                                        dacsck = 0;
                                        dacstate = 7;
                              end
                  7:    begin
                                        dacsck = 1;
                                        dacout = daccmd[0];
                                        dacstate = 8;
                              end
                  8:    begin
                                        dacsck = 0;
                                        dacstate = 9;
                              end
                  9:    begin
                                        dacsck = 1;
                                        dacout = dacdata[11];
                                        dacstate = 10;
                              end
                  10:   begin
                                        dacsck = 0;
                                        dacstate = 11;
                              end
{DAC data bits 10 through 0 are sent similarly in states 11 through 32}
                  33:   begin
                                        dacsync = 1;
                                        dacsck = 1;
                                        davdac = 1;        // DAC data ACK
                                        dacstate = 34;
                              end
                  34:   dacstate = 34;
                  default: dacstate = 34;
              endcase
          end
      end

endmodule
```

The DAC121S101 also requires a sync signal dacsync for a duration on one FSM transition (1/2) and a 16-bit data packet for 12-bit binary data to update a single analog output signal. The approximate maximum throughput data rate is then the same as the PmodDA1 8-bit DAC with R_{DAC} = 25 MHz / (1/2 + 16 bits/packet) = 1.515 Msamples/sec.

The data available signal dacdav from the controller sets the dacstate register to 0 if it is a logic 0 or activates the FSM on the positive edge of the clock signal (dacclk) if it is a logic 1. The datapath returns the status signal davdac as a logic 1 to the controller when the process of loading the DAC with a command and data is completed. The DAC SPI bus clock is set by the output register variable dacsck and on its negative edge clocks the 2-bit DAC command daccmd and the 12-bit DAC data dacdata as the DAC output signal dacout to either of the two data signals DACD0 and DACD1.

The PmodDA2 DAC datapath module *da2dac.v* is verified by the Verilog top module *ns3da2test.v*, which is in the *Chapter 3\DACtest\ns3da2test* folder. The top module *ns3da2test.v* is similar to the *ns3da1test.v* top module for the Pmod DA1 in Listing 3.28 and is not given here. The top module file also includes the controller module *gendac.v*. The complete Xilinx ISE project uses *ns3da2test.ucf* that uncomments the signals CLK, JA1 to JA4 in the Nexys 3 Board UCF of Listing

Trends in Embedded Design Using Programmable Gate Arrays

3.1. A PmodDA2 DAC Xilinx ISE project for the Atlys Board can be configured by replacing the UCF but is not implemented here.

The DAC 2-bit command daccmd is 00 binary which selects normal operation, as listed in Table 3.7. The DAC controller module *gendac.v* provides a signal and data to the DAC datapath using an FSM with the 2-bit state register gstate and generates an 12-bit (4096 level) linear ramp. The direct measurement of the period of the 4096 samples in the linear ramp voltage output at the PmodDA2 DAC header A is 3.03 msec, which indicates that the actual data rate $R_{DAC} = 4096/3.03 \times 10^{-3} \approx 1.352$ Msamples/sec (the maximum throughput data rate is 1.515 Msamples/sec).

As described in Chapter 2 Verilog Design Automation, the Design Utilization Summary for the top module *ns3da2test.v* shows the use of 58 slice registers (<1%) and 139 slice LUTs ($\approx$1%) in the Nexys 3 Board XC6SLX16 Spartan-6 FPGA synthesis. A Xilinx ISE project can be easily configured for the Atlys Board with the substitution of the UCF *atlys.ucf* but is not implemented here.

The second National Semiconductor DAC121S101 device on the PmodDA2 hardware module can be processed by a datapath module that produces coincident signals for the two data signals DACD0 and DACD1. This *da2dac2.v* module for the PmodDA2 DAC using two channels is similar to the *da2dac.v* module in Listing 3.29 and is in the *\Chapter 3\peripherals* folder. The direct measurement of the period of the 4096 samples in the two concurrent linear ramp voltage outputs at the DAC header A and B remains 3.03 msec, which indicates that the actual data rate $R_{DAC} \approx 1.352$ Msamples/sec for two concurrent channels of operation.

The parallel operation of the Verilog HDL FSM results in efficiency for digital signal processing, digital communications and digital control in embedded designs, as described in Chapter 2 Verilog Design Automation. Complete Xilinx ISE projects further illustrating the concept are described in Chapter 4 Digital Signal Processing, Communications and Control.

PmodDA3

The PmodDA3™ hardware module features an Analog Devices (*www.analog.com*) AD5541A 16-bit DAC, utilizes the SPI protocol described as one of the serial data link protocols in this Chapter, is referenced in the Digilent document 502-241 (*www.digilentinc.com*) and shown in Figure 3.17. Since the PmodDA3 only has one channel, there is no command register or the overhead of the command data transfer to the DAC.

For the PmodDA3 16-bit DAC the SPI data communication protocol begins with the chip select signal CS set to logic 0. The rising edge of the SPI bus clock signal SCLK is used to transmit a 16-bit data packet into the shift register of the DAC. If the load DAC signal LDAC is logic 0 the rising edge of CS transfer the 16-bit data packet from the shift register to the DAC output register. If LDAC is logic 1 no data transfer occurs. LDAC can be used to asynchronously load the DAC output register from the shift register.

Figure 3.17 Digilent PmodDA3 module with a 16 bit DAC

The PmodDA3 DAC is connected to the top 6 pins of the 12-pin peripheral hardware module connector (JA). The chip select signal CS is pin JA1, the input data signal DACDIN is pin JA3, the load DAC signal LDAC is pin JA3 and the SPI bus clock signal SCLK is pin JA4. Pins JA5 and JA6 are DC ground and power (VDD = +3.3 V DC). The analog output voltage for the 16-bit DAC is determined by Equation 3.3 with n = 16, D[15:0] ranging from 0 to 65535 and V_{REF} = 2.5 V. The unipolar analog output voltage appears on the SMA connector.

The module *da3dac.v* for the PmodDA3 DAC, which is in the *Chapter 3\peripherals* folder, is given in abbreviated form in Listing 3.30. The file download procedure is described in the Appendix. This module is a datapath utilizing a finite state machines (FSM) with the 6-bit state register dacstate and provides signals to the controller and the DAC device, as described in Chapter 1 Verilog Hardware Description Language.

The Analog Devices AD5541A of the PmodDA3 hardware module has a maximum SPI bus clock frequency of 50 MHz. The crystal clock oscillator of the Nexys 3 Board or the Atlys Board is 100 MHz which are be divided by the transitions of the FSM to produce a 50 MHz SPI bus clock signal dassck.

The AD5541A DAC requires a chip select signal daccs for a duration on one FSM transition and a 16-bit data packet for 16-bit binary data to update the analog output signal. The approximate maximum throughput data rate R_{DAC} = 50 MHz/16 bits/packet = 3.125 Msamples/sec.

Listing 3.30 Datapath module for the PmodDA3 DAC *da3dac.v*

```
// Digital-to-Analog Converter da3dac.v
// c 2012 Embedded Design using Programmable Gate Arrays  Dennis Silage

module da3dac(input dacclk, input dacdav, output reg davdac, output reg dacout,
              output reg dacsck = 0, output reg daccs = 1, output reg dacld = 0,
              input [15:0] dacdata);

reg [5:0] dacstate = 0;

always@(posedge dacclk)
    begin
        if (dacdav == 0)             // DAC data?
            begin
                dacstate = 0;
                daccs = 1;
                dacsck = 0;
                davdac = 0;          // DAC data NAK
            end

        if (dacdav == 1 && davdac == 0)
            begin
                case (dacstate)
                0:   begin
                        daccs = 0;
                        dacsck = 0;
                        dacout = dacdata[15];
                        dacstate = 1;
                     end
                1:   begin
                        dacsck = 1;
                        dacstate = 2;
                     end
{DAC data bits 14 through 0 are sent similarly in states 2 through 31}
                32:  begin
                        daccs = 1;
```

```
                        dacsck = 0;
                        davdac = 1;        // DAC data ACK
                        dacstate = 33;
                  end
            33:   dacstate = 34;
            default: dacstate = 33;
      endcase
   end
end

endmodule
```

The data available signal dacdav from the controller sets the dacstate register to 0 if it is a logic 0 or activates the FSM on the positive edge of the clock signal (dacclk) if it is a logic 1. The datapath returns the status signal davdac as a logic 1 to the controller when the process of loading the DAC with data is completed.

The PmodDA3 DAC datapath module *da3dac.v* is verified by the Verilog top module *ns3da3test.v*, which is in the *Chapter 3\DACtest\ns3da3test* folder. The top module *ns3da3test.v* is similar to the *ns3da1test.v* top module for the PmodDA1 in Listing 3.28 and is not given here. The clock divider module *clock.v* for the SPI bus clock is also not used here.

The top module file *ns3da3test.v* also includes the controller module *gendac.v*. The complete Xilinx ISE project uses *ns3da3test.ucf* that uncomments the signals CLK, JA1 to JA4 in the Nexys 3 Board UCF of Listing 3.1. A PmodDA3 DAC Xilinx ISE project for the Atlys Board can be configured by replacing the UCF but is not implemented here.

The DAC controller module *gendac.v* provides a signal and data to the DAC datapath using an FSM with the 2-bit state register gstate and generates a 16-bit (65 536 level) linear ramp. The direct measurement of the period of the 65 536 samples in the linear ramp voltage output at the PmodDA3 is 23.7 msec, which indicates that the actual data rate R_{DAC} = 65 536/23.7 × 10^{-3} ≈ 2.765 Msamples/sec (the maximum throughput data rate is 3.125 Msamples/sec).

As described in Chapter 2 Verilog Design Automation, the Design Utilization Summary for the top module ns3*da3test.v* shows the use of 31 slice registers (<1%) and 49 slice LUTs (<1%) in the Nexys 3 Board XC6SLX16 Spartan-6 FPGA synthesis. A Xilinx ISE project can be easily configured for the Atlys Board with the substitution of the UCF *atlys.ucf* but is not implemented here.

PmodDA4

The PmodDA4™ hardware module features an Analog Devices (*www.analog.com*) AD5628 8 channel, 12-bit DAC, utilizes the SPI protocol described as one of the serial data link protocols in this Chapter, is referenced in the Digilent document 502-245 (*www.digilentinc.com*) and is shown in Figure 3.18.

Figure 3.18 Digilent PmodDA4 module with an 8 channel, 12 bit DAC

For the PmodDA4 8 channel, 12-bit DAC the SPI data communication protocol begins with the sync signal SYNC set to logic 0. The falling edge of the SPI bus clock signal SCLK is used to transmit a 32-bit data packet, with the most significant bit (MSB) of the command, address and data sent first, as listed in Table 3.8. After all 32 bits have been sent the DAC process starts and the sync signal SYNC is reset to logic 1.

Table 3.8 PmodDA4 Analog Devices AD5628 DAC 32-bit data packet

Bits	Description	Contents (MSB…LSB)	
31-28	X (don't care)		
27-24	Command:	0000	Write to DAC input register N
		0001	Update DAC register N
		0010	Write to DAC input register N, update all registers
		0011	Write to and update DAC input register N and DAC register N
		0100	Power down/power up DAC
		0101	Load clear code register
		0110	Load LDAC register
		0111	Reset
		1000	Set up internal REF register
23-20	Address:	0000	DAC A
		0001	DAC B
		0010	DAC C
		0011	DAC D
		0100	DAC E
		0101	DAC F
		0110	DAC G
		0111	DAC H
		1111	All DACs
19-8	Data:		12-bit unsigned DAC data, MSB first
7-0	X (don't care)/Auxillary		

The PmodDA4 DAC is connected to the top 6 pins of the 12-pin peripheral hardware module connector (JA). The SYNC signal is pin JA1, the input data signal DIN is pin JA2 and the SPI bus clock signal SCLK is pin JA4. Pin JA3 is not connected and pins JA5 and JA6 are DC ground and power (VDD = +3.3 V DC). The analog output voltage for the 12-bit DAC is determined by Equation 3.3 with n = 12, D[11:0] ranging from 0 to 4095 and V_{REF} = 2.5 V. The eight unipolar analog output voltages appear on a 12-pin header at pins 1 through 8 and ground at pins 9 and 10.

The module *da4dac.v* for the PmodDA4 DAC, which is in the *Chapter 3\peripherals* folder, is given in abbreviated form in Listing 3.31. The file download procedure is described in the Appendix. This module is a datapath utilizing a finite state machines (FSM) with the 7-bit state register dacstate and provides signals to the controller and the DAC device, as described in Chapter 1 Verilog Hardware Description Language.

The Analog Devices AD5628 of the PmodDA4 hardware module has a maximum SPI bus clock frequency of 50 MHz. The crystal clock oscillator of the Nexys 3 Board or the Atlys Board is 100 MHz which are be divided by the transitions of the FSM to produce a 50 MHz SPI bus clock signal dassck.

The AD5628 DAC requires a chip select signal dacsync and a 32-bit data packet for 12-bit binary data to control the DAC and update the analog output signal. The maximum throughput data rate R_{DAC} = 50 MHz/32 bits/packet = 1.5625 Msamples/sec.

Trends in Embedded Design Using Programmable Gate Arrays

Listing 3.31 Datapath module for the PmodDA4 DAC *da4dac.v*

```verilog
// Digital-to-Analog Converter da4dac.v
// c 2012 Embedded Design using Programmable Gate Arrays  Dennis Silage

module da4dac (input dacclk, input dacdav, output reg davdac, output reg dacout,
               output reg dacsck = 1, output reg dacsync = 1, input [3:0] daccmd,
               input [3:0] dacaddr, input [11:0] dacdata, input [7:0] dacaux);
reg [6:0] dacstate = 0;

always@(posedge dacclk)
    begin
        if (dacdav == 0)            // DAC data?
            begin
                dacstate = 0;
                davdac = 0;          // DAC data NAK
            end

        if (dacdav == 1 && davdac == 0)
            begin
                case (dacstate)
                0:  begin
                        dacsync = 1;
                        dacsck = 1;
                        dacstate = 1;
                    end
                1:  begin
                        dacsync = 0;
                        dacout = 0;      // X1 don't care
                        dacstate = 2;
                    end
                2:  begin
                        dacsck = 0;
                        dacstate = 3;
                    end
{DAC don't care, bits 30 through 28 are sent similarly in states 3 through 8}
                9:  begin
                        dacsck = 1;
                        dacout = daccmd[3];
                        dacstate = 10;
                    end
                10: begin
                        dacsck = 0;
                        dacstate = 11;
                    end
{DAC command bits 2 through 0 are sent similarly in states 11 through 16}
                17: begin
                        dacsck = 1;
                        dacout = dacaddr[3];
                        dacstate = 18;
                    end
                18: begin
```

```
                        dacsck = 0;
                        dacstate = 19;
                end
{DAC address bits 2 through 0 are sent similarly in states 19 through 24}
        25:   begin
                        dacsck = 1;
                        dacout = dacdata[11];
                        dacstate = 26;
                end
        26:   begin
                        dacsck = 0;
                        dacstate = 27;
                end
{DAC data bits 10 through 0 are sent similarly in states 27 through 48}
        49:   begin
                        dacsck = 1;
                        dacout = dacaux[7];
                        dacstate = 50;
                end
        50:   begin
                        dacsck = 0;
                        dacstate = 51;
                end
{DAC auxillary bits 6 through 0 are sent similarly in states 51 through 64}
        65:   begin
                        dacsck = 1;
                        dacstate = 66;
                end
        66:   begin
                        dacsync = 1;
                        davdac = 1;            // DAC data ACK
                        dacstate = 67;
                end
        67:   dacstate = 67;
        default: dacstate = 67;
        endcase
   end
end

endmodule
```

The 32-bit data packet consists of the most significant 4 bits as don't care bits but the 8 least significant bits are either don't care bits or are used to control the DAC as auxillary bits for enabling the internal reference voltage or normal operation, as listed in Table 3.9 and Table 3.10. Additional command packets are available to set or clear the DAC or simultaneously update the DAC contents of selected channels as described in the data sheet for the AD5628 device (*www.analog.com*).

The data available signal dacdav from the controller sets the dacstate register to 0 if it is a logic 0 or activates the FSM on the positive edge of the clock signal (dacclk) if it is a logic 1. The datapath returns the status signal davdac as a logic 1 to the controller when the process of loading the DAC with data is completed.

The PmodDA4 DAC datapath module *da4dac.v* is verified by the Verilog top module *ns3da4test.v*, which is in the *Chapter 3\DACtest\ns3da4test* folder and given in Listing 3.32. The top

Trends in Embedded Design Using Programmable Gate Arrays

module file *ns3da4test.v* also includes the controller module *gendac.v*. The complete Xilinx ISE project uses *ns3da4test.ucf* that uncomments the signals CLK, JA1, JA2 and JA4 in the Nexys 3 Board UCF of Listing 3.1. A PmodDA4 DAC Xilinx ISE project for the Atlys Board can be configured by replacing the UCF but is not implemented here.

  The DAC controller module *gendac.v* enables the internal reference for the DAC, as listed in Table 3.9, since the power on default disables it. The controller module also selects DAC A for normal operation and disables the seven remaining DAC channels, as listed in Table 3.10.

  The DAC controller module *gendac.v* provides a signal and data to the DAC datapath using an FSM with the 3-bit state register gstate and generates a 12-bit (4096 level) linear ramp. The direct measurement of the period of the 4096 samples in the linear ramp voltage output at the PmodDA4 is 2.86 msec, which indicates that the actual data rate $R_{DAC} = 4096/2.86 \times 10^{-3} \approx 1.432$ Msamples/sec (the maximum throughput data rate is 1.5625 Msamples/sec).

Table 3.9 PmodDA4 Analog Devices AD5628 DAC 32-bit reference set-up command packet

Bits	Contents (MSB…LSB)		
31-28	X (don't care)		
27-24	Command:	1000	Set up internal REF register
23-1	X (don't care)		
0	Reference:	1/0	REF register on/off

Table 3.10 PmodDA4 Analog Devices AD5628 DAC 32-bit power/up/down command packet

Bits	Contents (MSB…LSB)		
31-28	X (don't care)		
27-24	Command:	0100	Power down/power up DAC
23-10	X (don't care)		
9-8	Power:	00	Normal operation
		01	Power down, 1 kΩ to ground
		10	Power down, 100 kΩ to ground
		11	Power down, high impedance
7-0	Select DAC:	HGFEDCBA	

Listing 3.32 Top module for the PmodDA4 DAC *ns3da4test.v*

```
// Nexys 3 Board
// Digital-to-Analog Converter ns3da4test.v
// c 2012 Embedded Design using Programmable Gate Arrays  Dennis Silage

module ns3da4test (input CLK, output JA1, JA2, JA4);

wire dacdav, davdac, dacout, dacsck, dacsync, dacclk;
wire [11:0] dacdata;
wire [3:0] daccmd;
wire [3:0] dacaddr;
wire [7:0] dacaux;

assign JA1 = dacsync;
assign JA2 = dacout;
assign JA4 = dacsck;
```

```
da4dac M0 (CLK, dacdav, davdac, dacout, dacsck, dacsync, daccmd, dacaddr, dacdata,
          dacaux);
gendac M1 (CLK, dacdav, davdac, daccmd, dacaddr, dacdata, dacaux);

endmodule

module gendac(input genclk, output reg dacdav = 0, input davdac, output reg [3:0] daccmd = 0,
          output reg [3:0] dacaddr = 0, output reg [11:0] dacdata = 0,
          output reg [7:0] dacaux = 0);

reg [2:0] gstate = 0;          // state register

always@(posedge genclk)
    begin
         case (gstate)
         0:    begin
                    daccmd = 8;      // 1000
                    dacaddr = 0;     // xxxx don't care
                    dacdata = 0;
                    dacaux = 1;      // internal reference ON
                    dacdav = 1;
                    gstate = 1;
              end
         1:    begin
                    if (davdac == 1)
                         begin
                              dacdav = 0;
                              gstate = 2;
                         end
              end
         2:    begin
                    if (davdac == 0)
                         begin
                              daccmd = 4;      // 0100
                              dacaddr = 0;     // xxxx don't care
                              dacdata = 0;     // LSBs 00 normal operation
                              dacaux = 1;      // select DAC A
                              dacdav = 1;
                              gstate = 3;
                         end
              end
         3:    begin
                    if (davdac == 1)
                         begin
                              dacdav = 0;
                              gstate = 4;
                         end
              end
         4:    begin
                    if (davdac == 0)
                         begin
```

```
                            dacaux = 0;
                            daccmd = 3;      // write to and update DAC N
                            dacaddr = 15;    // DAC A
                            dacdata = 0;
                            gstate = 5;
                    end
            end
    5:    begin
                    dacdata = dacdata + 1;
                    dacdav = 1;
                    gstate = 6;
            end
    6:    begin
                    if (davdac == 1)
                            begin
                                    dacdav = 0;
                                    gstate = 5;
                            end
            end
        default: gstate = 0;
    endcase
end

endmodule
```

As described in Chapter 2 Verilog Design Automation, the Design Utilization Summary for the top module ns3*da4test.v* shows the use of 30 slice registers (<1%) and 63 slice LUTs (<1%) in the Nexys 3 Board XC6SLX16 Spartan-6 FPGA synthesis. A Xilinx ISE project can be easily configured for the Atlys Board with the substitution of the UCF *atlys.ucf* but is not implemented here.

Analog-to-Digital Converter

An analog-to-digital converter (ADC) provides a discrete, sampled binary data output signal from a continuous analog input signal for embedded system design in audio processing, analog and digital baseband and bandpass communication and digital process control. The n-bit binary data output D[n-1:0] for the ADC that inputs a unipolar (only positive amplitude) analog signal is determined by Equation 3.4.

$$D[n-1:0] = G \frac{V_{IN} - V_{REF}}{V_{FS}} 2^{n-1} \qquad (3.4)$$

In Equation 3.4 G is the gain of any analog preamplifier that precedes the ADC, V_{REF} is the common reference voltage of the analog preamplifier and ADC, V_{FS} is the full-scale conversion voltage for the ADC, V_{IN} is the polar analog signal input at the input of the analog preamplifier and n is the number of bits of resolution.

Since V_{IN} could be less than V_{REF}, the n-bit binary data output D[n-1:0] is in two's complement format with the most significant bit (MSB) representing the sign bit and a number whose integer value is between -2^{n-1} and $2^{n-1} - 1$ [Wakerly00]. An external analog preamplifier can also support the function of the ADC in an embedded design by providing a differential to single-ended signal interface, significant gain for an analog transducer or an anti-aliasing filter for discrete data sampling. The maximum rate at which the ADC can sample an analog signal and produce n-bit binary data is its throughput rate R_{ADC} in samples per second.

Pmod ADC

Neither the Nexys 3 Board or the Atlys Board have an integral analog-to-digital converter (ADC). However, the Digilent PmodAD1™ and PmodAD2™ are available as an accessory ADC (*www.digilentinc.com*). Each of the Pmod ADCs have different specifications. The PmodAD1 uses a serial peripheral interface (SPI) bus interface and has two channels, each with 12-bits of resolution. The PmodAD2 uses an inter-integrated circuit (I2C) bus interface and has up to four channels, each with 12-bits of resolution.

PmodAD1

The PmodAD1™ hardware module features two National Semiconductor (now part of Texas Instruments, *www.ti.com*) ADCS7476 12-bit ADCs, utilize the SPI bus protocol described as one of the serial data link protocols in this Chapter, is referenced in the Digilent document 502-064 (*www.digilentinc.com*) and is shown in Figure 3.19.

The ADCs use an active low ADCCS signal and an SPI bus clock signal SCLK and output two data signals ADCD0 and ADCD1. The ADC SPI data communication protocol begins with the chip select signal ADCCS set to logic 0 which initiates analog data conversion.

Figure 3.19 Digilent PmodAD1 module with two 12-bit ADCs

The PmodAD1 ADCD7476 ADC uses the falling edge of the SPI clock signal SCLK to transmit a 16-bit data packet, with the first four bits as don't care bits and the most significant bit (MSB) of the data sent first, as listed in Table 3.11. After all 16 bits have been sent, the chip select signal ADCCS is set to logic 1.

Table 3.11 PmodAD1 National Semiconductor ADCS7476 ADC 16-bit data packet

Bits	Contents (MSB…LSB)
15-12	X (don't care)
11-0	ADC channel data

The PmodAD1 ADC is connected to the top 6 pins of a 12-pin peripheral hardware module connector (JA). The chip select signal ADCCS is pin JA1, the two output data signals ADCD0 and ADCD1 are pins JA2 and JA3 and the SPI bus clock signal SCLK is pin JA4. Pins JA5 and JA6 are DC ground and power (VDD = +3.3 V DC).

The n-bit binary data output D[n–1:0] for the ADC that inputs a unipolar (only positive amplitude) analog signal is determined by Equation 3.4, where the gain G = 1, V_{REF} = 0, V_{FS} = +3.3 V DC, V_{IN} is the analog signal input and n = 12 here. The range of the analog input signal is then $0 \leq V_{IN} \leq +3.3$ V and the 12-bit data output D[11:0] is in unsigned binary format with an integer value between 0 and 4095 [Wakerly00].

The analog inputs are on pin 1 (ADC0) and pin 3 (ADC1) and signal ground is on pins 2, 4 and 5 of the 6-pin external signal connector. Pin 6 is VDD. A two-pole Sallen-Key (−12 dB/octave) anti-aliasing filter on each of the analog input signals have a −3 dB cutoff frequency of 500 kHz.

Trends in Embedded Design Using Programmable Gate Arrays

The module *ad1adc.v* for the PmodAD1 ADC, which is in the *Chapter 3\peripherals* folder, is given in Listing 3.33. The file download procedure is described in the Appendix. This module is a datapath utilizing a finite state machine (FSM) with the 6-bit state register adcstate and provides signals to the controller and the ADC device, as described in Chapter 1 Verilog Hardware Description Language.

The National Semiconductor ASCS7476 ADC has a specified maximum SPI bus clock frequency of approximately 20 MHz and the master clock oscillators CLK of the Nexys 3 Board and the Atlys Board are 100 MHz. Rather than using the Clock Management Technology (CMT) frequency module of the Xilinx Spartan-6 FPGA to output a 20 MHz clock signal, the 100 MHz master clock oscillator can be simply divided by four by the *clock.v* nested module in the top module. The clockscale parameter of the module *clock.v* is 2, which provides a 25 MHz clock signal adcclk, as determined by Equation 3.1.

The transitions of the FSM in the ADC datapath module *ad1adc.v* further divide the clock signal by two to produce a 12.5 MHz ADC SPI bus clock, which is conservative but produces reliable ADC data here. The ADC uses a logic 0 chip select signal adccs for the conversion command.

A 16-bit data packet is used to convert two analog input signals to 12-bits of resolution, so the approximate maximum throughput data rate R_{ADC} = 12.5 MHz /16 bits/packet = 0.781 Msamples/sec, while the data rate with a 20 MHz SPI bus clock is 1.25 Msamples/sec. Note that the anti-aliasing filter of the PmodAD1 with a −3 dB cutoff frequency of 500 kHz implies that the sampling rate should be no more than 1 Msamples/sec, as described in Chapter 4 Digital Signal Processing, Communications and Control.

Listing 3.33 Datapath module for the PmodAD1 ADC *ad1adc.v*

```
// Analog-to-Digital Converter ad1adc.v
// c 2012 Embedded Design using Programmable Gate Arrays  Dennis Silage

module ad1adc (input adcclk, adcdav, output reg davadc, output reg [11:0] adc0data,
                output reg [11:0] adc1data, output reg adcsck, input adc0d, adc1d, output reg adccs);

reg [5:0] adcstate;
reg adcclk;

always@(posedge adcclk)
    begin
        if (adcdav == 0)
            begin
                adcstate = 0;
                adcsck = 1;
                adccs = 1;
                davadc = 0;       // ADC data NAK
            end

        if (adcdav == 1 && davadc == 0)
            begin
                case (adcstate)
                0:    begin
                            adccs = 0;        // ADC chip select
                            adcsck = 1;
                            adcstate = 1;
                      end
                1:    begin
```

```
                           adcsck = 0;        // 1  X
                           adcstate = 2;
                  end
          2:      begin
                           adcsck = 1;
                           adcstate = 3;
                  end
```
{ADC don't care data bits 14 through 12 are sent similarly in states 3 through 8}
```
          9:      begin
                           adcsck = 0;
                           adc0data[11] = adc0d;
                           adc1data[11] = adc1d;
                           adcstate = 10;
                  end
          10:     begin
                           adcsck = 1;
                           adcstate = 11;
                  end
```
{ADC channels 0 and 1 data bits 10 through 0 are sent similarly in states 10 through 32}
```
          33:     begin
                           adccs = 1;
                           davadc = 1;
                           adcstate = 34;
                  end
          34:     adcstate = 34;
          default: adcstate = 34;
      endcase
    end
  end

endmodule
```

The data available signal adcdav from the controller sets the adcstate register to 0 if it is a logic 0 or activates the FSM if it and the datapath signal davdac is logic 0. The data is transmitted on the falling edge of the SPI bus clock adcsck. The datapath returns the status signal davadc as a logic 1 to the controller when the process of analog conversion and the output of the data is completed. The ADC chip select signal is controlled by the module output register variable adccs.

The PmodAD1 ADC datapath module *ad1adc.v* is verified by the Verilog top module *ns3ad1test.v*, which is given in Listing 3.34. The top module *ns3ad1test.v* includes the controller module *genad1adc.v*.

Listing 3.34 Top module for the PmodAD1 ADC *ns3ad1test.v*

```
// Nexys 3 Board
// Analog-to-Digital Converter ns3ad1test.v
// c 2012 Embedded Design using Programmable Gate Arrays  Dennis Silage

module ns3ad1test(input CLK, BTND, SW0, output JC1, JC2, JC3, JC4, JC7, JC8, JC9, JC10, JD7,
                output JD8, JD9, JA1, JA4, input JA2, JA3);
wire [7:0] lcddatin;
wire [7:0] lcdd;
wire rslcd, rwlcd, elcd, adcdav, davadc, adcsck, adccs;
```

```
wire adc0d, adc1d, resetlcd, clearlcd, homelcd, datalcd, addrlcd;
wire initlcd, lcdreset, lcdclear, lcdhome, lcddata, lcdaddr;
wire [11:0] adc0data, adc1data;
wire [3:0] data;
wire [1:0] digitmux;

assign JC10 = lcdd[7];
assign JC9 = lcdd[6];
assign JC8 = lcdd[5];
assign JC7 = lcdd[4];
assign JC4 = lcdd[3];
assign JC3 = lcdd[2];
assign JC2 = lcdd[1];
assign JC1 = lcdd[0];
assign JD7 = rslcd;
assign JD8 = rwlcd;
assign JD9 = elcd;
assign JA1 = adccs;
assign adc0d = JA2;
assign adc1d = JA3;
assign JA4 = adcsck;

ad1adc M0 (adcclk, adcdav, davadc, adc0data, adc1data, adcsck, adc0d, adc1d, adccs);
adclcd M1 (CLK, BTND, resetlcd, clearlcd, homelcd, datalcd, addrlcd, initlcd, lcdreset, lcdclear,
          lcdhome, lcddata, lcdaddr, lcddatin, digitmux, data);
clplcd M2 (CLK, resetlcd, clearlcd, homelcd, datalcd, addrlcd, cmdlcd, initlcd, lcdreset, lcdclear,
          lcdhome, lcddata, lcdaddr, lcdcmd, rslcd, rwlcd, elcd, lcdd, lcddatin);
genad1adc M3 (CLK, SW0, adcdav, davadc, adc0data, adc1data, digitmux, data);
clock M4 (CLK, 2, adcclk);          // 25 MHz

endmodule

module genad1adc(input genclk, SW0, output reg adcdav=0, input davadc, input [11:0] adc0data,
                input [11:0] adc1data, input [1:0] digitmux, output reg [3:0] data);

reg gstate;            // state register
reg [3:0] adc4;        // ADC value BCD digits
reg [3:0] adc3;
reg [3:0] adc2;
reg [3:0] adc1;
reg [11:0] value;      // ADC value

integer i;

always@(digitmux)          // LCD digit mux
    begin
         case (digitmux)
         0:    data = adc4;
         1:    data = adc3;
         2:    data = adc2;
         3:    data = adc1;
         endcase
```

```
        end

always@(posedge genclk)
      begin
          case (gstate)
          0:    begin
                    adcdav = 1;              // ADC conversion
                    if (davadc == 1)
                          begin
                          adcdav = 0;
                          gstate = 1;
                    end
                end
          1:    begin
                    if (SW0 == 1)            // ADC channel 0/1
                          value = adc1data;
                    else
                          value = adc0data;

                    adc1 = 0;                // thousands digit
                    for (i = 1; i <= 9; i = i + 1)
                          begin
                              if (value >= 1000)
                                    begin
                                        adc1 = adc1 + 1;
                                        value = value − 1000;
                                    end
                          end

                    adc2 = 0;                // hundreds digit
                    for (i = 1; i <= 9; i = i + 1)
                          begin
                              if (value >= 100)
                                    begin
                                        adc2 = adc2 + 1;
                                        value = value − 100;
                                    end
                          end

                    adc3 = 0;                // tens digit
                    for (i = 1; i <= 9; i = i + 1)
                          begin
                              if (value >= 10)
                                    begin
                                        adc3 = adc3 + 1;
                                        value = value − 10;
                                    end
                          end

                    adc4 = value[3:0];    // units digit
                    gstate = 0;
                end
```

```
            endcase
        end

endmodule
```

The complete Xilinx ISE project is in the *Chapter 3\ADCtest\ns3ad1test* folder and uses *ns3ad1test.ucf* that uncomments the signals CLK, BTND, SW0, JA1 to JA4, JC1 to JC4, JC7 to JC10 and JD7 to JD9 in the Nexys 3 Board UCF of Listing 3.1. Note that the switch is initially given as array of eight switches (SW<n>) in the Nexys 3 Board UCF but is edited in *ns3ad1test.ucf* to be a single switch SW0. The file download procedure is described in the Appendix.

The slide switch SW0 selects one of the 12-bt straight binary numbers adc0data or adc1data, which is then converted to a four digit binary coded decimal (BCD) number adc1, adc2, adc3, and adc4. The 12-bit register value is used to manipulate the 12-bit input binary numbers adc0data or adc1data which cannot be modified since they are inputs. The BCD digits are calculated by the successive subtraction algorithm, as described in Chapter 2 Verilog Design Automation.

The five Verilog modules operate in parallel and some independently in the top module *ns3ad1test.v* in Listing 3.33. However, to reduce the complexity of the configuration of the controllers and datapaths in Figure 3.20, the *clplcd.v* module and its interconnections are not shown.

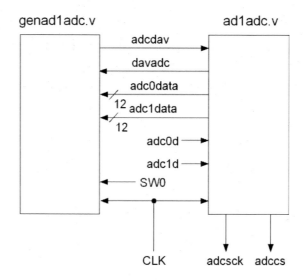

Figure 3.20 Partial controller and datapath modules for the top module *ns3ad1test.v*

The *adclcd.v* module used here is the controller for the parallel LCD *clplcd.v* datapath module, as described in Chapter 1 Verilog Hardware Description Language, and is similar to the *genlcd.v* module used for PS/2 keyboard data for the Nexys 3 Board, as given in Listing 3.22. The controller module *genad1adc.v* uses the 2-bit signal digitmux from the *adclcd.v* module and outputs the ADC digit values adc1, adc2, adc3 and adc4 to the LCD as a 4-digit decimal number (0000 to 4095).

As described in Chapter 2 Verilog Design Automation, the Design Utilization Summary for the top module *ns3ad1test.v* shows the use of 109 slice registers (<1%) and 664 slice LUTs (≈7%) in the Nexys 3 Board XC6SLX16 Spartan-6 FPGA synthesis.

A Xilinx ISE project can be configured for the Atlys Board but, because of the availability of only one 12-pin Pmod connector, the PmodCLS serial LCD peripheral would be used instead. Such an ISE project would also utilize a controller for the serial LCD and the substitution of the Atlys Board UCF *atlys.ucf*, as was accomplished for the PS/2 keyboard test demonstrated by the project in the folder *Chapter 3\keyboardtest\atlkeyboardtest* but this is not implemented here.

PmodAD2

The PmodAD2™ hardware module features an Analog Devices (*www.analog.com*) AD7991 4 channel, 12-bit ADC. The PmodAD2 utilizes the two wire, device addressable and bidirectional data inter-integrated circuit (I2C) bus described as one of the serial data link protocols in this Chapter. The PmodAD2 is referenced in the Digilent document 502-217 (*www.digilentinc.com*) and is shown in Figure 3.21.

Figure 3.21 Digilent PmodAD2 module with four 12-bit ADCs

The I2C bus protocol uses a serial bus clock SCL and a bidirectional serial data bus SDA. The AD7991 ADC is initially in a read-only mode and must first be configured at its device address and with the contents of a register, as listed in Table 3.12. The default 7-bit address for the AS7991 ADC is either 010 1000 or 101 1001 which permits two PmodAD2 modules to be interfaced on a single I2C bus.

The serial bus clock SCL signal is an open-collector output requiring an external pull-up resistor for the I2C bus. The SCL signal is initially logic 1 and is set to logic 0 to begin the I2C protocol data transfer. The serial data bus SDA signal is read on the rising edge of the SCL signal. The configuration register first is written to by the master with the 18-bit bidirectional data packet listed in Table 3.13, which includes two acknowledgements (ACK) by the ADC.

After the requisite write to the configuration register sequence by the master is completed, the AD7991 ADC initiates an analog data conversion on the ninth rising edge of the SCL signal after the correct I2C bus address is sent and an ACK from the ADC is received, as listed in Table 3.14. Included in the 27-bit bidirectional data packet is the channel number of the data outputted and the 12-bit data.

If the master sends a NACK (negative acknowledgement) on the ninth rising edge of the SCL signal in the second read byte, the data conversion sequence is ended. The analog channels are sampled and converted in the sequence set by the configuration register, as specified in Table 3.12 and Table 3.13.

The PmodAD2 ADC is connected to the 12-pin peripheral hardware module connector (JA). The serial bus clock SCL signal is on both pin JA3 and JA9 and the serial data bus SDA signal is on both pins JA4 and JA10. The I2C bus protocol pins are available on two Pmod pins to facilitate *daisy chaining* other devices. Pins JA5 and JA11 are DC ground and pins JA6 and JA12 are power (VDD = +3.3 V DC).

For normal operation n-bit binary data output D[n–1:0] for the ADC that inputs a unipolar (only positive amplitude) analog signal is determined by Equation 3.4, where the gain G = 1, the V_{REF} = 0, V_{FS} = +3.3 V DC, V_{IN} is the analog signal input and n = 12 here. The range of the analog input signal is then $0 \leq V_{IN} \leq +3.3$ V and the 12-bit data output D[11:0] is in unsigned binary format with an integer value between 0 and 4095 [Wakerly00].

The PmodAD2 ADC can also operate using V_{REF} = 2.048 V from the ADR380 voltage reference or from a voltage less than VDD at the channel 4 analog input if the reference selection bit 3 in the configuration register is enable. Jumper JP1 selects either the voltage reference or the external voltage.

Trends in Embedded Design Using Programmable Gate Arrays

The analog inputs are on pin 1 (ADC channel 1) through pin 4 (ADC channel 4) and signal ground is on pins 5 and 6 of the 6-pin external signal connector. A two-pole Sallen-Key (−12 dB/octave) anti-aliasing filter on each of the analog input signals have a −3 dB cutoff frequency of 50 kHz.

Table 3.12 PmodAD2 AD7991 ADC configuration register

Bits	Description	Contents (MSB...LSB)	
7-4	Channel selection	0000	No channels selected
		0001	Channel 1 selected
		0010	Channel 2 selected
		0100	Channel 3 selected
		1000	Channel 4 selected
		0011	Channels 1 and 2 selected
		0101	Channels 1 and 3 selected
		0110	Channels 2 and 3 selected
		0111	Channels 1, 2 and 3 selected
		1001	Channels 1 and 4 selected
		1010	Channels 1 and 3 selected
		1011	Channels 1, 2 and 4 selected
		1100	Channels 3 and 4 selected
		1101	Channels 1, 3 and 4 selected
		1110	Channels 2, 3 and 4 selected
		1111	Channels 1, 2, 3 and 4 selected
3	Reference selection	0	Internal reference voltage, 4 channel ADC
		1	External reference voltage, 3 channel ADC
2	Filter	0/1	SDA and SCL filtering enabled/bypassed
1	Bit trial delay	0/1	Implement/ignore bit trial delay
0	Sample delay	0/1	Implement/ignore sample delay

Table 3.13 PmodAD2 AD7991 ADC write configuration register 18-bit packet

Bits	Description	Contents (MSB...LSB)	
17-11	Address	010 1000	First AD7991 on I2C bus
10	Read/Write	0	Write
9	ACK	0	Acknowledgement by AD7991
8-1	Configuration		Configuration register
0	ACK	0	Acknowledgement by AD7991

The module *ad2adc.v* for the PmodAD2 ADC, which is in the *Chapter 3\peripherals* folder, is given in Listing 3.35. The file download procedure is described in the Appendix. This module is a datapath utilizing two finite state machines (FSM) with the 6-bit state registers adccstate for device configuration and adcstate for data. The two FSMs provide signals to the controller and the ADC device, as described in Chapter 1 Verilog Hardware Description Language.

The Analog Devices AD7991 ADC has a specified maximum I2C SCL bus clock frequency of approximately 100 kHz in normal mode. Fast and high speed modes with an enhanced and complex data transmission protocol have I2C SCL bus clock frequencies of 400 kHz and up to 3.4 MHz but are not implemented here.

The master clock oscillators CLK of the Nexys 3 Board and the Atlys Board are 100 MHz. Rather than using the Clock Management Technology (CMT) frequency module of the Xilinx Spartan-

6 FPGA to output a 100 kHz clock signal, the 100 MHz master clock oscillator can be simply divided by 500 by the *clock.v* nested module in the top module.

Table 3.14 PmodAD2 AD7991 ADC read data 27-bit packet

Bits	Description	Contents (MSB…LSB)	
26-20	Address	010 1000	First AD7991 on I2C bus
19	Read/Write	1	Read
18	ACK	0	Acknowledgement by AD7991
17-16	X (don't care)		
15-14	Channel	00	Channel 1
	identification	01	Channel 2
		10	Channel 3
		11	Channel 4
13-10	Data		4 MSBs
9	ACK	0	Acknowledgement by master
8-1	Data		8 LSBs
0	NACK	1	Negative Acknowledgement by master

Listing 3.35 Datapath module for the PmodAD2 ADC *ad2adc.v*

```
// Analog-to-Digital Converter ad2adc.v
// c 2012 Embedded Design using Programmable Gate Arrays  Dennis Silage

module ad2adc(input adcclk, adcdav, adccf, output reg davadc = 0, output reg cfadc = 0,
              output reg [11:0] adcdata, output reg [1:0] adcch, output reg adcscl = 1, inout adcsda,
              input [7:0] adcconf);

assign adcsda = sdaen ? 1'bz : sdaadc;        // inout port: enable ? true : false

reg [5:0] adcstate = 0;
reg [5:0] adccstate = 0;
reg sdaadc;        // inout port output
reg sdaen;         // inout port enable

always@(posedge adcclk)
    begin
        if (adcdav == 0)        // data available reset
            begin
                adcstate = 0;
                davadc = 0;
                adcscl = 1;
            end

        if (adccf == 0)         // configuration reset
            begin
                adccstate = 0;
                cfadc = 0;
                adcscl = 1;
            end
```

```
            if (adccf == 1 && cfadc == 0)   // configuration
        begin
                case (adccstate)
                0:    begin
                            adcscl = 0;
                            sdaen = 0;         // inout port output
                            sdaadc = 0;
                            adccstate = 1;
                        end
                1:    begin
                            adcscl = 1;        // 0: address bit 6
                            adccstate = 2;
                        end
                2:    begin
                            adcscl = 0;
                            sdaadc = 1;
                            adccstate = 3;
                        end
{address bits 5 through 0 are sent similarly in states 3 through 13}
                14:   begin
                            adcscl = 0;
                            adcstate = 15;
                        end
                15:   begin
                            adcscl = 1;        // WR_
                            adccstate = 16;
                        end
                16:   begin
                            adcscl = 0;
                            sdaen = 1;         // inout port input
                            adccstate = 17;
                        end
                17:   begin
                            adcscl = 1;        // ADC ACK
                            adccstate = 18;
                        end
                18:   begin
                            adcscl = 0;
                            sdaen = 0;         // inout port output
                            sdaadc = adcconf[7];
                            adccstate = 19;
                        end
                19:   begin
                            adcscl = 1;
                            adccstate = 20;
                        end
                20:   begin
                            adcscl = 0;
                            sdaadc = adcconf[6];
                            adccstate = 21;
                        end
{configuration bits 6 through 0 are sent similarly in states 21 through 33}
```

```
            34:   begin
                        adcscl = 0;
                        sdaen = 1;          // inout port input
                        adccstate = 35;
                  end
            35:   begin
                        adcscl = 1;         // ADC ACK
                        adccstate = 36;
                  end
            36:   begin
                        adcscl = 0;
                        adccstate = 37;
                  end
            37:   begin
                        adcscl = 1;
                        cfadc = 1;
                        adccstate = 37;
                  end
            default: adccstate = 37;
        endcase
   end

   if (adcdav==1 && davadc==0)  // data
        begin
            case (adcstate)
            0:    begin
                        adcscl = 0;
                        sdaen = 0;          // inout port output
                        sdaadc = 0;
                        adcstate = 1;
                  end
            1:    begin
                        adcscl = 1;         // 0: address bit 6
                        adcstate = 2;
                  end
            2:    begin
                        adcscl = 0;
                        sdaadc = 1;
                        adcstate = 3;
                  end
{address bits 5 through 0 are sent similarly in states 3 through 13}

            14:   begin
                        adcscl = 0;
                        sdaadc = 1;
                        adcstate = 15;
                  end
            15:   begin
                        adcscl = 1;         // RD
                        adcstate = 16;
                  end
            16:   begin
```

```
                          adcscl = 0;
                          sdaen = 1;        // inout port input
                          adcstate = 17;
                  end
          17: begin
                          adcscl = 1;        // ADC ACK
                          adcstate = 18;
                  end
          18: begin
                          adcscl = 0;
                          adcstate = 19;
                  end
{two don't care bits are received similarly in states 19 through 21}
          22:   begin
                          adcscl = 0;
                          adcstate = 23;
                  end
          23:   begin
                          adcscl = 1;
                          adcch[1] = adcsda;
                          adcstate = 24;
                  end
          24:   begin
                          adcscl = 0;
                          adcstate = 25;
                  end
          25:   begin
                          adcscl = 1;
                          adcch[0] = adcsda;
                          adcstate = 26;
                  end
          26:   begin
                          adcscl = 0;
                          adcstate = 27;
                  end
          27:   begin
                          adcscl = 1;
                          adcdata[11] = adcsda;
                          adcstate = 28;
                  end
          28:   begin
                          adcscl = 0;
                          adcstate = 29;
                  end
{data bits 10 through 0 are received similarly in states 29 through 52}
          52:   begin
                          adcscl = 0;
                          sdaen = 0;        // inout port output
                          sdaadc = 1;       // master NACK
                          adcstate = 53;
                  end
          53:   begin
```

```
                        adcscl = 1;
                        adcstate = 54;
                end
           54:  begin
                        adcscl = 0;
                        adcstate = 55;
                end
           55:  begin
                        adcscl = 1;
                        davadc = 1;
                        sdaen = 1;        // inout port input
                end
           default: adcstate = 55;
        endcase
    end
 end

endmodule
```

The clockscale parameter of the module *clock.v* is 250, which provides a 200 kHz clock signal adcclk, as determined by Equation 3.1. The transitions of the FSM in the ADC datapath module *ad2adc.v* further divide the clock signal by two to produce a 100 kHz ADC I2C bus clock, which produces reliable ADC data here.

The configuration signal adccf or the data available signal adcdav from the controller set the adccstate and adcstate state registers to 0 if they are a logic 0 or activate their FSMs independently if they and the datapath signals cfadc and davdac are logic 0. Data is transmitted or received on the rising edge of the I2C bus clock adcscl. The datapath returns the status signals cfadc or davadc as logic 1 to the controller when the process of configuration or analog conversion and the output of the data is completed.

After configuration of the AD7991 device a 27-bit address, acknowledgement and data packet is used to convert an analog input signal to 12-bits of resolution. The I2C bus clock frequency here is 100 kHz so the approximate maximum throughput data rate R_{ADC} = 100 kHz /27 bits/packet ≈ 3.7 ksamples/sec.

In fast and high speed I2C bus modes with clock frequencies of 400 kHz and up to 3.4 MHz the AD7991 is capable of R_{ADC} ≈ 14.8 and up to 125 ksamples/sec. Note that the anti-aliasing filter of the PmodAD1 with a −3 dB cutoff frequency of 50 kHz implies that the sampling rate should be no more than 100 ksamples/sec, as described in Chapter 4 Digital Signal Processing, Communications and Control.

The PmodAD2 ADC datapath module *ad2adc.v* is verified by the Verilog top module *ns3ad2test.v*, which is in the *Chapter 3\ADCtest\ns3ad2test* folder and is similar to that for the PmodAD1 module in Listing 3.34. The file download procedure is described in the Appendix.

The top module *ad2test.v* includes the controller module *genad2adc.v*. The five Verilog modules operate in parallel and some independently in the top module *ns3ad2test.v*. The configuration of the controllers and datapaths is similar to that in Figure 3.20 for the verification of the PmodAD1 ADC device.

As described in Chapter 2 Verilog Design Automation, the Design Utilization Summary for the top module *ns3ad2test.v* shows the use of 116 slice registers (<1%) and 581 slice LUTs (≈6%) in the Nexys 3 Board XC6SLX16 Spartan-6 FPGA synthesis.

A Xilinx ISE project can be configured for the Atlys Board but, because of the availability of only one 12-pin Pmod connector, the PmodCLS serial LCD peripheral would be used instead. Such an ISE project would also utilize a controller for the serial LCD and the substitution of the Atlys Board

Trends in Embedded Design Using Programmable Gate Arrays

UCF *atlys.ucf*, as was accomplished for the PS/2 keyboard test demonstrated by the project in the folder *Chapter 3\keyboardtest\atlkeyboardtest* but this is not implemented here.

AC97 Codec

AC97 is an audio frequency coder-decoder (codec) standard developed by the Intel Architecture Lab in 1997 for use on personal computers. The basic AC97 codec consists of a full duplex, 16-bit analog-to-digital converter (ADC) and digital-to-analog converter (DAC) which operates at a 48 kHz sampling rate. The Digilent Atlys Board utilizes a National Semiconductor (now part of Texas Instruments, *www.ti.com*) LM4550 AC97 standard codec, as shown in Figure 3.22.

Figure 3.22 Digilent Atlys Board AC97 codec peripheral

The four 1/8 inch audio jacks provide (left to right in Figure 3.22) stereo headphone output from an integral 50 milliwatt (mW) amplifier, stereo line output, stereo line input and monoaural microphone input. The LM4550 AC97 codec supports resolution of up to 18 bits and 48 kHz sampling rate and is AC97 revision 2.1 compliant.

AC97 is a bit serial protocol that outputs the signal AUDSDO to the codec and inputs the signal AUDSDI from the codec. AUDSO is outputted on the falling edge and AUDSI on the rising edge of a clock BITCLK, which is generated by the codec at a frequency of 12.288 MHz by dividing the external 24.576 MHz crystal oscillator.

A sync signal AUDSYNC coordinates the transfer of a 256 bit frame of data. The frame rate is $12.288 \times 10^6 / 256 = 48$ kframes/sec. Each frame provides up to 20 bits of data for the two DACs and ADCs in the codec. AUDSYNC is then a 48 kHz positive pulse with a duration of 16 bits and sampled on the rising edge of BITCLK.

The data frame is divided into a tag field of 16 bits and twelve slots of 20 bits each for a total of 256 bits. The most significant bit (MSB) of the tag field (bit 15) is sent first and if logic 1 indicates that the entire frame contains valid data. The remaining bits of the tag field are supervisory and are not utilized here.

Slots 1 and 2 are used to read and write the configuration configuration registers of the codec using AUDSDO and indicate the status of the codec using AUDSDI. Slots 3 and 4 transmit data to the left and right channel DACs using AUDSDO and receive.data from the left and right channel ADCs using AUDSDI. Slots 6, 7 and 8 are used with multiple codes for *surround sound* applications. The LM4550 codec is 18 bits and the two least significant bits (LSB) of the 20 bit data frame are ignored. Data is transmitted in two's complement binary format.

AUDRST is a logic 0 reset signal to initialize the LM4450 codec after power on. AUDRST returns all the configuration registers to their default values. The default condition includes muting the master, line in and headphone volume analog outputs.

The module *s6AC97.v* for the LM4550 AC97 codec of the Atlys Board, which is in the *Chapter 3\peripherals* folder, is given in Listing 3.36. The file download procedure is described in the Appendix. This module is an event driven datapath and provides signals to the controller and the AC97 codec, as described in Chapter 1 Verilog Hardware Description Language.

Listing 3.36 Datapath module for the AC97 codec *s6AC97.v*

```verilog
// Spartan-6 AC97 Codec s6AC97.v
// c 2012 Embedded Design using Programmable Gate Arrays  Dennis Silage
// LM4550 AC97 codec - Atlys Board, 100 MHz

module s6AC97 (input sysclk, sysrst, cmdvd, leftvd, rightvd, BITCLK, AUDSDI, output reg sdoaud,
               output reg syncaud, output reg rstaud, input [19:0] leftdac, input [19:0] rightdac,
               input [7:0] cmdaddr, input [15:0] cmddata, output reg ready, output reg framedone,
               output reg [19:0] leftadc, output reg [19:0] rightadc, output reg [19:0] regstatus,
               output reg [19:0] statusdata);

parameter rstlowtime = 8'd150;          //150 clock cycles (1.5 us at 100MHz)
parameter rst2clk = 5'd18;              //18 clock cycles (100 MHz)

reg [8:0] bitcount = 0;
reg [7:0] rstlow;
reg [15:0] status;
reg [19:0] slot1in;
reg [19:0] slot2in;
reg [19:0] leftin;
reg [19:0] rightin;
reg [19:0] cmdadr;
reg [19:0] cmddat;

always@(posedge sysclk) //reset
    begin
        if (sysrst == 1)
            begin
                rstlow = 0;
                rstaud = 0;
            end
        else if (rstlow == rstlowtime)
            begin
                rstaud = 1;
                rstlow = rstlowtime;
            end
        else
            rstlow = rstlow + 1;
    end

always@(posedge BITCLK)     //assert SYNC 1 bit before frame start
    begin                   //deassert SYNC on last bit of slot 0
        if (bitcount == 255)
            begin
                syncaud = 1;
                framedone = 1;
                cmdadr = {cmdaddr, 12'h000};
                cmddat = {cmddata, 4'h0};
            end
        else if (bitcount == 215)   //signify ready at an idle bit count
            ready = 1;
```

```
            else if (bitcount == 15)
                  syncaud = 0;
            else
                  begin
                        framedone = 0;
                        ready = 0;
                  end

//AC97 output frame
      //slot 0: tag
      if (bitcount >= 0 && bitcount <= 15)
            begin
                  case (bitcount[3:0])
                  0:    sdoaud = (cmdvd || leftvd || rightvd);  //valid frame bits
                  1:    sdoaud = cmdvd;       //command address valid
                  2:    sdoaud = cmdvd;       //command data valid
                  3:    sdoaud = leftvd;      //left data valid
                  4:    sdoaud = rightvd;     //right data valid
                  default: sdoaud = 0;
                  endcase
            end

      //slot 1: command address
      else if (bitcount > 16 && bitcount <= 35)
            begin
                  if (cmdvd == 1)
                        sdoaud = cmdadr[35-bitcount];
                  else
                        sdoaud = 0;
            end
      //slot 2: command data
      else if (bitcount >= 36 && bitcount <= 55)
            begin
                  if(cmdvd == 1)
                        sdoaud = cmddat[55-bitcount];
                  else
                        sdoaud = 0;
            end
      //slot 3: left DAC data
      else if (bitcount >= 56 && bitcount <= 75)
            begin
                  if(rightvd == 1)
                        sdoaud = rightdac[75-bitcount];
                  else
                        sdoaud = 0;
            end
      //slot 4: right DAC data
      else if (bitcount >= 76 && bitcount <= 95)
            begin
                  if(leftvd == 1)
                        sdoaud = leftdac[95-bitcount];
                  else
```

```
                        sdoaud = 0;
                end
        //default
        else
                sdoaud = 0;

        //count bits and reset at end of frame
        If (bitcount == 255)
                bitcount = 0;
        else
                bitcount = bitcount + 1;
        end

//AC97 link input frame
always@(negedge BITCLK)
        begin
                //slot 0: codec status bits
                if ((bitcount >= 1) && (bitcount <= 16))
                        begin
                                status = {status[14:0], AUDSDI};
                        end
                //slot 1: status registers
                else if ((bitcount >= 17) && (bitcount <= 36))
                        begin
                                slot1in = {slot1in[18:0], AUDSDI};
                        end
                //slot 2: status data
                else if((bitcount >= 37) && (bitcount <= 56))
                        begin
                                slot2in = {slot2in[18:0], AUDSDI};
                        end
                //slot 3: left ADC data
                else if ((bitcount >= 57) && (bitcount <= 76))
                        begin
                                leftin = {leftin[18:0], AUDSDI};
                        end
                //slot 4: right ADC data
                else if ((bitcount >= 77) && (bitcount <= 96))
                        begin
                                rightin = {rightin[18:0], AUDSDI};
                        end
                else
                        begin
                                leftadc = leftin;        //data transfer to ADC
                                rightadc = rightin;
                                regstatus = slot1in;    //data transfer to status
                                statusdata = slot2in;
                        end
        end

endmodule
```

Trends in Embedded Design Using Programmable Gate Arrays

The module *s6AC97.v* for the LM4550 AC97 codec of the Atlys Board is verified by the Verilog top module *atlAC97test.v*, which is given in Listing 3.37. The top module *atlAC97test.v* includes the controller module *genAC97.v*.

Listing 3.37 Top module for the AC97 codec for the Atlys Board *atlAC97test.v*

```
// Atlys Board
// AC97 Codec Test atlac97test.v
// c 2012 Embedded Design using Programmable Gate Arrays  Dennis Silage

module atlAC97test (input CLK, BTND, BITCLK, AUDSDI, output AUDSDO, AUDSYNC,
                    output AUDRST);

wire ready, framedone, sdoaud, syncaud, rstaud, led;;
wire [7:0] cmdaddr;
wire [15:0] cmddata;
wire [19:0] leftadc;
wire [19:0] adcleft;
wire [19:0] rightadc;
wire [19:0] adcright;
wire [19:0] regstatus;
wire [19:0] statusdata;
wire [19:0] leftdac;
wire [19:0] rightdac;

assign AUDSDO = sdoaud;
assign AUDSYNC = syncaud;
assign AUDRST = rstaud;
assign adcleft = leftadc;        //loopback
assign adcright = rightadc;

s6AC97 M0 (CLK, BTND, cmdvd, leftvd, rightvd, BITCLK, AUDSDI, sdoaud, syncaud, rstaud,
            leftdac, rightdac, cmdaddr, cmddata, ready, framedone, leftadc, rightadc, regstatus,
            statusdata);
genAC97 M1 (CLK, BTND, ready, framedone, adcleft, adcright, regstatus, statusdata, cmdvd, leftvd,
            rightvd, leftdac, rightdac, cmdaddr, cmddata);

endmodule

module genAC97(input genclk, BTND, ready, framedone, input [19:0] adcleft, input [19:0] adcright,
               input [19:0] regstatus, input [19:0] statusdata, output reg cmdvd, output reg leftvd,
               output reg rightvd, output reg [19:0] leftdac, output reg [19:0] rightdac,
               output reg [7:0] cmdaddr, output reg [15:0] cmddata);

reg set;
reg [3:0] ac97state;

always@(posedge genclk)
    begin
        if(BTND == 1)        //reset registers
            begin
                ac97state = 0;
```

```
                    cmdvd = 0;
                    leftvd = 0;
                    rightvd = 0;
                    leftdac = 0;
                    rightdac = 0;
                    cmdaddr = 0;
                    cmddata = 0;
                    set = 0;
            end

    else
        begin
            case(ac97state)
            0:    begin          //init state
                    if (ready == 1)   //check codec status
                            begin
                                    cmdaddr = 8'h80 + 8'h26;        //read + addr
                                    cmdvd = 1;
                                    if(statusdata[7:4] == 4'hF)      //ready
                                            ac97state = 1;
                            end
                    end
            1:    begin              //master volume
                    if (ready == 1)
                            begin
                                    cmdaddr = 8'h02;
                                    cmddata = 16'h0000;
                                    set = 1;
                            end
                    if ((framedone && set) == 1)
                            begin
                                    ac97state = 2;
                                    set = 0;
                            end
                    end
            2:    begin              //line-in gain
                    if (ready == 1)
                            begin
                                    cmdaddr = 8'h10;
                                    cmddata = 16'h0000;
                                    set = 1;
                            end
                    else
                            ac97state = 2;
                    if ((framedone && set) == 1)
                            begin
                                    ac97state = 3;
                                    set = 0;
                            end
                    end
            3:    begin              //record select
                    if (ready == 1)
```

```
                    begin
                        cmdaddr = 8'h1A;
                        cmddata = 16'h0404;
                        set = 1;
                    end
                else
                    ac97state = 3;
                    if ((framedone && set) == 1)
                        begin
                            ac97state = 4;
                            set = 0;
                        end
            end
    4:  begin               //record gain
            if (ready == 1)
                begin
                    cmdaddr = 8'h1C;
                    cmddata = 16'h0000;
                    set = 1;
                end
            else
                ac97state = 4;
                if ((framedone && set) == 1)
                    begin
                        ac97state = 5;
                        set = 0;
                    end
            end
    5:  begin               //send ADC directly to DAC
            cmdaddr = 8'h80;
            cmdvd = 0;
            leftdac = adcleft;
            rightdac = adcright;
            leftvd = 1;
            rightvd = 1;
        end
        endcase
    end
end

endmodule
```

The complete Xilinx ISE project is in the *Chapter 3\AC97test\atlAC97test* folder and uses *atlAC97test.ucf* that uncomments the signals CLK, BTND, BITCLK, AUDSDI, AUDSDO, AUDSYNC and AUDRST in the Atlys Board UCF of Listing 3.2. The file download procedure is described in the Appendix.

The controller module *genAC97.v* initializes the configuration registers of the LM4550 code utilizing slots 1 and 2 of the AC97 data frame. The MSB of slot 1 (bit 19) is logic 0 to indicate that a register is to be written and bits 18 through 12 specify the register address. The 16 MSBs of slot 2 is the register data.

The master volume register at address 02h controls the level of the line output of the codec. The MSB bit 15 of the 16-bit data is the mute bit which must be cleared. Bits 12 through 8 and bits 4 through 0 are the 5 bits of the left and right channel gain, respectively, with 00000b being the loudest output at 0 dB attenuation. A 5-bit data of 11111b produces an attenuation of 46.5 dB. The unspecified bits of the 16-bit data are not used. The line in volume register at address 10h is set in a similar manner.

The record select register at address 1Ah controls the source for the left and right channels of the codec. Line input is selected with bits 10 through 8 and bits 2 through 0 of the 16-bit data both set to 100b (04h). The single channel microphone input is selected with the data 000b.

The record gain register at address 1Ch sets the gain of the input selected. The MSB bit 15 of the 16-bit data is the mute bit which must be cleared. Bits 11 through 8 and bits 3 through 0 are the 4 bits of the left and right channel gain, respectively, with 1111b being a gain of 22.5 dB. A 4-bit data of 0000b produces 0 dB gain. The unspecified bits of the 16-bit data are not used.

The LM4450 codec has several more configuration registers that are used in a variety of applications and not discussed here. The controller module *genAC97.v* provides a basic setup of the AC97 codec through the datapath module *s6AC97.v* that *loops back* the ADC output to the DAC input without digital signal processing in the top module. The FSM in the controller module *genAC97.v* executes only once to configure the LM4550 codec unless reset with the BTND push button.

As described in Chapter 2 Verilog Design Automation, the Design Utilization Summary for the top module *atlAC97test.v* shows the use of 185 slice registers (<1%) and 197 slice LUTs (<1%) in the Atlys Board XC6SLX45 Spartan-6 FPGA synthesis.

Video Graphics Array Display

The video graphics array (VGA) display was first introduced in 1987 and remains a standard for text and graphics display in embedded design. The standard graphical resolution is 640 horizontal (x) and 480 vertical (y) picture elements (pixels) using a 15-pin D-subminiature connector. A text character is can be displayed as a font requiring 8 horizontal by 14 vertical pixels. Other common text fonts are presented as 8 x 8 pixels.

The VGA signal consists of horizontal and vertical sync pulses and analog data for the red, green and blue color signals. The Spartan-6 Nexys 3 Board uses a simple resistive summer from the three bits of red (RD), three bits of green (GR) and two bits of blue (BL) logic signals to form a red, green and blue analog signal for the VGA display port, as shown in Figure 3.23. The Atlys Board does not have a VGA display port but has an incompatible high definition multimedia interface (HDMI) port.

Figure 3.23 Digilent Nexys 3 Board VGA peripheral

The VGA color analog signal ranges from 0 V (fully off) to 0.7 V (fully on) and 256 distinct colors can be displayed. Compatible sync timing signals provide the active VGA display in the 640 horizontal by 480 vertical mode.

The horizontal sync (HS) pulse has a so-called *front porch* of 0.64 μsec, followed by a negative pulse width of 3.64 μsec and a *back porch* of 1.92 μsec. The vertical sync (VS) pulse has a front porch of 320 μsec (the so-called *retrace blanking* interval), followed by a negative pulse width of 64 μsec and a back porch of 962 μsec.

Trends in Embedded Design Using Programmable Gate Arrays

The module *vgavideo.v* for the VGA display port of the Nexys 3 Board, which is in the *Chapter 3\peripherals* folder, is given in Listing 3.38. The file download procedure is described in the Appendix. This module is a datapath utilizing two finite state machines (FSM) with the 3-bit horizontal state register vgahstate and the 2-bit vertical state register vgavstate.

Listing 3.38 Datapath module for the VGA display port of the Nexys 3 Board *vgavideo.v*

```
// VGA display vgavideo.v
// c 2012 Embedded Design using Programmable Gate Arrays  Dennis Silage

module vgavideo (input pixclk, vgareset, output reg [9:0] pixhloc = 0, output reg [8:0] pixvloc = 0,
                 output reg [1:0] pixsync = 3, output reg [1:0] pixdisplay = 0);

reg [2:0] vgahstate = 0;     // horizontal state register
reg [9:0] vgahcount = 0;     // horizontal pixel counter
reg [1:0] vgavstate = 0;     // vertical state register
reg [19:0] vgavcount = 0;    // vertical line counter

always@(posedge pixclk)
    begin
        if (vgareset == 1)
            begin
                pixsync = 3;
                pixdisplay = 0;
                vgahstate = 0;
                vgahcount = 0;
                pixhloc = 0;
                vgavstate = 0;
                vgavcount = 0;
                pixvloc = 0;
            end
        else
            begin
                case (vgahstate)        // horizontal sync
                0:    begin
                          vgahcount = vgahcount + 1;
                          if (vgahcount == 16)        // HS front porch
                              begin
                                  pixsync[1] = 0; //HS pulse
                                  vgahstate = 1;
                              end
                      end
                1:    begin
                          vgahcount = vgahcount + 1;
                          if (vgahcount == 112)       // HS pulse width, +96 counts
                              begin
                                  pixsync[1] = 1;
                                  vgahstate = 2;
                              end
                      end
                2:    begin
                          vgahcount = vgahcount + 1;
```

```
                if (vgahcount == 160)      //  HS back porch, +48 counts
                    begin
                        pixdisplay[1] = 1;
                        vgahstate = 3;
                    end
            end
3:    begin
          pixhloc = pixhloc + 1;
          if (pixhloc == 640)          // end of display
              begin
                  pixdisplay[1] = 0;
                  pixhloc = 0;
                  vgahcount = 0;
                  pixvloc = pixvloc + 1;
                  if (pixvloc == 480)
                      begin
                          pixdisplay[0] = 0;
                          pixvloc = 0;
                          vgavcount = 0;
                          vgavstate = 1;
                          vgahstate = 4;
                      end
                  else
                      vgahstate = 0;
              end
      end
4:    begin
          pixsync[1] = 1;
      end
default: vgahstate = 0;
endcase

case (vgavstate)       // vertical sync
0:    begin
          pixsync[0] = 1;
      end
1:    begin
          vgavcount = vgavcount + 1;
          if (vgavcount == 8000)     // VS front porch
              begin
                  pixsync[0] = 0; // VS pulse
                  vgavstate = 2;
              end
      end
2:    begin
          vgavcount = vgavcount + 1;
          if (vgavcount == 9600)     // VS pulse width, +1600 counts
              begin
                  pixsync[0] = 1;
                  vgavstate = 3;
              end
      end
```

```
                    3:    begin
                              vgavcount = vgavcount + 1;
                              if (vgavcount == 32800)   // back porch, +23 200 counts
                                   begin
                                        pixdisplay[0] = 1;
                                        vgavstate = 0;
                                        vgahstate = 0;
                                   end
                          end
                   endcase
             end
      end

endmodule
```

The horizontal state register initiates the vertical state register after 480 vertical display lines from its idle state 0 to generate the VS pulse. When complete in state 3, the vertical state register releases the horizontal state register from its idle state 4 and returns to its idle state 0. The horizontal state register generates the HS pulse starting in state 0. The horizontal and vertical pixel count registers vgahcount and vgavcount determine the position and extent of the horizontal and vertical sync pulses.

The datapath module *vgavideo.v* inputs a 25 MHz clock pixclk, a reset signal vgareset and outputs the horizontal (x) and vertical (y) pixel location registers pixhloc and pixvloc whose ranges respectively are 0 to 639 and 0 to 479. The upper left corner of the display is the location x, y = 0, 0. The 2-bit pixel sync register pixsync provides the horizontal and vertical sync pulses to the VGA display. The 2-bit pixel display register pixdata indicates the active video data when both bits are logic 1. The red, green and blue pixel color data pixdata is generated externally to the datapath module *vgavideo.v*.

The VGA display datapath module *vgavideo.v* is verified by the Verilog top module *ns3vgatest.v*, which is in the *Chapter 3\vgatest\ns3vgatest* folder and given in Listing 3.39. The file download procedure is described in the Appendix.

Listing 3.39 VGA display test top module for the Nexys 3 Board *ns3vgatest.v*

```
// Nexys 3 Board
// VGA Display Test ns3vgatest.v
// c 2012 Embedded Design using Programmable Gate Arrays  Dennis Silage

module ns3vgatest (input CLK, BTND, output [2:0] RD, output [2:0] GR,  output [2:1] BL,
                   output HS, VS);

wire pixclk, pbbtnd;
wire [1:0] pixsync;
wire [1:0] pixdisplay;
wire [7:0] pixdata;
wire [9:0] pixhloc;
wire [8:0] pixvloc;

assign RD[2:0] = pixdata[7:5];  // red
assign GR[2:0] = pixdata[4:2];  // green
assign BL[2:1] = pixdata[1:0];  // blue
assign HS = pixsync[1];         // horizontal sync
assign VS = pixsync[0];         // vertical sync;
```

```
assign vgareset = pbbtnd;        // debounced push button 0 reset

vgavideo M0 (pixclk, vgareset, pixhloc, pixvloc, pixsync, pixdisplay);
vgadatgen M1 (pixclk, vgareset, pixhloc, pixvloc, pixdisplay, pixdata);
pbdebounce M2 (pbclk, BTND, pbbtnd);
clock M3 (CLK, 1000000, pbclk);     // 50 Hz
clock M4 (CLK, 2, pixclk);          // 25 MHz

endmodule

module vgadatgen (input pixclk, vgareset, input [9:0] pixhloc, input [8:0] pixvloc,
                  input [1:0] pixdisplay, output reg [7:0] pixdata = 0);

always@(negedge pixclk)
    begin
        if (vgareset == 1)
            pixdata = 0;
        else
            begin
                if (pixdisplay == 3)
                    begin
                        if (pixhloc <= 319 && pixvloc < 239)
                            pixdata = 224;        // red
                        if (pixhloc > 320 && pixvloc < 239)
                            pixdata = 28;         // green
                        if (pixhloc <= 319 && pixvloc >= 240)
                            pixdata=3;            // blue
                        if (pixhloc >320 && pixvloc >= 240)
                            pixdata = 255;        // white
                    end
                else
                    pixdata=0;        // black
            end
    end

endmodule
```

The top module *ns3vgatest.v* includes the controller module *vgagendat.v*, which generates a red, green, blue and white quadrant pattern on the VGA display. The input 2-bit register pixdisplay indicates an active video region. The clock module *clock.v* provides the 25 MHz pixel clock by dividing the 100 MHz master clock CLK, as given by Equation 3.1.

The values in the input horizontal and vertical pixel 8-bit registers pixhloc and pixyloc set the quadrants of the VGA display. Colors are arbitrarily set in the 8-bit output register pixdata to red ($11100000_2 = 224$), green ($00011100_2 = 28$), blue ($00000011_2 = 3$) and white ($11111111_2 = 255$). However, drawing VGA display patterns in this manner is cumbersome.

Alternatively, an external memory can provide an *image* of the $640 \times 480 \times 8$ bit = 2 457 600 bits = 307 200 bytes of the VGA display. The pixxloc and pixvloc pixel registers are the effective address to the memory storage of the image and the output data byte is then the input pixel data pixdat.

The complete Xilinx ISE project is in the *Chapter 3\VGAtest\ns3vgatest* folder and uses *ns3vgatest.ucf* that uncomments the signals CLK, BTND, RD<0> to RD<2>, GR<0> to GR<2>, BL<1>, BL<2>, HS and VS in the Nexys 3 Board UCF of Listing 3.1. The file download procedure is described in the Appendix. As described in Chapter 2 Verilog Design Automation, the Design

Trends in Embedded Design Using Programmable Gate Arrays

Utilization Summary for the top module *ns3vgatest.v* shows the use of 129 slice registers (<1%) and 264 slice LUTs (≈3%) in the Nexys 3 Board XC6SLX16 Spartan-6 FPGA synthesis.

Serial Data Link Protocols

Serial data link protocols were first are used in telecommunications and later extended to embedded computer systems. The serial data communication standard RS-232 is described in Chapter 4 Digital Signal Processing, Communications and Control. In this Chapter the serial peripheral interface (SPI) and inter-integrated circuit (I2C) bus protocols are introduced for peripheral component interfaces to the FPGA.

These serial protocols have the distinct advantage of utilizing a minimum number of signals to provide data communication. This and improvements in signal integrity and data rates for the serial protocols have now outweighed the advantage of simplicity of the parallel data bus. Other examples of common serial data link protocols for computer systems include the universal serial bus (USB), FireWire, Ethernet, serial ATA and PCI Express.

Serial Peripheral Interface

The serial peripheral interface (SPI) bus is a synchronous, full duplex serial data link protocol developed by Motorola Semiconductor (now Freescale) in 1985. The SPI bus is described in the Xilinx application note XAPP348 (*www.xilinx.com*). SPI is a single master, multiple slave, four wire, unidirectional serial bus with a serial clock (SCLK), master output, slave input (MOSI), master input and slave output (MISO) and slave select (SS) signals. The SPI bus can operate with a single master and slave, as shown in Figure 3.24.

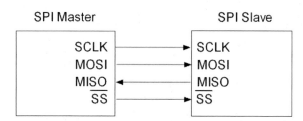

Figure 3.24 Serial peripheral interface bus

Multiple SPI bus slave devices can be configured from a single master with multiple independent SS signals but sharing the MOSI and MISO signals. This effectively places the SPI bus slave devices in parallel but requires tri-state logic for the MISO signals of the slave devices.

Multiple SPI bus slave devices can be connected in series or *daisy chained* with the MISO output of a slave device connected to the MOSI input of the next slave device in sequence. The MISO output of the last SPI bus slave device is then connected to the MISO input of the master and a single SS signal is connected to the slave devices. This effectively places the SPI bus slave devices in series but requires that each device decode the serial data into appropriate commands.

However, SPI bus slave device operation in parallel or in series limit the data rate because of the single SPI master. The intrinsic parallel operation of the FPGA as multiple SPI bus masters obviates this and increases the overall serial data rate.

SPI bus serial data transmission begins with the SS signal at logic 0. Either the rising or falling edge of SCLK as specified by the slave device signifies valid MOSI data with the most significant bit (MSB) sent first. The default value of the SCLK signal for a rising edge valid data transmission is logic 0 and for a falling edge it is logic 1. Concurrently, the MISO signal outputs the MSB of the last data transmission to the SPI bus slave device. This serial data transmission continues with any number of SCLK cycles until the SS signal returns to logic 1. Unless required for data verification in critical embedded system design, the MISO signal is usually ignored.

Minimum timing specifications for the SCLK signal and setup of valid MOSI data determine the SPI bus data rate. SPI slave devices usually ignore serial transmissions with an incorrect number of data bits. The rising edge of the SS signal indicates completion of the data transmission and the start of the operation intended for the SPI bus slave device.

The SPI slave devices in this Chapter have SCLK frequencies from 50 kHz (PmodJSTK) to 50 MHz (PmodDA3 and PmodDA4), transmitted data bytes from two (typically, PmodAD1) to five (PmodJSTK) and either use a rising edge (typically, PmodDA1) or falling edge (typically, PmodDA4) SCLK signal to indicate valid data.

Inter-Integrated Circuit

The inter-integrated circuit (I2C) bus is a synchronous full duplex serial data link protocol developed by Phillips Semiconductors (now NXP) in 1982. The I^2C bus is described in the Xilinx application note XAPP333. I2C is a multiple master, multiple slave two wire, bidirectional serial bus with a serial data line (SDA) and serial clock (SCL). The SDA and SCL signals are often, but not always, *open drain* and require external *pull up* resistors, as shown in Figure 3.25.

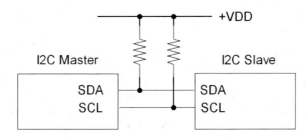

Figure 3.25 Inter-integrated circuit bus

I2C devices utilize a unique 7 or 10 bit address rather than a select signal and can utilize multiple masters on the bidirectional SDA bus. Standard mode SCL clock frequency is 100 kHz, although specialized devices can use a frequency as high as 3.4 MHz. Arbitrary low clock frequencies are also allowed. The I2C master generates the SCL clock signal and issues the requisite address for the slave devices as the SDA data signal. The maximum number of I2C slave devices is limited not only by the addresses available which are fixed but also the total bus capacitance from multiple devices that limits the data transmission rate.

The I2C slave devices can affect flow control by setting the SCL serial clock line to logic 0. After a complete data transmission setting the SDA data signal line to logic 1 or to high impedance (z) indicates the end of bus transmission. Every 8 SDA data bits an acknowledge (ACK) bit is sent.

There are four possible modes of operation: the master or slave can either transmit or receive. If the I2C slave device recognizes its address it responds with an ACK during the data transmission. The master also responds with an ACK with a negative acknowledge (NACK), as listed for the PmodAD2 I2C slave device in Table 3.13 and Table 3.14.

Trends in Embedded Design Using Programmable Gate Arrays

Summary

In this Chapter the Digilent Nexys 3 Board and the Atlys Board that utilize the Xilinx Spartan-6 FPGA are described. The integral components of these evaluation boards, such as the crystal clock, push buttons, slide switches, light emitting diodes and video graphics adapter, and external peripherals, such as the rotary shaft encoders, keypad, joystick, serial and parallel liquid crystal displays, PS/2 keyboard and mouse and digital-to-analog and analog-to-digital converters, are presented in operation by complete Xilinx ISE projects. The projects in this Chapter utilize the controller and datapath and finite state machine construct, as described in Chapter 1 Verilog Hardware Description Language [Ciletti04]. These projects in this Chapter illustrate the some of the uses of the components, ports and external hardware peripherals in embedded design.

Chapter 4 Digital Signal Processing, Communications and Control presents Xilinx ISE projects in the Verilog HDL and the tenants of digital filtering, digital modulation in communication systems, digital data transmission and display and digital control system design. Chapter 5 Extensible Processing Platform introduces the Xilinx Zynq all programmable *system-on-chip* with an ARM Cortex™-A9 hard core processor, AMBA bus and integral FPGA.

References

[Ashenden08]   Ashenden, Peter J., *Digital Design – An Embedded System Approach using Verilog*. Morgan Kaufman, 2008.

[Botros06]   Botros, Nazeih M., *HDL Programming Fundamentals*. Thomson Delmar, 2006.

[Chu08]   Chu, Pong P., *FPGA Prototyping by Verilog Examples*. Wiley, 2008.

[Ciletti99]   Cilletti, Michael D., *Modeling, Synthesis and Rapid Prototyping with the Verilog HDL*. Prentice Hall, 1999.

[Ciletti04]   Cilletti, Michael D., *Starter's Guide to Verilog 2001*. Prentice Hall, 2004.

[Lee06]   Lee, Sunguu, *Advanced Digital Logic Design*. Thomson, 2006.

[Navabi06]   Navabi, Zainalabedin, *Verilog Digital System Design*. McGraw-Hill, 1999.

[Wakerly00]   Wakerly, John F., *Digital Design Principles and Practice*, Prentice Hall, 2000.

4

Digital Signal Processing, Communications and Control

Electronic design automation (EDA) tools and hardware are available for embedded system design in the Verilog hardware description language (HDL) using a field programmable gate array (FPGA). Structural and behavioral models, finite state machines (FSM) and controller and datapath constructs are presented in Chapter 1 Verilog Hardware Description Language. The Xilinx Integrated Synthesis Environment (ISE®) EDA is presented in Chapter 2 Verilog Design Automation. The Digilent Nexys 3 Board and the Atlys Board using the Xilinx Spartan®-6 FPGA and peripheral hardware modules are described in Chapter 3 Programmable Gate Array Hardware with complete Xilinx ISE projects.

This Chapter presents the tenants of digital signal processing (DSP) and applications in digital communications and digital control with emphasis on embedded design in the Verilog HDL using the FPGA. The Xilinx LogiCORE blocks provide additional functionality for the projects in this Chapter. The LogiCORE FIR Compiler implements the finite impulse response (FIR) digital filter. The LogiCore Sine-Cosine Look-Up Table is used for a dual tone multiple frequency (DTMF) audio signal generator. The LogiCORE DDS Compiler is used for a sinusoidal frequency generator and frequency and phase shift keying modulators in digital communication.

Serial data communication is facilitated by the implementation in Verilog HDL of a *soft-core* universal asynchronous receiver transmitter (UART) peripheral. Embedded design in Verilog HDL for digital control is facilitated by real-time clock and calendar, thermometer and thermostat, gyroscope and accelerometer peripherals.

The Verilog source modules and project files are located in the Chapter 4 folder as subfolders identified by the name of the appropriate project. The complete contents and the file download procedure are described in the Appendix. The projects in this Chapter illustrate not only the use of the components, ports and external hardware peripherals in applications in DSP, digital communications and digital control, but the versatility of the Xilinx ISE EDA and the Verilog HDL for real-time embedded design.

Sampling and Quantization

Analog sources of information are often derived from transducers which provide continuous electrical voltage signals from physical phenomenon such as light, pressure, temperature, vibration, and acceleration. These analog *baseband* signals are bandlimited to a maximum frequency. Analog baseband signals are continuous in time and amplitude and are *sampled* and *quantized* for digital signal processing (DSP) [Silage09].

Analog signals are first sampled at discrete intervals of time but continuous in amplitude. Quantization then is the *roundoff* of the continuous amplitude sample to a discrete preset value, represented as binary number. The preset values are equally spaced in *uniform quantization* and the total number of binary bits is the resolution. The *ideal* sampling operation can be described as a multiplication of the baseband analog signal $x(t)$ by a periodic series of unit impulse functions $\delta(t - mT_s)$, where T_s is the *sampling interval* and m is an arbitrary index. The ideal sampling process is determined by Equation 4.1.

$$x(mT_s) = \sum_m x(t)\, \delta(t - mT_s) \qquad (4.1)$$

Trends in Embedded Design Using Programmable Gate Arrays

The response of the ideal sampling process is described in the spectral domain by the normalized (the load resistor $R_L = 1\ \Omega$) power spectral density (PSD), as determined by Equation 4.2 [Lathi98].

$$\text{PSD} = f_s^2 \sum_k |X(f - k\,f_s)|^2 \qquad (4.2)$$

The Fourier transform of the baseband analog signal $x(t)$ is $X(f)$ and the *sampling rate* $f_s = 1/T_s$ samples/sec. The normalized PSD of $x(t)$ is $|X(f)|^2$ which is bandlimited to a maximum frequency of f_{max}. However, the ideally sampled signal $x(mT_s)$ has a PSD which is not bandlimited but repeats the baseband PSD centered at multiples of the sampling rate f_s, as determined by Equation 4.2. The direct implication is that to avoid spectral overlay or *aliasing* the sampling rate $f_s > 2 f_{max}$, where $2 f_{max}$ is the *Nyquist rate* [Haykin01]. To avoid aliasing, an analog filter with a *cutoff frequency* $f_{cutoff} < f_s/2$ is often placed before the ideal sampler.

The output of the ideal sampler $x(mT_s)$ is inputted to an first order sample-and-hold process, whose output $y_{s\text{-}h}(t)$ is determined by Equation 4.3.

$$y_{s\text{-}h}(t) = \sum_m x(mT_s)\, h(t - mT_s) \quad mT_s \le t < (m+1)T_s$$

$$\text{where} \quad h(t) = 1 \quad 0 \le t < T_s \qquad (4.3)$$

$$h(t) = 0 \quad \text{otherwise}$$

The sample-and-hold output $y_{s\text{-}h}(t)$ is continuous in time but represents a fixed amplitude signal during the sampling interval T_s. This analog signal is then inputted to an analog-to-digital converter (ADC) peripheral to affect the process of quantization. This fixed amplitude signal facilitates the ADC process by maintaining a constant input signal during the finite time required for conversion. The n-bit binary data output D[n-1:0] for the ADC that inputs a unipolar (only positive amplitude) analog signal is determined by Equation 4.4.

$$D[n\text{-}1:0] = G\,\frac{V_{IN} - V_{REF}}{V_{FS}}\,2^{n\text{-}1} \qquad (4.4)$$

In Equation 4.4 G is the gain of any analog preamplifier that precedes the ADC, V_{REF} is the common reference voltage of the analog preamplifier and ADC, V_{FS} is the *full-scale* conversion voltage for the ADC, V_{IN} is the polar analog signal input at the input of the analog preamplifier and n is the number of bits of resolution. The most significant bit (MSB) of the n-bit binary data output D[n-1:0] represents the sign bit and a number whose integer value is between $-2^{n\text{-}1}$ and $2^{n\text{-}1} - 1$. The ideal uniform ADC quantizer voltage step size Δ is determined by Equation 4.5.

$$\Delta = \frac{2\,V_{MAX}}{L} \qquad (4.5)$$

V_{MAX} is the equal positive and negative maximum input voltage with respect to V_{REF}, $L = 2^n$ is the number of levels in the output of the ideal uniform ADC quantizer and n is the number of bits. If the ideal uniform ADC quantizer only has a positive input voltage range from 0 to V_{FS} then $V_{MAX} = V_{FS}/2$ in Equation 4.5. The maximum *quantization error* q that can occur in the sampled output of the ideal uniform quantizer is $\pm \Delta/2$ V. Assuming that all values of quantization error as a random variable within the range $+\Delta/2$ to $-\Delta/2$ are equally likely and from Equation 4.4, the mean square quantizing error E_q is determined by Equation 4.6 [Haykin01].

$$E_q = \frac{1}{\Delta} \int_{-\Delta/2}^{\Delta/2} q^2 \, dq = \frac{\Delta^2}{12} = \frac{V_{MAX}^2}{3 \, L^2} \qquad (4.6)$$

E_q is also the normalized power in the resulting quantizing noise. The root mean square (RMS) quantizing noise is $\Delta/\sqrt{12} = \Delta/3.464$. If the normalized power in the analog signal is S_o then, from Equation 4.5 and Equation 4.6, the signal to quantization noise ratio (SNR_q) is determined by Equation 4.7.

$$SNR_q = \frac{12 \, S_o}{\Delta^2} = 3 \, L^2 \frac{S_o}{V_{MAX}^2} \qquad (4.7)$$

SNR_q is a linear function of the normalized power in the signal S_o and a second order function of the number of levels $L = 2^n$ of the ideal uniform quantizer. If S_o and V_{max} remain constant but the number of bits n increases to n+1 (the number of levels L doubles) and from Equation 4.7, SNR_q quadruples or increases by +6.02 dB ($10 \log_{10} 4$). For a sinusoidal input analog signal with a positive and negative maximum input voltage equal to V_{MAX}, the normalized power in the signal $S_o = V_{MAX}^2/2$ V^2-sec and, from Equation 4.6, the signal to quantization noise ratio $SNR_q = 1.5L^2$.

The two channel Digilent Pmod AD1 ADC hardware module described in Chapter 3 has 12 bits of resolution or n = 12, $V_{REF} = 0$ V, $V_{FS} = 2V_{MAX} = 3.3$ V and G = 1. In this instance $\Delta = 3.3/4096$ V ≈ 0.8056 mV and for an offset or unipolar sinusoidal input signal of V_{MAX}, $SNR_q = 1.5 \times (4096)^2 = 74.01$ dB. This SNR_q performance is as expected for a 12-bit ADC compared to a 14-bit ADC since $84.05 - 2 \times 6.02$ dB $= 74.01$ dB.

The PmodAD1 peripheral hardware module ADC has an operational amplifier (*op amp*) two pole, anti-aliasing active filter with a –3 dB cutoff frequency f $_{-3 \, dB} = 500$ kHz at the analog input. The conservative sampling frequency f_s utilized in the PmodAD1 project in Listing 3.28 is 0.781 Msamples/sec and the ideal cuttoff frequency $f_{cutoff} < f_s/2 \approx 390$ kHz.

Discrete Time Sequences

The uniformly sampled and n-bit quantized data output of the ADC is described by a sequence $x_q(mT_s)$ where m is an arbitrary index, T_s is the *sampling interval* and x_q is a discrete binary number ranging from 0 to $2^n - 1$. To facilitate the description of the analysis $x_q(mT_s)$ is often written simply as $x(m)$. An input sequence $x(m)$ is processed by a general DSP system, or *digital filter*, to produce an output sequence $y(m)$, as determined by Equation 4.8 [Ifeachor02].

$$y(m) = \sum_{q}^{Q-1} b_q x(m-q) + \sum_{p=0}^{P-1} a_p y(m-p) \qquad (4.8)$$

Usually the output sequence $y(m)$ is considered to be the sum of the current (indices $q = 0$ and $p = 0$) and a finite number ($Q - q$ and P) of the past input and output sequences multiplied by coefficients (b_q and a_p). However, the index q for the input sequence $x(m)$ can be a negative ($q = -r$). This implies that output sequence $y(m)$ is also a sum of apparent future input sequences $x(m+r)$ multiplied by coefficients (b_{-r}), but this is interpreted as the output sequence is merely delayed by the index $| -r |$. The finite impulse response (FIR) class of digital filter has $a_p = 0$ for all p. FIR digital filters are also known as moving average (MA) filters since the output sequence is a weighted average of the input sequence, as determined by Equation 4.9 [Proakis07].

$$y(m) = \sum_{q}^{Q-1} b_q x(m-q) \qquad (4.9)$$

The coefficients b_q of the FIR digital filter are identical to a finite length *impulse response* sequence [Chen01]. The determination of the coefficients an FIR filter can therefore be accomplished in the frequency domain by the *inverse discrete Fourier transform* (IDFT) of the specified frequency response [Mitra06]. In many digital communication and digital image processing applications a linear phase response is important to minimize distortion. The coefficients b_q of the FIR digital filter have a simple relationship that mandates a linear phase sequence response, which is obtained by setting pairs of coefficients equal to each other, as determined by Equation 4.10.

$$b_0 = b_{Q-1} \quad b_1 = b_{Q-2} \quad b_3 = b_{Q-3} \quad K \qquad (4.10)$$

The infinite impulse response (IIR) class of digital filter includes the autoregressive (AR) filter, as determined by Equation 4.11 [Mitra06].

$$y(m) = x(m) - \sum_{p=0}^{P-1} a_p y(m-p) \qquad (4.11)$$

The general form of the IIR digital filter is the autoregressive, moving average (ARMA) filter determined by Equation 4.8 [Cavicchi00]. Since the output sequence of the IIR digital filter at least includes a weighted sum of the past output sequences, stability of the output can be problematical.

There is no simple relationship between the coefficients b_q and a_q of the IIR digital filter and the impulse response sequence or that for a linear phase sequence response as there is for the FIR digital filter. However, IIR digital filters require a lesser number of multiplicative coefficients to provide a specified digital filter frequency response than an FIR digital filter. Therefore IIR digital filters are less computationally intense and utilize fewer resources within the FPGA [Mitra06].

Discrete Frequency Response

DSP requires that the characteristics of the digital filter be assessed in the frequency domain. The discrete time sequence can be readily transformed to the discrete frequency domain [Mitra06]. The discrete time input and output sequences $x(m)$ and $y(m)$ is assumed to have a discrete frequency transforms $X(z)$ and $Y(z)$, where the temporal delay d is replaced by the discrete frequency delay parameter z^{-d}, as determined by Equation 4.12. The IIR ARMA digital filter in Equation 4.8 has the discrete frequency transfer or system function $H(z) = Y(z) / X(\underline{z})$, as then determined by Equation 4.13.

$$Y(z) = \sum_{q}^{Q} b_q X(z) z^{-q} + \sum_{p=1}^{P} a_p Y(z) z^{-p}$$

$$Y(z) - \sum_{p=1}^{P} a_p Y(z) z^{-p} = \sum_{q}^{Q} b_q X(z) z^{-q} \qquad (4.12)$$

$$Y(z) \left[1 - \sum_{p=1}^{P} a_p z^{-p} \right] = X(z) \sum_{q}^{Q} b_q z^{-q}$$

$$H(z) = \frac{Y(z)}{X(z)} = \frac{\displaystyle\sum_{q}^{Q} b_q z^{-q}}{1 - \displaystyle\sum_{p=1}^{P} a_p z^{-p}} \qquad (4.13)$$

The discrete frequency system function $H(z)$ for the FIR or MA digital filter in Equation 4.9 is then determined by Equation 4.14.

$$H(z) = \frac{Y(z)}{X(z)} = \sum_{q}^{Q} b_q z^{-q} \qquad (4.14)$$

Finally, the discrete frequency system function $H(z)$ for the IIR AR filter in Equation 4.11 is then determined by Equation 4.15.

$$H(z) = \frac{Y(z)}{X(z)} = \frac{1}{1 - \displaystyle\sum_{p=1}^{P} a_p z^{-p}} \qquad (4.15)$$

The frequency domain for a discrete frequency transform is the *unit circle* in the complex plane [Proakis07]. The discrete sequence sinusoidal excitation of the discrete system $H(z)$ exists then as a point P on the unit circle in the range $0 \le 2\pi f T_s \le \pi$, where f is the frequency of excitation and T_s is the sampling interval.

As a first example, a simple IIR digital filter rendered as the output sequence $y(m)$ in terms of the input sequence $x(m)$ and coefficients from Equation 4.13 will illustrate the discrete frequency response analysis. Here $Q = 0$, $q = -1$, $b_{-1} = 0.25$, $b_0 = 0.5$, $P = 1$, and $a_1 = 0.25$, as determined by Equation 4.16.

$$y(m) = 0.5\, x(m) + 0.25\, x(m+1) + 0.25\, y(m-1) \qquad (4.16)$$

The discrete frequency transfer function $H(z)$ from Equation 4.12 is determined by Equation 4.17.

$$H(z) = \frac{Y(z)}{X(z)} = \frac{0.5 + 0.25\, z}{1 - 0.25\, z^{-1}}$$
$$H(z) = \frac{0.25\, z\,(z+2)}{z - 0.25} \qquad (4.17)$$

This simple IIR digital filter has one transfer function *pole* (where the response is infinite) at $z = 0.25$, two transfer function zeros (where the response is zero) at $z = 0$ and $z = -2$ and a multiplicative term of 0.25. The pole (indicated by ×) and the zeros (indicated by ○) of the transfer function are plotted on the complex frequency domain plane, as shown in Figure 4.1. Vectors are drawn from the pole and zeros to an arbitrary point P on the unit circle which represents the sinusoidal excitation of the discrete system $H(z)$ [Mitra06].

The magnitude of the discrete frequency response $|H(z)|$ is determined by the product of the gain G and the length of the vector(s) from the zero(s) divided by the product of the length of the vector(s) from the poles. The angle from the origin of the complex plane to the point P on the unit circle where the sinusoidal excitation occurs is in the range $0 \leq 2\pi f T_s \leq \pi$ and the simple geometry allows the length of these vectors and the magnitude of the discrete frequency response to be determined as in Equation 4.18.

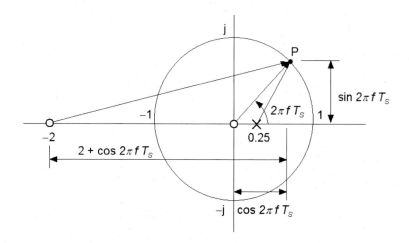

Figure 4.1 IIR digital filter discrete frequency transfer function plotted on the complex plane

$$G = 0.25 \qquad L_{z=0} = 1$$

$$L_{z=-2} = \sqrt{\left(2 + \cos 2\pi f T_s\right)^2 + \sin^2 2\pi f T_s}$$

$$L_{p=0.25} = \sqrt{\left(\cos 2\pi f T_s - 0.25\right)^2 + \sin^2 2\pi f T_s} \qquad (4.18)$$

$$|H(z)| = 0.25 \frac{\sqrt{\left(2 + \cos 2\pi f T_s\right)^2 + \sin^2 2\pi f T_s}}{\sqrt{\left(\cos 2\pi f T_s - 0.25\right)^2 + \sin^2 2\pi f T_s}}$$

The magnitude of the discrete frequency response of this IIR digital filter is shown in Figure 4.2 on a *log-log* scale plotted against frequency Hz with $T_s = 4 \times 10^{-6}$ sec or $f_s = 1/T_s = 250$ kHz. This IIR digital filter has a *low pass* characteristic with a -3 dB (magnitude $= 0.707$) cutoff frequency of approximately 44.5 kHz and a low frequency gain of 1. This IIR low pass digital filter is efficient because the coefficients are all negative powers of the binary base 2 (2^{-n}) and can be performed with integer scaling (shifting).

The phase angle ψ of the discrete frequency response $H(z)$ is determined by the sum of the angles subtended counter-clockwise with the real axis and the vectors drawn from the zeros of the discrete frequency response $H(z)$ to an arbitrary point P on the unit circle less the angles subtended with the real axis and the vectors drawn from the poles [Cavicchi00]. The phase angle ψ of the IIR low pass digital filter, derived from Figure 4.1 and Equation 4.18, is determined by Equation 4.19.

$$\psi = 2\pi f T_s + \tan^{-1}\left(\frac{\sin 2\pi f T_s}{2 + \cos 2\pi f T_s}\right) - \tan^{-1}\left(\frac{\sin 2\pi f T_s}{\cos 2\pi f T_s - 0.25}\right) \qquad (4.19)$$

The ambiguous calculation of the arctangent ($\tan^{-1}$) must also be considered in the analytical determination of the phase angle. A requirement for no distortion in the *baseband* region is that the phase angle should be a linear function of frequency there. The phase angle ψ is only approximately linear in frequency f due to the first term of Equation 4.18 ($2\pi f T_s$) for this simple IIR low pass digital filter.

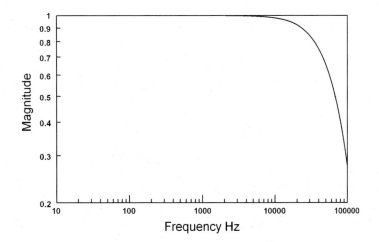

Figure 4.2 IIR low pass digital filter discrete frequency response magnitude
for $T_s = 4 \times 10^{-6}$ sec ($f_s = 250$ kHz)

The IIR low pass digital filter from Equation 4.16 can be rendered as a *building block* in a *direct* form, as shown in Figure 4.3 [Ifeachor02]. The building block uses delay elements (z^{-1}) from storage registers, the gain elements from multipliers, dividers or shifters and an adder from an accumulator. Although the direct form usually requires more storage registers than the *canonic* form, it is less susceptible to internal overflow error and may demonstrate an improved noise performance [Mitra06].

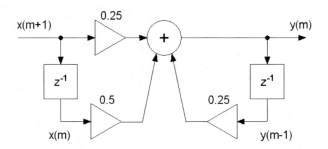

Figure 4.3 IIR low pass digital filter direct form

As a second example, a simple FIR digital filter rendered as the output sequence $y(m)$ in terms of the input sequence $x(m)$ and coefficients from Equation 4.14 will illustrate the discrete frequency response analysis. Here $Q = 1$, $q = -1$, $b_{-1} = -0.5$, $b_0 = 2$ and $b_1 = -1.5$ as determined by Equation 4.20.

$$y(m) = 2\,x(m) - 1.5\,x(m-1) - 0.5\,x(m+1) \qquad (4.20)$$

The discrete frequency transfer function $H(z)$ from Equation 4.13 is determined by Equation 4.21.

$$H(z) = \frac{Y(z)}{X(z)} = 2 - 1.5\,z^{-1} - 0.5\,z = \frac{2\,z - 1.5 - 0.5\,z^2}{z}$$

$$H(z) = \frac{0.5\,(z-3)\,(1-z)}{z}$$

(4.21)

This simple FIR digital filter has one transfer function *pole* (where the response is infinite) at $z = 0$, two transfer function zeros (where the response is zero) at $z = 3$ and $z = 1$ and a multiplicative term of 0.5. The pole (indicated by ×) and the zeros (indicated by ○) of the transfer function are plotted on the complex frequency domain plane, as shown in Figure 4.4. Vectors are drawn from the pole and zeros to an arbitrary point P on the unit circle which represents the sinusoidal excitation of the discrete system $H(z)$.

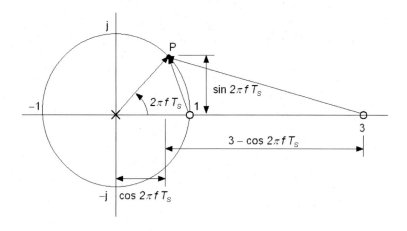

Figure 4.4 FIR digital filter discrete frequency transfer function plotted
on the complex plane

As for the IIR digital filter analyzed previously, the magnitude of the discrete frequency response $|H(z)|$ is determined by the product of the gain G and the length of the vector(s) from the zero(s) divided by the product of the length of the vector(s) from the poles. The simple geometry allows the length of these vectors and the magnitude of the discrete frequency response to be determined as in Equation 4.22.

$$G = 0.5 \qquad L_{p=0} = 1$$

$$L_{z=3} = \sqrt{\left(3 - \cos 2\pi f\,T_s\right)^2 + \sin^2 2\pi f\,T_s}$$

$$L_{z=1} = \sqrt{\left(1 - \cos 2\pi f\,T_s\right)^2 + \sin^2 2\pi f\,T_s}$$

(4.22)

$$|H(z)| = 0.5\sqrt{\left(3 - \cos 2\pi f\,T_s\right)^2 + \sin^2 2\pi f\,T_s} \quad \times$$

$$\sqrt{\left(1 - \cos 2\pi f\,T_s\right)^2 + \sin^2 2\pi f\,T_s}$$

The magnitude of the discrete frequency response of this FIR digital filter is shown in Figure 4.5 on a *log-log* scale plotted against frequency Hz with $T_s = 4 \times 10^{-6}$ sec or $f_s = 1/T_s = 250$ kHz. This FIR digital filter has a *derivating* (d/dt) characteristic because of its approximately linear magnitude response with frequency [Proakis07]. As for the IIR digital filter analyzed previously, this FIR

234

derivating digital filter is efficient because the coefficients and multiplicative gain term are positive and negative powers of the binary base 2 (2^n or 2^{-n}) and can be performed with integer scaling or are formed with a low order addition.

The phase angle ψ of the FIR derivating digital filter then derived from Figure 4.1 and is determined by Equation 4.23.

$$\psi = \pi - 2\pi f\, T_s - \tan^{-1}\left(\frac{\sin 2\pi f\, T_s}{3 - \cos 2\pi f\, T_s} \right) + \tan^{-1}\left(\frac{\sin 2\pi f\, T_s}{1 - \cos 2\pi f\, T_s} \right) \qquad (4.23)$$

The phase angle of a derivating filter should be a constant $\pi / 2$ but the phase angle ψ of the simple FIR derivating digital filter does not strictly meet this requirement.

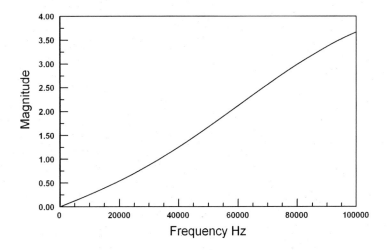

Figure 4.5 FIR derivating digital filter discrete frequency response magnitude
for $T_s = 4 \times 10^{-6}$ sec ($f_s = 250$ kHz)

The FIR derivating digital filter from Equation 4.20 can be rendered as a building block in a direct or *transversal* form, as shown in Figure 4.6 [Ifeachor02]. The transversal FIR digital filter represents a *tapped delay line* and is particularly simple to implement. [Proakis07]. The building block uses delay elements (z^{-1}) from storage registers, the gain elements from multipliers, dividers or shifters and an adder/subtractor from an accumulator.

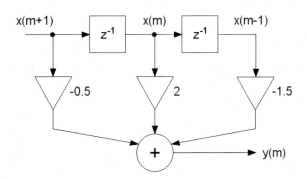

Figure 4.6 FIR derivating digital filter direct or transversal form

Trends in Embedded Design Using Programmable Gate Arrays

IIR and FIR digital filters generally do not have coefficients that are relatively small integer numbers. Often the coefficients are expressed as floating-point numbers during the digital filter design process which must be approximately scaled for integer processing [Chen01]. DSP using floating-point numbers for the coefficients of a digital filter and the data obviates the concern to some degree for *overflow* but may execute relatively slowly.

The determination of the frequency response magnitude and phase angle is tedious if the number of terms in the discrete frequency system function $H(z)$ is large. The difficulty in factoring the resulting expression to determine the location of the poles and zeros is daunting. However, a direct substitution of the equivalence $z = \exp(2\pi f T_s)$ provides a complex value for the discrete frequency system function $H(z)$, as determined here by Equation 4.24 for the FIR digital filter in Equation 4.14 with $q = 0$.

$$H(z) = \sum_{q=0}^{Q} b_q z^{-q} = b_0 + b_1 z^{-1} + b_2 z^{-2} + \ldots + b_Q z^{-Q}$$

$$H(e^{j2\pi f T_s}) = b_0 + b_1 e^{-j2\pi f T_s} + b_2 e^{-j4\pi f T_s} + \ldots + b_Q e^{j2Q\pi f T_s}$$

(4.24)

Substitution of Euler's Identity transforms the sum of complex exponentials in Equation 4.24 to a discernible form in Equation 4.25 where A and B represent the real and imaginary parts of the expansion of $H(\exp(2\pi f T_s))$ evaluated at a frequency f. The computation of the frequency response magnitude and phase angle from Equation 4.25 can be implemented easily in a computer language such as C [Ifeachor02].

MATLAB™ (*www.mathworks.com*) provides a direct function *zplane* which computes and plots the poles and zeros of the discrete frequency system function $H(z)$ directly from the a_p and b_q coefficients. MATLAB also provides a function *freqz* that utilizes a fast Fourier transform (FFT) technique to compute the frequency response magnitude and phase angle [Mitra06].

$$\text{Euler's Identity} \quad e^{-j2\pi f T_s} = \cos 2\pi f T_s - j\sin 2\pi f T$$

$$H(e^{j2\pi f T_s}) = b_0 + b_1[\cos 2\pi f T_s - j\sin 2\pi f T_s] + b_2[\cos 4\pi f T_s - j\sin 4\pi f T_s] + \ldots + b_Q[\cos 2Q\pi f T_s - j\sin 2Q\pi f T_s]$$

$$H(e^{j2\pi f T_s}) = [b_0 + b_1 \cos 2\pi f T_s + b_2 \cos 4\pi f T_s + \ldots + b_Q \cos 2Q\pi f T_s] - j[b_1 \sin 2\pi f T_s + b_2 \sin 4\pi f T_s + \ldots + b_Q \sin 2Q\pi f T_s]$$

$$H(e^{j2\pi f T_s}) = A - jB = \sqrt{A^2 + B^2} \angle \tan^{-1}[-B/A]$$

(4.25)

Analog Output

The output sequence $y(m)$ is converted to a *step-wise* but continuous analog output signal $y(t)$ by a digital-to-analog converter (DAC) peripheral. The analog output voltage resolution (or *step size*) ΔV for a DAC that inputs an unsigned n-bit binary values is determined by Equation 4.26.

$$\Delta V = \frac{V_{REF}}{2^n}$$

(4.26)

V_{REF} is the reference voltage for the DAC and n is the number of bits of resolution. The number of bits of resolution of the discrete time input sequence from the ADC, the resolution in bits of the DSP digital filter or the number of bits of resolution for the DAC need not all be equal.

The analog output signal $y(t)$ from the DAC is a sample-and-hold process, as determined by Equation 4.3. The normalized PSD of the analog output signal from the DAC then is determined by Equation 4.27 [Haykin01].

$$\text{PSD} = f_s^2 \sum_k \left| Y(f - k\,f_s) \right|^2 T_s^2 \operatorname{sinc}^2(2\pi f\,T_s) = \sum_k \left| Y(f - k\,f_s) \right|^2 \operatorname{sinc}^2(2\pi f\,T_s) \qquad (4.27)$$

The normalized PSD of the DAC analog output signal $y(t)$ is $|\,Y(f)\,|^2$. The PSD is not theoretically bandlimited but repeats the baseband PSD centered at multiples of the sampling rate f_s, as determined by Equation 4.26. However, the PSD is practically bandlimited because of the sinc^2 (sinc x = sin x/x) term which decreases in magnitude as the frequency increases. An analog low pass filter is often placed after the DAC analog output to *smooth* the discrete time step-wise response.

The four channel Digilent PmodDA1 DAC hardware module, as described in Chapter 3, has n = 8 and V_{REF} = 3.3 V DC with ΔV = 3.3/256 ≈ 12.89 mV. The two channel Digilent Pmod DA2 DAC hardware module, as described in Chapter 3, has n = 12 and V_{REF} = 3.3 V DC with ΔV = 3.3/4096 ≈ 0.806 mV. Neither of these DACs provide an integral analog output filter to smooth the discrete time signal and produce an analog step-wise response.

Digital Signal Processing Embedded System

The digital signal processing (DSP) embedded hardware system consists of an ADC, field programmable gate array (FPGA) and DAC, as shown in Figure 4.7. The ADC provides n-bit data to the FPGA processor and receives an a-bit data packet for command and control. The DAC receives both m-bit data and a d-bit data packet for command and control from the FPGA processor.

A crystal oscillator provides a clock signal (CLOCK) to the FPGA for synchronization and timing of the data transfers and to establish the sampling rate f_s of the DSP system. The DSP embedded hardware system can optionally also have input/output (I/O) devices such as light emitting diodes (LED), liquid crystal display (LCD), switches and data communication ports, as described in Chapter 3 Programmable Gate Array Hardware.

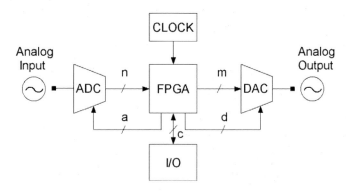

Figure 4.7 DSP embedded hardware system

The DSP system executes on the FPGA hardware using Verilog HDL structural and behavioral synthesis modules that are developed using software electronic design automation (EDA) tools, as described in Chapter 2 Verilog Design Automation. The Verilog modules are configured as finite state machines (FSM) and the controller and datapath constructs, as described in Chapter 1

Trends in Embedded Design Using Programmable Gate Arrays

Verilog Hardware Description Language. These Verilog HDL modules and simple applications were introduced in Chapter 3 Programmable gate Array Hardware but are extended here to applications in DSP.

A DSP system is initially implemented as a *straight-through* processor that inputs and outputs an analog signal without any manipulation to assess the maximum data throughput rate. The DSP system to be benchmarked is the Digilent PmodAD1 and Pmod DA2 hardware modules both processed by the FPGA, as described in Chapter 3 Programmable Gate Array Hardware.

This straight-through DSP system utilizing the PmodAD1 ADC and PmodDA2 DAC is implemented with the Verilog top module *ns3ad1da2.v* for the Nexys 3 Board, which is in the *Chapter 4\adcdac\ns3ad1da2* folder, as given in Listing 4.1. The Xilinx ISE project uses the UCF *ns3ad1da2.ucf* which uncomments the signals CLK, SW0, JA1 to JA4, JB1 to JB4 and JC1 in the Nexys 3 Board UCF of Listing 3.1. The four Verilog modules operate in parallel and some independently in the top module. The file download procedure is described in the Appendix.

Listing 4.1 DSP PmodAD1 ADC and PmodDA1 DAC DSP system top module *ns3ad1da2.v*

```
// Nexys 3 Board
// DSP System ns3ad1da2.v
// c 2012 Embedded Design using Programmable Gate Arrays  Dennis Silage

module ns3ad1da2 (input CLK, SW0, JA1, JA3, output JA1, JA4, JB1, JB2, JB3, JB4, JC1);

wire adcdav, davadc, adcsck, adc0d, adc1d, adccs;
wire dacdav, davdac, dacsck, dacout, dacsync, sysclk;
wire [11:0] dacdata;
wire [1:0] dacmd;
wire [11:0] adc0data, adc1data;

assign JA1 = adccs;        // ADC AD1 on JA
assign adc0d = JA2;
assign adc1d = JA3;
assign JA4 = adcsck;
assign JB1 = dacsync;      // DAC DA1 on JB
assign JB2 = dacout;
assign JB3 = 0;
assign JB4 = dacsck;
assign JC1 = adccs;        // monitor sampling rate

ad1adc M0 (sysclk, adcdav, davadc, adc0data, adc1data, adcsck, adc0d, adc1d, adccs);
da2dac M1 (sysclk, dacdav, davdac, dacout, dacsck, dacsync, daccmd, dacdata);
genad1da2 M2 (CLK, SW0, adcdav, davadc, adc0data, adc1data, dacdav, davdac, dacdata, daccmd);
clock M3 (CLK, 2, sysclk);      // 25 MHz

endmodule

module genad1da2 (input genclk, SW0, output reg adcdav = 0, input davadc, input [11:0] adc0data,
                  input [11:0] adc1data, output reg dacdav = 0, input davdac,
                  output reg [11:0] dacdata, output reg [1:0] daccmd = 0);

always@(posedge genclk)
    begin
        adcdav = 1;                // ADC conversion
```

238

```
        dacdav = 1;              // DAC conversion, in parallel

     if (davadc == 1 && davdac == 1)      // ADC and DAC status
          begin
               adcdav = 0;
               davdac = 0;
               if (SW0 == 0)   // select one ADC channel
                    dacdata = adc0data;
               else
                    dacdata = adc1data;
          end
     end

endmodule
```

The Verilog top module *ns3ad1da2.v* utilizes the *ad1adc.v* module for the PmodAD1 ADC and the *da2dac.v* module for the PmodDA2 DAC, as described in Chapter 3 Programmable Gate Array Hardware. The PmodAD1 hardware module is connected to JA and the PmodDA2 hardware module is connected to JB on the Nexys 3 Board. The *clock.v* module provides a 25 MHz system clock sysclk to the *ad1adc.v* and *da2dac.v* modules, as determined by Equation 3.1.

The 12-pin peripheral hardware module connector JC is used to monitor the ADC conversion command signal adccs on JC1 and the sampling rate is $f_s \approx 714$ ksamples/sec. One half the sampling rate $f_s/2$ is above the −3 dB cutoff frequency f_{cutoff} of the anti-aliasing filter of the Digilent PmodAD1 ADC (500 kHz). To avoid aliasing, an analog filter with a cutoff frequency $f_{cutoff} < f_s/2$ or $f_{cutoff} < 357$ kHz would be appropriate here.

Figure 4.8 shows the ADC analog input and DAC analog output of the straight-through DSP system for a 5 kHz (left) and 50 kHz (right) sinusoid. At a frequency of 50 kHz the output sinusoid in Figure 4.8 (right) is *discrete step-wise* due to the sampling rate and displays inherent noise due to the processing system and lack of analog filtering of the DAC output. At 50 kHz there are only 714/50 ≈ 14 samples per cycle, whereas at 5 kHz there are ≈ 140 samples per cycles.

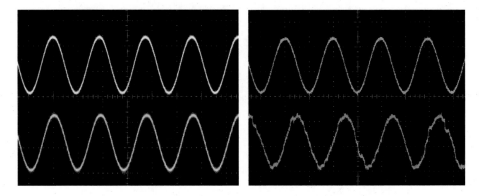

Figure 4.8 ADC input (top) and DAC output (bottom) of the straight-through
DSP system *ns3ad1da2.v* for a sinusoidal input at 0.5 V/div and
100 μsec/div (left) and 0.5 V/div and 10 μsec/div (right)

Although data from the two ADC channels are available simultaneously as adc0data and adc1data, only one channel of the PmodDA2 DAC is used. The output data of the PmodAD1 ADC and the input data of the PmodDA2 DAC are both 12-bit, utilize a straight binary data representation and no data conversion is required.

Trends in Embedded Design Using Programmable Gate Arrays

The module *genad1da2.v* does not use an FSM controller for the DSP system. The PmodAD1 ADC and PmodDA2 DAC status signals davadc and davdac from the datapath modules *ad1adc.v* and *da2dac.v* are processed in parallel and both provide a logic 1 signal to indicate that conversion has completed. This implies that the slower peripheral sets the ultimate sampling rate of the DSP system.

Without an FSM, the module *genad1da2.v* is event driven on the positive edge of the 100 MHz master clock. On the first event the ADC and DAC conversion is initiated by the controller command adcdav and dacdav to the *ad1adc.v* and *da2dac.v* datapath modules. On the second and succeeding events in the sequence if the ADC and DAC status signals davadc and davdac are both logic 1, then the data exchange occurs. These events occur at an interval of $1/(100 \times 10^6) = 10$ nsec.

The PmodAD1 ADC has a maximum data rate of 0.781 Msamples/sec or a minimum conversion period of 1.28 µsec, as described in Chapter 3 Programmable Gate Array Hardware. similarly, the PmodDA2 DAC has a maximum data rate of 1.515 Msamples/sec or a minimum conversion period of 0.66 µsec. The slower peripheral here is the ADC which requires 1280 positive edge master clock events to occur for signal conversion.

The DAC is outputting the previous analog signal sampled by the ADC while the ADC is obtaining the current analog signal sample. Slide switch SW0 selects one of the two available ADC channels. Thus there is a one sample delay of the DAC output of $1/f_s = 1/(714 \times 10^5) \approx 1.4$ µsec, as shown clearly by the phase delay between input and output sinusoids in Figure 4.8 (left).

As described in Chapter 2 Verilog Design Automation, the Design Utilization Summary for the top module *ns3ad1da2.v* shows the use of 60 slice registers (<1%) and 96 slice LUTs (1%) in the Nexys 3 Board XC6SLX16 Spartan-6 FPGA synthesis.

IIR Digital Filter

The simple IIR low pass digital filter in Equation 4.16 is implemented as a DSP system, as shown in Figure 4.3 and Figure 4.7. The Verilog top module *ns3ad1lpfda1.v* is given in Listing 4.2, which is in the *Chapter 4\adcdac\ns3ad1lpfda2* folder. The Xilinx ISE project uses the UCF *ns3ad1lpfda2.ucf* which uncomments the signals CLK, SW0, SW1, JA1 to JA4, JB1 to JB4 and JC1 in the Nexys 3 Board UCF of Listing 3.1. The five Verilog modules operate in parallel and some independently in the top module. The file download procedure is described in the Appendix.

The Verilog top module *ns3ad1lpfda2.v* utilizes the *ad1adc.v* module for the PmodAD1 ADC and the *da2dac.v* module for the PmodDA2 DAC, as described in Chapter 3 Programmable Gate Array Hardware, is given in Listing 4.2. The first *clock.v* module provides a 25 MHz system clock sysclk to the *ad1adc.v* and *da2dac.v* modules, as determined by Equation 3.1.

The second clock module *clock.v* provides a 500 kHz clock genclock used to set the sampling rate $f_s = 250$ ksamples/sec. As described for the straight-through DSP system in Listing 4.1, the module *genad1lpfda2.v* is event driven on the positive edge of the 500 kHz clock or at a period of 2 µsec. This period is larger than that required for either the ADC and DAC conversion to occur. On the second event the IIR filter processing occurs and is completed within the available 2 µsec period. Thus IIR filter samples data on every other event, or a sampling rate $f_s = 250$ ksamples/sec which is monitored on port JC1.

Listing 4.2 Simple IIR low pass digital filter DSP system top module *ns3ad1lpfda1.v*

```
// Nexys 3 Board
// IIR Low Pass Filter ns3ad1lpfda2.v
// c 2012 Embedded Design using Programmable Gate Arrays  Dennis Silage

module ns3ad1lpfda2 (input CLK, SW0, SW1, JA2, JA3, output JA1, JA4, JB1, JB2, JB3, JB4, JC1);

wire adcdav, davadc, adcsck, adc0d, adc1d, adccs;
wire dacdav, davdac, dacsck, dacout, dacsync, sysclk, genclk;
```

```
wire [11:0] dacdata;
wire [1:0] dacmd;
wire [11:0] adc0data, adc1data;

assign JA1 = adccs;        // ADC PmodAD1 on JA
assign adc0d = JA2;
assign adc1d = JA3;
assign JA4 = adcsck;
assign JB1 = dacsync;      // DAC PmodDA2 on JB
assign JB2 = dacout;
assign JB3 = 0;
assign JB4 = dacsck;
assign JC1 = adccs;        // monitor sampling rate

ad1adc M0 (sysclk, adcdav, davadc, adc0data, adc1data, adcsck, adc0d, adc1d, adccs);
da2dac M1 (sysclk, dacdav, davdac, dacout, dacsck, dacsync, daccmd, dacdata);
genad1lpfda2 M2 (smpclk, SW0, SW1, adcdav, davadc, adc0data, adc1data, dacdav, davdac, dacdata,
                 daccmd);
clock M3 (CLK, 2, sysclk);      // 25 MHz
clock M4 (CLK, 100, genclk);    // 500 kHz

endmodule

module genad1lpfda2 (input genclk, SW0, SW1, output reg adcdav = 0, input davadc,
                     input [11:0] adc0data, input [11:0] adc1data, output reg dacdav = 0,
                     input davdac, output reg [11:0] dacdata, output reg [1:0] daccmd = 0);

reg [11:0] value;
reg [11:0] xa;        // x(m)
reg [11:0] xb;        // x(m+1)
reg [11:0] ya;        // y(m)
reg [11:0] yc;        // y(m−1)

always@(posedge smpclk)
    begin
            adcdav = 1;      // ADC conversion
            dacdav = 1;      // DAC conversion, in parallel

            if (davadc == 1 && davdac == 1)      // ADC and DAC status
                begin
                    adcdav = 0;
                    dacdav = 0;
                    if (SW0 == 0)            // select one ADC channel
                        value = adc0data;
                    else
                        value = adc1data;
                    if (SW1 == 0)
                        begin
                            xa = xb;    // IIR filter
                            xb = value;
                            yc = ya;
                            ya = (xa/2) + (xb/4) + (yc/4);
```

```
                        dacdata = ya;
                end
        else
                dacdata = value;        // bypass filtering
        end
    end

endmodule
```

The module *genadclpfdac.v* does not use an FSM for the IIR low pass digital filter DSP system, as described for the straight-through DSP system in Listing 4.1. From Equation 4.16, the IIR filter utilizes four 12-bit registers which represent $x(m+1)$ as xb, $x(m)$ as xa, $y(m)$ as ya and $y(m-1)$ as yc. The registers must be *pushed-down* to store the immediate values before being updated and the Verilog blocking assignment statement assures this, as described in Chapter 1 Verilog Hardware Description Language.

The register xb is stored as the register xa before being updated with the current ADC output signal as the register value. Similarly, the immediate output register ya is stored as the register yc before the IIR filter calculation is performed.

Slide switch SW0 selects one of the two available ADC channels and SW1 is used to bypass the IIR low pass digital filter to provide the straight-through response. The frequency response can then be assessed on an oscilloscope by comparing the input sinusoidal excitation as the straight-through response to that of the output of the IIR low pass digital filter.

Figure 4.9 shows the ADC analog input and DAC analog output of the IIR low pass digital filter DSP system for a 500 Hz (left) and 5 kHz (right) square wave. The 5 kHz low pass filtered square wave shows a reduction in high frequency content [Haykin01]. The discrete step-wise response in Figure 4.9 (right) is due to the sampling rate $f_s = 250$ ksamples/sec and displays inherent noise due to the processing system and lack of analog filtering of the DAC output. At 5 kHz there are 250/5 = 50 samples per cycle, whereas at 500 Hz there are 500 samples per cycles.

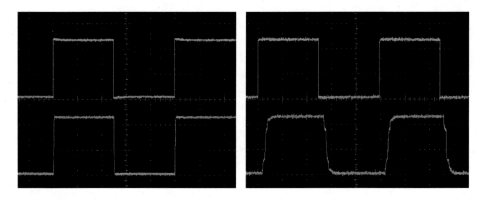

Figure 4.9 ADC input (top) and DAC output (bottom) of the IIR low pass
DSP system *ns3ad1lpfda2.v* for a square wave input at 0.5 V/div and
400 µsec/div (left) and 0.5 V/div and 40 µsec/div (right)

As described in Chapter 2 Verilog Design Automation, the Design Utilization Summary for the top module *ns3ad1lpfda2.v* shows the use of 148 slice registers (<1%) and 303 slice LUTs (3%) in the Nexys 3 Board XC6SLX16 Spartan-6 FPGA synthesis.

FIR Digital Filter

The simple FIR derivating digital filter in Equation 4.20 is implemented as a DSP system, as shown in Figure 4.6 and Figure 4.7. The Verilog top module *ns3adcddtdac.v* is given in Listing 4.3, which is in the *Chapter 4\adcdac\ns3adcddtdac* folder. The Xilinx ISE project uses the UCF *ns3ad1ddtda2.ucf* which uncomments the signals CLK, SW0, SW1, JA1 to JA4, JB1 to JB4 and JC1 in the Nexys 3 Board UCF of Listing 3.1. The five Verilog modules operate in parallel and some independently in the top module. The file download procedure is described in the Appendix.

The Verilog top module *ns3adcddtdac.v* is similar to the *ns3adcdlpfdac.v* module in Listing 4.2 and illustrates the concept of *design reuse*. The modules operate in a similar manner and utilize the PmodAD1 ADC and PmodDA2 DAC, as described in Chapter 3 Programmable Gate Array Hardware. The sampling rate remains f_s = 250 ksamples/sec. However, the module *genadcddtdac.v* for the derivating digital filter is different.

Listing 4.3 Simple FIR derivating digital filter DSP system *ns3adcddtdac.v*

```
// Nexys 3 Board
// FIR Derivating Filter ns3ad1ddtda2.v
// c 2012 Embedded Design using Programmable Gate Arrays  Dennis Silage

module ns3ad1ddtda2 (input CLK, SW0, SW1, JA2, JA3, output JA1, JA4,
                     output JB1, JB2, JB3, JB4, JC1);

wire adcdav, davadc, adcsck, adc0d, adc1d, adccs;
wire dacdav, davdac, dacsck, dacout, dacsync, sysclk, genclk;
wire [11:0] dacdata;
wire [1:0] dacmd;
wire [11:0] adc0data, adc1data;

assign JA1 = adccs;          // ADC PmodAD1 on JA
assign adc0d = JA2;
assign adc1d = JA3;
assign JA4 = adcsck;
assign JB1 = dacsync;        // DAC PmodDA2 on JB
assign JB2 = dacout;
assign JB3 = 0;
assign JB4 = dacsck;
assign JC1 = adccs;          // monitor sampling rate

ad1adc M0 (sysclk, adcdav, davadc, adc0data, adc1data, adcsck, adc0d, adc1d, adccs);
da2dac M1 (sysclk, dacdav, davdac, dacout, dacsck, dacsync, daccmd, dacdata);
genad1ddtda2 M2 (genclk, SW0, SW1, adcdav, davadc, adc0data, adc1data, dacdav, davdac,
                 dacdata, daccmd);
clock M3 (CLK, 2, sysclk);      // 25 MHz
clock M4 (CLK, 100, genclk);  // 500 kHz

endmodule

module genad1ddtda2 (input genclk, SW0, SW1, output reg adcdav=0, input davadc,
                     input [11:0] adc0data, input [11:0] adc1data, output reg dacdav=0,
                     input davdac, output reg [11:0] dacdata, output reg [1:0] daccmd=0);
```

```
reg [11:0] value;
reg [11:0] xa;        // x(m)
reg [11:0] xb;        // x(m+1)
reg [11:0] xc;        // x(m-1)
reg [11:0] ya;        // y(m)

always@(posedge genclk)
    begin
            adcdav = 1;      // ADC conversion
            dacdav = 1;      // DAC conversion, in parallel

        if (davadc == 1 && davdac == 1)     // ADC and DAC status
            begin
                adcdav = 0;
                dacdav = 0;
                if (SW0 == 0)        // select one ADC channel
                    value = adc0data;
                else
                    value = adc1data;
                if (SW1 == 0)
                    begin
                        xc = xa;    // FIR filter
                        xa = xb;
                        xb = value;
                        ya = (2*xa) - (xb/2) - ((xc+xc+xc)/2);
                        dacdata = ya + 2048; // DC offset
                    end
                else
                    dacdata = value;         // bypass filtering
            end
    end

endmodule
```

From Equation 4.20, the FIR filter utilizes three 12-bit registers which represent $x(m+1)$ as xb, $x(m)$ as xa and $x(m-1)$ as xc. The registers must also be *pushed-down* to store the immediate values before being updated. The register xb is stored as the register xa before being updated with the current ADC output signal as the unsigned 12-bit register value. However, the derivating digital filter can provide negative output values during the computation and a half-scale (2048) DC offset is added for the DAC output.

Slide switch SW0 selects one of the two available ADC channels and SW1 is used to bypass the FIR derivating digital filter to provide the *straight-through* response. The derivating response can then be assessed on an oscilloscope by comparing an input sinusoidal excitation as the straight-through response to that of the output of the FIR digital filter.

Figure 4.10 shows the PmodAD1 ADC analog input and PmodDA2 DAC analog output of the FIR derivating digital filter DSP system for a 5 kHz sine wave (left) and triangle wave (right). The horizontal cursor lines in Figure 4.10 are at 0 V. The response in Figure 4.10 (left, bottom) to the input sinusoid is also a sinusoid with an approximate phase relationship of $\pi / 2 = 90°$ that is expected for a derivative.

The expected phase relationship of the derivating output of 90° (50 μsec at 5 kHz) is further delayed by approximately 14 μsec. This is due in part to the non-ideal phase response of the derivating filter, as described in Equation 4.23. A small amount of this delay though is due to the processing inherent in the FIR digital filter. The output data $y(m)$ is delayed by one sample interval $T_s = 1/f_s = 4$ μsec from the input data $x(m+1)$, as determined by Equation 4.20. Note that the derivative of the triangle wave in Figure 4.10 (right, bottom) as expected is a square wave.

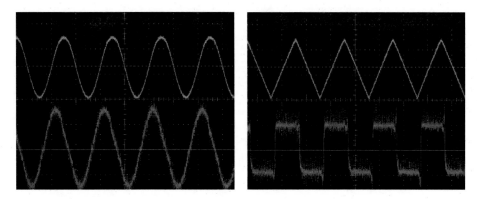

Figure 4.10 ADC input (top) and DAC output (bottom) of the FIR derivating DSP system *ns3ad1ddtda2.v* for a sine wave (left) and triangle wave (right) input at 0.5 V/div and 100 μsec/div

As described in Chapter 2 Verilog Design Automation, the Design Utilization Summary for the top module *ns3ad1ddtda2.v* shows the use of 151 slice registers (<1%) and 314 slice LUTs (3%) in the Nexys 3 Board XC6SLX16 Spartan-6 FPGA synthesis.

FIR Compiler LogiCORE Block

The Xilinx CORE Generator provides a FIR Compiler LogiCORE block, as in Chapter 2 Verilog Design Automation. The Xilinx FIR Compiler is a common interface for the design of FPGA resource efficient FIR digital filters with either multiply-accumulate (MAC) or distributed arithmetic (DA) architectures [Ifeachor02]. The Xilinx FIR Compiler provides sufficient arithmetic precision to avoid overflow and is described in data sheet DS534 (*www.xilinx.com*).

FIR digital filters can be implemented as single-rate, interpolated or multi-rate [Mitra06]. The single-rate FIR digital filter is conceptualizes as a tapped-delay line, as shown in Figure 4.11 and where the index $q = 0$ as determined by Equation 4.9 [Proakis07]. Although correct in essence, the actual implementation using an FPGA is different. If the MAC architecture is selected in the FIR Compiler, one or more MAC functional units are used to provide the Q sum-of-product calculations for the specified data throughput. If the DA architecture is selected only look-up tables (LUT), shift registers and an accumulator are used.

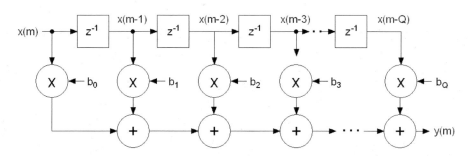

Figure 4.11 Tapped-delay line, single rate FIR digital filter

Trends in Embedded Design Using Programmable Gate Arrays

The Xilinx FIR Compiler LogiCORE block provides from 2 to 1024 *taps* (equivalent to $Q+1$ in Figure 4.11) and integer signed or unsigned coefficients that range from 2 to 35 bit precision. The signed or unsigned integer data widths can be as large as 35 bits in the Xilinx Spartan-6 FPGA. The FIR Compiler is evoked from within a Xilinx ISE project, as described in Chapter 2 Verilog Design Automation.

The first design window of the FIR Compiler LogiCORE block is shown in Figure 4.12. The component name (fir1) is specified, the coefficients are inputted directly as a vector, a single-rate FIR digital filter type is chosen, one data channel is used (although up to 64 channels are possible), the sample frequency (or sampling rate) is 0.25 MHz (250 ksamples/sec) and the clock frequency is 100 MHz. The clock and sample frequency parameters specified here are those utilized with the Nexys 3 Board and the PmodAD1 ADC and PmodDA2 DAC in the previous DSP systems in this Chapter.

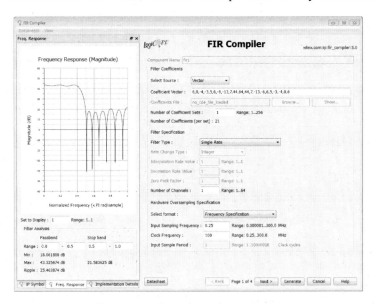

Figure 4.12 First design window of the FIR Compiler LogiCORE block

The coefficients can also be inputted as a ASCII text data file with the file extension *.coe*. (*fir1.coe*), as given in Listing 4.4. The 21 symmetrical coefficients here are 8-bit signed integers (range −128 to 127) specified by an ASCII text data file The first line of the file is the declaration of the coefficient radix, which can be 2 (binary), 10 (decimal) or 16 (hexadecimal), terminated by a semicolon (;). The integer FIR digital filter coefficients are then separated by a comma (,) and terminated with a semicolon. This arbitrary set of symmetrical, signed integer coefficients is essentially the sampled impulse response of a low pass FIR digital filter [Mitra06].

Listing 4.4 FIR Compiler coefficent file *fir1.coe*

radix = 10;
coefdata = 6, 0, −4, −3, 5, 6, −6, −13, 7, 44, 64, 44, 7, −13, −6, 6, 5, −3, −4, 0, 6;

The second design window of the FIR Compiler LogiCORE block is shown in Figure 4.13. This window specifies the filter architecture as either systolic MAC, transpose MAC or DA, the coefficient structure as inferred, symmetric or non-symmetric, the coefficient type as signed or unsigned, the quantization as integer, quantize or maximum dynamic range, the coefficient width, the number of data paths, the input data type, width and fractional bits, output rounding mode and registered outputs. The input data is derived from the 12-bit unsigned PmodAD1 ADC. The output rounding mode as truncate the least significant bits (LSB) specifies the output bit width. The data is outputted to the 12-bit PmodDA2 DAC. The FIR Compiler determines that the full precision output rounding mode results in 21 bits.

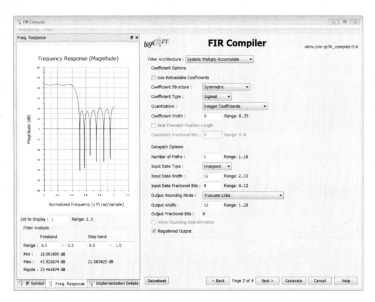

Figure 4.13 Second design window of the FIR Compiler LogiCORE block

The third design window of the FIR Compiler LogiCORE block specifies the control and implementation options of the digital filter, as shown in Figure 4.14. Using the *tab menu* the IP symbol for the LogiCORE device is shown in Figure 4.14.

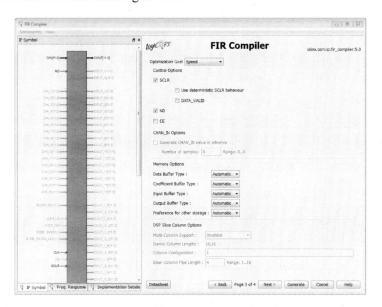

Figure 4.14 Third design window of the FIR Compiler LogiCORE block

The FIR Compiler is a controller and datapath construct optimized for speed or area, as described in Chapter 1 Verilog Hardware Description Language. The synchronous clear input signal

Trends in Embedded Design Using Programmable Gate Arrays

sclr resets the internal state machine of the FIR digital filter with the clock input clk. The new data input signal nd loads the data sample input into the FIR digital filter core.

The ready for input data status signal rfd is asserted as a logic 1 to load new data. The data ready status signal rdy indicates that the FIR digital filter data output is available. The memory buffer for the data and coefficients of the FIR digital filter can utilize block or distributed FPGA random access memory (RAM), as described in Chapter 2 Verilog Design Automation. Here the FIR Compiler automatically selects the implementation.

Finally, the fourth design window of the FIR Compiler LogiCORE block is the summary screen for the parameters of the digital filter, as shown in Figure 4.15. The tab menu can display the magnitude of the low pass frequency response of the digital filter. The frequency axis is normalized and 1.0 represents a frequency of $f_s/2$ Hz, where f_s is the sampling rate. Here $f_s = 250$ ksamples/sec and the FIR digital filter displays a -2-2 dB *roll off* for the first spectral notch at a frequency of $f_s/4 = 62.5$ kHz.

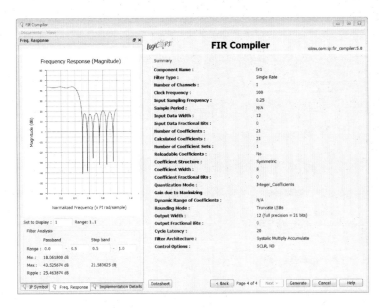

Figure 4.15 Fourth design window of the FIR Compiler LogiCORE block

Another tab menu provides a resource estimate for the implementation of the digital filter. The generation of the FIR Compiler LogiCORE block provides Verilog components, including the module instantiation template file *fir1.veo*, as given in Listing 4.5. The template file for the FIR Compiler is instantiated into the design by adding the module to the project, as described in Chapter 2 Verilog Design Automation. *YourInstanceName* is changed to M3 in the top module of the FIR Compiler LogiCORE block DSP system in Listing 4.6 and the port connections by name are changed to reflect the actual connections in the Xilinx ISE project, as described in Chapter 1 Verilog Hardware Description Language.

Listing 4.5 FIR Compiler LogiCORE block instantiation template file *fir1.veo*

```
// The following must be inserted into your Verilog file for this
// core to be instantiated. Change the instance name and port connections
// (in parentheses) to your own signal names.
//----------- Begin Cut here for INSTANTIATION Template ---// INST_TAG
fir1 YourInstanceName (
    .sclr(sclr), // input sclr
```

```
        .clk(clk),    // input clk
        .nd(nd),      // input nd
        .rfd(rfd),    // output rfd
        .rdy(rdy),    // output rdy
        .din(din),    // input [11 : 0] din
        .dout(dout));    // output [11 : 0] dout
// INST_TAG_END ------ End INSTANTIATION Template ---------
```

The FIR Compiler has the capability to reload coefficients on a separate data bus and change the digital filter function with an external command. The FIR Compiler can also utilize different coefficient sets for multiple data channel. However, these and other advanced capabilities of the FIR Compiler LogiCORE block are not used here but are described in the data sheet DS534 (*www.xilinx.com*).

FIR Compiler Digital Filter

The FIR Compiler digital filter is implemented as a *wavefront* digital signal processing (DSP) system in which the processing tasks of the ADC, FIR filter and DAC essentially occur in parallel, as shown in Figure 4.7. The PmodAD1 ADC and PmodDA2 DAC provide data conversion in parallel, as for the IIR and FIR digital filters in Listing 4.2 and Listing 4.3, but here the digital filter is also implemented in parallel.

The Verilog top module *ns3ad1firda2.v* is given in Listing 4.6, which is also located in the *Chapter 4\adcdac\s3ead1firda2* folder. The Xilinx ISE project uses the UCF *ns3ad1firda2.ucf* which uncomments the signals CLK, SW0, SW1, JA1 to JA4, JB1 to JB4 and JC1 to JC4 in the Nexys 3 Board UCF of Listing 3.1. The six Verilog modules operate in parallel and some independently in the top module. The file download procedure is described in the Appendix.

Listing 4.6 FIR Compiler LogiCORE block DSP system *nsead1firda2.v*

```
// Nexys 3 Board
// FIR Compiler ns3ad1firda2.v
// c 2012 Embedded Design using Programmable Gate Arrays  Dennis Silage

module ns3ad1firda2 (input CLK, SW0, SW1, JA2, JA3, output JA1, JA4, JB1, JB2, JB3, JB4, JC1,
                     JC2, JC3, JC4);

wire adcdav, davadc, adcsck, adc0d, adc1d, adccs;
wire dacdav, davdac, dacsck, dacout, dacsync, sysclk, genclk;
wire [11:0] dacdata;
wire [1:0] dacmd;
wire [11:0] adc0data, adc1data;
wire [11:0] firdin, firdout;

assign JA1 = adccs;        // ADC PmodAD1 on JA
assign adc0d = JA2;
assign adc1d = JA3;
assign JA4 = adcsck;
assign JB1 = dacsync;      // DAC PmodDA2 on JB
assign JB2 = dacout;
assign JB3 = 0;
assign JB4 = dacsck;
assign JC1 = adccs;        // monitor sampling rate
```

```
assign JC2 = rfd;        // FIR ready for data
assign JC3 = rdy;        // FIR data ready
assign JC4 = nd;         // FIR new data

ad1adc M0 (sysclk, adcdav, davadc, adc0data, adc1data, adcsck, adc0d, adc1d, adccs);
da2dac M1 (sysclk, dacdav, davdac, dacout, dacsck, dacsync, daccmd, dacdata);
genad1firda2 M2 (genclk, CLK, SW0, SW1, adcdav, davadc, adc0data, adc1data, dacdav, davdac,
            dacdata, daccmd, sclr, rfd, rdy, nd, firdout, firdin);
fir1 M3 (.sclr(sclr),.clk(CLK),.nd(nd),.rfd(rfd),.rdy(rdy),.din(firdin),.dout(firdout));
clock M4 (CLK, 2, sysclk);      // 25 MHz
clock M5 (CLK, 100, genclk);   // 500 kHz

endmodule

module genad1firda2 (input genclk, firclk, SW0, SW1, output reg adcdav = 0, input davadc,
            input [11:0] adc0data, input [11:0] adc1data, output reg dacdav = 0,
            input davdac, output reg [11:0] dacdata, output reg [1:0] daccmd = 0,
            output reg sclr = 0, input rfd, rdy, output reg nd = 0, input [11:0] firdout,
            output reg [11:0] firdin);

always@(posedge genclk)
     begin
          adcdav = 1;        // ADC conversion
          dacdav = 1;        // DAC conversion, in parallel
          if (davadc == 1 && davdac == 1)      // ADC and DAC status
               begin
                    adcdav = 0;
                    dacdav = 0;
                    if (SW0 == 0)   // select one ADC channel
                         firdin = adc0data;
                    else
                         firdin = adc1data;
               end
     end

always@(posedge firclk)
     begin
          if (SW1 == 0)
               begin                     // FIR filter
                    if (rfd == 1)        // FIR filter ready for data
                         nd = 1;         // load new FIR filter data
                    if (rdy == 1)        // FIR filter data ready
                         begin
                              nd = 0;
                              dacdata = firdout;
                         end
               end
          else
               dacdata = firdin;      // bypass filtering
     end

endmodule
```

The Verilog top module *ns3ad1firda2.v* is similar to the *ns3ad1lpfda2.v* in Listing 4.2. The 12-pin peripheral hardware module connector JC is used to monitor the ADC conversion command signal adccs as JC1, the FIR Compiler digital filter ready for input data signal rfd as JC2, the data ready output signal rdy as JC3 and the new data input signal nd as JC4. The sampling rate f_s = 250 ksamples/sec is the same as for the IIR and FIR digital filters in Listing 4.2 and Listing 4.3.

The estimated cycle latency of the FIR filter from the FIR Compiler LogiCORE block, as shown in Figure 4.15, is $20 \times T_{clock}$ = 0.2 μsec, where T_{clock} = 10 nsec since the frequency of the master clock CLK of the Nexys 3 Board f_{clock} = 100 MHz. The actual latency of the digital filter calculation can be determined from the time interval between the assertion of the new data input signal nd on the hardware module connector JC4 and the appearance of the data ready output signal rdy on JC3 and is measured to be 0.2 μsec.

The sampling period here $T_s = 1/f_s$ = 4 μsec and the sampling rate for the wavefront DSP system is limited by the execution time of the longest task. The data conversion for the PmodDA2 DAC requires 0.66 μsec and that for the PmodAD1 ADC requires 1.28 μsec, as described in Chapter 3 Programmable Gate Array Hardware. Thus the PmodAD1 ADC limits the sampling rate of the DSP system to approximately $1/1.28 \times 10^{-6} \approx 780$ ksamples/sec.

The controller module *genad1firda2.v* utilizes two event driven processes for the digital filter DSP system. The first event occurs on the positive edge of the clock genclk (500 kHz) and initiates ADC and DAC data conversion. The second event occurs in parallel on the positive edge of the clock firclk but at a faster rate (100 MHz) and controls the FIR Compiler datapath. The control signal nd loads new 12-bit data and the status rdy indicates that the 12-bit output is available.

Slide switch SW0 selects one of the two available ADC channels and SW1 is used to bypass the FIR digital filter to provide the straight-through response. The frequency response can then be assessed on an oscilloscope by comparing the input sinusoidal excitation as the straight-through response to that of the output of the FIR Compiler digital filter.

The low frequency gain of the digital filter $G_{lf} \approx 148$, which is obtained by summing the coefficients in Listing 4.4 [Proakis07]. The low frequency voltage gain is $20 \log_{10}(148)$ = 43.4 dB, as shown in Figure 4.15. The output is the 12 most significant bits (MSB) of the full precision output of 21 bits since the 9 least significant bits (LSB) are truncated here, as shown in Figure 4.15. The nominal low frequency gain of the FIR Compiler digital filter then is given by $2^{12}/2^{21} \times 148 \approx 0.289$.

As described in Chapter 2 Verilog Design Automation, the Design Utilization Summary for the module *ns3ad1firda2.v* shows the use of 210 slice registers (1%), 218 slice LUTs (2%) and 1 multiply-accumulate (MAC, type DSP48A1) in the Nexys 3 Board XC6SLX16 Spartan-6 FPGA synthesis. The FIR Compiler determines that only one time-shared MAC is required to service the sum-of-product calculations in the FIR filter based on the specified clock (100 MHz) and sample rate (250 ksamples/sec).

FIR Complier Implementations

The FIR Compiler coefficient file facilitates the convenient restructuring of the digital filter without the necessity of modifying a Verilog HDL structure, as is required for the IIR and FIR digital filters in Listing 4.2 and Listing 4.3. For example, a new coefficient file generates new frequency response parameters and reconfigures the FIR filter. The FIR Compiler also provides the half-band, Hilbert transform, interpolator and decimator implementations of the FIR digital filter [Chen01].

The half-band FIR digital filter provides a low-pass filter response with as cutoff frequency at $f_s/4$ Hz, where f_s is the sampling rate, with equal *passband* δ_p and *stopband* δ_s amplitude *ripples*, as shown in Figure 4.16. Approximately half of the half-band digital filter coefficients are *interleaved* zeros which can be exploited to provide an efficient implementation [Ifeachor02]. The passband to stop band attenuation performance of the half-band digital filter is similar to that of the single rate FIR filter but has less latency in the output because of a reduced number of taps [Proakis07].

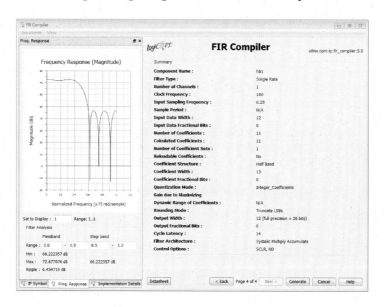

Figure 4.16 FIR Compiler LogiCORE block half-band filter
frequency response and summary

The FIR Compiler 11-tap half-band coefficient file *hb1.coe* is given in Listing 4.7. These coefficients are presented in the FIR Compiler data sheet DS534 as Figure 47 (*www.xilinx.com*).

Listing 4.7 FIR Compiler half-band coefficient file *hb1.coe*

radix = 10;
coefdata = 220, 0, −375, 0, 1283, 2047, 1283, 0, −375, 0, 220;

The FIR Compiler half-band digital filter is implemented as a DSP system, as shown in Figure 4.7. The Verilog top module s3eadchbdac.v is similar to Listing 4.7 and is in the *Chapter 4 \adcdac\ns3ad1hbda2* folder. The estimated cycle latency of the half-band FIR filter is $14 \times T_{clock} = 0.14$ μsec and the total latency is measured to be 0.14 μsec.

The low frequency gain of the half-band digital filter $G_{lf} \approx 4303$ or $20 \log_{10} (4303) = 72.7$ dB, as shown in Figure 4.16. The output is the 12 MSBs of the full precision output of 26 bits since the 14 LSBs are truncated here, as shown in Figure 4.16. The nominal low frequency gain of the FIR Compiler half-band digital filter then is given by $2^{12}/2^{26} \times 4303 \approx 0.263$. As described in Chapter 2 Verilog Design Automation, the Design Utilization Summary for the *ns3ad1hbda2.v* shows the use of 202 slice registers (1%), 216 slice LUTs (2%) and 1 MAC in the Nexys 3 Board XC6SLX16 Spartan-6 FPGA synthesis.

The Hilbert transform FIR digital filter is utilized in digital communication systems [Lathi98]. An ideal Hilbert transform provides a 90° phase shift for positive frequencies and a −90° phase shift for (so-called) negative frequencies, which converts a real signal into its in-phase and quadrature components [Silage06]. The coefficients of the Hilbert transform FIR digital filter have odd symmetry and interleaved zeros.

The interpolated FIR digital filter replaces the discrete frequency unit delay parameter z^{-1} with $k–1$ units of delay z^{-k+1}, where k is the *zero-packing factor* [Chen01]. Interpolated FIR digital filters provide efficient implementation of both narrow-band and wide-band discrete frequency response. Finally, the decimator FIR digital filter is a parallel construct in which the discrete signal input $x(m)$ is provided in sequence to M sub-filters and the output is obtained as the sum with an output sampling rate of f_s / M Hz [Mitra06]. The decimator FIR digital filter is well suited to the parallel architecture of the FPGA. These implementations are also described in the FIR Compiler LogiCORE block data sheet DS534 (*www.xilinx.com*).

The requisite number of MACs required for the FIR digital filter is a function of the number of implicit multiplications in the tapped delay line representation, as shown in Figure 4.11, divided by the number of clock cycles available to process each input sample. The input data and coefficient storage of a single MAC can be reloaded and the MAC reused for efficiency, if sufficient processing time is available. A conceptual block diagram of the MAC architecture is shown in Figure 4.17.

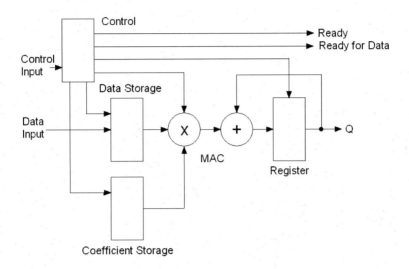

Figure 4.17 Conceptual block diagram of the MAC architecture

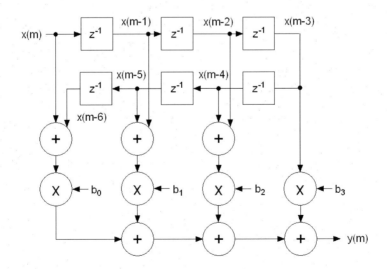

Figure 4.18 FIR digital filter architecture with an odd number
of symmetrical coefficients ($N = 7$)

The FIR Complier also provides the distributed arithmetic (DA) bit serial architecture which requires look-up tables (LUT), adders, subtractors and shift registers and can be efficiently mapped to fine-grained architecture of the FPGA. With the MAC architecture the maximum sample rate of the

FIR digital filter is related to the number of coefficients. However, with the DA architecture the maximum sample rate is related to the bit precision of the input data [Ifeachor02].

For N-bit precision N clock cycles are required to process an output sample for a non-symmetrical coefficient FIR digital filter. As the number of coefficients increases the DA FIR digital filter utilizes more FPGA resources to maintain the sample rate.

The discrete finite impulse response of many digital filters displays a degree of symmetry in the coefficients which can be exploited to provide FPGA resource efficient realizations. The tapped-delay line, single rate FIR digital filter, as shown in Figure 4.11, can be reconfigured when coefficient symmetry occurs [Chen01].

The tapped-delay line FIR digital filter requires approximately N multiplications and $N-1$ additions. The FIR digital filter architecture with an odd number of symmetrical coefficients requires only approximately $N/2$ multiplications and N additions, as shown in Figure 4.18 with $N = 7$.

The FIR digital filter architecture with negative coefficient symmetry is similar to Figure 4.18 but with subtractors in the intermediate layer. The FIR digital filter architecture with an even number of symmetrical coefficients also requires only approximately $N/2$ multiplications and N additions, as shown in Figure 4.19 with $N = 8$.

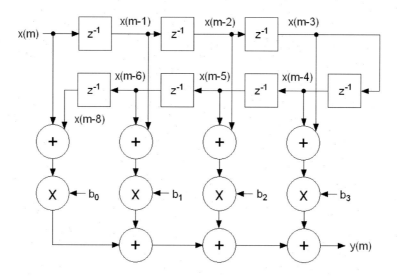

Figure 4.19 FIR digital filter architecture with an even number
of symmetrical coefficients ($N = 8$)

Direct Digital Synthesis Compiler LogiCORE Block

The Xilinx Direct Digital Synthesis (DDS) Compiler LogiCORE block is an essential building block in a digital signal processing and digital communication systems. The DDS forms the basis for digital frequency synthesizers, up and down converters, and coherent demodulators and modulators [Haykin01]. The DDS, which is also known as a numerically controlled oscillator (NCO), utilizes a phase accumulator as a digital integrator and a sine-cosine lookup table. The DDS Compiler LogiCORE block is described in the data sheet DS558 (*www.xilinx.com*).

Sine-Cosine Lookup Table

The sine-cosine lookup table (LUT) component of the Xilinx DDS Compiler LogiCORE block accepts an unsigned input angle *phase_in* and produces a two's complement output of sine(*phase_in*) and cosine(*phase_in*). The phase accumulator is not implemented in this component of the DDS. The input *phase_in* is specified as a *phase_width* of 3 to 16 bits for the distributed ROM of the Spartan-6 FPGA as the LUT, as described in Chapter 3 Programmable Gate Array Hardware. The sine and cosine *output_width* can be from 3 to 26 bits and either a full or a quarter of a sinusoid is store in the distributed ROM. The quarter sinusoid can be used to generate a full sinusoid using additional internal logic and the selection is determined by the LogiCORE block for the most efficient implementation. The actual radian angle θ is determined by Equation 4.28.

$$\theta = \text{phase\_in} \frac{2\pi}{2^{\text{phase\_width}}} \qquad (4.28)$$

The two's complement sine and cosine output are fractional fixed-point values and in the range as determined by Equation 4.29. With an arbitrary output width of 4 bits, for example, the range is −1 to +0.875. For the 12-bit sine and cosine output, the values range from − 1 to approximately +0.9995. For computation, if not the actual representation, the 12-bit fractional fixed-point values here can be considered as signed binary numbers in the range from −2048 to +2047.

$$\frac{-2^{\text{output\_width}-1}}{2^{\text{output\_width}-1}} \rightarrow \frac{2^{\text{output\_width}-1}-1}{2^{\text{output\_width}-1}} \qquad (4.29)$$

DTMF Generator

The sine-cosine lookup table component of the Xilinx DDS LogiCORE block is used to generate a dual-tone multiple frequency (DTMF) audio signal. DTMF is the standard method for instructing a telephone switching system of the telephone number to be dialed or to issue commands to switching systems or related telephony or embedded equipment.

The standard DTMF keypad is a 4 by 4 matrix where each row represents a low frequency and each column represents a high frequency, as shown in Figure 4.20 (left). Depressing a single key causes a low and a high frequency audio tone to be generated. The PmodKYPD™ keypad, shown in Figure 4.20 (right) and described in Chapter 3 Programmable Gate Array Hardware, moves the location of the supervisory asterisk (*) and hashtag (#) keys.

Figure 4.20 Standard DTMF keypad (left), dual tone frequencies and PmodKYPD keypad (right)

The tone frequencies are selected such that harmonics and intermodulation products do not cause an unreliable decoding of the DTMF signal. No frequency is a multiple of another and the difference between and the sum of any two frequencies does not equal any of the individual frequencies. The ITU-T Recommendation Q.23 for the DTMF signal specifies that the frequencies may not vary more than ± 1.5%. The signal amplitude ratio between the high and low frequencies must be within 3 decibels (0.707). The minimum duration of the DTMF signal must be at least 70 msec.

Trends in Embedded Design Using Programmable Gate Arrays

The sine-cosine lookup table (LUT) component of the DDS Compiler LogiCORE block is implemented with four LogiCORE design windows, as in Chapter 2 Verilog Design Automation. The first design window of the DDS Compiler LogiCORE block specifies the configuration option to be the sine-cosine LUT architecture, the *phase_width* as 7 bits (expanded display as *phase_in*), and the *output_width* as 12 bits (expanded display as *sine*), as shown in Figure 4.21. The second design window specifies a sine output only, as shown in Figure 4.22.

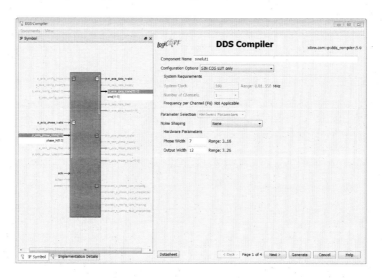

Figure 4.21 First design window of the DSS Compiler for sine-cosine LUT

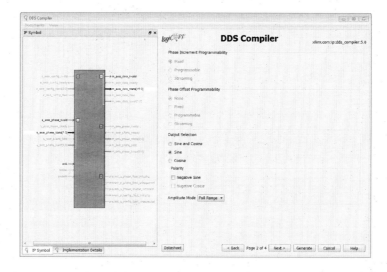

Figure 4.22 Second design window of the DSS Compiler for sine-cosine LUT

The third design window selects the distributed ROM LUT implementation in the Spartan-6 FPGA, optimizes the design for area and not latency, disables the asynchronous clock enable and reset, as shown in Figure 4.23. The status of the datapath module with the ready RDY output signal is automatically enable. The control and status signals for the advanced extensible interface (AXI) are not required here. The AXI is utilized for the Xilinx Zynq *system-on-chip* and described in Chapter 5 Extensible Processing Platform. Finally, Figure 4.24 is the summary window of the DDS Compiler LogiCORE block.

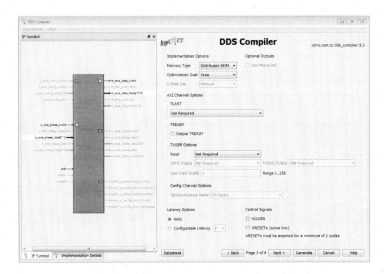

Figure 4.23 Third design window of the DSS Compiler for sine-cosine LUT

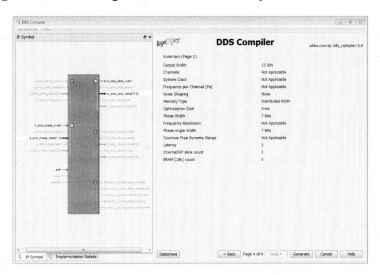

Figure 4.24 Summary window of the DSS Compiler for sine-cosine LUT

The generation of the sine-cosine lookup table component of the DSS Compiler LogiCORE block provides Verilog components, including the module instantiation template file *sinlut1.veo*, as given in Listing 4.8. The template file for the sine-cosine LUT LogiCORE block is instantiated into the parent design by adding the module to the project, as described in Chapter 2 Verilog Design Automation. There are two such modules, *sinlut1.xco* and *sinlut2.xco*, which are independent for the high and low frequency components of the DTMF signal.

YourInstanceName, a dummy name from the instantiation template file *sinlut1.veo* in Listing 4.8, is changed to M7 and M8 in the top module in Listing 4.9 and the port connections by name, as described in Chapter 1 Verilog Hardware Description Language, are changed to reflect the actual connections in the Xilinx ISE project.

The DTMF generator Verilog top module *ns3sincosdtmf.v* is given in Listing 4.9, which is in the *Chapter 4\sincoslut\ns3sincosdtmf* folder. The Xilinx ISE project uses the UCF *ns3sincosdtmf.ucf* which uncomments the signals CLK, BTNL, BTND, BTNR, JA1 to JA4, JC1 to JC4

Trends in Embedded Design Using Programmable Gate Arrays

and JC7 to JC10 in the Nexys 3 Board UCF of Listing 3.1. The six Verilog modules operate in parallel and some independently in the top module. The file download procedure is described in the Appendix.

Listing 4.8 Sine-Cosine Lookup Table LogiCORE instantiation template file *sinlut1.veo*

```
// The following must be inserted into your Verilog file for this
// core to be instantiated. Change the instance name and port connections
// (in parentheses) to your own signal names.
//----------- Begin Cut here for INSTANTIATION Template ---// INST_TAG
sinelut1 your_instance_name (
      .aclk(aclk), // input aclk
    .s_axis_phase_tvalid(s_axis_phase_tvalid),      // input s_axis_phase_tvalid
    .s_axis_phase_tdata(s_axis_phase_tdata),        // input [7 : 0] s_axis_phase_tdata
    .m_axis_data_tvalid(m_axis_data_tvalid),        // output m_axis_data_tvalid
    .m_axis_data_tdata(m_axis_data_tdata)           // output [15 : 0] m_axis_data_tdata);
// INST_TAG_END ------ End INSTANTIATION Template
```

Listing 4.9 DDS Complier LogiCORE block DTMF generator *ns3sincosdtmf.v*

```
// Nexys 3 Board
// Sine-Cosine DTMF ns3sincosdtmf.v
// c 2012 Embedded Design using Programmable Gate Arrays  Dennis Silage

module ns3sincosdtmf (input CLK, input BTNL, BTND, BTNR, output JA1, JA2, JA3, JA4,
                output JC1, JC2, JC3, JC4, input JC7, JC8, JC9, JC10);

wire dacdav, davdac, dacsck, dacsync;
wire [1:0] daccmd;
wire [11:0] dacdata;
wire [31:0] clkdiva, clkdivb;
wire clka, clkb;
wire [3:0] column;
wire [3:0] row;
wire [7:0] keydata;
wire [6:0] phasein1;
wire [6:0] phasein2;
wire [11:0] sine1;
wire [11:0] sine2;
wire pdav1, pdav2, rdy1, rdy2;

assign JA1 = dacsync;
assign JA2 = dacout;
assign JA3 = 0;
assign JA4 = dacsck;
assign JC1 = column[3];
assign JC2 = column[2];
assign JC3 = column[1];
assign JC4 = column[0];
assign row[3] = JC7;
assign row[2] = JC8;
assign row[1] = JC9;
assign row[0] = JC10;
```

```
clock M0 (CLK, clkdiva, clka);          //low frequency LUT clock
clock M1 (CLK, clkdivb, clkb);          //high frequency LUT clock
clock M2 (CLK, 1, dacclk);              //25 MHz
clock M3 (CLK, 1000000, kpdclk);   //50 Hz
da2dac M4 (dacclk, dacdav, davdac, dacout, dacsck, dacsync, daccmd, dacdata);
keypad M5 (kpdclk, column, row, 0, resetkpd, keydata);
gendtmf M6 (CLK, BTND, BTNL, BTNR, clkdiva, clka, clkdivb, clkb, keydata,
                pdav1, phasein1, rdy1, sine1, pdav2, phasein2, rdy2, sine2, dacdav,
                davdac, dacdata, daccmd);
sinelut1 M7 (.aclk(CLK), .s_axis_phase_tvalid(pdav1), .s_axis_phase_tdata(phasein1),
                .m_axis_data_tvalid(rdy1), .m_axis_data_tdata(sine1));
sinelut2 M8 (.aclk(CLK), .s_axis_phase_tvalid(pdav2), .s_axis_phase_tdata(phasein2),
                .m_axis_data_tvalid(rdy2), .m_axis_data_tdata(sine2));

endmodule

module gendtmf (input genclk, BTND, BTNL, BTNR, output reg [31:0] clkdiva, input clka,
                output reg [31:0] clkdivb, input clkb, input [7:0] keydata, output reg pdav1=0,
                output reg [6:0] phasein1=0, input rdy1, input [11:0] sine1, output reg pdav2=0,
                output reg [6:0] phasein2=0, input rdy2, input [11:0] sine2, output reg dacdav=0,
                input davdac, output reg [11:0] dacdata, output reg [1:0] daccmd=0);

reg gstate1 = 0;            // state register
reg gstate2 = 0;
reg [1:0] gstate3 = 0;
reg signed [12:0] lowf;     // low frequency tone
reg signed [12:0] highf;    // high frequency tone
reg [1:0] lowreg = 0;
reg [1:0] highreg = 0;
reg [7:0] temp;

always@(posedge genclk)
    begin
        if ((keydata >= 49 && keydata <= 51) || keydata == 65)
            begin
                lowreg = 0;
                temp = keydata − 49;
                if (temp > 2)
                    highreg = 3;
                else
                    highreg = temp[1:0];
            end

        if ((keydata >= 52 && keydata <= 54) || keydata == 66)
            begin
                lowreg = 1;
                temp = keydata − 52;
                if (temp > 2)
                    highreg = 3;
                else
                    highreg = temp[1:0];
            end
```

```
if ((keydata >= 55 && keydata <= 57) || keydata == 67)
    begin
        lowreg = 2;
        temp = keydata − 55;
        if (temp > 2)
            highreg = 3;
        else
            highreg = temp[1:0];
    end

if (keydata == 48 || (keydata >= 68 && keydata <= 70))
    begin
        lowreg = 3;
        if (keydata == 68)
            highreg = 3;
        if (keydata == 69)
            highreg = 2;
        if (keydata == 70)
            highreg = 0;
        if (keydata == 48)
            highreg = 1;
    end

case (lowreg)
    0:  clkdiva = 560;      // 697 Hz
    1:  clkdiva = 507;      // 770 Hz
    2:  clkdiva = 458;      // 852 Hz
    3:  clkdiva = 415;      // 941 Hz
endcase

case (highreg)
    0:  clkdivb = 323;      // 1209 Hz
    1:  clkdivb = 292;      // 1336 Hz
    2:  clkdivb = 266;      // 1471 Hz
    3:  clkdivb = 239;      // 1633 Hz
endcase

case (gstate1)                  // generate low frequencies
    0:  begin
            if (clka == 1)
                begin
                    pdav1 = 0;
                    if (BTND == 1)
                        phasein1 = 0;
                    else
                        phasein1 = phasein1 + 1;
                    gstate1 = 1;
                end
        end
    1:  begin
            pdav1 = 1;
            if (clka == 0)
```

```
                        gstate1 = 0;
            end
    endcase

    case (gstate2)              // generate high frequencies
        0:   begin
                 if (clkb == 1)
                     pdav2 = 0;
                     begin
                         if (BTND == 1)
                             phasein2 = 0;
                         else
                             phasein2 = phasein2 + 1;
                         gstate2 = 1;
                     end
             end
        1:   begin
                 pdav2 = 1;
                 if (clkb == 0)
                     gstate2 = 0;
             end
    endcase

    case (gstate3)              // output DTMF
        0:   begin
                 if (rdy1 == 1)
                     begin
                         lowf[11:0] = sine1[11:0];  // output low frequencies
                         lowf[12] = lowf[11];       //sign extension
                         lowf = lowf + 2048;
                     end

                 if (rdy2 == 1)
                     begin
                         highf[11:0] = sine2[11:0]; // output high frequencies
                         highf[12] = highf[11];     //sign extension
                         highf = highf + 2048;
                     end

                 if (BTNR == 1)        // DAC output only low frequencies
                     dacdata[11:0] = lowf[12:1];
                 if (BTNL == 1)        // DAC output only high frequencies
                     dacdata[11:0] = highf[12:1];
                 if (BTNR == 0 && BTNL == 0)       // DAC output DTMF
                     dacdata[11:0] = lowf[12:1] + highf[12:1];

                 gstate3 = 1;
             end
        1:   begin
                 dacdav = 1;                // DAC conversion
                 gstate3 = 2;
             end
```

```
        2:   begin
                  if (davdac == 1)
                        begin
                              dacdav = 0;
                              gstate3 = 0;
                        end
              end
        default: gstate3 = 0;
      endcase
   end


endmodule
```

The low and high frequency tones are generated by two sine-cosine look-up table components of the DSS Compiler LogiCORE block. Two clock modules provide the rate at which the 128 (*phase_in* width of 7 bits) sine table values are retrieved. For the highest tone of 1633 Hz, there would be $128 \times 1633 = 209\ 024$ sine table data retrievals per second. The clock scale factor for the clock module is determined by Equation 3.1 and would be $50\ 000\ 000\ /\ 209\ 024 \approx 239.21$.

Since the tone frequency need only be accurate to $\pm\ 1.5\%$ the clock scale factor for 1633 Hz is rounded to 239. If 256 (*phase_in* width of 8 bits) or more sine table entries are used, rounding of the clock scale factor can produce an inaccurate tone. Additionally, the nominal data throughput rate of the PmodDA2 DAC $R_{DAC} \approx 1.352$ Msamples/sec, as described in Chapter 3 Programmable Gate Array Hardware, and would be exceeded for the highest tone of 1633 Hz with 1024 (10-bit) sine table entries.

The controller module *gendtmf.v* utilizes three FSM controllers for the DTMF system. Separate clock signals clka and clkb are provided by the two modules *clock.v*. The requisite timing for the low and high frequency tones of the DTMF signal is set with the clock scale factors clkdiva and clkdivb. The DTMF system here uses two 2-bit signals lowreg and highreg derived from the keypad signal keydata to select one of the 16 possible sets of dual tones. Two case statements for lowreg and highreg then select the low and high frequency tone clock scale factors clkdiva and clkdivb.

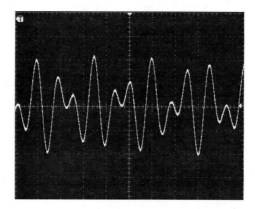

Figure 4.25 DTMF generator *ns3sincosdtmf.v* output at 1 V/div and 1 msec/div
for the dual tone 770 Hz and 1209 Hz (keypad 4)

Two FSM controllers using the clock signals clka and clkb increment the two input signals phasein1 and phasein2 to the two sine-cosine LUTs. If BTND is logic 1 phasein1 and phasein2 are set to 0 which effectively cancels the DTMF tone output. If BTNL and BTNR are logic 1 individually only the high and low frequency tones of the DTMF signal is outputted for verification. The phase input data available control signals pdav1 and pdav2 indicate that valid phase data is present. The status signals rdy1 and rdy1 are logic 1 for a valid sine output.

The 12-bit two's complement sine outputs sine1 and sine2, which are effectively in the range from −2048 to +2047, are converted to 12-bit unsigned binary data as the DTMF signal for the DAC. The sine outputs are sign extended to signed 13-bits as the signals lowf and highf then offset by +2048. The signals, each now in the range from 0 to 4095, are then added together and divided by 2 by taking the 12 most significant bits (MSB) of the 13-bit values. The combined lowf and highf signals as the signal dacdata now are in the proper range for the 12-bit PmodDA2 DAC.

Figure 4.25 shows the DAC output of the DTMF system *ns3sincosdtmf.v* for the dual tone of 770 and 1209 Hz which corresponds to keypad 4. As described in Chapter 2 Verilog Design Automation, the Design Utilization Summary for the top module *ns3sincosdtmf.v* shows the use of 170 slice registers (1%) and 331 slice LUTs (3%) in the Nexys 3 Board XC6SLX16 Spartan-6 FPGA synthesis.

Direct Digital Synthesizer

The direct digital synthesizer (DDS) or numerically controlled oscillator (NCO) of the Xilinx DDS Compiler LogiCORE block can generate sinusoidal signals and phase and frequency modulate sinusoidal carriers with digital information [Haykin01]. The DDS can utilize the phase accumulator and sine-code LUT architecture. The DDS Compiler accepts a phase increment $\Delta\theta$ and clock signal of frequency f_{clock} to a phase accumulator of B_θ bits and produces a discrete sinusoidal signal with an output frequency f_{out} determined by Equation 4.30.

$$f_{out} = \frac{f_{clock} \, \Delta\theta}{2^{B_\theta}} \quad \text{Hz} \qquad (4.30)$$

Equation 4.31 gives the phase increment $\Delta\theta$ required to generate an output frequency f_{out} Hz.

$$\Delta\theta = \frac{f_{out} \, 2^{B_\theta}}{f_{clock}} \qquad (4.31)$$

The spectral purity of the output sinusoidal is affected by the number of bits in the phase accumulator and the amplitude quantization of the samples from the look-up table. The clock frequency and the bit width of the phase accumulator determine the frequency resolution of the DDS. As a result, a large number of bits are usually allocated to the phase accumulator to satisfy these requirements. If the required frequency resolution is Δf then the number of bits B_θ of the phase accumulator is determined by Equation 4.32.

$$B_\theta = \log_2 \left\lceil \frac{f_{clock}}{\Delta f} \right\rceil \qquad (4.32)$$

The number of bits B_θ from Equation 4.32 is *rounded-up*. If $f_{clock} = 100$ MHz and $\Delta f = 0.5$ Hz then $B_\theta = 28$ bits. However, a phase accumulator of 28 bits requires an excessive amount of entries in the sine-cosine look-up table and a truncated version or quantized version of the phase angle is used. Although this quantization allows a reasonable memory requirement, the resulting *jitter* in the time base produces an undesired phase modulation.

The DDS Compiler LogiCORE block is evoked from within a Xilinx ISE project with now six design windows, as described in Chapter 2 Verilog Design Automation. The first design window of the DDS Compiler LogiCORE block is shown in Figure 4.26.

Here the component name (dds1) is specified, the phase generator and sine-cosine LUT architecture is chosen, the DDS clock rate f_{clock} is 100 MHz, the spurious free dynamic range (SFDR) is 72 dB (decibel), the frequency resolution Δf is 0.5 Hz and auto noise shaping is selected. The clock frequency 100 MHz is that provided by the clock oscillator of the Nexys 3 Board. The specification of the SFDR determines the requisite number of bits in the discrete sinusoidal output signal of the DDS.

The analog sinusoidal output is derived from this discrete signal here by using the 12-bit PmodDA2 DAC. The first design window specifies the SDFR as 72 dB and determines and displays the resulting size of the phase increment input B_θ as 28 bits (expanded display as *pinc*) and sinusoidal output as 12 bits (expanded display as *sine*), as shown in Figure 4.26. The second design window of the DDS Compiler LogiCORE block specifies a sinusoidal output with no phase offset but a programmable phase increment, as shown in Figure 4.27.

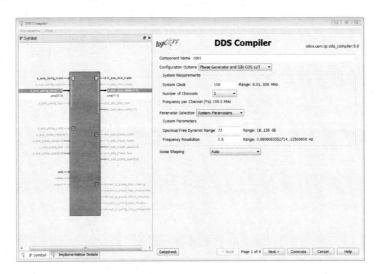

Figure 4.26 First design window of the DDS Compiler for phase increment

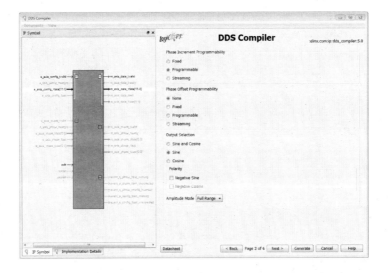

Figure 4.27 Second design window of the DDS Compiler for phase increment

The programmable phase increment allows the output frequency to be set or provides frequency shift keying (FSK) in digital modulation [Silage06]. A programmable phase offset provides phase shift keying (PSK) in digital modulation or adjusts the phase of a reference sinusoid in the matched filter or correlator to that of the received signal in bandpass digital demodulation [Sklar01].

The third design window of the DDS Compiler LogiCORE block selects the distributed ROM LUT implementation in the Spartan-6 FPGA, optimizes the design for area and not latency, disables the asynchronous clock enable and reset signals and selects a minimal use of the DSP48 hardware multiplier resources. The third design window is similar to that in Figure 4.23 and not shown here.

The fourth design window of the DDS Compiler LogiCORE block specifies the output frequency f_{out} as 25 kHz, as shown in Figure 4.28. The fifth design window is a summary similar to that in Figure 4.24 and not shown here. The sixth design window of the DDS Compiler LogiCORE block indicates that the actual output frequency is approximately 24.9997 kHz, as shown in Figure 4.29.

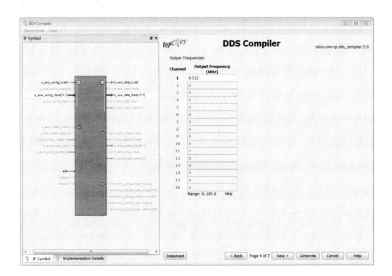

Figure 4.28 Fourth design window of the DDS Compiler for phase increment

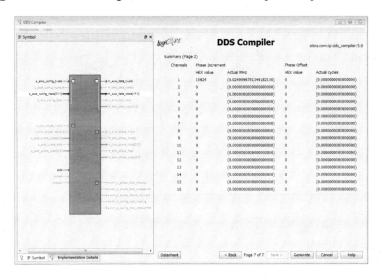

Figure 4.29 Sixth design window of the DDS Compiler for phase increment

The generation of the DDS Compiler LogiCORE block provides Verilog components, including the module instantiation template file *dds1.veo*, as given in Listing 4.10. The template file for the DDS Compiler LogiCORE block is instantiated into the parent design by adding the module to the Xilinx ISE project, as described in Chapter 2 Verilog Design Automation.

Trends in Embedded Design Using Programmable Gate Arrays

YourInstanceName, a dummy name from the instantiation template file dds1.veo in Listing 4.10, is changed to M1 in the top module in Listing 4.11 and the port connections by name, as described in Chapter 1 Verilog Hardware Description Language, are changed to reflect the actual connections in the Xilinx ISE project.

The DDS Compiler uses a quantized version of the phase angle producing jitter and an undesired phase modulation. The LogiCORE block here does not use either the phase dithered or Taylor series corrected DDS, referred to as noise shaping, to ameliorate the jitter. The phase dithered DDS provides an additional 12 dB of SFDR even with two fewer bits in the quantized phase angle. Additional logic implements a randomizing or dithering sequence to improve performance. The Taylor series corrected DDS use FPGA multiplier resources to decrease the undesired phase modulation.

Listing 4.10 DDS Compiler LogiCORE instantiation template file *dds1.veo*

```
// The following must be inserted into your Verilog file for this
// core to be instantiated. Change the instance name and port connections
// (in parentheses) to your own signal names.
//----------- Begin Cut here for INSTANTIATION Template ---// INST_TAG
dds1 your_instance_name (
    .aclk(aclk), // input aclk
    .s_axis_config_tvalid(s_axis_config_tvalid),    // input s_axis_config_tvalid
    .s_axis_config_tdata(s_axis_config_tdata),      // input [31 : 0] s_axis_config_tdata
    .m_axis_data_tvalid(m_axis_data_tvalid),        // output m_axis_data_tvalid
    .m_axis_data_tdata(m_axis_data_tdata)           // output [15 : 0] m_axis_data_tdata);
// INST_TAG_END ------ End INSTANTIATION Template ---------
```

The fifth and sixth design windows of the DDS Compiler LogiCORE block provides a summary with the latency of the design and the value of the phase increment $\Delta\theta$ required for the output frequency f_{out} specified, as determined by Equation 4.31. For an output frequency f_{out} = 25 kHz with B_θ = 28 bits and f_{clock} = 100 MHz the phase increment $\Delta\theta$ = 10624h (67 108). The estimated latency for the DDS task is $5 \times T_{clock}$ = 50 nsec.

The DDS Compiler phase generator and sine-cosine LUT architecture is inherently more efficient and versatile than only the sine-cosine LUT since the discrete sinusoidal data is accessed continuously without providing argument angles. The synthesized discrete sinusoid from the DDS Compiler LogiCORE block can be used to generate an analog sinusoidal signal by outputting the data samples to a DAC.

A carrier sinusoid from the LogiCORE DDS Compiler can be frequency and phase modulated from a digital information source [Sklar01]. Thus the implementation of baseband frequency generation and bandpass digital modulation as a transmitter is straightforward and the output can be conveniently viewed on an oscillographic display. However, the development of a baseband or bandpass receiver requires complex bit and carrier synchronization in the demodulation process [Silage06] and is not attempted here.

Frequency Generator

A synthesized frequency generator is implemented with the DSS Compiler LogiCORE block in the Verilog top module *ns3ddsfreqgen.v* in Listing 4.11, which is in the *Chapter 4\dds\ns3ddsfreqgen* folder. The Xilinx ISE project uses the UCF *ns3ddsfreqgen.ucf* which uncomments the signals CLK, BTND, JA1 to JA4 , JB1 to JB3 and JC1 in the Nexys 3 Board UCF of Listing 3.1. The six Verilog modules operate in parallel and some independently in the top module. The file download procedure is described in the Appendix.

The DDS Compiler LogiCORE block initially generates a 12-bit discrete 25 kHz sinusoid and outputs an analog signal using the PmodDA2 DAC. The maximum data throughput rate of the DAC

R_{DAC} = 1.515 Msamples/sec (660 nsec period), as described in Chapter 3 Programmable Gate Array Hardware. The data throughput rate of the synthesized frequency generator $R_{freqgen}$ is measured at the 6-pin peripheral hardware module connector JC1 as 1.389 Msamples/sec (720 nsec period) and reduced by the latency of the DDS Compiler and the datapath module *genddsfreq.v*.

The datapath module *genddsfreq.v* utilizes one FSM controller for the synthesized frequency generator. The phase increment Δθ is incremented or decremented from its initial value of 10624h (67 108), which provides an 12-bit discrete 25 kHz sinusoidal, by the debounced rotary shaft encoder described in Chapter 3 Programmable Gate Array Hardware. The observed rotation of the shaft encoder is an event driven task independent of the FSM.

Listing 4.11 Synthesized frequency generator top module for the Nexys 3 Board *ns3ddsfreqgen.v*

```
// Nexys 3 Board
// DDS Frequency Generator  ns3ddsfreqgen.v
// c 2012 Embedded Design using Programmable Gate Arrays  Dennis Silage

module ns3ddsfreqgen (input CLK, BTND, JB1, JB2, JB3, output JA1, JA2, JA3, JA4, JC1);

wire dacclk, dacdav, davdac, dacout, dacsck, dacsync;
wire [1:0] daccmd;
wire [11:0] dacdata;
wire we, rdy;
wire [27:0] data;
wire [11:0] sine;
wire rotclk, rotA, rotB, rotCTR, rotAreg, rotBreg, rotCTRreg;

assign JA1=dacsync;
assign JA2=dacout;
assign JA3=dacclk;
assign JA4=dacsck;
assign rotA=JB1;
assign rotB=JB2;
assign rotCTR=JB3;
assign JC1=dacdav;        //monitor data rate

da2dac M0 (dacclk, dacdav, davdac, dacout, dacsck, dacsync, daccmd, dacdata);
dds1 M1 (.aclk(CLK), .s_axis_config_tvalid(we), .s_axis_config_tdata(data),
         .m_axis_data_tvalid(rdy), .m_axis_data_tdata(sine));
rotary M2 (rotclk, rotA, rotB, rotCTR, rotAreg, rotBreg, rotCTRreg);
genddsfreq M3 (CLK, rotAreg, rotBreg, rotCTRreg, BTND, we, data, rdy, sine, dacdav, davdac,
               dacdata, daccmd);
clock M4 (CLK, 1, dacclk);        //25 MHz
clock M5 (CLK, 50000, rotclk);    //1 kHz

endmodule

module genddsfreq (input genclk, rotAreg, rotBreg, rotCTRreg, BTND, output reg we = 0,
                   output reg [27:0] data = 27'h10624, input rdy, input [11:0] sine,
                   output reg dacdav = 0, input davdac, output reg [11:0] dacdata = 0,
                   output reg [1:0] daccmd = 0);

reg [1:0] gstate = 0;  // state register
```

```verilog
always@(posedge rotAreg)
    begin
        if (rotBreg == 0 && rotCTRreg == 0)
            begin
                if (BTND == 0)
                    data = data + 268;      // fine increment
                else
                    data = data + 2680;   // coarse increment
            end
        else
            begin
                if (BTND == 0)
                    data = data - 268;      // fine decrement
                else
                    data=data - 2680;     // coarse decrement
            end
        if (rotCTRreg == 1)
            data = 27'h10624;                // reset frequency
    end

always@(posedge genclk)
    begin
        case (gstate)
            0: begin
                    we = 1;            // write DDS data
                    gstate = 1;
                end
            1: gstate=2;
            2:   begin
                    we = 0;
                    if (rdy == 1)
                        begin
                            dacdata[11:0] = sine[11:0];
                            dacdata[11] = ~dacdata[11];
                            gstate=3;
                        end
                end
            3: begin
                    dacdav = 1;        // DAC conversion
                    if (davdac == 1)
                        begin
                            dacdav = 0;
                            gstate = 0;
                        end
                end
        endcase
    end

endmodule
```

While depressing the push button BTND the rotary shaft encoder provides coarse incrementation or decrementation of the phase increment $\Delta\theta$ by $\pm$ 2680 resulting in an approximate $\pm$ 1000 Hz change (2680*25 000/67 108 ≈ 1000) in the analog sinusoidal output frequency. Depressing and rotating the shaft encoder in either direction resets the output frequency to 25 kHz.

The output frequency can be changed in the first design window of the LogiCORE DDS Compiler and the resultant change in the phase increment $\Delta\theta$ can be read in the sixth design window without finishing the design to ascertain the value needed. The 12-bit two's complement sinusoidal output sine is converted to 12-bit straight binary data for the PmodDA2 DAC by complementing bit 11.

As described in Chapter 2 Verilog Design Automation, the Design Utilization Summary for the top module *ns3ddsfreqgen.v* shows the use of 131 slice registers (1%) and 289 slice LUTs (3%) in the Nexys 3 Board XC6SLX16 Spartan-6 FPGA synthesis.

Frequency Shift Keying Modulator

Frequency shift keying (FSK) is a digital bandpass modulation technique that encodes information as the frequency of a sinusoidal carrier. Binary FSK shifts the carrier frequency to one of two discrete frequencies during the bit time T_b for the representation of binary logic signals for the transmission of information. The modulated sinusoidal carrier signal has an amplitude of A V, a frequency of f_c Hz, and a 0° reference phase angle, as given by the *analytical expression* in Equation 4.33 [Silage06].

$$s_j(t) = A\sin(2\pi(f_c + k_f m_j(t))\,t) \quad (i-1)T_b \le t \le iT_b \quad j = 0, 1 \qquad (4.33)$$

The information signal or data source is $m_j(t)$ ($j = 0, 1$) and for binary FSK $m_j(t) = \pm 1$ V for one bit time T_b. The factor k_f, whose units are Hz/V, is the *frequency deviation factor* (or the modulation gain) and the *frequency deviation* ΔF is given by Equation 4.34.

$$\Delta F = k_f m_j(t) \qquad (4.34)$$

Since $m_j(t) = \pm 1$ V the magnitude of the frequency deviation ΔF is equal on either side of the carrier frequency f_c.

An FSK modulator can be implemented with the DSS Compiler LogiCORE block and programmable phase increments $\Delta\theta$. The FSK modulator implementation is an extension of the synthesized frequency generator and provided in the prior text [Silage08].

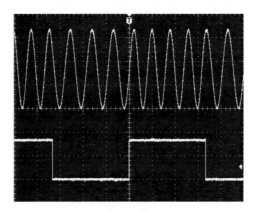

Figure 4.30 FSK modulator output with 1270 Hz for binary 1 and 1070 Hz for binary 0 at 500 mV/div (top) and 300 b/sec data at 2 V/div (bottom) and 1 msec/div

Trends in Embedded Design Using Programmable Gate Arrays

There the FSK modulator uses the Bell type 103 standard for an originating modem with a data rate r_b = 300 b/sec, f_c = 1170 Hz and ΔF = 100 Hz (or 1070 Hz and 1270 Hz), as shown in Figure 4.30. The 300 b/sec data is provided by a linear feedback shift register (LFSR) Verilog module *lfsr.v* in the prior text [Silage08].

The output of the LFSR is a *pseudorandom* binary bit stream as test data [Sklar01]. For a clock frequency f_{clock} = 100 MHz, the number of bits of the phase accumulator B_θ = 28 bits, a frequency resolution Δf = 0.5 Hz and the spurious free dynamic range SFDR = 72 dB, the fixed phase increment $\Delta\theta$ is B38h for 1070 Hz and D51h for 1270 Hz.

Phase Shift Keying Modulator

Phase shift keying (PSK) is a digital bandpass modulation technique that encodes information as the phase of a sinusoidal carrier. Binary phase shift keying (BPSK) shifts the phase angle of the carrier frequency to one of two discrete phases during the bit time T_b for the representation of binary logic signals for the transmission of information. The modulated sinusoidal carrier signal has an amplitude of A V, a frequency of f_c Hz, as given by the analytical expression in Equation 4.35 [Silage06].

$$s_j(t) = A\sin(2\pi f_c t + k_p m_j(t)) \quad (i-1)T_b \le t \le iT_b \quad j = 0, 1 \qquad (4.35)$$

The information signal or data source is $m_j(t)$ (j = 0, 1) and for BPSK $m_j(t)$ = 0 V and 1 V for one bit time T_b. The factor k_p, whose units are 2π (radians)/V, is the *phase deviation factor* (or the modulation gain) and the *phase deviation* $\Delta\varphi$ is given by Equation 4.36.

$$\Delta\varphi = k_p m_j(t) \qquad (4.36)$$

A PSK modulator is implemented with the DSS Compiler LogiCORE block and programmable phase deviations $\Delta\varphi$ or phase offsets. The BPSK modulator implementation is an extension of the DDS Compiler and provided in the prior text [Silage08].

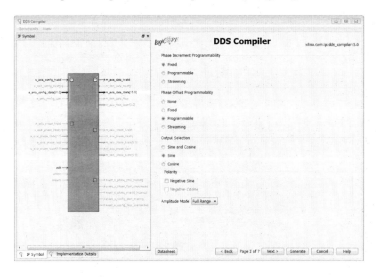

Figure 4.31 Second design window of the DDS Compiler for phase offset

The second design window of the DDS Complier now selects a programmable phase offset to support PSK, as shown in Figure 4.31, rather than programmable phase increment for FSK, as shown in Figure 4.27. The third and fourth design windows of the DDS Compiler remain the same, as shown

270

in Figure 4.23 and Figure 4.27, but a new fifth design window selects the phase offset, as shown in Figure 4.32.

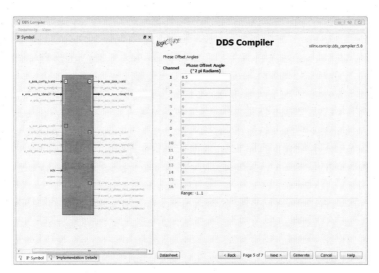

Figure 4.32 Fifth design window of the DDS Compiler for phase offset

The phase offset which is multiplied by 2π radians is in the range ± 1 and can be read in the now seventh summary design window to ascertain the value needed for processing. The phase offset The BPSK modulator provided in the prior text uses a data rate r_b = 250 b/sec, f_c = 1 kHz and $\Delta\varphi$ = 0, 180°, as shown in Figure 4.33 [Silage08].

The 250 b/sec data is provided by a linear feedback shift register (LFSR) Verilog module *lfsr.v* described in the prior text [Silage08]. For a clock frequency f_{clock} = 100 MHz, the number of bits of the phase accumulator B_θ = 28 bits, a frequency resolution Δf = 0.5 Hz and the spurious free dynamic range SFDR = 72 dB, the fixed phase increment $\Delta\theta$ is A7Ch for 1 kHz and the binary phase offset φ_j is 0 or 8000000h.

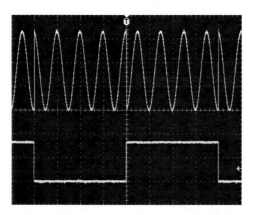

Figure 4.33 DDS Compiler BPSK modulator output with 1 kHz at 180° for binary 1 and 1 kHz at 0° for binary 0 at 500 mV/div (top) and 250 b/sec data at 2 V/div (bottom) and 1 msec/div

Trends in Embedded Design Using Programmable Gate Arrays

Data Communication

Several serial data communication protocols with various degrees of complexity and application properties are used in embedded design. The serial peripheral interface (SPI) can connect local devices such as an analog-to-digital converter, digital-to-analog converter, or flash memory PROM to the programmable gate array in an embedded design, as described in Chapter 3 Programmable Gate Array Hardware.

The SPI is a *synchronous* bus and utilizes a SPI clock to coordinate bi-directional binary data transfers on separate output and input signals. The inter-integrated circuit (I^2C) bus is a serial data communication interface that uses only a clock and a single data line to transfer bi-directional data to multiple devices, as described in Chapter 3 Programmable Gate Array Hardware.

More complicated serial data communication protocols include the universal serial bus (USB), FireWire (IEEE1394) and Ethernet (IEEE 802.3). These protocols require extensive hardware and software support and are not featured here. However, an established protocol for serial data communication with equipment external to an embedded system is the RS-232 standard. The Manchester encoder-decoder for serial data communication is *self-synchronizing* and described in the prior text [Silage08].

RS-232 Standard

The RS-232 (Recommended Standard 232, now EIA/TIA-232F) standard is a binary serial data communication bus that is usually *asynchronous* and which connects data terminal equipment (DTE) to data circuit-terminating equipment (DCE) commonly used in computer ports. Although a synchronous clock is part of the RS-232 standard it is not usually employed. The synchronous binary serial data communication RS-422 standard (now EIA/TIA-422B) uses differential signaling for high speed and noise immunity.

Unlike the complexity of the protocol of USB which is replacing it in many computer systems, the RS-232 protocol is simple and easily implemented. The RS-232 standard remains commonly in use to connect legacy data terminal and communication equipment (DTE and DCE) and industrial apparatus. The RS-232 protocol includes signals which indicate the availability of the equipment with data terminal ready (DTR) and data set ready (DSR).

However, there are some disparities and limitations in the RS-232 protocol. Although the RS-232 standard requires the transmitter data TXD to use –12 V and +12 V for the binary data, the receiver must distinguish binary data RXD with voltages as low as –3 V and +3 V. The large voltage required for the transmitter increases power consumption and complicates power supply design. As a result, so-called RS-232 compatible serial ports using –5 V and +5 V, or even 0 V and +5 V, are often employed.

The *hardware flow control* lines, request to send (RTS) and clear to send (CTS), are problematic and are often not used in simple data communication. Alternatively *software flow control* is implemented by the use of character codes for transmission on, XON or DC1 ASCII 17, and transmission off, XOFF or DC3 ASCII 19. Finally, the asymmetry of the DTE and DCE data protocol and connector induces problems in the correct equipment interface.

The frame format for RS-232 binary serial data transmission is shown in Figure 4.34. The transmitter *idles* at $-V_S$ volts until data are available. The start of transmission is asynchronous and begins with a *start bit* of one bit time (T_b) duration and $+V_S$ volts. The 8 bit data is sent least significant bit (LSB) first where logic 1 is $-V_S$ volts and at least one *stop bit* concludes the transmission.

Binary serial data communication using the RS-232 standard utilizes the universal asynchronous receiver transmitter (UART) to provide serial-to-parallel and parallel-to-serial conversion, bit rate generation, control functions and buffering. The type 16550 hardware UART (National Semiconductor, *www.national.com*) can be implemented in an embedded design as a *soft-core* peripheral. A simple soft core UART originally configured for a Xilinx complex programmable logic device (CPLD) is described in the Xilinx application note XAPP341 and is used with modifications here.

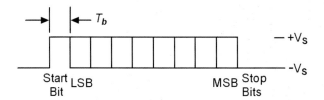

Figure 4.34 RS-232 frame format for binary serial data transmission

The UART RS-232 standard transmitter datapath module *txmit.v* is shown in Listing 4.12. The 8-bit data is inputted from the variable tdin to the 8-bit buffer register variable tbr with logic 1 on the *write strobe* wrn. Register variable tsr receives the data from tbr and is used to sequentially shift the data out as txd. The input variable clk16x is the reference clock at 16 times the nominal bit rate $r_b = 1/T_b$. The register variable tbuf as logic 0 indicates that the input buffer tbr is empty.

Listing 4.12 UART transmitter module *txmit.v*

```
// UART Transmitter txmit.v
// c 2000 Xilinx, Inc. XAPP341
// c 2012 Embedded Design using Programmable Gate Arrays  Dennis Silage

module txmit (input [7:0] tdin, output reg tbuf, input clk16x, wrn, output reg txd = 1);

reg clk1x_en = 0;
reg parity;
reg wrn1 = 1;
reg wrn2 = 1;
reg [7:0] tsr = 0;
reg [7:0] tbr = 0;
reg [3:0] clkdiv = 0;
reg [3:0] no_bits_sent = 0;

assign clk1x = clkdiv[3];        // generate 1x clock

always @(posedge clk16x)
    begin
            wrn2 = wrn1;         // async detection for write
            wrn1 = wrn;
            if (wrn1 == 0 && wrn2 == 1)
                begin
                    clk1x_en = 1;
                    tbuf = 1;  // transmit buffer not empty
                end
            if (no_bits_sent == 2)
                tbuf=1;
            if (no_bits_sent == 13)
                begin
                    clk1x_en = 0;
                    tbuf = 0;  // transmit buffer empty
```

```
                end
            if (clk1x_en)
                    clkdiv = clkdiv + 1;
        end

always @(posedge wrn)      // write transmit data
        tbr = tdin;

always @(negedge clk1x)
        begin
            if (no_bits_sent == 1)
                    tsr=tbr;
            if (no_bits_sent == 2)
                    txd=0;
            if (no_bits_sent >= 3 && no_bits_sent <= 10)
                    begin
                            txd = tsr[0];
                            tsr[6:0] = tsr[7:1];
                            tsr[7] = 0;
                            parity = parity ^ tsr[0];
                    end
            if (no_bits_sent == 11)
                    txd = parity;
            if (no_bits_sent == 12)
                    txd = 1;

        end

always @(posedge clk1x or negedge clk1x_en)
        begin
            if (clk1x_en == 0)
                    no_bits_sent = 0;
            else
                    no_bits_sent = no_bits_sent + 1;
        end

endmodule
```

The *txmit.v* Verilog module is in the *Chapter 4\peripherals* folder and utilizes multiple concurrent cyclical behavioral events to affect the serial data transmission, as described in Chapter 1 Verilog Hardware Description Language.

The UART RS-232 standard receiver datapath module *rcvr.v* is given in Listing 4.13. The binary serial data is inputted as rxd and the 8-bit data is outputted from the reg variable rbr. Register variables rxd1 and rxd2 are used to adjust the read timing for the receiver. The register variable rdrdy indicates that received data is available with logic 1. Register variable rbr receives the data from the receive shift register rsr. The input signal clk16x is the reference clock at 16 times the nominal bit rate $r_b = 1/T_b$ and is divided by 16 to produce the bit clock clk1x. An asynchronous input signal rdrst is used to reset the functionality of the UART receiver.

The *rcvr.v* Verilog module is in the *Chapter 4\peripherals* folder and also utilizes multiple concurrent cyclical behavioral events to affect the serial data reception, as described in Chapter 1 Verilog Hardware Description Language.

Listing 4.13 UART receiver module *rcvr.v*

```
// UART Receiver rcvr.v
// c 2000 Xilinx, Inc. XAPP341
// c 2012 Embedded Design using Programmable Gate Arrays  Dennis Silage

module rcvr (output reg [7:0] rbr, output reg rdrdy, input rxd, input clk16x, rdrst);

reg rxd1, rxd2, clk1x_en;
reg [3:0] clkdiv = 0;
reg [7:0] rsr = 0;              // receive shift register
reg [3:0] no_bits_rcvd;

assign clk1x = clkdiv[3];   // generate 1x clock

always @(posedge clk16x or posedge rdrst)
    begin
        if (rdrst == 1)
            begin
                rxd1 = 1;
                clk1x_en = 0;          // clk1x enable
                clkdiv = 0;
            end
        else
            begin
                rxd2 = rxd1;           // async edge detection for start bit
                rxd1 = rxd;
                if (rxd1 == 0 && rxd2 == 1)
                    clk1x_en = 1;
                if (no_bits_rcvd == 9) // start bit + 8 data bits
                    begin
                        clk1x_en = 0;
                        clkdiv = 0;
                    end
                if (clk1x_en == 1)                 // clk16x divider for clk1x
                    clkdiv = clkdiv + 1;
            end
    end

always @(posedge clk1x or posedge rdrst)
    begin
        if (rdrst == 1)   // reset
            begin
                rsr = 0;
                rbr = 0;
                rdrdy = 0;
            end
        else
            begin
                if (no_bits_rcvd >= 1 && no_bits_rcvd <= 7)
                    begin
                        rsr[7] = rxd;
```

```
                            rsr[6:0] = rsr[7:1];
                    end
                else if (no_bits_rcvd == 8)
                        begin
                            rsr[7] = rxd;
                            rbr = rsr;
                            rdrdy = 1;          // receive data ready
                        end
                end
        end

always @(negedge clk1x or posedge rdrst or negedge clk1x_en)
    begin
        if (rdrst == 1 || clk1x_en == 0)
            no_bits_rcvd = 0;
        else
            no_bits_rcvd = no_bits_rcvd + 1;
    end

endmodule
```

The RS232 standard transmit *txmit.v* and receive *rcvr.v* modules are verified by the top module *altusbuart.v* for the Spartan-6 Atlys Board which is in the *Chapter4\rs232\atlusbuart* folder and given in Listing 4.14. The Xilinx ISE project uses the UCF *atlusbuart.ucf* which uncomments the signals CLK, BTND, RXD and TXD in the Atlys 3 Board UCF of Listing 3.2. The five Verilog modules operate in parallel and some independently in the top module. The file download procedure is described in the Appendix. A Xilinx ISE project similar to that in Listing 4.14 can be configured for the Nexys 3 Board and is available in the *Chapter4\rs232\ns3usuuart* folder.

The Atlys Board has only one 12 pin Pmod connector for external peripherals and the use of an integral USB-UART bridge provides the capability of a convenient keyboard and display for embedded design using a terminal emulator on the host. The USB-UART bridge port (J17) uses an Exar XR21V410 device (*www.exar.com*) and is effectively a serial port for data communication using the USB protocol and appropriate COM port drivers on the host.

The Atlys Board USB-UART bridge does not utilize the hardware flow control signal CTS and RTS. Data transmission can be controlled by the XON and XOFF character codes with the appropriate host terminal and embedded protocols but not implemented here. The *atlusbuart.v* top module includes the *genusbuart.v* controller module for the datapath which transmit the received data back to the host at 9600 b/sec, no parity and no software or hardware flow control.

Listing 4.14 UART transmit and receive top module for the Atlys Board *atlusbuart.v*

```
// Atlys Board
// USB-UART atlusbuart.v
// c 2012 Embedded Design using Programmable Gate Arrays  Dennis Silage

module atlusbuart (input CLK, BTND, RXD, output TXD);

wire [7:0] tdin;
wire [7:0] rbr;
wire tbuf, rdrst, clk16x, wrn, txd, rxd, rdrdy, rdn, genclk, en;
assign rxd = RXD;
assign TXD = txd;
```

```
clock M0 (CLK, 326, clk16x);          // 9600 b/sec
clock M1 (CLK, 5000, genclk);         // 10 kHz
rcvr M2 (rbr, rdrdy, rxd, clk16x, rdrst);
txmit M3 (tdin, tbuf, clk16x, wrn, txd);
genusbuart M4 (genclk, BTND, rdrst, rbr, rdrdy, tdin, tbuf, wrn);

endmodule

module genusbuart (input genclk, BTND, output reg rdrst = 0, input [7:0] rbr, input rdrdy,
                   output reg [7:0] tdin, input tbuf, output reg wrn);

reg [2:0] gstate = 0;          // state register

always@(posedge genclk)
    begin
        if (BTND == 1)          // reset
                gstate = 0;
        else

        case (gstate)
            0:   begin
                    rdrst = 1;          // reset UART
                    gstate = 1;
                 end
            1:   begin
                    rdrst = 0;
                    gstate = 2;
                 end
            2: begin
                    if (rdrdy == 1)  // receive data ready?
                        begin
                            tdin = rbr; // receiver buffer->transmit input
                            gstate = 3;
                        end
                 end
            3: begin
                    if (tbuf == 0)     // transmit buffer empty?
                        begin
                            wrn = 1;   // write transmit input to txmit
                            gstate = 4;
                        end
                 end
            4: begin
                    wrn = 0;
                    if (tbuf == 0)     // transmit buffer cleared?
                        gstate = 0;
                 end
            default: gstate = 0;
        endcase
    end

endmodule
```

Trends in Embedded Design Using Programmable Gate Arrays

One *clock.v* module from the *Chapter 3\peripherals* folder divides the 100 MHz master clock CLK by 326 as given by Equation 3.1 to output the clk16x clock signal at 16 times the data rate or 153.374 kHz ≈ 16 × 9600 b/sec. The other clock.v module generates a 10 kHz clock for the FSM controller *genusbuart.v* which is adequate for the receive reset event. Figure 4.35 shows the RS232 standard serial data signal reception.

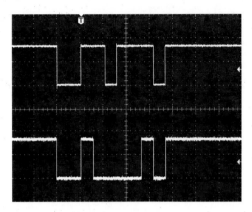

Figure 4.35 RS232 9600 b/sec serial data reception for ASCII *v* (top)
and transmission for ASCII *B* (bottom) at 2V/div and 200 μsec/div

Figure 4.36 demonstrates the use of a host terminal emulator (Tera Term Pro, *www.ayera.com/teraterm/*) to *echo* the characters from the keyboard through the *atlusbuart.v* top module Xilinx ISE project to its display. Set the host terminal emulator for 9600 b/sec, 7 data bits, odd parity, 1 stop bit and no flow control.

Figure 4.36 Host terminal emulator echoing keyboard characters on its display

As described in Chapter 2 Verilog Design Automation Verilog Design Automation, the Design Utilization Summary for the top module *atlusbusart.v* shows the use of 133 slice registers (<1%) and 252 slice LUTs (1%) in the Atlys Board XC6SLX45 Spartan-6 FPGA synthesis.

The RS232 standard transmit *txmit.v* and receive *rcvr.v* modules can also be verified by the top module *ns3usbuart.v* for the Spartan-6 Nexys 3 Board which is in the *Chapter4\rs232\ns3ubuuart* folder and is essentially the same as that given in Listing 4.14. The Nexys 3 Board uses the FTDI FT232RQ device, the same as that used for the PmodUSBUART module, and not the Exar XR21V410 device of the Atlys Board. The host terminal emulator and the USB-UART bridge, rather than the more elaborate but integral LCD display and keypad, is more convenient and used in many embedded design applications.

PmodUSBUART UART Bridge

The Digilent PmodUSBUART™ is an external USB to UART bridge peripheral using the FTDI (*www.ftdichip.com*) FT232RQ device, is referenced in the Digilent document 502-212 (*www.digilentinc.com*) and is shown in Figure 4.37.

Figure 4.37 Digilent PmodUSBUART USB to UART bridge module

The PmodUSBUART module provides hardware flow control with the RTS and CTS signals. The controller module in an embedded design can supervise the data transmission to the remote device with these signals. Two LEDs indicate data transfer to and from the RS232 device and USB port. The PmodUSBUART module can utilize the RS232 serial data transmit *txmit.v* and receive *rcvr.v* Verilog modules in Listing 4.12 and Listing 4.13.

PmodRS232 Voltage Converter

The Digilent PmodRS232™ is an RS232 standard voltage converter module using the Analog Devices (*www.analog.*com) ASM3232E device, is referenced in the Digilent document 502-068 (*www.digilentinc.com*) and is shown in Figure 4.38.

The PmodRS232 module converts the 0 and +3.3 V logic signals of the FPGA to at least −3 to +3 V to at most −12 to +12 V for RS232 standard compatible data transmission. The PmodRS232 can be configured by the jumpers JP1 and JP2 as either a three wire (TXD, RXD and ground) or five wire (TXD, RXD, RTS, CTS and ground) DTE device.

The hardware flow control RTS and CTS signals can be jumpered together which effectively ignores them for an input DCE device. The RS232 port is a standard female DB9 connector. The PmodRS232 module can utilize the RS232 serial data transmit *txmit.v* and receive *rcvr.v* Verilog modules in Listing 4.12 and Listing 4.13.

Figure 4.38 Digilent PmodRS232 voltage converter module

Manchester Encoder-Decoder

The binary data source code represented by the RS232 serial data communication is termed a unipolar *non-return to zero* (NRZ) line code and utilizes a rectangular pulse p(t) of +V volts for one bit time T_b, as shown in Figure 4.39 [Haykin01]. Alternatively, a unipolar *return-to*-zero (RZ) line code uses a rectangular pulse p(t) of +V volts for half a bit time $T_b/2$ and then returns to 0 V for the remaining half a bit time $T_b/2$. The pulse p(t) of +V volts can represent either a logic 1 or logic 0 which is set by the *protocol* (specification) of the line code.

Some desirable properties of a line code include a power spectral density (PSD) which is 0 (a null) at a frequency of 0 Hz (DC) because many data communication systems utilize AC coupling and magnetic transformers and *transparency* in which there are no long strings of binary 1s or 0s regardless of the data source information [Sklar01].

One protocol for the unipolar Manchester NRZ or split phase line code uses +V for $T_b/2$ then 0 for $T_b/2$ as logic 1 and 0 for $T_b/2$ then +V for $T_b/2$ as logic 0. Figure 4.39 shows the Manchester NRZ serial data transmission with this protocol. The Machester encoder-decoder Xilinx ISE project and a discussion of the properties of various lines codes is in the prior text [Silage08].

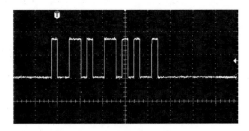

Figure 4.39 Manchester NRZ 9600 b/sec serial data transmission for ASCII *v* at 2V/div and 200 μsec/div [Silage08]

PmodBT2 Bluetooth Wireless Communication

The Digilent PmodBT2™ is a fully integrated Bluetooth wireless data communication module using the Roving Networks RN-42 device (*www.rovingnetworks.com*), is referenced in the Digilent document 502-214 (*www.digilentinc.com*) and is shown in Figure 4.40.

Figure 4.40 Digilent PmodBT2 Bluetooth module

The PmodBT2 module provides a standard UART serial data interface and hardware flow control with the RTS and CTS signals. The jumpers JP1 through JP4 configure the RN-42 device. After three transitions of short-to-open, open-to-short of jumper JP1 the default conditions of a

Bluetooth slave, pin code 1234, serial data rate of 115.2 kb/sec, no flow control and lower power mode disabled is restored.

Jumper JP2 facilitates data communication with a specific class of devices and jumper JP3 permits auto-connectioned to an address both defined during command initialization. Jumper JP4 sets a serial data rate of 9600 b/sec.

The RN-42 device has a serial data communication command code with a complex set of instructions described in the Roving Networks *Bluetooth Data Module Command Reference* (RN-BT-DATA-UG). The PmodBT2 can utilize the RS232 transmit *txmit.v* and receive *rcvr.v* Verilog modules in Listing 4.12 and Listing 4.13 to transmit commands and receive and transmit data to external devices in embedded designs.

The PmodBT2 module is a datapath and, in addition to the UART signals (TXD, RXD, RTS, and CTS) of a DTE device, provides reset RST and STATUS signals to a controller Verilog module. Reset initializes the RN-42 device and registers the setting of the jumpers. Commands sent to the RN-42 device with serial data are followed by a reset. A logic 1 on the STATUS signal indicates that a valid Bluetooth connection is available.

Sensors

External sensors provide measurement of physical variables as an integral component of embedded design. However, many available sensors are not simply transducers but processing and data communication systems as well. This inherently increases their functionality but also increases the complexity of the interface.

PmodACL Accelerometer

The Digilent PmodACL™ is a three axis digital accelerometer module using the Analog Devices ADXL345 device, is referenced in the Digilent document 502-097 (*www.digilentinc.com*) and is shown in Figure 4.41.

Figure 4.41 Digilent PmodACL three axis acceleration module

The PmodACL provides both I2C and SPI bus interfaces to a complex series of configuration and data registers, as partially listed in Table 4.1. The register address is 6-bits. Additional information is available in the ADXL345 data sheet and the application note *AN-1077 ADXL345 Quick Start Guide* (*www.analog.com*). The ADXL345 has a resolution of 3.9 mg/bit which enables measurement of inclination changes of less than 1° as described in the Analog Devices application note *AN-1057 Using an Accelerometer for Inclination Sensing*.

The ADXL345 is both a sensor and an autonomous processing system. The device monitors either activity or inactivity by autonomously comparing measured acceleration along any axis to a set of thresholds. Tap sensing detects single and double taps in any direction. Free fall is sensed if the device is falling. A 32-level first-in, first-out (FIFO) buffer stores acceleration data for later retrieval.

Table 4.1 PmodACL ADXL345 digital accelerometer configuration and data registers

Address	Contents (MSB…LSB)	Description
1Eh		X-axis offset
1Fh		Y-axis offset
20h		Z-axis offset
2Ch	000PRRRR	Data rate and low power control
	0000	0.1 Hz
	0001	0.2
	0010	0.39
	0011	0.78
	0100	1.56
	0101	3.13
	0110	6.25
	0111	12.5 #
	1000	25 #
	1001	50 #
	1010	100 # default value
	1011	200 #
	1100	400 #
	1101	800
	1110	1600
	1111	3200
2Dh	00LAMSWW	Power control
2Eh	RSDAIFWO	Interrupt enable
2Fh	RSDAIFWO	Interrupt mapping
31h	TSI0FJRR	Data format
	00	±2 g
	01	±4 g
	10	±8 g
	11	±16 g
32h	XXXXXXXX	X-axis data 0
33h	Sxx(XXX)XX	X-axis data 1
34h	YYYYYYYY	Y-axis data 0
35h	Sxx(YYY)YY	Y-axis data 1
36h	ZZZZZZZZ	Z-axis data 0
37h	Sxx(ZZZ)ZZ	Z-axis data 1

The X, Y and Z axis offset read/write (R/W) data registers are 8-bit signed integers with a scale factor of 15.6 mg/bit or 7Fh ≈ +1.98 g. This offset can be used to compensate for the effect of gravity on the accelerometer. The data rate and low power control R/W configuration register sets a low power mode (P = 1) with limited data rates (#) or a normal mode (P = 0) with the data rates listed in Table 4.1. The default register value is 0000 1010 or a normal mode with 100 Hz data rate.

The power control R/W configuration register links (L = 1) or correlates the interaction of activity or inactivity as sensed by the accelerometer, enables the auto sleep mode on inactivity (A = 1), sets the measurement mode (M = 1), enables the sleep mode (S = 1) and sets the activity data acquisition rate in sleep mode (WW). Since the default value of the register is 0000 0000 the ADXL345 device must be set for measurement.

The interrupt enable R/W configuration register designates which of the signals, data ready (D), single tap (S), double tap (D), activity (A), inactivity (I), free fall (F) watermark (W) or overrun (O), can generate an interrupt. The watermark interrupt occurs when the number of data samples stored in the FIFO equals the value in the FIFO control register. The overrun interrupt occurs when new data samples replace unread data.

The interrupt enable register operates in conjunction with the interrupt mapping R/W configuration register. An interrupt from any signals whose matching bits in this register are set to 0 are logically ORed and sent to the interrupt 1 pin (INT1). A matching bit set to 1 sends the ORed interrupt signal to the interrupt 2 pin (INT2).

The data format R/W configuration register implements a self-test mode (T = 1), an unconventional three wire SPI bus (S = 1), inversion of the interrupt logic value (I = 1) and a full resolution mode (F = 1) where the number of output data bits increases to maintain a scale factor of 3.9 mg/bit up to 13 bits or a fixed 10-bit mode (F = 0) used here. The additional up to 3 bits are listed as, for example, (XXX) in Table 4.1.

The range bits (RR) determine the full scale factor and the selection of left justified most significant bit (J = 1) or right-justified with sign extension (J = 0). The sign bit S of the fixed 10 bit or up to 13 bit X, Y and Z-axis acceleration data is the MSB of the second byte, as listed in Table 4.1.

The PmodACL three axis accelerometer module *acl.v*, which is in the *Chapter 4\peripherals* folder is given in Listing 4.15. This module is a datapath with two finite state machines (FSM) each with a 3-bit state register aclstate and provides signals to the controller and the accelerometer device, as described in Chapter 1 Verilog Hardware Description Language.

Listing 4.15 Datapath module for the PmodACL three axis accelerometer *acl.v*

```
// PmodACL Accelerometer acl.v
// c 2012 Embedded Design using Programmable Gate Arrays  Dennis Silage

module acl (input aclclk, aclwdav, output reg wdavacl = 0, input [5:0] acladdr, input [7:0] aclwdata,
            input aclrdav, output reg rdavacl = 0, output reg [7:0] acldata, output reg aclsclk,
            output reg aclsdi, input aclsdo, output reg aclss = 1);

integer i;
reg [2:0] aclstate = 0;      // state register
reg [7:0] aclcadr;           // command, address

always@(posedge aclclk)
    begin
        if (aclrdav == 0 && rdavacl == 1)     // reset read status
                begin
                    rdavacl = 0;
                    aclstate = 0;
                end
        if (aclwdav == 0 && wdavacl == 1)  //reset write status
                begin
                    wdavacl = 0;
                    aclstate = 0;
                end

        if (aclrdav == 1 && rdavacl == 0)     // read data
            begin
                case (aclstate)
                0:    begin
                        aclcadr[5:0] = acladdr[5:0];
                        aclcadr[7:6] = 2'b10;       // read, MB=0
                        i = 9;
```

```
                    aclss = 0;
                    aclsclk = 1;
                    aclstate = 1;
            end
    1:      begin
                    aclsclk = 0;
                    i = i - 1;
                    if (i == 0)
                            aclstate = 3;
                    else
                            begin
                                    aclsdi = aclcadr[i -1];
                                    aclstate = 2;
                            end
            end
    2:      begin
                    aclsclk = 1;
                    aclstate = 1;
            end
    3:      begin
                    i = 9;
                    aclsclk = 1;
                    aclstate = 4;
            end
    4:      begin
                    aclsclk = 0;
                    i = i - 1;
                    if (i == 0)
                            aclstate = 6;
                    else
                            aclstate = 5;
            end
    5:      begin
                    aclsclk = 1;
                    acldata[i−1] = aclsdo;
                    aclstate = 4;
            end
    6:      begin
                    aclss=1;
                    rdavacl=1;
            end
    default: aclstate = 6;
    endcase
end

if (aclwdav == 1 && wdavacl == 0)  // write data
begin
    case (aclstate)
    0:      begin
                    aclcadr[5:0] = acladdr[5:0];
                    aclcadr[7:6] = 0;           // write, MB=0
                    i = 9;
```

```
                        aclss = 0;
                        aclsclk = 1;
                        aclstate = 1;
                end
        1:      begin
                        aclsclk=0;
                        i = i − 1;
                        if (i == 0)
                                begin
                                        i = 9;
                                        aclstate = 3;
                                end
                        else
                                begin
                                        aclsdi = aclcadr[i−1];
                                        aclstate = 2;
                                end
                end
        2: begin
                        aclsclk = 1;
                        aclstate = 1;
                end
        3: begin
                        aclsclk = 0;
                        i = i − 1;
                        if (i == 0)
                                aclstate = 5;
                        else
                                begin
                                        aclsdi = aclwdata[i−1];
                                        aclstate = 4;
                                end
                end
        4: begin
                        aclsclk = 1;
                        aclstate = 3;
                end
        5: begin
                        aclss = 1;
                        wdavacl = 1;
                        aclstate = 5;
                end
        default: aclstate = 5;
        endcase
    end
 end

endmodule
```

The first FSM has 7 states and writes an 8-bit control and address packet then reads 8-bits of sensor data. The second FSM has 6 states and writes an 8-bit control and address packet followed by writing an 8-bit parameter to a configuration register. The reduction in source code complexity for the

Trends in Embedded Design Using Programmable Gate Arrays

alternative FSM in Listing 1.46 can be afforded here because of the low speed of execution of the ADXL345 SPI interface with a maximum clock frequency of 5 MHz.

The contents of the control, address, data and parameter data packets are given in Table 4.2. SDI and SDO are the SPI interface serial data input and output signals. The read bit ($R = 1$) and write bit ($W = 0$) indicate the type of packet. Multiple data bytes or parameters can be utilized if the MB bit is logic 1. The 6-bit register addresses and 8-bit parameters as register contents are listed in Table 4.1. Some bytes are ignored (X).

Table 4.2 PmodACL ADXL345 digital accelerometer control, address, data and parameter packet

Write/Read	SDI	R MB [5:0] address [7:0] X
	SDO	[7:0] X [7:0] data
Write/Write	SDI	W MB [5:0] address [7:0] parameter
	SDO	[15:0] X

The Analog Devices ADXL345 digital accelerometer has a maximum SPI clock frequency of 5 MHz, while the master clock oscillator CLK of the Nexys 3 Board or the Atlys Board is 100 MHz. Rather than using the Clock Management Technology (CMT) frequency module of the Xilinx Spartan-6 FPGA to output a conservative 2.5 MHz clock signal, the 100 MHz master clock oscillator can be simply divided by 20 by the *clock.v* nested module in the top module. The clockscale parameter of the module *clock.v* is 10, which provides a 5 MHz clock signal, as determined by Equation 3.1.

The resulting 5 MHz clock signal is then divided by two again by the transitions of the FSM to produce a 2.5 MHz SPI bus clock signal. The ADXL345 utilizes two 16-bit control, address and data packets to obtain a single axis accelerometer sample, so the approximate maximum throughput data rate for three axes $R_{ACL} = 2.5$ MHz/($3 \times 2 \times 16$ bits/packet) $\approx$ 26 ksamples/sec. However since the maximum data rate as listed in Table 4.1 is 3.2 ksample/sec, the low speed SPI interface does not determine the actual data rate.

The read or write data available signals aclrdav and aclwdav from the controller sets the aclstate register to 0 and resets the datapath status signals rdavacl and wdavacl to logic 0 when the data available signals are logic 0 and the status signals are logic 1. The appropriate FSM is activated on the positive edge of the clock signal aclclk if one of the data available signal is a logic 1 and the status signal is logic 0. The datapath returns the status signals rdavacl and wdavacl as a logic 1 to the controller when the process of reading from or writing to the ADXL345 is completed.

The data transfer begins with the SPI slave select signal aclss set to logic 0. The ADXL345 SPI bus clock is set by the output register variable aclsclk and on its positive edge clocks the 16-bit control, address and data packets, as listed in Table 4.2, as the SPI bus input and output signals aclsdi and aclsdo.

The PmodACL digital accelerometer datapath module *acl.v* is verified by the Verilog top module *ns3acltest.v* for the Nexys 3 Board, which is in the *Chapter 4\sensors\ns3acltest* folder and is given in Listing 4.16. The top module file also includes the controller module *genacl.v*. The file download procedure is described in Appendix A.

Listing 4.16 Top module for the PmodACL digital accelerometer *ns3acltest.v*

```
// Nexys3 Board
// Accelerometer ns3acltest.v
// c 2012 Embedded Design using Programmable Gate Arrays  Dennis Silage

module ns3acltest (input CLK, BTND, [2:0] SW, output JC1, JC2, JC3, JC4, output JC7, JC8, JC9,
                   output JC10, JD7, JD8, JD9, JA1, JA2, input JA3, output JA4);
```

```
wire [7:0] lcddatin;
wire [7:0] lcdd;
wire rslcd, rwlcd, elcd;
wire resetlcd, clearlcd, homelcd, datalcd, addrlcd;
wire initlcd, lcdreset, lcdclear, lcdhome, lcddata, lcdaddr, sign;
wire aclclk, aclwdav, wdavacl, aclrdav, rdavacl;
wire aclsclk, aclsdi, aclsdo, aclss, int1;
wire [5:0] acladdr;
wire [7:0] aclwdata;
wire [7:0] acldata;
wire [3:0] data;
wire [1:0] digitmux;

assign JC10=lcdd[7];
assign JC9=lcdd[6];
assign JC8=lcdd[5];
assign JC7=lcdd[4];
assign JC4=lcdd[3];
assign JC3=lcdd[2];
assign JC2=lcdd[1];
assign JC1=lcdd[0];
assign JD7=rslcd;
assign JD8=rwlcd;
assign JD9=elcd;
assign JA1=aclss;
assign JA2=aclsdi;
assign aclsdo=JA3;
assign JA4=aclsclk;

acl M0 (aclclk, aclwdav, wdavacl, acladdr, aclwdata, aclrdav, rdavacl,acldata, aclsclk, aclsdi, aclsdo,
        aclss);
acllcd M1 (CLK, BTND, resetlcd, clearlcd, homelcd, datalcd, addrlcd, initlcd, lcdreset, lcdclear,
        lcdhome, lcddata, lcdaddr, lcddatin, digitmux, data, sign);
clplcd M2 (CLK, resetlcd, clearlcd, homelcd, datalcd, addrlcd, cmdlcd, initlcd, lcdreset, lcdclear,
        lcdhome, lcddata, lcdaddr, lcdcmd, rslcd, rwlcd, elcd, lcdd, lcddatin);
genacl M3 (aclclk, aclwdav, wdavacl, acladdr, aclwdata, aclrdav, rdavacl, acldata, digitmux, data, sign,
        SW);
clock M4 (CLK, 10, aclclk);     // 5 MHz

endmodule

module genacl (input aclclk, output reg aclwdav = 0, input wdavacl, output reg [5:0] acladdr,
            output reg [7:0] aclwdata, output reg aclrdav = 0, input rdavacl, input [7:0] acldata,
            input [1:0] digitmux, output reg [3:0] data, output reg sign, input [2:0] SW);

reg [3:0] gstate = 0;  // state register
reg [3:0] acl4;        // acl value BCD digits
reg [3:0] acl3;
reg [3:0] acl2;
reg [3:0] acl1;
reg [9:0] value;       // acl value
reg [13:0] delay = 0; // startup delay
```

```
integer i;

always@(digitmux)          // LCD digit mux
    begin
        case (digitmux)
            0:    data=acl4;
            1:    data=acl3;
            2:    data=acl2;
            3:    data=acl1;
        endcase
    end

always@(posedge aclclk)
    begin
        case (gstate)
            0:   begin
                    aclrdav = 0;
                    aclwdav = 0;
                    delay = delay + 1;    // startup delay
                    if (delay == 8192)    // 8192 x 0.2 usec = 1638 msec
                        gstate = 1;
                 end
            1:   begin
                    acladdr = 8'h31;     // data format
                    aclwdata = 8'h00;    // 10 bit, + − 2g
                    aclwdav = 1;
                    gstate = 2;
                 end
            2: begin
                    if (wdavacl == 1)
                        begin
                            aclwdav = 0;
                            gstate = 3;
                        end
                 end
            3: begin
                    if (wdavacl == 0)
                        begin
                            acladdr = 8'h2D;
                            aclwdata = 8'h08;    // measure
                            aclwdav = 1;
                            gstate = 4;
                        end
                 end
            4: begin
                    if (wdavacl == 1)
                        begin
                            aclwdav = 0;
                            gstate = 5;
                        end
                 end
            5: begin
```

```
                if (wdavacl == 0)
                        gstate = 6;
        end
6: begin

        acladdr = 8'h32;            // xdata0
        if (SW[1] == 1 && SW[2] == 0 && SW[0] == 0)
                acladdr = 8'h34;      // ydata0
        if (SW[2] == 1 && SW[1] == 0 && SW[0] == 0)
                acladdr = 8'h36;      // zdata0
        aclrdav = 1;
        gstate = 7;
        end
7: begin

        if (rdavacl == 1)
                begin
                        aclrdav = 0;
                        value[7:0] = acldata[7:0];
                        gstate = 8;
                end
        end
8: begin

        if (rdavacl == 0)
                begin
                        acladdr = 8'h33;            // xdata1
                        if (SW[1] == 1 && SW[2] == 0 && SW[0] == 0)
                                acladdr = 8'h35;      // ydata1
                        if (SW[2] == 1 && SW[1] == 0 && SW[0] == 0)
                                acladdr = 8'h37;      // zdata1
                        aclrdav=1;
                        gstate=9;
                end
        end
9: begin

        if (rdavacl == 1)
                begin
                        aclrdav = 0;
                        value[9:8] = acldata[1:0];
                        sign = acldata[7];
                        gstate = 10;
                end
        end
10: begin

        if (rdavacl == 0)
                gstate = 11;
        end
11: begin

        acl1 = 0;                // thousands digit
        for (i = 1; i <= 9; i = i + 1)
                begin
                        if (value >= 1000)
                                begin
                                        acl1 = acl1 + 1;
```

```
                                        value = value − 1000;
                                end

                        end
                acl2 = 0;                   // hundreds digit
                for (i = 1; i <= 9; i= i + 1)
                        begin
                                if (value >= 100)
                                        begin
                                                acl2 = acl2 + 1;
                                                value = value − 100;
                                        end
                        end
                acl3 = 0;                   // tens digit
                for (i = 1; i <= 9; i = i + 1)
                        begin
                                if (value >= 10)
                                        begin
                                                acl3 = acl3 + 1;
                                                value = value − 10;
                                        end
                        end

                acl4 = value[3:0];     // units digit
                gstate = 6;
        end
    default: gstate = 0;
    endcase
end

endmodule
```

The complete Xilinx ISE project uses *ns3acltest.ucf* that uncomments the signals CLK, BTND, SW<0> to SW<2>, JA1 to JA4, JC1 to JC4, JC7 to JC10 and JD7 to JD9 in the Nexys 3 Board UCF of Listing 3.1. The five Verilog modules operate in parallel and some independently in the top module.

This Xilinx ISE project utilizes the PmodCLP parallel LCD display in ports JC and JD, the PmodACL in port JA and is similar to that for the PmodAD1 ADC in Listing 3.34. The PmodACL requires a startup delay of at least 1.1 msec which is providing by a delay register clocked from the 5 MHz aclclk signal. Next the data format in register 31h is set to 10 bits of resolution and a range of ± 2g and the power control in register 2Dh enables accelerometer measurements. The three slide switches select the X, Y or Z axis for display. The datapath *acllcd.v* is similar to *adclcd.v* in Listing 3.34 but modified here to accept a sign bit for display as the ASCII character 43 (+) or 45 (−).

PmodGYRO Gyroscope

The Digilent PmodGYRO™ is a three axis digital gyroscope with a temperature sensor module using the STMicroelectronics L3G4200D device, is referenced in the Digilent document 502-215 (*www.digilentinc.com*) and is shown in Figure 4.42.

The PmodGYRO provides both I2C and SPI bus interfaces to a complex series of configuration and data registers, as partially listed in Table 4.3. The register address is 6-bits. Additional information is available in the L3G4200D data sheet (*www.st.com*). The L3G4200D is an angular rate sensor and has a full scale range of ± 250, ± 500 or ± 2000 degrees/sec.

Figure 4.42 Digilent PmodGYRO three axis digital gyroscope module

The L3G4200D produces a signed 16-bit output of angular rate for counterclockwise rotation around its axis in the X, Y and Z directions independently. The device has control registers that select high pass and low pass cutoff frequencies, interrupt and data ready signals, full scale, first-in, first-out (FIFO) buffer configuration, status register for data acquisition and FIFO buffer and interrupt operation. The default configuration selects a continuous data updating, a ± 250 degree/sec full scale range, the SPI bus interface and disables the FIFO buffer and high pass filter.

The L3G4200D is both a sensor and an autonomous processing system. The device monitors activity by autonomously comparing measured angular rate along any axis to a set of programmable thresholds. The FIFO buffer can store up to the last 32 sets of complete X, Y and Z-axis angular rate measurements.

The default configuration for the control register 1 (CTRL_REG1) sets X, Y and Z bits to logic 1 which enables the X, Y and Z-axis output, but sets the P bit to logic 0 which powers down the device. The data rate bits RR and angular rate bandwidth bits BB are also set in CTRL_REG1. An 8-bit temperature reading is available from the OUT_TEMP register. The low and high byte of the signed 16-bit X, Y and Z-axis angular rate measurements are read from separate registers, as listed in Table 4.3.

The PmodGYRO three axis digital gyroscope module *gyro.v*, which is in the *Chapter 4\peripherals* folder is similar to that for the PmodACL accelerometer in Listing 4.15 and not given here. The file download procedure is described in the Appendix. This module is a datapath with two finite state machines (FSM) each with a 3-bit state register gyrostate and provides signals to the controller and the gyroscope device, as described in Chapter 1 Verilog Hardware Description Language.

The first FSM has 6 states and reads 8-bits of sensor data gyrordata at the 6-bit address gyroaddr. The second FSM also has 6 states and writes an 8-bit parameter gyrowdata to a configuration register at the 6-bit address gyroaddr. The reduction in source code complexity for the alternative FSM in Listing 1.46 can be afforded here because of the low speed of execution of the L3G4200D SPI interface with a maximum clock frequency of 10 MHz.

The PmodGYRO three axis digital gyroscope datapath module *gyro.v* is verified by the Verilog top module *ns3gyrotest.v* for the Nexys 3 Board, which is in the *Chapter 4\sensors\ns3gyrotest* folder, and similar to that for the PmodACL accelerometer in Listing 4.16 and not given here. The top module file also includes the controller module *gengyro.v*.

The complete Xilinx ISE project uses *ns3gyrotest.ucf* that uncomments the signals CLK, BTND, SW<0> to SW<3>, JA1 to JA4, JC1 to JC4, JC7 to JC10 and JD7 to JD9 in the Nexys 3 Board UCF of Listing 3.1. The five Verilog modules operate in parallel and some independently in the top module. The file download procedure is described in the Appendix.

This Xilinx ISE project also utilizes the PmodCLP parallel LCD display in ports JC and JD, the PmodGYRO in port JA and is similar to that for the PmodAD1 ADC in Listing 3.34. The PmodGYRO requires that the CTRL_REG1 register be written to several times on startup which also sets data rate to 100 Hz (RR = 00), bandwidth to 12.5 Hz (BB = 00) and enables the device with the power control bit (P = 1) and the three axis enable bits (XYZ = 111), as listed in Table 4.3.

Table 4.3 PmodGYRO L3G4200D digital gyroscope configuration and data registers

Address	Contents (MSB…LSB)	Description		Name
20h	RRBB PZYX	Data rate	Bandwidth	CTRL_REG1
	0000	100 Hz	12.5 Hz	
	0001	100	25	
	0010	100	25	
	0011	100	25	
	0100	200	12.5	
	0101	200	25	
	0110	200	50	
	0111	200	70	
	1000	400	20	
	1001	400	25	
	1010	400	50	
	1011	400	110	
	1100	800	30	
	1101	800	35	
	1110	800	50	
	1111	800	110	
26h	TTTT TTTT	Temperature		OUT_TEMP
28h	XXXX XXXX	X-axis low byte		OUT_X_L
29h	SXXX XXXX	X-axis high byte		OUT_X_H
2Ah	YYYY YYYY	Y-axis low byte		OUT_Y_L
2Bh	SYYY YYYY	Y-axis high byte		OUT_Y_H
2Ch	ZZZZ ZZZZ	Z-axis low byte		OUT_Z_L
2Dh	SZZZ ZZZZ	Z-axis high byte		OUT_Z_H

Four slide switches select the X, Y or Z axis (SW<0> to SW<2>) and the temperature (SW<3>) for display. The datapath *gyrolcd.v* is similar to *adclcd.v* in Listing 3.34 but modified here to accept a sign bit for display as the ASCII character 43 (+) or 45 (−) and provide an addition BCD digit for the 16-bits of resolution for the angular rate measurement. The default full scale measurement of ± 250 degrees/sec is used here.

As described in Chapter 2 Verilog Design Automation, the Design Utilization Summary for the top module *ns3gyrotest.v* shows the use of 161 slice registers (1%) and 2 622 slice LUTs (28%) in the Nexys 3 Board XC6SLX16 Spartan-6 FPGA synthesis.

PmodTMP2 Temperature Sensor and Thermostat

The Digilent PmodTMP2™ is a temperature sensor module and thermostat control board using the Analog Devices ADT7420, is referenced in the Digilent document 502-221 (*www.digilentinc.com*) and is shown in Figure 4.43.

The PmodTMP2 provides an I2C bus interfaces to a complex series of configuration and data registers, as listed in Table 4.4. Additional information is available in the ADT7420 data sheet (*www.analog.com*). The ADT7420 is a temperature sensor with up to 16-bits of data, an effective resolution of ± 0.25 °C (± 0.45 °F) over a measurement range from. −20 °C to +105 °C.

The ADT7420 is also a thermostat where the bits of the flags and status register indicates that low (L), high temperature (H) or critical (C) temperature event has occurred. The ready bit (R) is logic 0 when a temperature conversion result is available.

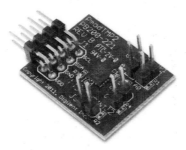

Figure 4.43 Digilent PmodTMP2 temperature sensor and thermostat module

Table 4.4 PmodTMP2 ADT7420 temperature sensor and thermostat data and configuration registers

Address	Contents (MSB…LSB)	Description	Type
00h	STTT TTTT	Sign bit (S) and high bits of temperature (T)	R
01h	TTTT TCHL	Low bits (T) of temperature and flags (CHL)	R
02h	LHCR 0000	Flags (LCH) and ready status register	R/W
03h	ROOI PCFF	Configuration register	R/W
04h	STTT TTTT	Sign bit (S) and high bits of T_{HIGH} setpoint	R/W
05h	TTTT TTTT	Low bits of T_{HIGH} setpoint	R/W
06h	STTT TTTT	Sign bit (S) and high bits of T_{LOW} setpoint	R/W
07h	TTTT TTTT	Low bits of T_{LOW} setpoint	R/W
08h	STTT TTTT	Sign bit (S) and high bits of T_{CRIT} setpoint	R/W
09h	TTTT TTTT	Low bits of T_{CRIT} setpoint	R/W
0Ah	0000 TTTT	Temperature hysteresis T_{HYST} value	R/W

The resolution bit R of the configuration register sets 13-bit (R = 0) or 16-bit (R = 1) of temperature data. If 16-bits of resolution is set then the flag bits CHL of the low bits of temperature are used for data TTT. The operation mode bits OO sets a continuous (00), one-shot (01) or one per second (10) temperature conversion or shutdown (11). The interrupt bit I enables an event signal INT if logic 0 which appears at J3-1 on the PmodTMP2 module. If I is logic 1 the device operates in comparator mode without the interrupt signal INT. The comparator even signal CT appears at J2-1. The polarity bit P sets INT as logic 0 (P = 0) or logic 1 (P = 1). The comparator polarity bit C sets CT as logic 0 (C = 0) or logic 1 (C = 1). The fault queue bits F sets the number of under or over temperature faults that can occur before setting either the INT or CT signals. One, two, three or four faults can be set (FF = 00, 01, 10, 11).

The setpoints for the events for over, under and critical temperature are set by the T_{HIGH}, T_{LOW} and T_{CRIT} registers. The temperature hysteresis T_{HYST} register stores a 4-bit number in the range of 0° to 15° C which is subtracted from the setpoints T_{HIGH} and T_{CRIT} and added to T_{LOW} to affect a hysteresis to improve the performance of the thermostat.

The module *temp.v* for the PmodTMP2 temperature sensor and thermostat module, which is in the *Chapter 4\peripherals* folder, is similar to that for the I2C bus PmodAD2 module in Listing 3.35 and not given here. The file download procedure is described in the Appendix. This module is a datapath utilizing two finite state machines (FSM) with the 6-bit state registers twbstate for writing a byte and trwwstate for reading or writing two bytes of data to a register. The control signal input temprw to the *temp.v* module determines if a read or write to a register occurs. The two FSMs provide signals to the controller and the ADC device, as described in Chapter 1 Verilog Hardware Description Language.

Table 4.5 describes the 28-bit packet to write a byte of data to a register. Table 4.6 describes the 37-bit to read or write two bytes to a register. The first 5 bits of the I2C bus interface address are fixed. The two additional address bits aa are set by JP1 and JP2 with an open read as logic 1. The 8-bit address pointer determines which register is to be read or written.

Table 4.5 PmodTMP2 ADT7420 write byte 28-bit packet

Bits	Description	Contents (MSB...LSB)	
27-21	Address	100 10aa	
20	Read/Write	0	Write
19	ACK	0	Acknowledgement by ADT7420
18-11	Address pointer	pppp pppp	
10	ACK	0	Acknowledgement by ADT7420
9-2	Byte data	dddd dddd	
1	ACK	0	Acknowledgement by ADT7420
0	Stop	1	Stop from master

Table 4.6 PmodTMP2 ADT7420 read/write word 37-bit packet

Bits	Description	Contents (MSB...LSB)	
36-30	Address	10010aa	
29	Read/Write	1/0	Read/write
28	ACK	0	Acknowledgement by ADT7420
27-20	Address pointer	pppp pppp	
19	ACK	0	Acknowledgement by ADT7420
18-11	High byte data	dddd dddd	
10	ACK	0	Acknowledgement by ADT7420
9-2	Low byte data	dddd dddd	
1	ACK	0	Acknowledgement by ADT7420
0	Stop	1	Stop from master

The Analog Devices ADT7420 temperature sensor and thermostat has a specified maximum I2C SCL bus clock frequency of approximately 400 kHz. The master clock oscillators CLK of the Nexys 3 Board and the Atlys Board are 100 MHz. The clockscale parameter of the module *clock.v* is 125, which provides a 400 kHz clock signal tmpclk, as determined by Equation 3.1. The transitions of the FSM in the datapath module *temp.v* further divide the clock signal by two to produce a conservative 200 kHz I2C bus clock, which produces reliable data here.

The I2C bus protocol uses a serial bus clock SCL and a bidirectional serial data bus SDA. The ADT7420 thermometer and thermostat must first be configured at its device address, address pointer for the various register and with the contents of those registers, as listed in Table 4.4. The default 7-bit addresses for the ADT7420 is 100 1000 through 100 1011 which permits four PmodTMP2 modules to be interfaced on a single I2C bus.

The serial bus clock SCL signal is an open-collector output requiring an external pull-up resistor for the I2C bus. The SCL signal is initially logic 1 and is set to logic 0 to begin the I2C protocol data transfer. The serial data bus SDA signal is read on the rising edge of the SCL signal. The bidirectional data packets for writing a byte or reading or writing a word listed in Table 4.5 and Table 4.6, which includes several acknowledgements (ACK) by the ADT7420 device.

The PmodTMP2 is connected to the 12-pin peripheral hardware module connector (JA). The serial bus clock SCL signal is on both pin JA3 and JA9 and the serial data bus SDA signal is on both pins JA4 and JA10. The I2C bus protocol pins are available on two Pmod pins to facilitate *daisy chaining* other devices. Pins JA5 and JA11 are DC ground and pins JA6 and JA12 are power (VDD = +3.3 V DC).

Digital Signal Processing, Communications and Control

The PmodTMP2 temperature sensor and thermostat datapath module *temp.v* is verified by the Verilog top module *ns3temptest.v* for the Nexys 3 Board, which is in the *Chapter 4\sensors\ns3temptest* folder. This Xilinx ISE project also utilizes the PmodCLP parallel LCD display in ports JC and JD, the PmodTMP2 in port JA and is similar to that for the PmodAD1 ADC in Listing 3.34 and not given here. The top module file also includes the controller module *gentemp.v*. Four slide switches select current temperature and the T_{HIGH}, T_{LOW}, T_{CRIT} and T_{HYS} setpoints for display.

The complete Xilinx ISE project uses *ns3temptest.ucf* that uncomments the signals CLK, BTND, SW<0> to SW<4>, JA1 to JA4, JC1 to JC4, JC7 to JC10 and JD7 to JD9 in the Nexys 3 Board UCF of Listing 3.1. The five Verilog modules operate in parallel and some independently in the top module. The file download procedure is described in the Appendix.

As described in Chapter 2 Verilog Design Automation, the Design Utilization Summary for the top module *ns3temptest.v* shows the use of 148 slice registers (1%) and 482 slice LUTs (5%) in the Nexys 3 Board XC6SLX16 Spartan-6 FPGA synthesis.

Digital Control

The digital control of a process can be provided by an embedded design with various degrees of complexity. Sensors are used to convert physical properties, such as temperature, pressure, electromagnetic field intensity, electrical current, voltage or power, mechanical position, velocity, and acceleration, as the input to the system usually to an analog electrical signal. The analog signal is then sampled and quantized by an analog-to-digital converter (ADC) or a threshold logic interface to a discrete signal as described in this Chapter.

The discrete signal can be processed by a programmable gate array (PGA) using the controller and datapath construct and the basic tenants of digital signal processing and digital control. The sensor can also be an inherent processor which facilitates embedded system development. The processed signals are used to affect or control the output of the system using a digital-to-analog converter (DAC) or digital logic with actuators, servomotors, valves and electronic devices [Kuo97].

An *open-loop controller* has no direct connection between the actual output of a system or response and the desired or reference input, as shown in Figure 4.44. Thus the open-loop controller does not use *feedback* to determine if the input has produced the desired response. However, an open-loop controller is reasonable for well-defined systems not subject to unpredictable responses and is often used in simple control processes.

Figure 4.44 An open-loop controller

A *closed-loop controller* monitors the actual output of the system through a reference sensor and *feeds back* a signal to the input. The reference feedback signal is subtracted from the desired input producing an error signal which is then inputted to the controller, as shown in Figure 4.45. A closed-loop controller cancels errors and obviates the effects of changes in the parameters of operation.

A common type of closed loop control with feedback for a process utilizes the proportion-integral-derivative (PID) controller in which the error signal is processed by three distinct algorithms operating in parallel, as determined by Equation 4.37. The term e(t) is the error signal, sp(t) is the desired *set point* for the process, o(t) is the output from and i(t) is the input to the process. The constants K_p, K_i, and K_d in Equation 4.37 describes the PID controller algorithm.

$$e(t) = sp(t) - o(t)$$

$$i(t) = K_p \, e(t) + K_i \int e(\tau) \, d\tau + K_d \, \frac{de(t)}{dt} \qquad (4.37)$$

The constants K_p, K_i, and K_d of the PID controller have appropriate magnitudes and the proper conversion units to provide the input i(t) to the process. Proportional control processes the weighted error, integral control processes the weighted accumulated error and derivative control processes the weighted rate of change of the error [Kuo97].

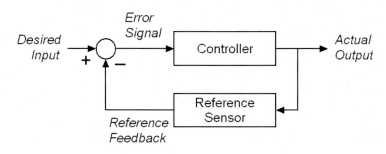

Figure 4.45 A closed-loop controller with feedback

The processed weighted error signals are used to affect the output of the system. Separation of the controller into three distinct algorithms facilitates the adjustment of the output response to various desired inputs. However, the PID controller does not assure that *optimal control* actually occurs in the system and more complex *state space control* is often required [Ogata02].

Some applications may not require all three algorithms of the PID controller and proportional (P), proportion-integral (PI) or proportion-derivative (PD) controllers are used in embedded design. The PID, P, PI and PD controllers have associated gains for the error signal, however these control adjustments can lead to instability, oscillation or overshoot in the output [Kuo97].

The PI controller is often utilized since the derivative process is very sensitive to noise on the desired input. However, integral control responds to the accumulated error signal of the past it can cause the instability and overshoot in the response. Finally, although proportional control can also lead to instability and usually produces a steady-state offset in the desired output, it is the foremost contributor to the actual output.

Pulse Width Modulation

A prevalent application in open-loop control is setting the speed of a *DC servomotor* in industrial processes and robotics using pulse width modulation (PWM) in an embedded design. In PWM a rectangular pulse is modulated by an input signal which increases or decreases the pulse width T_w for a fixed period T_p, as shown in Figure 4.46.

The ratio T_w/T_p is the *duty cycle* of the PWM signal. In one protocol a unipolar input signal V_{input} is sampled at a rate $f_p = 1/T_p$ and the magnitude of the discrete sample determines the pulse width T_w. Other protocols include pulse position modulation (PPM), in which the location of a fixed pulse within the period T_p is varied and pulse amplitude modulation (PAM) in which the amplitude of a fixed pulse within the period T_p is varied.

PWM can be implemented with a programmable gate array counter in an embedded design. The counter is used to set the pulse width T_w with the pulse on by counting a clock signal with a rate f_s where $f_s \gg f_p$. A high sampling rate f_s increases the resolution of the pulse width T_w. The counter then sets the fixed period T_p with the pulse off before the PWM cycle repeats.

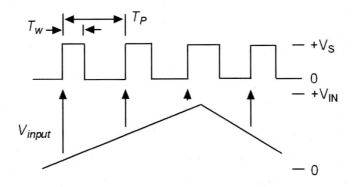

Figure 4.46 Pulse width modulation

DC Servomotor Speed Control

The output of the pulse width modulator (PWM) is connected to a DC servomotor by an *H-bridge* circuit, a portion of which is shown in Figure 4.47. The H-bridge circuit provides voltage isolation for the programmable gate array (PGA) to the higher operating voltage of the DC servomotor. It also isolates deleterious voltage spikes that can occur during operation of the DC servomotor. An H-bridge system has additional combinational logic which uses control inputs from the PGA, commonly direction and enable control signals, to affect the motion of the DC servomotor.

If the MOSFET transistors Q1 and Q4 are turned on by the control logic, the DC servomotor turns in one direction since the voltage supply V_{supply} is connected to the left terminal and the right terminal is grounded. If Q2 and Q3 are turned on, then the DC servomotor turns in the opposite direction since the voltage supply V_{supply} is connected to the right terminal and the left terminal is grounded.

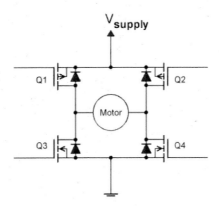

Figure 4.47 H-bridge DC servomotor circuit

If the pulse width T_w equals the period T_p, from Figure 4.46, then the maximum amount of power is delivered to DC servomotor resulting in maximal torque and speed. If $T_w = 0$ then the delivered power is zero and the friction of the load of the DC servomotor eventually will stop its rotation. For critical embedded design applications the direction control signal can be reversed for a short period of time.

A DC servomotor provides feedback of its rotational speed and direction by quadrature encoder logic signals (A and B) from Hall effect magnetic sensors, as shown in Figure 4.48. The quadrature encoder signals have a period which is proportional to the rotational speed of the DC servomotor and are 90° out of phase.

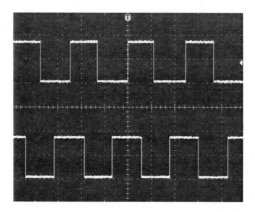

Figure 4.48 DC servomotor quadrature encoder signals A (top) and
B (bottom) at 2 V/div and 2 msec/div

The period of the encoder signal in Figure 4.48 is approximately 4.9 msec. The direction of rotation of the DC servomotor is sensed by which quadrature encoder signal (A or B) leads in phase. In Figure 4.48 the positive pulse of quadrature encoder signal B leads that of A by 90°.

PmodHB5 H-Bridge

The Digilent PmodHB5 is a MOSFET H-bridge module with interface CMOS logic that can provide up to 2 A of output current at up to 12 VDC for an appropriate DC servomotor, is referenced in the Digilent documents 502-106 (*www.digilentinc.com*) and is shown in Figure 4.49.

Figure 4.49 Digilent PmodHB5 MOSFET H-bridge module

Closed-loop speed control of a DC servomotor using a proportional feedback controller is implemented with the Verilog top module *ns3servocontrol.v* in Listing 4.17, which is in the *Chapter 4 \servo\ns3servocontrol* folder. The file download procedure is described in the Appendix. The Xilinx ISE project uses the UCF *ns3servocontrol.ucf* which uncomments the signals CLK, BTND, JA1 to JA4, JC1 to JC4, JC7 to JC10 and JD7 to JD9 in the Nexys 3 Board UCF of Listing 3.1. The six Verilog modules operate in parallel and some independently in the top module.

The clock module *clock.v* and rotary shaft encoder module *rotary.v* are in the *Chapter 3 \peripherals* folder. The *clock.v* module provides a 1 MHz clock signal mclk by dividing the 100 MHz crystal oscillator and the *rotary.v* module provides debounced shaft encoder rotational signals rotAreg and rotBreg and a debounced shaft pushbutton signal rotCTRreg, as described in Chapter 3 Programmable gate Array Hardware.

Listing 4.17 DC servomotor closed-loop proportional speed control *ns3servocontrol.v*

```verilog
// Nexys 3 Board
// Servomotor Control ns3servocontrol.v
// c 2012 Embedded Design using Programmable Gate Arrays  Dennis Silage

module ns3servocontrol (input CLK, BTND, SW0, JA1, JA2, JA3,  output JB1, JB2, input JB3, JB4,
                        output JC1, JC2, JC3);

wire mclk, rotAreg, rotBreg, rotCTRreg, spddav, flagpwm, dir, enable;
wire [14:0] speed;
wire [14:0] dspeed;
wire [8:0] pwm;

assign rotA = JA1;
assign rotB = JA2;
assign rotCTR = JA3;
assign JB1=dir;
assign JB2=enable;
assign sa=JB3;
assign sb=JB4;
assign JC1=sa;         // monitor
assign JC2=sb;
assign JC3=enable;

servospeed M0 (mclk, sa, spddav, speed);
servomotor M1 (mclk, speed, spddav, rotAreg, rotBreg, rotCTRreg, pwm);
servocontrol M2 (mclk, BTND, SW0, pwm, dir, enable);
rotary M3 (rotclk, rotA, rotB, rotCTR, rotAreg, rotBreg, rotCTRreg);
clock M4 (CLK, 50, mclk);         // 1 MHz
clock M5 (CLK, 50000, rotclk);    // 1 kHz clock

endmodule

module servomotor (input smmclk, input [17:0] speed, input spddav, rota, rotb, rotctr,
                   output reg [8:0] pwm);

reg [17:0] dspeed = 5000;         // desired speed
reg [8:0] tpwm = 200;             // temporary PWM on count
reg davspd = 0;

always@(posedge smmclk)
    begin
        if (rota)                 // increment speed
            begin
                dspeed = dspeed + 50;
                if (dspeed > 50000)
                    dspeed = 50000;
            end
        if (rotb == 1)                    // decrease speed
            begin
                dspeed = dspeed – 50;
```

```
                    if (dspeed == 0)
                         dspeed = 1000;
             end
      if (rotctr == 1)                    // reset speed and PWM on
             begin
                    dspeed = 5000;
                    pwm = 200;     // 50% duty cycle
             end

      if (spddav == 1 && davspd == 0)
             begin
                    pwm = tpwm;
                    davspd = 1;
                    if (dspeed > speed)
                         begin
                              tpwm = tpwm – 4;
                              if (tpwm <= 50)
                                   tpwm = 50;
                         end
                    if (dspeed <= speed)
                         begin
                              tpwm = tpwm + 4;
                              if (tpwm <= 350);
                                   tpwm = 350;
                         end
             end

      if (spddav == 0)
             davspd = 0;
   end

endmodule

module servospeed (input ssmclk, sa, output reg spddav = 0, output reg [14:0] speed = 0);

reg [17:0] cspeed = 0;          // calculated speed
reg flagsa = 0;

always@(posedge ssmclk)
      begin
           cspeed = cspeed + 1;

           if (sa == 1 && flagsa == 0)
                 begin
                       speed = cspeed;
                       spddav = 1;
                       cspeed = 0;
                       flagsa = 1;
                 end

           if (sa == 0)
                 begin
```

```
                    spddav = 0;
                    flagsa = 0;
              end
      end

endmodule

module servocontrol (input scsclk, input encmd, dircmd, input [8:0] pwm, output reg dir,
                     output reg en = 0);

reg [8:0] pwmon;          // PWM on
reg [8:0] pwmcount;       // PWM count
reg flagpwm;

always@(posedge scsclk)        // 1 MHz
      begin
            dir = dircmd;

            if (flagpwm == 1)
                  begin
                        pwmon = pwm;
                        flagpwm = 0;
                        pwmcount = 0;
                  end

            if (flagpwm == 0)
                  begin
                        pwmcount = pwmcount + 1;
                        if (pwmcount <= pwmon)
                              en = encmd;
                        else
                              en = 0;

                        if (pwmcount > 400)
                              flagpwm = 1;
                  end
      end

endmodule
```

The complete ISE Verilog project utilizes three modules which demonstrate the capability of the PGA to process signals in parallel. The *servospeed.v* module uses the clock signal mclk to measure the count period as the output register variable speed of the quadrature encoder signal A as the signal sa. The period is recorded as a count of the 1 MHz clock signal with a resolution of 1 µsec.

The register variable flagsa is use to *flag* when the net variable sa has completed a complete period. The output register variable spddav as logic 1 indicates to the *servomotor.v* module that an updated DC servomotor speed measurement is available.

The *servomotor.v* module increments or decrements the desired speed register variable dspeed with the rotation of the shaft encoder. The desired speed is initialed or reset with the debounced shaft pushbutton signal rotCTRreg to a count of 5000. If the desired speed count is greater than the actual speed count of the DC servomotor then the PWM pulse width T_w as the output register pwm is decreased. If the desired speed count is less than the actual speed count, the output register pwm is increased.

The recommended PWM pulse period T_p for the DC servomotor is 0.4 msec or a count of 0.4 msec/1 μsec = 400. The output register pwm as the PWM pulse width T_w is limited to a count range of 50 to 350, which is equivalent to width of 0.05 to 0.35 msec and a resulting duty cycle of 12.5% to 87.5%.

Finally, the *servocontrol.v* module generates the two command signals for the DC servomotor. The direction control signal is set from slide switch SW0. The enable command signal of the DC servomotor is set by the pushbutton BTND. The direction of the DC servomotor should not be changed if the enable control signal set is logic 1 which can damage or destroy the H-bridge MOSFET transistors, as shown in Figure 4.47.

The register variable pwmon, determined by the net variable pwm from the *servomotor.v* module, is the PWM pulse width T_w count in the range from 50 to 350. The register variable pwmcount determines the interval during which the DC servomotor enable control signal is determined either by the enable command signal net variable encmd or set to 0 to disable.

As described in Chapter 2 Verilog Design Automation, the Design Utilization Summary for the top module *ns3servocontrol.v* shows the use of 168 slice registers (2%) and 522 slice LUTs (5%) in the Nexys 3 Board XC6SLX16 Spartan-6 FPGA synthesis.

The modules in the ISE Verilog project for the closed-loop proportional digital controller for the speed of a DC servomotor are a connection of interrelated modules and not an evident controller and datapath. The servomotor.v and servocontrol.v modules together represent a near datapath construct with an input command signal spddav but no status signal in return.

The module *servospeed.v* is a processing module which determines the speed count as a data input to the near datapath construct. Using several smaller modules in Verilog HDL facilitates the efficient development and hardware synthesis of a project.

The stability and response of the closed-loop proportional digital controller for the speed of a DC servomotor is determined by the electromechanical characteristics of the servomotor and its mechanical load, the sampling rate f_s and the choice of the proportionality constant K_p [Ogata02]. The proportionality constant K_p relates the difference in the desired and actual speed count as the error signal to the incrementation or decrementation of PWM signal. The process of *tuning* of this parameter and the selection of the sampling rate f_s is an iterative process but could be facilitated by inputting them as variables from an external peripheral.

The DC servomotor is connected to Pmod HB5 H-bridge hardware module peripheral and operates with an external +6 V DC power supply. The Pmod HB5 H-bridge hardware module outputs the quadrature encoder signals to and receives the direction and enable control signals for the DC servomotor from the PGA.

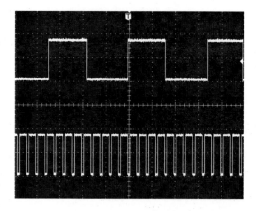

Figure 4.50 DC servomotor quadrature encoder signal A (top) and enable control signal (bottom) at 2 V/div and 1 msec/div

Figure 4.50 shows DC servomotor the quadrature encoder signal A and the enable control signal. The speed count from the quadrature encoder signal A is approximately 3.4 msec/1 μsec = 3400. The duty cycle of the enable control signal is approximately 75% here and the DC servomotor is rotating at a relatively high rate. Figure 4.51 shows a lower rotation rate where the speed count from the quadrature encoder signal A is approximately 10 msec/1 μsec = 10 000 and the duty cycle of the enable control signal is approximately 25%.

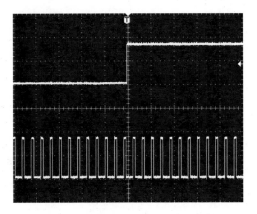

Figure 4.51 DC servomotor quadrature encoder signal A (top) and enable control signal (bottom) at 2 V/div and 1 msec/div

Expansion Peripherals

Both the Digilent Nexys 3 Board and the Atlys Board feature a 68-pin very high density cable (VHDC) connector for expansion. The 40 input/output (I/O) pins available on the VHDC connector facilitate additional peripherals.

The Digilent VmodMIB VHDC module interface board provides four additional 12-pin Pmod connectors, one 12-pin Pmod connect with series and pulldown resistors intended for interfacing to an I2C bus, and four HDMI-D connectors which are shared with the Pmod connectors. The VmodMIB is a useful adjunct to the Atlys Board since it features only one 12-pin Pmod connector, is referenced in the Digilent document 502-190 (*www.digilentinc.com*) and is shown in Figure 4.52.

Figure 4.52 Digilent VmodMIB expansion connector

Trends in Embedded Design Using Programmable Gate Arrays

The Digilent VmodWW wirewrap prototype board and VmodBB solderless breadboard can be used for the fabrication or additional perpherals and are referenced in the Digilent document 502-184 (*www.digilentinc.com*).

VmodCAM Stereo Camera

The Digilent VmodCAM module is a stereo camera module using two Aptina MT9D112 2 megapixel CMOS digital image sensor (*www.aptina.com*), is referenced in the Digilent document 502-179 (*www.digilentinc.com*) and is shown in Figure 4.53. A male-to-male VHDCI cable is required to connect the VmodTFT to the Nexys 3 Board or the Atlys Board.

Figure 4.53 Digilent VmodCAM stereo digital camera module

The digital image sensors feature a maximum resolution of 1600 by 1200 10-bit pixels at 15 frames/sec. The MT9D112 has an I2C control bus and an image flow processor that enables selectable output formats, cropping, scaling and special effects. Image output formats include YCrCb (CCIR 601 standard), RGB and Bayer. The two digital image sensors can be controlled independently and the stereo baseline for ranging is 63 mm.

The MT9D112 digital image sensor utilizes a microcontroller and a programmable general purpose I/O module (GPIO), which can be used to control an external auto focus, an optical zoom or a mechanical shutter. The microcontroller manages all the components and sets key operational parameters to optimize the quality of the digital image data.

The image flow processor provides algorithms for the enhancement and optimization of the digital image sensor performance. These algorithms include black level conditioning, lens shading and defect correction, noise reduction, color interpolation, edge detection, color and aperture correction and image formatting.

An I2C control bus provides read/write access to control registers, variables, and special function registers. The hardware registers include sensor, color pipeline and output controls. Variables are located in the RAM accessible by the microcontroller and are used for auto exposure, auto white balance and auto focus. Special function registers connected to the local bus of the microcontroller and include the GPIO and the sensor waveform generator.

Developmental Verilog ISE projects using the VmodCAM are in the *Chapter 4\camera* folder. The file download procedure is described in the Appendix.

VmodTFT Color LCD and Touchscreen

The Digilent VmodTFT module is a color LCD with resistive touchscreen, is referenced in the Digilent document 502-210 (*www.digilentinc.com*) and is shown in Figure 4.54. A male-to-male VHDCI cable is required to connect the VmodTFT to the Nexys 3 Board or the Atlys Board.

Figure 4.54 Digilent VmodTFT color LCD with resistive touchscreen

The VmodTFT module is a 4.3 inch LED-backlit LCD screen with 480 by 272 pixel resolution with a color depth of 24 bits per pixel. The LCD screen is an Innolux AT043TN24-V7 (*www.innolux.com*) and uses a display enable (DE), pixel clock (PCLK) and pixel data (PDATA) signals.

The touchscreen controller is an Analog Devices AD7873 device (*analog.com*) and reports the X,Y touch position by a resistive divider with 12 bits of resolution. However, the actual X,Y readings are required to calibrate the touch screen and are not optimal.

The VmodTFT module has a power-on timing sequence using an Fairchild Semiconductor FDG6331L load switch (*fairchildsemi.com*) which provides an enable signal (TFT-EN). The power-on sequence requires no more than 100 msec from the TFT-EN signal as logic 1 to the initial appearance of PDATA and no more than 200 msec from PDATA to the DISP signal as logic 1.

PDATA is sent as parallel 8-bit data for the red, green and blue signals (RGB) on the negative edge of PCLK. The setups and hold times for PDATA are a minimum of 10 nsec.

The LED-backlight can be fixed or set by a pulse wide modulated (PWM) signal in the frequency range from 100 Hz to 50 KHz at the jumper JP1. The pixel clock is 9 MHz and the timing is similar to that of the Verilog VGA datapath module *vgavideo.v* in Listing 3.38.

Developmental Verilog ISE projects using the VmodTFT are in the *Chapter 4\tft* folder. The file download procedure is described in the Appendix.

Trends in Embedded Design Using Programmable Gate Arrays

Summary

In this Chapter several embedded design projects in digital signal processing, digital communications and digital control are presented using the Xilinx ISE for the Spartan-6 Nexys 3 Board. The controller-datapath construct is utilized for these embedded projects that require multiple parallel processes to execute and the resulting real-time performance. Chapter 5 Extensible Processing Platform describes the Xilinx Zynq all programmable *system-on-chip* with an ARM Cortex™-A9 hard core processor, AMBA bus and integral FPGA.

References

[Cavicchi00]   Cavicchi, Thomas J., *Digital Signal Processing*. Wiley, 2000.

[Chen01]   Chen, Chi-Tsong, *Digital Signal Processing: Spectral Computation and Filter Design*. Oxford, 2001.

[Haykin01]   Haykin, Simon, *Communication Systems*. Wiley, 2001.

[Ifeachor02]   Ifeachor, Emmanuel C. and Barrie W. Jervis, *Digital Signal Processing: A Practical Approach*. Prentice Hall, 2002.

[Kuo97]   Kuo, Benjamin, *Digital Control Systems*. Oxford, 1997.

[Lathi98]   Lathi, B.P., *Modern Digital and Analog Communication*. Oxford, 1998.

[Mano07]   Mano, M. Morris and Michael D. Cilletti, *Digital Design*. Prentice Hall, 2007.

[Ogata02]   Ogata, Katsuhiko, *Modern Control Engineering*, Prentice Hall, 2002.

[Mitra06]   Mitra, Sanjit K., *Digital Signal Processing: A Computer Based Approach*. McGraw-Hill, 2006.

[Proakis07]   Proakis, John G. and Dimitris G. Manolakis, *Digital Signal Procesing*. Prentice Hall, 2007.

[Silage06]   Silage, Dennis, *Digital Communication Systems using SystemVue*. Cengage Publishing, 2006.

[Silage08]   Silage, Dennis, *Embedded Design Using Programmable Gate Arrays*, Bookstand Publishing, 2008.

[Silage09]   Silage, Dennis, *Digital Communication Systems using MATLAB and Simulink*. Bookstand Publishing, 2009.

[Simon01]   Simon, Marvin et al., *Spread Spectrum Communications Handbook*, Mc-Graw-Hill, 2001.

[Sklar01]   Sklar, Bernard, *Digital Communications*, Prentice-Hall, 2001.

[Xiong00]   Xiong, Fuqin, *Digital Modulation Techniques*, Artech, 2000.

5

Extensible Processing Platform

Embedded design utilizing the Verilog hardware description language (HDL), electronic design automation (EDA) tools and the programmable gate array (PGA) can supplement finite state machines (FSM) and controller and datapath constructs by the implementation of a processor. Although the constraints of real-time processing in digital signal processing, communications and control often require the rapid execution and parallel processing capabilities of the Verilog HDL controller and datapath construct, other embedded projects are well suited to a resource efficient sequential processor or microprocessor.

The soft core processor, exemplified by the Xilinx 8-bit PicoBlaze and 32-bit MicroBlaze, provides one solution with a traditional microprocessor architecture, albeit not as a hard core implementation. These processors are programmable with sequential instructions in either assembly language in the case of the PicoBlaze or in both assembly and C languages for the MicroBlaze.

The recent introduction (2011) of the Xilinx Zynq™ Extensive Processing Platform (EPP) has significantly altered the paradigm for embedded design and the concomitant tradeoff between the sequential processor and the inherently parallel PGA. An IBM PowerPC 32-bit hard core processor and a dominant PGA coexisted on the Xilinx VirtexII (2004) but this device did not feature a bus interconnection in hardware.

The Xilinx Zynq EPP though is processor system and not programmable logic centric with dual ARM® Cortex™-A9 hard core processors. The Zynq EPP is a *system-on-chip* (SoC) with a high bandwidth Advanced Microcontroller Bus Architecture (AMBA®) Advanced Extensive Interface (AXI™) interconnection in hardware. This Chapter introduces the Zynq-7000 EPP, its EDA tools and its implementation as an evaluation board.

Xilinx Zynq-7000

The Xilinx Zynq-7000 All Programmable SoC is a first generation architecture featuring a dual-core ARM Cortex-A9 processing system and programmable logic in a single device, as shown in Figure 5.1 and described in the data sheet DS190 (*www.xilinx.com*). The Zynq-7000 EPP provides an SoC solution with enhanced performance and integration.

Zynq EPP Processing System

The features of the Xilinx Zynq EPP XC7Z020 device processing system (PS), consisting of an application processing unit (APU) with dual-core ARM Cortex-A9 32-bit processors and an operating frequency of up to 800 MHz, is described here. The set of integral hardware subsystems provided by the Zynq EPP insures the complete SOC solution for embedded design.

The Zynq EPP has a 32 KB instruction and 32 KB data L1 cache for each processor, a 512 KB L2 cache and 256 KB of dual-ported RAM. The integral memory interface unit (MIU) includes a static memory 8-bit controller (SMC) which supports up to 64 MB of SRAM and 64 MB of NOR flash memory.

The MIU also provides a dynamic memory 64-bit controller (DMC), which supports DDR2 and DDR3 memory, can be configured to provide 16-bit or 32-bit data accesses for up to 1 GB. The DMC is multi-ported and facilitates access to memory by both the PS and PL with four ports. One 64-bit port is dedicated to the PS via the L2 cache controller. Two 64-bit ports are used by the PL and the remaining port is for an AXI interconnection.

The input/output peripherals (IOP) interface provides the integral data communication capability of the Zynq EPP with a variety of standards, as shown in Figure 5.2. Two 10/100/1000

Trends in Embedded Design Using Programmable Gate Arrays

Mb/sec tri-mode Ethernet media access controllers (MAC) support both the IEEE-802.3 and the IEEE-1588 standard with an external physical (PHY) layer interface.

Two USB 2.0 On-the-Go (OTG) ports can connect up to 12 endpoints. The USB ports utilize 32-bit Advanced High Performance Bus (AHB) direct memory access (DMA) master and slave interfaces. The ports have an 8-bit USB transceiver macrocell, low pin interface (ULPI), as shown in Figure 5.2, and use an external PHY interface.

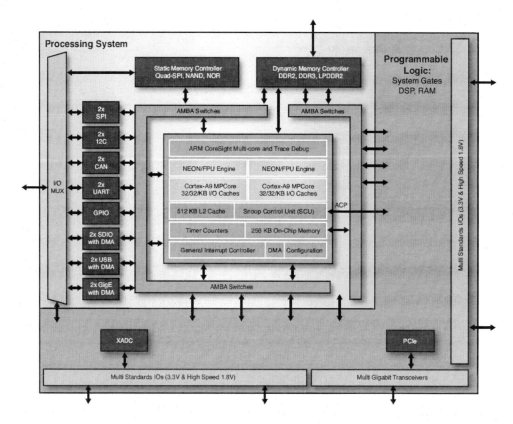

Figure 5.1 Xilinx Zynq-7000 EPP (*Xcell Journal*, 75: 2011)

Two Secure Digital (SD/SDIO) non-volatile memory card interfaces with DMA controller are provided. Two conventional full duplex one data bit serial peripheral interfaces (SPI) have three chip select signals. The Zynq EPP also features a four parallel data bit Quad-SPI interface, as shown in Figure 5.2 Two controller area network (CAN) bus interfaces are 2.0-B (BOSCH Gmbh) compliant. There are two UARTs that utilizes an external RS232 standard voltage converter and two master and slave I2C interfaces.

The IOP interfaces communicates with external devices through up to 543 dedicated multiuse IO (MIO) pins. Although each of the available IOP interfaces can access any of several predefined groups of MIO pins, there are not enough pins for simultaneous access by all. However, most IOP interfaces can be accessed by the PL and its standard IO pins that are not part of the MIO.

The APU, MIU, IOP and PL are interconnected by a multilayered ARM AMBA AXI bus which is non-blocking and supports multiple simultaneous master-slave activities. The interconnection is supported by latency sensitive data paths and high bandwidth PL bus masters.

The Zynq EPP PS external interface has dedicated pins for clock, reset, boot mode and voltage reference. Up to 54 MIO pins are configurable for any of the integral IOP and SMC connections. If more than 54 pins are required, signals can be routed as an extendable multiplexed IO

(EMIO) through the PL to the IOP associated with the PL, as shown in Figure 5.2. Port pin mapping exist in multiple locations and can be accessed by the PS Configuration Wizard.

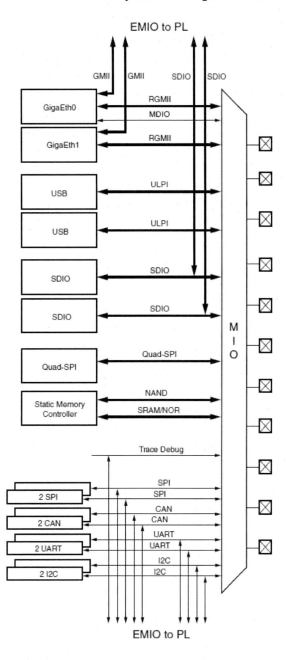

Figure 5.2 Zynq EPP multiuse I/O (*DS190, www.xilinx.com*)

The PS to PL interface includes the AMBA AXI interface for primary data communication by two 32-bit master and two 32-bit slave interfaces. There are also four high performance AXI ports as 64-bit or 32-bit configurable, buffered slave interfaces with direct access to DDR and on-chip memory (OCM) and one 64-bit accelerator coherency port (ACP) for access to the PS memory. The high performance AXI ports provide access from the PL to the DDR MIU controller in the PS, as shown in Figure 5.3.

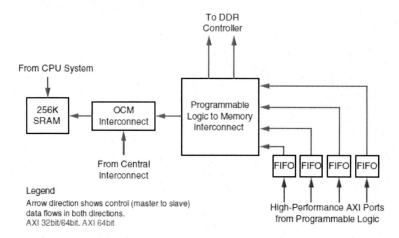

Figure 5.3 Zynq EPP PL to PS DDR memory (*DS190, www.xilinx.com*)

The high performance AXI port features reduced latency between the PL and PS DDR memory. The first-in, first-out (FIFO) buffers, as shown in Figure 5.3, are 1 KB. The ACP is a 64-bit AXI slave interface for connectivity between the APU and a PGA hardware accelerator function in the PL. The ACP provides a low latency data path between the PS and a PL-based accelerator.

Zynq EPP Programmable Logic

The Xilinx Zynq EPP XC7Z020 device contains a programmable logic (PL) equivalent to the architecture of the Xilinx Artix™-7 field programmable gate array (FPGA) here with 2 200 control logic block (CLB). Each CLB features eight look-up tables (LUT) for logic implementation and distributed memory and configurable memory LUTs as 64×1 or 32×2 bit RAM or shift registers. The CLB also has 16 registers and a 2×4 bit cascadeable adder for arithmetic functions. In comparison the Spartan-6 XC6SLX45 FPGA, as on the Digilent Nexys 3 Board, has only two LUTs for each of its 3 411 CLBs.

The Xilinx Zynq EPP XC7Z020 device has 60 36 Kb (270 KB) block RAM, which are up to 36 bits wide, that can be configured as dual 18 Kb block RAM. There are 80 DSP48 18×25 signed multiply, 48-bit added/accumulator slices. Uniquely, the Zynq also provides two 12-bit, I Msample/sec analog-to-digital converters (XADC) with voltage regulation and an analog multiplexer with up to 17 external differential input channels. The Spartan-6 XC6SLX45 FPGA has 116 18 Kb (261 KB) block RAM, 58 DSP48 slices and no integral ADC capability.

ZedBoard

The Digilent and Avnet Zynq Evaluation Board or ZedBoard is a system configured for the Xilinx Zynq EPP XC7Z020, is described in the *ZedBoard Hardware User's Guide* (*www.zedboard.*org™) and shown in Figure 5.4. The external memory of the ZedBoard consists of 512 MB DDR3 dynamic RAM, 256 Mb Quad-SPI flash memory and a removable 4 GB SD memory card. The ZedBoard has four 12-pin Pmod ports connected to the PL and one Pmod port to the PS. Data communication consists of a gigabit Ethernet port, USB OTG port and a USB UART bridge. There are eight user LEDs and slide switches, five push buttons connected to the PL (BTNU, BTNL, BTNR, BTND and BTNC) and two push buttons to the PS.

An Analog Devices ADV7511 provides an HDMI video port and there is a 12-bit VGA port with 4 bits for red, green and blue. An Analog Devices ADAU1761 audio codec provides integrated digital audio processing for stereo 48KHz record and playback. Sample rates from 8KHz to 96KHz are supported. The Analog Devices ADAU1761 provides a digital volume control. A Inteltronic/Wisechip UG-2832HSWEG04 OLED display provides a 128x32 pixel, passive-matrix, monochrome display.

Figure 5.4 Digilent and Avnet Zynq EPP XC7Z020 ZedBoard

A Micron MT41K128M16JT DDR3 dynamic memory is connected DMC and configured for 32-bit wide accesses to a 512 MB address space at interface speeds up to 533MHz. A Spansion S25FL256S Quad-SPI NOR flash memory provides non-volatile code, and data storage and is used to initialize the PS subsystem as well as configure the PL subsystem. The ZedBoard 4 GB class 4 SD Card (A 4GB Class 4 card is used for non-volatile external memory storage and for boot loading the PS.

The Zynq-7000 PS uses a dedicated 33.3333 MHz clock source. The PS can generate up to four phase-locked loop (PLL) based clocks for the PL system. An integral 100 MHz oscillator provides the clock for the PL.

In addition to the five 12-pin Pmod connectors, a low-pin count (LPC) FPGA mezzanine card (FMC) slot is provided on the ZedBoard to support plug-in modules. The LPC FMC utilizes 68 single-ended I/O which can be configured as 34 differential pairs.

Zynq EPP Design Automation

The Zynq EPP design automation requires additional steps because of the SoC architecture, the processor centric processing system and the availability of hard core peripheral and programmable logic. The EDA is described in the *Zynq-7000 All Programmable SoC Software Developers Guide* and the *Zynq-7000 EPP Concepts, Tools and Techniques* (UG821 and UG873, *www.xilinx.com*). Three EDA tools are used: the Xilinx Platform Studio (XPS), the Xilinx Integrated Software Environment (ISE) and the Xilinx Software Development Kit (SDK). A JTAG programmer is also required and the ZedBoard has a USB-JTAG interface for device programming.

Trends in Embedded Design Using Programmable Gate Arrays

XPS was used to develop an embedded design using the soft core 32-bit MicroBlaze processor and here is used for the Zynq EPP PS. The configuration, interfaces, device timing constraints and physical address ranges are specified in XPS and the output is a hardware description language (HDL) netlist. ISE is the EDA description for Verilog HDL design automation and here integrates the both the PL and PS HDL netlists. The SDK is used to develop software for the PS but requires that the hardware configuration be defined.

Figure 5.5 Xilinx PlanAhead initial options

The incorporation of these three disparate EDA tools in the design process can be problematic. The Xilinx PlanAhead tool conveniently integrates them and simplifies the development, as shown in Figure 5.5. After clicking *Create New Project*, a series of option screen are available for *Project Type*, *Add Sources*, *Add Existing IP* and *Add Constraints*.

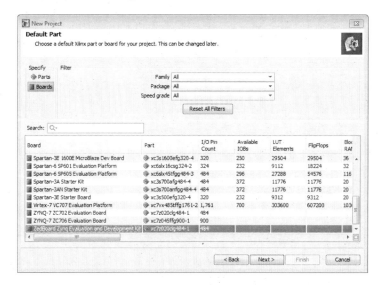

Figure 5.6 Xilinx PlanAhead Default Part

The next option screen is *Default Part* where Boards is specified and the ZedBoard is selected, as shown in Figure 5.6. After reviewing the selected options and clicking *Finish*, the New Project Wizard closes and the PlanAhead tool opens, as shown in Figure 5.7.

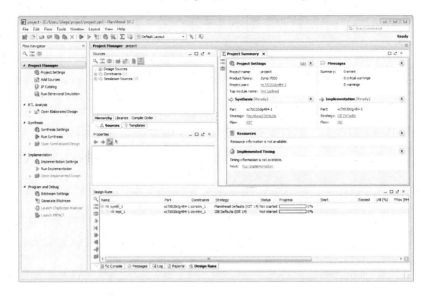

Figure 5.7 Xilinx PlanAhead design window

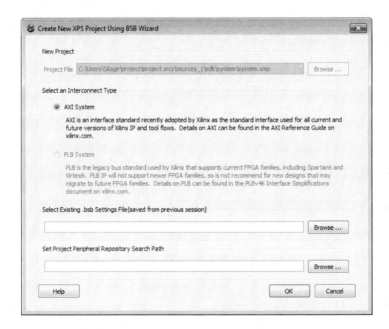

Figure 5.8 Xilinx Create New XPS Project Using BSB Wizard

The Project Manager *Add Sources* facilitates the insertion of sources, constraints or IP in the design. Specifying *Add or Created Embedded Sources*, followed by *Create Subdesign*, allows the selection of a module name which here is *system*. The PlanAhead tool creates an embedded processor systems and launches XPS to build a project using the Base System Builder (BSB) wizard and an AXI system, as shown in Figure 5.8. After the board and system and peripheral configuration option screens are selected, XPS displays a view of the Zynq EPP PS, as shown in Figure 5.9.

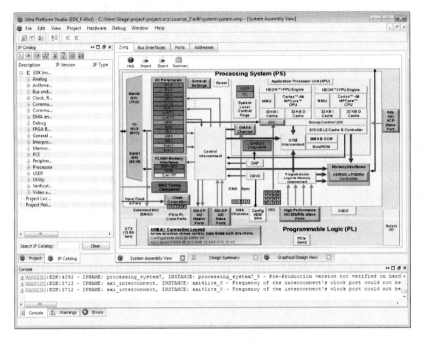

Figure 5.9 Xilinx Platform studio view of the Zynq EPP PS

After closing XPS and returning to PlanAhead the register transfer language (RTL) netlist for the PS in Verilog is generated. Here also Verilog HDL sources for the PL can also be added to the project and an RTL netlist created. Right-clicking on the module name *system.xmp* in the Design Sources and selecting *Create Top HDL* creates the *system_stub.v* top level module for the design, as shown in Figure 5.10.

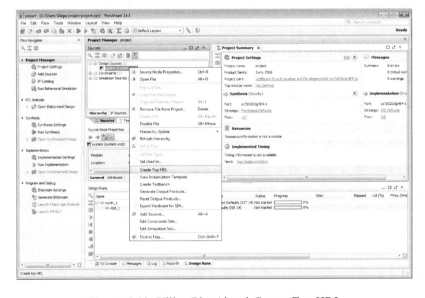

Figure 5.10 Xilinx PlanAhead *Create Top HDL*

The constraint file and board support package (BSP) for the Zynq EPP project is predefined here for the ZedBoard and also for other Zynq-7000 evaluation boards. The complete Zynq EPP XPS and possible ISE project is exported to the SDK from the PlanAhead tool by *File…Export…Export Hardware*, as shown in Figure 5.11. The *Launch SDK* checkbox should be selected.

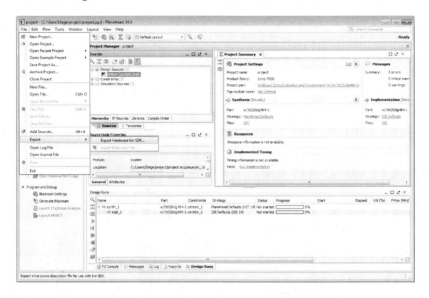

Figure 5.11 Xilinx PlanAhead *Export Hardware*

The Xilinx SDK then opens for the Zynq EPP project, as shown in Figure 5.12. PlanAhead exported the Hardware Platform Specification for your design *system.xml* to SDK with four other files: *ps7_init.c*, *ps7_init.h*, *ps7_init.tcl*, and *ps7_init.html*.

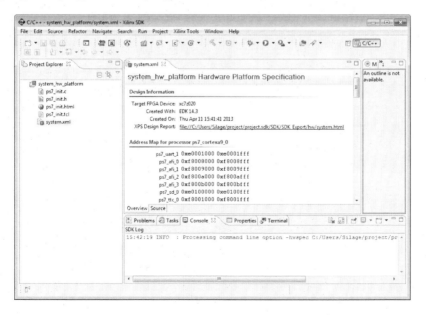

Figure 5.12 Xilinx Software Development Kit

Trends in Embedded Design Using Programmable Gate Arrays

The *system.xml* file opens by default and the address map of your system is shown by default in the SDK window, as shown in Figure 5.12. The *ps7_init.c* and *ps7_init.h* files contain the initialization code for the Zynq EPP PS and initialization settings for the DMC, clocks, PLLs, and the MIO pins. The SDK adjusts the Zynq EPP PS to these hardware settings so that applications can be executed.

The application software in either the C or C++ language is edited and complied in the SDK. There are template files for simple console *hello world* programs to first stage boot loaders. The project can be selected to execute with a *bare-metal* system, essentially no operating system (OS) at all, or with a Linux OS or a real-time OS (RTOS), such as FreeRTOS. More concise information for the Zynq EPP EDA is available in *Zynq-7000 All Programmable SoC: Concepts, Tools and Techniques* (UG873, *www.xilinx.com*).

Zynq EPP Operating Systems

The Xilinx Zynq EPP PS can utilize various operating systems (OS) environments to execute an application. Bare-metal is not an OS and is devoid of many advanced features. However, OS utilize some processor throughout and can be less deterministic in execution than a bare-metal system.

The bare-metal BSP has libraries and device drivers for a single-threaded applications. The bare-metal system provides boot code, cache functions, exception handling, basic file I/O, C library support for memory allocation and timer functions. The bare-metal OS can can be configured as an asymmetric multiprocessing (AMP) system executing separate software stacks and executables utilizing both ARM Cortex-A9 processors of the Zynq EPP (XAPP 1079, *www.xilinx.com*). The processors then communicate through shared memory.

Linux is a popular, open-source OS often used in some embedded designs. Figure 5.13 shows the Xilinx Zynq Linux kernel diagram and the relationship between functions within the various layers of the OS.

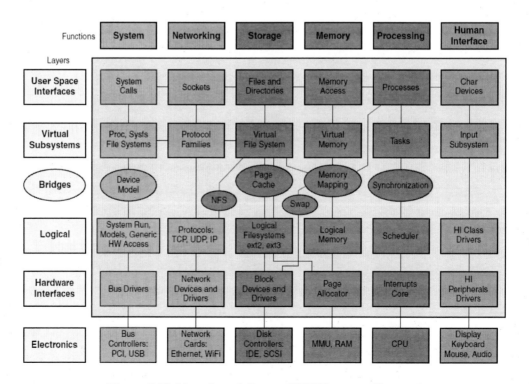

Figure 5.13 Linux kernel diagam (UG821, *www.xilinx.com*)

Although Linux is not inherently an RTOS it is a full-featured OS that utilizes the memory management unit (MMU) of the ARM Cortex-A9 32-bit processor. Linux also provides support for symmetric multiprocessing (SMP) for the dual ARM Cortex-A9 processors of the Zynq EPP. A distributions of Linux for the ZedBoard is available at eLinux (*www.elinux.org/zedboard*). Linux inherently supports symmetric multiprocessing (SMP) on multiple cores. Also Linux and the bare-metal OS can provide AMP excuting on the two ARM Cortex-A9 processors of the Zynq EPP (XAPP 1078, *www.xilinx.com*).

Finally, an RTOS provides the deterministic and predicable response required for sensitive timing application in embedded design. As an example of an RTOS, FreeRTOS has been ported to not only the Zynq EPP but many other hard and soft core processors since it is written mostly in the C language. However, the more advanced features of other OSs, including Linux, are not available.

FreeRTOS emphasizes compactness and speed of OS execution evident with Rhealstone perfromance benchmarking [Gumzej10]. FreeRTOS implements multiple threads of execution utilizing priorities and *round-robin* scheduling as described in *Using the FreeRTOS Real Time Kernel* (Real Time Engineers Ltd, *www.freertos.org*).

FreeRTOS provides support for multiple threads, mutual exclusions (*mutexs*), semaphores and software timers. Memory allocation is by four schemes: allocate, simple allocate and free, fast allocate and free with memory coalescence and the normal C library allocate and free with mutex protection.

Additional information for the Zynq EPP OS configurations is available in *Zynq-7000 All Programmable SoC Software Developers Guide*, (UG821, *www.xilinx.com*).

Trends in Embedded Design Using Programmable Gate Arrays

Summary

In this Chapter an introduction to the Xilinx Zynq Extensive Processing Platform is presented as a sea change for embedded design. The Zynq EPP is processor centric featuring a dual-core ARM Cortex-A9 32-bit processing system and programmable logic in a single device. The ZedBoard Zynq EPP evaluation board is described and the electronic design automation tools and techniques reviewed. The potential of the Zynq EPP system-on-chip represents a new paradigm and an emerging technology.

References

[DSD412]   *Getting Started With Embedded Linux – ZedBoard*, Digilent, Inc.

[DS190]   *Zynq-7000 All Programmable SoC Overview*, Xilinx, Inc.

[FRTOSK]   *Using the FreeRTOS Real Time Kernel*, Real Time Engineers Ltd.

[FRTOSRM]   *The FreeRTOS Reference Manual*, Real Time Engineers Ltd.

[Gumzej10]   *Real Time Systems' Quality of Service*, Roman Gumzej and Wolfgang Halang, Springer, 2010.

[UG821]   *Zynq-7000 All Programmable SoC Software Developers Guide*, Xilinx, Inc.

[UG873]   *Zynq-7000 All Programmable SoC: Concepts, Tools and Techniques*, Xilinx, Inc.

[XAPP1079]   *Simple AMP Running Linux and Bare-Metal System on Both Zynq SOC Processors*, Xilinx, Inc.

[XAPP1079]   *Simple AMP: Bare-Metal System Running on Both Cortex-A9 Processors*, Xilinx, Inc.

[ZCTT]   *ZedBoard: Zynq-7000 AP SoC Concepts, Tools and Techniques*, Xilinx, Inc.

[ZHWUG]   *ZedBoard Hardware User's Guide*, ZedBoard.org

Appendix

Project File Download

The Xilinx ISE projects and Verilog hardware description language (HDL) modules described in the Chapters are available for download in a ZIP file archive format from the website *astro.temple.edu/~silage/trendembeddes*. An alternative website for the ZIP file archive format is *www.dennis-silage.com/trendembeddes*. The ZIP archive file download is password protected with *XUECE13T*.

These copyrighted materials are provided in support of this text and no other rights or license is implied by their availability for non-commercial use. Comments on the Xilinx ISE projects and this file download procedure can be directed to the author via email at *silage@temple.edu*.

Although these embedded design projects target the Digilent Spartan-6 Nexys 3 Board and Atlys Board some have the capability of being easily ported to other Xilinx FPGA evaluation boards. Additional embedded design projects and corrections not described in the Chapters are to be available on the websites as further development continues. The ZIP file archive on the websites contains the most recent and verified Xilinx ISE projects and other information.

Install the folders and subfolders in the directory *C:\TEDPGA*. The Verilog modules (*.v*), user control files (*.ucf*) and Xilinx project files (*.xise*) are organized into folders and subfolders by Chapters, for example *C:\TEDPGA\Chapter 2\ns3elapsedtime*. Project files beginning with *ns3* are for the Digilent Spartan-6 Nexys 3 Board and those with *atl* are for the Digilent Sparatn-6 Atlys Board. Modifications to existing projects, hardware synthesis using other Xilinx programmable gate array devices or evaluation boards and the programming of the volatile bit map file (*.bit*) require the Xilinx ISE electronic design automation environment (*www.xilinx.com*).

About the Author

Dennis Silage is a Professor in the Department of Electrical and Computer Engineering at Temple University. He has a PhD in Electrical Engineering from the University of Pennsylvania. He is a Senior Member of IEEE and Director of the System Chip Design Center *www.temple.edu/scdc* of Temple University which researches the application of programmable gate arrays in digital signal processing and digital communication. He is the author of *Digital Communication Systems Using SystemVue* (Thomson Delmar 2006), *Digital Communication Using MATLAB and Simulink* (Bookstand 2009) and *Embedded Design Using Programmable Gate Arrays* (Bookstand 2008). He has published over 90 articles on digital signal processing, digital image processing and digital communication implementations.

His email address is *silage@temple.edu* and academic website is *astro.temple.edu/~silage*.